The Marriage Diaries of
Robert & Clara Schumann

Also by Peter Ostwald and published by Robson Books

Vaslav Nijinsky: A Leap into Madness

The Marriage Diaries of
ROBERT & CLARA SCHUMANN

Edited by Gerd Nauhaus

Translated, with a preface, by Peter Ostwald

First published in Great Britain in 1994 by Robson Books Ltd, Bolsover House,
5-6 Clipstone Street, London W1P 7EB, by arrangement with
Northeastern University Press, Boston.

Originally published in German in 1987 by Deutscher Verlag für Musik,
Leipzig, as part of *Robert Schumann: Tagebücher, 1836–1854,*
edited by Gerd Nauhaus. Translation and Preface copyright 1993
by Peter Ostwald. The right of Peter Ostwald to be identified as
translator of this work has been asserted by him in accordance
with the Copyright, Designs and Patents Act 1988.

British Library Cataloguing in Publication Data
A catalogue record for this title is available from the British Library

Designed by Virginia Evans
All rights reserved. No part of this publication may be reproduced, stored
in a retrieval system, or transmitted in any form or by any means,
electronic, mechanical, photocopying, recording or otherwise,
without the prior permission in writing of the publishers.

Printed in the USA

CONTENTS

List of Illustrations   /*vii*

Preface   /*ix*

Foreword to the German Edition   /*xxi*

One   Diary 1   /*1*

Two   Diary II   /*95*

Three   Diary III   /*175*

Four   The Trip to Russia   /*227*

Five   Russian Customs   /*301*

Six   Poems from Moscow   /*311*
by Robert Schumann

Notes   /*339*

Biographical Directory   /*357*

Index   /*399*

ILLUSTRATIONS

Following page 210

1. Robert and Clara Schumann's residence in Leipzig
2. A page from Marriage Diary I
3. The singer Sophie Schloss
4. The sisters Elise and Lina List
5. Hammerclavier piano belonging to the Schumanns
6. The Bastei Bridge in the Saxon Alps
7. The Royal Theater in Copenhagen
8. A view of Carlsbad
9. Königswart Castle
10. Courtyard in Königsburg
11. Adolph Henselt
12. Nevsky Prospect and the Anichkov Bridge, Petersburg
13. View of the city of Tver (Kalinin)
14. Concert program of the Petersburg Philharmonic Society
15. Honorary diploma given to Clara Schumann
16. Ivan's Square in the Kremlin, Moscow

17. Ink sketch of Ivan's Square by Robert Schumann
18. Portrait of Robert Schumann
19. Clara and Marie Schumann, ca. 1844

PREFACE

Would Clara Wieck and Robert Schumann ever get married? Early in 1840 the prospects for that seemed unlikely. They had known each other for twelve years, having first met at a party given by Dr. and Mrs. Ernst August Carus in Leipzig, on 31 March 1828. Clara, then an eight-year-old child prodigy, performed some brilliant virtuoso pieces on the piano under the watchful eyes of her father, who was also her teacher. Robert, seventeen at the time, had just graduated from high school and was still vacillating between wanting to be a writer, like his recently deceased father, or pursuing the career of a musician, for which there was no adequate role model in either his family or the small town of Zwickau, where he grew up. (Although his mother had an attractive singing voice and was influential in that respect, she by no means supported his musical ambitions. On the contrary, Frau Schumann firmly opposed Robert's desire for further training as a pianist and preferred that he study law and then, like his three older brothers, enter the family publishing business.) Robert's conflicts had worsened after his father died, following the suicide of his sister. This double tragedy had precipitated his first emotional breakdown, at age fifteen, but thanks to his capacity for creative work, and with the help of his first psychiatrist, Dr. Carus, and Carus's wife, a singer, Robert had recovered from the crisis.

When he first met Clara, she epitomized something he had wanted very much to be: a clever and charming performer, socially outgoing, and enthusiastically backed by both parents. (Although Clara's parents were divorced, her mother, the celebrated Leipzig pianist and singer Marianne Tromlitz, was an excellent role model for her, while her father, the influential pedagogue and businessman Friedrich Wieck, supervised her education and trained her daily at the keyboard.) There were also qualities in Robert that had immediately attracted the young Clara. He seemed a quiet and gentle soul, more refined than her own brothers, and, with his ear for poetry, quaint sense of humor, and fund of ghost stories, a desirable playmate. Besides, Robert was older and brought to the Wieck household, where he actually boarded for some time, the personal qualities that her father lacked: tolerance, kindness, and openness to the romantic spirit then gaining popularity among German artists and intellectuals.

Despite their immediate mutual attraction, a strong current of ambivalence and rivalry had permeated Robert and Clara's relationship from the beginning. He found her father's authoritarianism highly offensive and deeply resented Clara's docile submission to this aggressively controlling man. He also objected to the superficiality of Clara's repertoire and the shallowness of her education in general. Unlike Robert, Clara did not attend high school or go to the university. She in turn was exasperated by his passion (and perhaps, on an unconscious level, stimulated by it), by his crushes on male friends and his flirtations with various women, including one of the servants in the Wieck household, with whom he actually had an affair.

Clara's affection had nearly ceased completely when Robert, in 1834, decided to marry one of her girlfriends, Ernestine von Fricken, also a boarder and student of Wieck's. But by this time he had gained some recognition as well as respect as a music critic, and he was beginning to write those miraculous piano pieces that today are considered among his most inspired compositions. By now he had also suffered another breakdown, a severe panic and depression associated with an injury to his right hand, chronic dependence on alcohol, dangerous suicidal tendencies, and other health problems.

Preface

If anything, it was the music—his composing and her performing—that had sustained their relationship during those trying years when both Robert and Clara were looking for other potential spouses. She was the only pianist interested in and capable of playing his highly original compositions. And thus she became, as he himself put it, Robert's "right hand," performing the works he could no longer play himself because of severe stage fright and the disabled right hand. Although some of these early compositions were dedicated to other pianists, including Moscheles and Liszt (whom Clara disliked especially), many were intended specifically for her.

Not until 1836 did what had been a flirtation, suspiciously observed and harshly condemned by her father, truly catch fire. Now Clara was well into adolescence and beginning to respond more erotically—she had nearly fainted in November 1835 when Robert bestowed on her what was probably his first passionate kiss. (His engagement to Ernestine had ended, and his close friend Ludwig Schuncke, with whom he had been living and who was a cofounder of the *New Journal for Music,* had died.) That same year, 1836, Robert had to face the death of his mother. (Frau Schumann died at age sixty-nine. Six years her husband's senior, she had been forty-three and close to menopause when Robert was born. Toward the end of her life she had actively encouraged Clara to marry him.) Too distraught to attend his mother's funeral, Robert (accompanied by his current roommate, Wilhelm Ulex) rushed to see Clara in Dresden instead. Their rendezvous had been surreptitiously arranged during her father's brief absence. Exactly what then happened we will never know, but their letters refer to a secret engagement.

At what point Robert and Clara became physically intimate is also unclear. Some of the letters suggest considerable passion, and the possibility of at least one premarital pregnancy and miscarriage has recently been raised by a German biographer. Wieck of course was horrified when he discovered the marriage plans. His entire professional life had been devoted to Clara's musical development, and he was not about to sanction her attachment to someone he considered mentally unstable, financially irresponsible, sexually promiscuous, and musically incompetent, which is how he described Schumann in numerous public accusations. Wieck predicted—correctly, as it turned out—that marriage to Robert would drastically curtail Clara's career, and that when the marriage failed she would have to support their children. Consequently, Wieck did everything possible to destroy the relationship. He smeared Schumann's reputation through malicious gossip and publications; he prevented any further contact between the lovers by intercepting their correspondence and separating them physically. Only by routing letters circuitously through the elaborate grapevine of friends and journalists he had established as editor of the *New Journal for Music* did Schumann manage to keep in contact with his fiancée. He even moved to Vienna, hoping thus to circumvent the Saxon law that made marriage without parental consent illegal for a woman before her twenty-first birthday. Finally, he and Clara decided to take legal action against Wieck.

The year of the court trial, 1839–1840, saw Robert again close to suicide, but this time he threatened to kill Clara as well as himself. One reason for this was that she often expressed considerable sympathy for her father, a problem (one of many) that persisted throughout their marriage. It was also during the year of the trial that Robert, agonizingly separated from Clara and having to face the possibility of losing her forever, entered one of the most creatively fertile periods of his life, composing hundreds of incredibly beautiful songs, many about the loneliness and terror of abandonment he was then experiencing. (Program booklets

Preface   *xiii*

and record jackets often report, incorrectly, that Schumann's great song year began after his marriage, and that his creative fervor thus demonstrates newfound happiness. In fact, his abrupt return to vocal music, something he had tried unsuccessfully ten years earlier, coincides with the terrible ordeal of the trial, the outcome of which seemed precarious.)

The miracle was that Robert and Clara finally did marry, deliberately choosing 12 September 1840, as the date for the wedding. It was the *coup de grâce* for Wieck, who had been found guilty of slandering Schumann and was sentenced to prison. One day later Clara would turn twenty-one, and become legally of age. That is where the present book begins.

What makes the Schumann marriage diaries so moving and informative is that they show in graphic detail the essential, deeper, spiritual aspects of marriage—a couple's mutual love, loyalty, and devotion—in juxtaposition to the often mundane, uninspiring, and irritating realities of cohabitation between two musicians who were equally determined to follow their individual destinies and pursue independent careers. The tension and excitement of this marriage almost typifies the two-income family of today: two gifted, productive, and successful people struggling to maintain a household, achieve sexual happiness, raise children, and preserve their sanity in the face of unrelenting social, psychological, and, in this case, artistic demands.

All this has been described in much greater detail in my biography *Schumann: The Inner Voices of a Musical Genius,* published in 1985. While writing that book I was privileged to read and consult the composer's voluminous diaries, and after the book was finished Deborah Kops, then Editorial Director of Northeastern University Press, asked about a possible translation of Schumann's diaries. My immediate reaction was one of guarded enthusiasm.

In favor of such a plan was the remarkably detailed view of musicians' lives in the nineteenth century that the Schumann diaries provide. They show his involvement in numerous responsibilities—writing and editing his newspaper, meeting friends, composing, rehearsing, conducting, traveling with Clara, raising children, seeing his doctors, worrying about his health, and engaging in other daily activities that would surely interest the many admirers and performers of Schumann's music who do not read German.

But against the idea of translating *all* of his diaries was their incredible bulk and the overabundance of routine facts—financial statements, weather reports, lists of items he purchased, and other minutiae that Schumann, in his distinctly methodical way, felt compelled to record each day. Much of this material, I felt, would be of interest primarily to scholars, who might be better served by reading the diaries in their original language. My other reservation was that so much of Schumann's diary writing is in a telegraphic style, with observations loosely strung together without any explanatory narrative. How was the general reader to make sense of all that material without a large number of footnotes and very extensive commentaries?

There were two remarkable exceptions to this pattern, however: (1) the diaries of Schumann's youth, written at a time when he was thinking of himself as a future novelist and poet, and (2) the marriage diaries he wrote conjointly with his wife. In both these sets of diaries Schumann expressed himself much more fully, using complete sentences and a style that is eminently readable and surely invites translation. The youthful diaries[1] depict his transformation from a visionary, ambitious, troubled adolescent into a sensitive, disturbed, and extraordinarily productive writer and musician, and they include Schumann's fantastic discovery of the alter egos Eusebius and Florestan as both a useful artistic de-

Preface xv

vice and a symbol of his divided self. The marriage diaries reveal just as clearly his evolution from a composer of extraordinary piano pieces and lieder into a creative artist able to engage the full range of musical forms, including symphonies, chamber music, and choral and operatic works. Along with that came Schumann's maturation from lonely bachelorhood to his new role as husband and father, all accompanied and complemented by Clara Wieck's transition from an independent artist to a housewife and mother confronting the difficulties of balancing family and career.

Here, then, is the ideal place for starting a translation. Not only do the marriage diaries reward performers and musicologists looking for insight into Robert Schumann's compositions and an understanding of Clara Schumann's career, but they also allow the reader to see what marriage was like for these young musicians— the daily joys and travails of their intertwined lives, organizing work schedules, entertaining friends, coping with family, giving lessons, preparing concerts, planning vacations, finding places to stay, cooking meals, along with the vicissitudes of love and procreation. In addition, the marriage diaries describe the Schumanns' long-anticipated tour of Russia in 1844, the fourth year of their marriage. Such a trip was full of surprises, stresses, excitements, and difficulties, as it can be even today. Their description is of interest to anyone curious about nineteenth-century Russia, its people, landscape, architecture, culture, and musical resources.

The marriage diaries, when I used them as resource material for my Schumann biography, had not yet been made available even in a published German edition. In 1987, however, Dr. Gerd Nauhaus, then the associate director and now the director of the Robert Schumann Haus in Zwickau, brought them out as part of a definitive scholarly edition,[2] and he sent me a copy inscribed "in hope of further collaboration concerning this book." But I had already started the research for a new biography of the great

Russian dancer Vaslav Nijinsky, and thus had to delay translating the diaries until that book was published.[3] Fortunately, by that time Dr. Nauhaus had accomplished something that would greatly favor a successful translation from German into English. In preparation for a new special edition of the three marriage diaries and the Russia trip, he had separated that material from the sixteen additional books published in his 1987 edition of the Schumann diaries. For this new edition (not yet published in Germany) Dr. Nauhaus had also removed much of the scholarly paraphernalia that would have made translating the 1987 version so daunting: hundreds of detailed footnotes, and comments on every error, elision, ink blot, insertion, correction, and so on, to be found in the handwritten originals.

What we have here then, in translation, is a far more readable version of the marriage diaries, introduced by Dr. Nauhaus's own foreword, and with explanatory notes for his new edition. Included are the Russia trip, some of Robert Schumann's random jottings about Russian customs, and poems he wrote while in Moscow.

Technical questions about style and content inevitably arose. My initial desire had been to do a rather free translation, modern sounding, fairly colloquial, and devoid of the many clumsy, archaic expressions found in the original. We must remember that the Schumanns were using a Saxon dialect and writing in a now outdated German. I soon discovered, however, that updating the style, which might have been easier on the reader, would have disguised the authors' personalities and destroyed many of their idiosyncratic ways of self-expression. The fascinating contrast between Robert Schumann's more journalistic and rather pedantic style and Clara Schumann's rambling and at times even incoherent writing would have been lost. The contrast (which she herself frequently alludes to) is significant: as was mentioned earlier, he

Preface   *xvii*

came from a bookish household, had been to college, and was a professional writer about music and musicians, while she, raised as a piano virtuoso, had a more limited formal education and relatively less experience with literary forms (it should also be noted that her early diaries had been penned largely by her father and teacher, Friedrich Wieck). Clara, even more than her husband, frequently relies on French expressions that were then entering the German language.

Therefore, I decided it would be better to stay with the original, and to reproduce as honestly as possible the clumsy grammar, odd punctuation patterns, excessive underlining, and other personal stylistic characteristics of the authors. Wherever it was absolutely necessary I have added, in brackets, explanatory words and phrases to those already introduced by the editor, Dr. Nauhaus. Out of respect for the superb musicianship of both writers of these diaries, I have tried whenever possible to preserve the lilt and rhythm if not the tone color of their language. As for the translation of poetry, always a thankless task, I've tended to aim more for the meaning than the sound of the words, especially when it came to the poems from Moscow. These poems, as the original German (which is included) will show, were quite clumsily rhymed in the first place. Indeed, the poems surely do not represent Robert Schumann at his best—he was often ill during the Russia trip. I at first hesitated to include them, but then decided to do so, not because of any inherent beauty, but because they tell us something of the composer's disturbed mood. His attention in Moscow was repeatedly drawn to the Kremlin and fixed on the gigantic broken bell displayed there, a sight that evoked fantasies of Napoleon, who had been one of his childhood heroes and whose downfall (along with the bell's) may have symbolized the composer's own fear of breakdown and confinement.

At other places as well the marriage diaries hint at Robert Schumann's precarious state of health. Clara Schumann cannot keep from voicing her anxieties about it, along with her adoring comments about her husband and her playful teasing. Of great interest is her gradual assumption of more responsibility for making decisions within the marriage, and her insistence upon returning to the concert stage and earning money, while Robert's resentment of her leadership grows accordingly. One of the most poignant incidents described is when Clara Schumann, regretting her self-imposed separation from their two young daughters left at home, drags Robert to an orphanage, where she plays the piano and then observes at great length and quite movingly how very well Moscow's abandoned children were cared for.

Because the "Trip to Russia" not only represents a critical turning point in their marriage—indeed, the joint diaries came to an end after this trip—but also offers such a wealth of information about that country, I have separated it from Diary III, to which it originally belonged, and given it a place of its own in this book.

Finally, I must acknowledge the most valuable assistance of Gregor Hens, M.A., of the Department of German at the University of California at Berkeley, who conscientiously went over the entire translation and offered many extremely helpful suggestions before it was reviewed by Gunther Schuller in Boston and Gerd Nauhaus in Zwickau. I also wish to express my thanks to Professors Irmengard Rauch and Leon Epstein of the University of California for their significant support and advice. To my wife, Lise Deschamps Ostwald, I am grateful for assistance with French terms and for her ever-constant love.

San Francisco, 26 April 1993   PETER OSTWALD, M.D.

Notes

1. Robert Schumann, *Tagebücher, 1827–1838,* ed. Georg Eismann (Leipzig: Deutscher Verlag für Musik, 1971).

2. Robert Schumann, *Tagebücher,* vol. 2, *1836–1854,* ed. Gerd Nauhaus (Leipzig: Deutscher Verlag für Musik, 1987).

3. Peter Ostwald, *Vaslav Nijinsky: A Leap into Madness* (New York: Lyle Stuart/Carol Publishing Group, 1991).

✥ FOREWORD TO THE GERMAN EDITION

The three joint diaries that Robert and Clara Schumann kept in the early years of their marriage belong, as does their extensive correspondence during their courtship and marriage, to the most valuable documents of this unique artistic and personal relationship. Begun the day after their wedding and continued until the couple's return from their great concert tour of Russia, the diaries cover a period full of important events: not only was the Schumanns' household established and the two oldest children born, but important orchestral works, chamber music, and an oratorio by Robert Schumann, together with sensitively conceived songs and piano compositions by Clara Schumann, saw the light of day as well. Furthermore, a variety of personal experiences are described in colorful detail; these are partly about private but mostly about public—especially cultural—matters.

As is known, until the late nineteenth and early twentieth centuries keeping diaries was a widespread practice, particularly among artists and the middle class. Conjoint records of persons involved in a close relationship are much rarer. During their honeymoon, Felix Mendelssohn-Bartholdy and his young wife, Cécile, had filled a notebook and sketchbook with intriguing observations and skillful drawings (as Schumann noted with a sense of amused wonder), but then soon abandoned it. Their effort seems like an innocent game compared to the three-and-a-half-year-long effort of Robert and Clara Schumann to comply with their self-imposed "statutes of the secret marriage vows" for keeping a joint diary. Yet concealed behind the solemn foreword of the first diary, written by the newly hatched head of the household, there is—as Clara likes to point out—a prankster whose favorite means of expression are humor and self-mockery. Thus, while on the one hand we should not take too seriously the somewhat soberly philistine motto of their married life—"industry, thrift, and loyalty"—which they both endorsed, on the other hand we should view it in the context of the difficult early history of their marriage: coming to fruition in the face of vehement obstacles, that union had to prove its bourgeois utility even now, while the idealistic, artistic aspects of their relationship were of such importance for both partners.

The twelfth of September 1840 was their wedding day; the thirteenth, the first day of their married life, was also Clara Schumann's twenty-first birthday and the date of the first entry in their joint diary. These dates mark a double end point to the period of their separation. The year 1840 had begun full of worries, with "terrible harassment from the angry old man" (Clara's father, Friedrich Wieck), and yet already in the spring it had taken a happy direction when Robert Schumann's creativity produced "a rich harvest of songs," only to lead quickly to that "most happy day" of summer marking the end of the wearisome legal obstructions to their marriage. Now, cheerfully optimistic, the couple could rent their first lodgings together in the then newly constructed Friedrichstadt in Leipzig (today unfortunately a place of sadness and decay), which henceforth provided the primary arena for their alternating diary entries—unless they happened to go walking, go to the theater or to concerts, pay visits, or take excursions and trips. "Domestic bliss"—once scornfully derided by Clara's father—now becomes a source of comfort and contentment for the young couple, although they in no way recede into self-sufficiency. Their participation in social and cultural affairs—always practiced in moderation—is something to be taken for granted. Soon the young wife, whose household and cooking chores are not too demanding at first, revives her professional ambitions. She does not want to neglect her art but instead, in an interesting reversal of traditional roles, hopes to "use her hands

Foreword to the German Edition

to support" her husband—that is, to be able to create the leisure for him to cultivate his own genius.

The tensions that subsequently arise in this (as in any) marriage are mainly due to the conflict between Clara Schumann's artistic and domestic existence. They are resolved through growing flexibility and reciprocal adaptation and lead, in addition to Clara's performances in Leipzig and later in Dresden as well as Robert's steady encouragement of her activities as a composer, to the trips to Russia and Copenhagen. The hostility of Clara's father places another strain on their marriage, at least until Schumann and Friedrich Wieck are reconciled to each other for the sake of appearance at Christmas in 1843. The young couple bravely confronts his resentment, and at times even laughs about it—for example, when the successful composer of the *Frühlingssymphonie* (*Spring* Symphony) finds out that Wieck, thinking it was composed merely to defy him, has christened it the *Widerspruchssymphonie* (*Opposition* Symphony).

But all this amounts to little in view of what at the core is a harmonious and happy union, freed of the preceding fears and worries, as the diary intends to—and does in fact—reflect. It turns out to be especially intimate during excursions, walking tours, and journeys—to mention just a few: the birthday outing to Grimma, the short summer trips to the Saxon Alps and to Bohemia. Somewhat more problematic are the concert tours, specifically the one they take together to Hamburg, from where Clara continues on her very successful stay in Copenhagen. Not to have accompanied her there seems to Robert like one of his "most foolish mistakes"—he had thought he ought to stay with their infant daughter, Marie, and remain in his studio, but in doing so he soon sinks into melancholia. By contrast, along with several humiliating situations for Robert that at the beginning actually make him sick, the grand tour of Russia provides such an abundance of stimulating and interesting impressions for both travelers that in summing up—even if one ignores the valuable travel memorabilia and the poems Schumann wrote in Moscow—it turns out unconditionally positive.

Clara's report of this trip of several months, based on her husband's travel notebook, marks the end of their joint records, in May 1844. Thereafter Robert reverted to noting daily events most succinctly in his household books[1] or, on journeys, in small notebooks,[2] while Clara kept her own diary almost until her death.[3] The purpose of the marriage diaries, "to be a true friend, to which we can confide everything, and to which our hearts are open," has been achieved, inasmuch as the partners are now so intimately fused with one another that they no longer need the written medium and can quietly discard the "statute" of 1840.

During the span of time from 1840 to 1844 Germany enjoyed a period free of dramatic political events, yet essentially within the time of the *Vormärz*. That period formed an important epoch for Robert Schumann's personal development, in which he was no longer the unknown, obscure composer (or the respected music critic) of his early years, but had not yet become the acknowledged artist of later times, firmly established in public musical life. Stimulated by his newly won private fulfillment and marital harmony, his creative energy developed with special richness. By comparison, it was somewhat more difficult for Clara Schumann to pursue her artistic career along with her family and household obligations; nevertheless, she made progress and achieved success at the piano, in pedagogy, and in composition. Every friend and admirer of Robert and Clara Schumann and everyone who loves their musical work—whose genesis and first performances are so impressively witnessed here—will enjoy accompanying the artists along the stages of their shared life outlined here, and will be stimulated to explore both of their biographies more thoroughly. In the diaries we also meet a colorful array of contemporaries,

Foreword to the German Edition

illustrious and obscure, attractive and repulsive, interesting and dull; we learn about places and situations that have ceased to exist as such, but whose past seems worth recording.

It was the objective of the editor and the publisher to produce this first separate edition (the first complete critical edition has been available only since 1987), to present the marriage diaries of Robert and Clara Schumann to a wider public, in an attractive form without compromising the accuracy of the text, and to provide additional information for the reader. We hope to do justice to Robert Schumann's wish, expressed as early as 1838 in a letter to Clara Wieck, which seems to us to be the motto of these artists' love and marriage: "Posterity shall regard us completely as one heart and one soul." Still, we should not forget that we encounter here two distinctive individuals, who both singly and as partners in their unique relationship deserve all our respect and admiration.

Zwickau, 12 September 1990   GERD NAUHAUS, PH.D.
(the 150th wedding anniversary of
Robert and Clara Schumann)

Notes

1. Robert Schumann, *Tagebücher,* ed. Gerd Nauhaus, vol. 3, *Household Books 1837–1856,* parts 1 and 2 (Leipzig: Deutscher Verlag für Musik, 1982.

2. Edited as part of Robert Schumann, *Tagebücher,* vols. 1 and 2 (see Preface, notes 1 and 2).

3. Clara Schumann, *Ein Künstlerleben nach Tagebücher und Briefen,* ed. (in part) Berthold Litzman, vols. 2 and 3 (Leipzig: Breitkopf & Härtel, 1905, 1908).

One

MARRIAGE DIARY I

13 September 1840 – 6 July 1841

Diary   [RS]

of

Robert and Clara Schumann

from 12 September 1840 to July 1841

On 13th September 1840.

My dearly beloved young wife,

First of all let me kiss you most tenderly on this day, your first day as a wife, the first of your 22nd year. This little book, which I inaugurate today, has a very intimate meaning; it shall be a diary about everything that touches us mutually in our household and marriage; our wishes, our hopes shall be recorded therein; it should also be a little book of requests that we direct toward one another whenever words are insufficient; also one of mediation and reconciliation whenever we have had a misunderstanding; in short, it shall be our good, true friend, to whom we entrust everything, to whom we open our hearts. If you agree with that, dear wife, then promise me to hold strictly to the statutes of our secret marriage vows, as I hereby promise you.

Once a week we will trade the secretarial duties, exchanging the diary every Sunday (early, at coffee time, if possible) so that nobody can be kept from also adding a kiss. Then the text will be read, silently or aloud, depending on what the content demands, forgotten items will be added, wishes will be listened to, proposals made and granted, indeed all events of the week carefully evaluated to see whether they were worthy and efficient, whether our inner and outer values have been strengthened, and whether we have gained ever more perfection in our beloved art.

The recording of one week may never amount to less than a single page; whoever fails in this respect shall receive some sort of punishment, which we will have to figure out. Should it occur to one member of our marital team not to turn anything in for a whole week, then the penalty will be made very much harsher— an almost unimaginable circumstance, considering our well-known mutual high esteem and sense of duty.

All these statements and rules are also to be adhered to on travels and the like, and the diary must always come along.

One of the highlights of our little diary, as I say, will be the criticism of our artistic accomplishments; e.g., what you have been studying especially, what you are composing, what new things you have learned, and what you think about them will be entered in detail; the same holds for me. Another major adornment of the book will be character descriptions, e.g., of important artists we have closely encountered. Anecdotes and humorous matters shall by no means be excluded.

However, the most beautiful and heartfelt content of the book I would rather not yet mention, my dear wife: your beautiful hopes and mine, which heaven might bless; your and my worries, which married life brings with it; in short, all the joys and sorrows of marital life should be written down here as a true history, which should give us pleasure even in old age.

If you agree with all this, wife of my heart, then sign your name underneath mine, and let us pronounce three words as a talisman on which all happiness in life depends:

Industry, Thrift, and *Loyalty.*

I am truly your sincerely loving husband Robert, and you?

Marriage Diary I 5

[CS]

I too, your wife, Clara, who is devoted to you with her entire soul.

First week
[RS]

From 13th to 20th September

Only a few events, abundant happiness. My wife is truly a treasure that increases every day. If she only knew how happy she makes me. The 13th[1] we celebrated in real style. In the morning to Grimma, all alone in very clear weather. Then we walked up to the Rudelsburg.[2] Grabau and her husband were there. In the meantime, our relatives and friends prepared for the birthday celebration. Clara was genuinely pleased with everything. Included were her mother [Marianne Bargiel], the Carls, the Lists, Madame Devrient, Becker from Freiberg, Wenzel, Reuter, Hermann. Elise [List] sang, with some inhibition. Clara also played, quite superbly, and I did too, a little bit. It all went quite smoothly, everything remained under control and yet everything was there in profusion.

We now have a relative of the Carls in the house, Agnes [Röller], a good girl who keeps the household in the best order.

We parted around 9 P.M. All the joy and happiness had made us tired.

Monday the 14th. First meal. Suspense on the faces of the participants. It tasted excellent. Afternoon Becker, for whom we played many songs. Evening farewell from Becker.

Tuesday the 15th. Emilie [List] came early to see us. The first roast with Mama. Our little household is really very intimate, and must also impress our guests that way. Lorenz & Julius Becker visited us.

My Clara plays the hostess most charmingly. One can hardly say the same about me, and I often consider myself to be rather simpleminded, but only when I think too much about my good fortune.

In the evening at the Carls'. Farewell from [Clara's] mother, who wanted to leave for Magdeburg on Wednesday.

On *Wednesday,* official visits to Härtel, Kistner, Madame Mendelssohn, David, Voigt, and Friese. Champagne with the latter, which strongly went to the young woman's head. The young *Rieffel;* renewal of her acquaintance with Clara.

I haven't yet been able to engage fully in my own work; I'll soon be catching up. Clara is starting to practice, and now plays the fugues of Bach and Mendelssohn. Emilie [List] with us this afternoon. Songs in my room. Dr. *Oesterlei* from Hanover, a cultivated gentleman. A Professor *Kittl* from Prague, who just missed me. In the evening Madame Friese and the Rieffel girl visited us; the latter a young woman of feeling and character, which also expresses itself that way in the music [she played].

Thursday the 17th. Quiet day. Happiness within our four walls. Clara is generally well and cheerful. Elise was with us this morning with Händel arias.

Friday the 18th. Uncomplicated day. Dr. *Kahlert* from Breslau joined me in the afternoon, I played a few songs for him; he swallowed them with praise, like a critic. In the evening I picked up my wife (!) at Madame List's. I asked Elise (modestly) "might I dare dedicate the Eichendorff Songs to her?"[3]—My Clara already makes the impression of a very respectable wife.

Saturday the 19th. Intention: to go piece by piece through [J. S. Bach's] "Well-Tempered Clavier" with Clara. I am looking through Hiller's Oratorio "The Destruction of Jerusalem."[4] In the

Marriage Diary I 7

morning cousin Pfund, whom we showed a piece of our paradise. Together into town. In the afternoon Dr. Kahlert came to see me and played some of his compositions, which he seems to hold in high regard; but he is really more of a journalist.[5] With him and the List girls to Voigt, who began behaving with incredible silliness, enough to make one want to stop associating with him forever. One wants so much to associate with people. And yet how often the kindhearted ones are stupid, while the intelligent ones lack kindness. I told this to Clara, who in her modesty thought this [mistake] served her right.

[Ferdinand] David played a quartet by Mendelssohn with Eckert, Klengel, and Grenser, and Clara played the Trio by Mendelssohn[6]—actually both groups against my will. May Heaven forgive me, but I can't listen to so much music; I let Clara know this, and it troubled her; but she soon calmed down, since at the end of our first week I can certify that she possesses everything to make a man happy, and it is truly my greatest wish, beloved wife, for you to be as satisfied and happy with me.

Second week [CS]
from 20th to 27th September

Before I begin with the new week, I must confess to you, my dear husband, that I have never lived such happy days as those just passed, and surely I am the happiest wife on earth. To me it seems as though I love you more every minute, and I can truly say I *only* live through you. It is my greatest happiness when you are completely satisfied with me, and should something not be right for you, tell me so right away, really, my beloved husband, will you do that?—Now about Sunday the 20th. The architect Limberger visited us and implored that I should play in the Gewandhaus concert, but I have a feeling of opposition within me, and Robert also doesn't wish it. Limberger is a good but somewhat boring old man.

Wenzel came to play, fourhanded, the Sonata in *E♭ Major* by *Moscheles*. It is a masterpiece! The *Carls, Dr. Reuter, Wenzel* came to have dinner with us. I lost my appetite because of all my house-wife anxieties, which are that the guests might not like the food, or that there wouldn't be enough to eat, and so on and so forth.

After dinner Emilie came with Linna [List]—I was in a very bad mood, because Robert was not well.

David came also, with his wife. She is very kind, but one can never become intimate with her—is it her social position that holds one back?[7] I almost believe that, since her personality is really so simple!—

In the evening we had time yet for a little promenade. Robert spoke to me in such a friendly way that I became really happy again. I depend so much on his moods; it may not be good per-haps, but I can't help myself.

Emilie returned home with me, which I didn't like, because my maid had to bring her home in the storm and bad weather. It's often going to happen this way, and that is very annoying for me. I wonder why Emilie can't see this herself and let herself be picked up. Incidentally, she was in a very agreeable, friendly mood, and will always be my most loyal friend.

The 21st. So far I haven't been really industrious, but today I arose with the best intentions.

We have started with the Fugues of *Bach;* Robert marks those places where the theme always returns—studying these fugues is really quite interesting and gives me more pleasure each day. Rob-ert reprimanded me very strongly; I had doubled one place in oc-taves, and thus impermissibly added a fifth voice to the four-voice texture. He was right to denounce this, but it pained me not to have sensed it myself.

Marriage Diary I   9

There still continue to be distractions; Elise, August Kietz, in the afternoon Madame Devrient, [and] Emma Meyer kept me from working. It's annoying that when I am playing Robert can hear me from his room, for thus I cannot use the morning hours, the best ones for serious study.

Emma Meyer took me into town to her home. I found myself among a lot of Jews; one really feels a little uncomfortable there, although one hardly notices that the Meyers are Jewish. Emma is a dear good girl, who, I believe, loves me with complete sincerity.

Robert picked me up and displayed his complete affection in the most friendly way—it really makes me like him too much.

It really seems to me as though Emma loves him more than she herself wants to admit—but I'm not worried.

Tuesday the 22nd. Emilie visited me for a few hours—I was studying. Were I to allow myself to be disturbed, then I'd accomplish nothing anymore—my girlfriends will have to tolerate that.

In the afternoon a visit from Herr *Nathan* from Copenhagen. He played a *Chopin* etude, not without dexterity, but without a spark of inspiration. He is also one of those deplorable musicians who lacks the most important thing—talent.

In the evening I again began to study really earnestly the Concerto in *E Minor* by *Chopin,* also I'm now seriously looking into my husband's compositions. I have a dangerous female competitor in *Rieffel* by whom, rather than me, Robert prefers hearing his compositions played, as I was able to conclude from his remarks— that really irked me quite a bit! He said she plays the things more exactly; that may well be, because I always, when looking at the whole of a composition, overlook the details of performance, [such as] accents, of which Robert's compositions contain very many— one could say that almost every note has its meaning. I look at a composition in terms of performance, and that should no longer be; I shall strive to approach his ideals.

Friedrich Kistner visited us, and he too urged me to play in the first Gewandhaus concert. I don't want in the least to play, not in any case, but it's getting to be terribly difficult for me to refuse.

Kistner is an agreeable man and I like him; but it's amusing when he appears as a representative of the Gewandhaus administration, speaking with the greatest authority about *"we* are doing everything that is in *our* power," "*We* have had this artist come," etc.

Thursday the 24th. Bertha Constantin visited me. We spoke a lot about the late Madame Voigt.

In the evening I was at the *Lists'*; Robert came for me. I am always happy when he arrives, because by the time he does I have always been overcome with yearning; whenever he is not with me, I think about him constantly.

It's odd that Elise, despite her heavenly, beautiful voice, has never until now stirred me, as they say, but today she enchanted me with an aria by Rossini—I myself hardly know how; she sang it with unusual animation. Of Robert's lieder she sang a few, but it seems to me that with German lieder she lacks deeper emotion, an intimate understanding of the text; I really can't express myself very well about this, it is something that I don't know how to put into words. The same feeling once forced itself on me while listening to Pauline *Garcia* sing the Gretchen by Schubert, which she performed more for its effect on the audience than with that inner glow expressed so magnificently by the words as well as Schubert's music. Pauline *Garcia* delighted me every time, but just with this *German* lied she left me unsatisfied, which I really can't comprehend when it comes to this thoroughly musical creature who otherwise grasps everything with greatest speed in its complete truthfulness!—

The 25th. Duvigno, my old language teacher, visited me, to bring me his congratulations. He is a good old man and full of knowledge; he speaks and writes 12 languages.

Marriage Diary I 11

Saturday the 26th. Today it is already 14 days that we have been married! How beautifully and happily we've spent these days! But this week we were also fairly busy. Our fugal studies are continuing; every time we play one it becomes more interesting for me. Such great art with such a natural flow; one can say this about almost every one of the fugues. Compared to Bach's, Mendelssohn's fugues really strike one as impoverished, also it is too apparent how they are made, and how difficult it probably was for him at times. Perhaps it's foolish for me to want to make a comparison, but this forces itself upon me involuntarily whenever I (as I almost always do) play the Mendelssohn fugues after Bach's. Incidentally, I truly believe there is no one alive today who could write such fugues other than Mendelssohn, who since childhood has lived only with Bach, Händel, Haydn, and other old masters.

[RS, in the margin:] (*Cherubini*, Spohr, Klengel)

[CS continues:] The attorney *Schleinitz* came once more as delegate of the concert administration—they are in the greatest quandary; I'm supposed to play, but I absolutely cannot do it; in anticipation I wouldn't have a single quiet moment.

I played one hour for Amalie *Rieffel;* I grow fonder of her all the time, since it really seems to me that she pursues her art with complete love.

She wept bitterly; she said it's owing to dissatisfaction with herself—I know the feeling, it's also given me many bitter hours.

Emma Meyer came in the afternoon with her cousin to listen to me—I played, and sang many of Robert's lieder with an especially animated mood.

Robert's lieder book that he gave me for my birthday, and the one received from him earlier,[8] are real treasures for me; I sometimes want to bury myself in them completely. What a wealth of imagination and deep emotion is in these lieder.—

Emilie [List] visited me with her mother. I like to see some of my friends occasionally and thus feel quite happy in my home.

I close this week with the request to you, my dear Robert, that you might have patience with me and might pardon me when here and there I've said something stupid, which surely will happen frequently.

Third week [RS]
from 27 September to 4 October

"Every beginning is difficult." You are right, dear wife. How to begin reporting about this week, which was a joyful, a truly happy week of marriage. I swear that you agree with me. In a hundred instances I've again perceived you as a loving, solicitously unpretentious wife, and every day I observe your new accomplishments. We quarreled once because of the way you interpret my compositions. But you are not in the right, Klärchen. The composer, and only he alone, knows how his compositions are to be presented. If you were to believe you could do it better, that would be the same as a painter, for example, wanting to make a tree better than God had created it. He can paint a more beautiful one—but then it is a different tree from the one he wanted to represent. In short, that's the way things are. Surely no one would object when it comes to a few interesting exceptions made by very distinguished individuals. But it's always better for the virtuoso to present the work of art, not himself.

My Clara has been very diligent; yes, she burns for music. I heard her study new and old etudes by Chopin, also by Henselt, diverse things by Bach, [and] my "Fantasie" and "Kreisleriana." Also the F Minor Sonata by Beethoven. We are pursuing our daily studies of the Well-Tempered Clavier. I made two little

Marriage Diary I

duets, "Wenn ich ein Vöglein wär" and "Herbstlied" by Mahlmann. Clara is also so nice as to clean up a Ballade Album (including the "Löwenbraut"),[9] whereby she relieves me of a sour task. She likes so much to do everything, if it is for my benefit.

We often saw the Lists; the old man [List] is now here. Last Sunday morning [we were] together in the Kuchengarten. A strange family, equally interesting for painters and writers.

In addition many disturbances by visitors. Carl has been arrested on account of debts. We should help, but even with the best intentions that could only be a little.

Julius Becker brought new songs; everything peculiarly delicate, small, and fragile. One of them we liked especially.

[Gustav] Kellner from Weimar, a student of [Carl] Montag, visits us more frequently. Every evening he runs all around our house, making me madly jealous.

I think about the Russia trip with apprehension, and believe Clara does too. To get out of our small warm nest and go up there, when we have barely organized our things! Ugh. And yet we will have to undertake it.

I gave Clara a song by Burns to compose; but she doesn't dare to do it.[10]

A ballade by Chopin appeared yesterday, dedicated to me,[11] which gave me more pleasure than an official medal. Today is the first subscription concert. [Ferdinand] David will conduct it, since Mendelssohn is still in England. Besides Elise [List],[12] Schloss will also be singing.

The little Rieffel keeps herself completely hidden.

A strange year. The most magnificent fruit harvest I've ever seen—and no thunderstorms as yet.

This week for the first time I read more of [Pierre de] Beranger,[13] probably the most important French poet.

Nothing but jottings today. Don't be angry, little Clara. For me everything swims in music today; I have to get to the piano.

Fourth week [CS]
[4 to 10 October]

The 4th. Finally I heard a subscription concert again, but it gave me little satisfaction, except for the *Eroica* by *Beethoven,* which compensated for the first part, consisting of various shallow compositions. One is truly edified by such a Beethoven symphony; the more I hear it the greater the enjoyment—no music other than this gets all my feelings stirred up. The performance was very good except for a few mistakes in the last movement, and if one missed *Mendelssohn* it was really only visually, since one has gotten used to seeing him on the podium. By the way, I don't want to apply that to myself, because I must admit it came back to me vividly that Robert once said or wrote that the conducting of symphonies embarrasses him, and I have to agree with him that one gains a freer, almost poetic impression when the conductor's baton isn't constantly beating time.

The last movement of the *Eroica* has always seemed somewhat unclear to me, but that was due to the interpretation, for example, the one I heard in Berlin, where the various entrances of the theme did not emerge clearly—this time however it all seemed much more understandable to me, particularly because it was executed so very exactly (except for the few mistakes mentioned above).

Sophie Schloss has a full, strong voice, but it does not have a beautiful noble character, like Elise's. She does a lot of coloratura, but how well? nobody should ask that.

Marriage Diary I

Uhlrich played a concerto by David with much diligence but a rather small tone.

A Madame *Moody* has written asking whether I give lessons. Here in Leipzig I wouldn't do it for any price, but since she is a foreigner I would be more inclined to do so, which I also wrote her. If she is an Englishwoman, as I presume from the name, then I am afraid, because they don't take lessons in order to learn, but just because taking lessons is fashionable.

The 5th. In the evening I visited my aunt [Emilie] Carl. She is very self-controlled! Will misfortune never teach her to be a better housekeeper! —

On Sunday *Uhlmann* from Schneeberg and Kellner from Weimar had their noon meal at our house. The afternoon was tedious, we didn't know what to do with our guests. *Uhlmann* isn't musical at all, and *Kellner* still a beginner. He played some things by Hummel, showing good training. Like most young people from smaller places he lacks sophistication in life. He didn't leave us alone the whole day, followed each of our steps, and today already we let excuses be made a number of times, which otherwise I do most reluctantly; one just can't escape from these young people! A Rakemann *senior.* —[14]

The 6th. Tuesday. The *Lists* spent the evening at our house. *Elise* suffers and complains of stagefright; she wants to please everyone, and that won't work. Everyone gives her different advice, and thus she finally gets completely confused, unless she makes her appearance resolutely and decisively and sings what *she* wants [to sing]. I pity her: she has neither a musical father nor a musical mother who could advise her. But it is astonishing how broadly this girl has educated herself without any guidance and despite resistance on the part of the parents (earlier that is). The little *Lina* has a great talent for music, but it will be suppressed in her; the mother wants to make a housewife of her because that did not work out with the two oldest [daughters]. How pitiful is such a thing!—

The 7th. Today I studied fairly diligently, *Ballade* by *Chopin, C Major* Sonata by *Beethoven, Kreisleriana* etc: If I wanted to pursue my own pleasure I sometimes would gladly play more, but I get tired so easily, and so exhausted that after 2 hours of practicing I fall into the most terrible mood—I've noticed that so often, and I can only think that it stems from mental exhaustion.

My Robert is composing very industriously. Today he completed a "Gypsy Chorus"[15] that has a uniquely magical effect on me when I hear it—how beautiful that must sound, well sung!

Regarding our trip to St. Petersburg, things look bad—as for the war with the pasha of Egypt, things seem to be getting serious,[16] and then "adieu virtuosos"!

If I could only persuade Robert to travel with me to Holland and Belgium, so that use can be made of next winter—it's terrible for me to be unable to put my talents to use for him, now while I have the power for that. Think it over again once more, my dear husband! Let us use *only a few more* winters—I really also owe it to my reputation not yet to withdraw completely at this time. It is a feeling of responsibility toward you and myself that speaks within me.

Last week we finished the first book of the Well-Tempered Clavier by *Bach,* but did not continue our study of the second book— Robert wanted to rest for a week!

Thursday the 8th. I spent the evening at the *Lists'.* I met Elise in deepest melancholy, Emilie crying, Madame List imploring me not to leave; in short, it was an interesting scene! I did my best to cheer them all up a bit, and to inspire courage in Elise, in which I was finally somewhat successful. It really is a nice family, and Elise has her days when she is irresistably kind—as today, despite her melancholia, which on the contrary made her even more interesting.

Marriage Diary I 17

The 9th. Elise's anxiety is gaining ground in a way I have never seen it happen before. Several times she had already decided not to sing, to give up singing in public (and has not even started to); the parents are beside themselves, poor Emilie cries the bitterest tears, but most of all I pity Elise herself, who really has no one to depend on, whose parents, so completely unmusical, can inspire no courage in her. She tortures herself terribly with the illusion and regards her downfall next Sunday with certainty. Sometimes one has to laugh, but I almost don't feel like it any longer—I tremble about Sunday; if only she doesn't stop in the middle of the piece!—

For two days I haven't been able to study properly, on the *Lists'* account, and when I don't study for a day I always seem to see my retrogressions right away; also today I couldn't withstand the *Lists'* pleading and in the evening went along again.—Emilie read some things from *Lord Byron's* biography that interested me very much, since I've never yet known anything about him and even his writings are still very unfamiliar to me. I sometimes really feel my ignorance in the humanities, my lack of exposure to literature, quite oppressively! but when should I read? I don't find the time as others do, and then I believe I actually lack the drive for reading, which I cannot give to myself at all. I like to read, yes, but I can also leave a book long untouched, which Elise and Emilie for example are incapable of doing; they immediately go after everything there is to read, hence also their knowledge, their familiarity with everything that is happening in the world.

Sometimes I feel really unhappy with myself—when I look around thus in my empty head. Now it's all right so long as my Robert still is satisfied with me, but if that were not the case, then it would all be over for me!—

Saturday the 10th. Saturday always looks at me in a very uniquely friendly way! It always reminds me that a week of marriage has happily gone by. No weeks have gone by for me as fast as the last four; it wouldn't be good for that to continue—at the end one would be gray and old and hardly know *how that happened!* —

I'm chattering really stupid stuff, isn't that true my dear Robert?—but if in accordance with our agreement I have to write everything that I'm thinking at the moment, then the stupid stuff cannot be left out, that you will see, and accordingly proceed mildly in judging your wife.

With trembling I went to the Gewandhaus rehearsal today, but everything went well; despite her great anxiety one noticed nothing about Elise's voice, it only seemed a little weaker than usual to me. She sang well except for her idiosyncratic tempi, which are somewhat too slow; but she is right to sing slowly and distinctly rather than fast and unclean *à la Schloss.* If only Sunday were already over!

Moscheles was at the rehearsal—he came from England with *Mendelssohn.* I'm supposed to play for him, and am more afraid of that than of playing in front of a whole audience. In general I feel that my performance anxiety increases steadily; what might be causing that! I don't know!—

Since I may not disturb you in your little studio just now, then please give me permission, my dear husband, to give you, in spirit, a truly intimate kiss at the end of the week. I am ever happier being with you, and if it sometimes seems that I am not so happy, this is only because of other scruples that I demand of myself— mostly dissatisfaction with myself. I want to be worthy of standing at your side—surely you will not be angry at me for that!—

Fifth week [RS]
From 11th–18th October

The week has gone by under all kinds of interesting distractions. Elise's first appearance,[17] visits by Moscheles and others, prepara-

Marriage Diary I 19

tions for fêtes pp pp [praemissis praemittendis]—all this has unsettled us somewhat. Dreary impressions also were not lacking. Clara's father, who always seeks to damage me through words and deeds, spent the week here. Uncle Carl's affairs similarly became rather worse. Thus the balance between joy and sorrow always shifts. Nevertheless my Clara remains equally loving and comforting and wants to help wherever she can. She clings to her art more enthusiastically than ever, and last week she played occasionally in a way that made me forget the woman for the master and very often [I] had to praise her to others while she was looking on. Thus last Sunday morning she played the C Major Sonata by Beethoven in a way I've never heard it before; she also played several of the Kreisler pieces that way for Moscheles, and Thursday evening the trios of Moscheles and Mendelssohn in a soirée that we gave. As much I would have to say about Clara, so little does she have [to say] about me. Despite every effort to work and create, right now nothing wants to go right for me, which often fills me with depression. Where that comes from, I know well. I wasn't completely idle, however, and have ventured into a territory in which every first step surely does not always succeed.[18] About that later.—

Elise's first appearance took place passably; for a while she still ought to sing under the daily supervision of a master, a composer, who would understand how to bring this beautiful instrument to life. Her anxiety was certainly severe and affected even the quality of the voice.

On *Monday* the 12th there were many visitors. Bürck from Weimar, David with a Herr Landsberg from Rome for whom Clara played, then Moscheles and a celebrated author, Chorley,[19] whom Moscheles brought along, afternoon List's girls, then Mendelssohn with his wife.

The study of Bach has been at a standstill for 14 days already; instead I now read Shakespeare, in order to mark everything pertaining to music, which Clara then writes down in a nice book.[20] Later I think I'll write an article about Shakespeare's relationship to music, a theme that Mendelssohn should handle were he also a writer. Nothing more beautiful and pertinent has ever been said about music than by Shakespeare, and this at a time when it was still in its infancy. Here the genius of the poet reveals itself once again, rising above and observing every age.

But soon Bach will also be taken up again.

On *Tuesday* Zuccalmaglio (Gottschalk Wedel) came over, a poetic temperament, in whose presence I always feel particularly calm and secure. Count Reuss was also with us, with whom it is possible to converse only disjointedly; but an amiable gentleman.

On *Wednesday* we made our return visit to Moscheles; he was very well behaved, spoke slowly and thoroughly like a master. We enjoyed that. He is staying at Mendelssohn's.

Thursday evening must be marked in red. "First Soirée at Madame Schumann's"—Clara looked very fine in her little bonnet. Almost 20 guests, including a prince. Clara played the trios I mentioned above; Elise [List] sang several of my songs, and one by Mendelssohn, but none very well. Instead Clara bathed the entire company in beautiful music, which also made her seem thoroughly bathed and fresh and cheerful. And so was also the farewell at midnight.

Madame Mendelssohn burns as steadily as a wax candle. A strange image. Mendelssohn was lovable and had his artist's day. Moscheles as well; he played his Sonata in E Flat with Clara, then also by himself; the last however insecurely, stiffly, not even once with virtuosity.

On *Friday,* dinner at Friedrich Kistner's with almost exactly the same company that was with us. Clara sat between Mendelssohn and Count Reuss and carried on a lot; one nice word from Mendelssohn makes her glow for hours. Next to Moscheles I felt in a

Marriage Diary I 21

fairly good mood. All that excellent food and drink finally makes the mind sleepy, and we were happy at last to get up. The weather, incidentally, was even worse than normal.

In the evening I met Verhulst, who had returned from his trip to Vienna and reported many interesting things. Clara could barely conceal her pleasure over the news—

Yesterday finally, *Saturday,* there was music at *David's* with nearly the same company. Octet by Mendelssohn; a work written with the most magnificent freshness of youth. Septet by Moscheles, which came off badly after that. Schloss also sang. My sister-in-law Therese [Schumann] is here in Fleischer's house;[21] I was at her place yesterday.

Today I can't [write] any more.

Sixth week [CS]
[18–24 October]

Sunday the 18th. We, *Moscheles, Mendelssohn,* and I, rehearsed the D Minor Concerto by *Bach* for 3 pianos, and other things as well. It really seems to me that recently *Moscheles* has retrogressed significantly in his playing as well as in composing. It's natural of course—he is getting older now. Why do so many artists overlook the fact that they outlive themselves! I should think everyone should be aware of it when he retrogresses, and withdraw from the public in good time! poor Moscheles, I pity him; he must notice how little by little the enthusiasm for him is quenched, and that must be painful for him indeed!

Monday the 19th. Last week my Robert has expressed himself with considerable affection about me; after several sentences, however, I want to allow myself to interpolate ?: "one nice word from *Mendelssohn* makes her glow for hours" furthermore "she could barely conceal her pleasure over *Verhulst's* return"—those are defamatory jokes, which I will not allow to have written about myself so seriously!—

It troubles me greatly that Robert believes he cannot create anything now, and that this depresses him. Doesn't he think about what he has created in the year gone by? shouldn't the mind sometimes also take a rest? afterward he will break forth with even greater force. Or do you believe it couldn't happen anymore because now you have me for a wife, or do you have other worries because of me? that would be terrible for me, and could darken my happiness in being with you. You say "I know well where that comes from"—why don't you express yourself more clearly? Next week I will ask you please to tell it to me—you really don't want to conceal anything from me, that was your promise!

Mendelssohn's soiree in the Gewandhaus[22] was brilliant, but there was too much music, and no real *anima* ruled the whole, as it was supposed to have been in Liszt's presence that time.

Performed were the two overtures by *Beethoven* for *Leonora*, the Psalm "Wie der Hirsch schreit" by *Mendelssohn*, the *Hebrides* Overture, *Hommage à Händel* by *Moscheles*, performed by him and *Mendelssohn*, the *G Minor* by *Moscheles*, and the Triple Concerto by *Bach*. The *Leonora* Overture (the First) was the crown of the evening for me; the Second, also in *C major*, seems not from the same mold, appears more to me like the sketch for the big one, but contains some magnificent things and is most interesting, especially when one knows the First exactly. [Livia] *Frege* sang in the *Psalm* with a beautiful sonorous voice and good delivery. I was happy to hear her again after many years.[23] The *Hommage à Händel* and the *G Minor* Concerto by *Moscheles* did not please me. The composition of both *pieces* is quite beautiful, the *G Minor Concerto* written in such a noble style, but wasn't performed at all masterly by the composer. I regret to have this last impression of the composer!—

Marriage Diary I   23

The *Bach* Concerto went fairly well; I wasn't excited; that really can't happen at all when one is mentally exhausted by 2 hours of music, as I was! *Bach* must always be approached with fresh energy.

Now, I hope, a bit more tranquillity will again come into our lives—we yearn for that very much.

Tuesday the 20th. Visits from *Dr. Tischendorf* and in the evening from Madame *Friese* and *Amalie Rieffel*. Always the old stories! Madame *Friese* yammers about her household, the kitchen, cellar, husband, children, and she has no joy in living anymore; Amalie is in accord with the last statement; she lives in other spheres, she sees an unattainable goal ahead of herself, she is always in a terribly agitated mood and can't stand having anyone be her superior, because that makes her unhappy. I am the one who gives her the bitterest hours, she admits this to me, and yet because of her love wants to squeeze me to death—how does all this fit together? She can't stand to see me, to hear me, and yet she is completely exalted when she sees and hears me—a peculiar creature, who by and by must rub herself raw in this schism with herself. I have the most profound pity for her!—

Wednesday the 21st. I paid a visit to Madame Schmidt (wife of the theater singer). I found the two of them still just as tender with one another as shortly after their marriage. I thought to myself, "If only your Robert will also maintain his love for you like that, and for years yet, then your happiness will lack nothing"— and I believe it; he will of course always see my love for him, and that I intend to be good to him. Isn't that true, my dear husband?

Thursday the 22nd. the 3rd subscription concert. Symphony by *Mozart, Overture* to Berggeist by *Spohr, David* with a new concerto, *Schloss, Elise* [List], *etc.* The Adagio from the Symphony[24] enchanted me the most; it is so simple, so quiet, that it really puts one in a very calm mood. How Mozart succeeds so well with the simplest, most modest means—I think Mozart must always have had a cheerful, peaceful soul, because his music puts one in that mood. The Berggeist Overture left me unsatisfied. I didn't find it sufficiently flowing—Robert thinks that was due to the performance.

David played masterfully, but his composition is poor in inventiveness—the man has no calling whatsoever as a composer.

Schloss sang well, better than I've ever heard her—for sure, one always has to put up with a few unsuccessful passages! her voice is full and strong, I must admit, but has a mean streak in its character. How Elise [List] would be able to charm everyone with her noble voice, what a furor she would make here were she to sing only half as well in a concert as she does at home. Her anxiety tortured her terribly also today, she sang very feebly and received little applause—oh God, how that hurts one! the poor girl has already studied and learned so much, she lacks nothing to have the biggest success in the world, and now she has to have this tormenting anxiety, which spoils everything. I hardly believe that it will ever abate; she is so sensitive that yesterday's diminished applause surely will be unforgettable for her and possibly increase her anxiety even more. She will grieve a lot, that I know; I know all her feelings exactly.

A new piece of music, "Klänge aus Osten" by Marschner, left me cold except for a few moments. Only a few leftovers are to be found in it—its spirit is no longer fresh, but the striving for beauty, spirituality, cannot be missed.

The 24th. Yesterday and today were sad for me—I was and still am most depressed! I have neither energy nor desire for playing, and play noticeably worse these days than before. It may well be a physical condition, since I feel limp and exhausted, and sometimes I'm seized by a terrible fear for my health, which for the past year has always been shaky.

The *Lists, Reuter, Wenzel* spent a bit of the evening with us. Elise sang and tinkled the piano a lot—the first pleased, the last angered me. There is nothing I hate more than when someone

Marriage Diary I 25

tinkles small pieces from any Italian aria, and on top of that always with the wrong harmonies. That's a real trial of patience for a musical ear. If I could only break Elise of this habit—but this fault has rooted itself deeply; for as long as I've known her it has always been a favorite occupation of hers.

Robert thinks the only thing Elise's singing lacks is *heart, emotion.* That has already occurred to me many times, since her singing has never moved me as much as, e.g., a lied sung by *Devrient* or *Pauline Garcia,* but it always seemed to me as though she had emotion in her everyday life; why should she not be able to express this in singing as well? I don't understand it!—I believe that once she falls in love, she will also sing with more soul. It's certain that love has much to do with it, I discovered this in myself. When I began to love my Robert really intimately, then for the first time I felt what I was playing, and people said it must be a deeper impulse that makes me play so soulfully.

The sixth happy week is now over! every day I love my Robert more, and he was completely right to say, as he once did in a tender, fine poem with which he surprised me:

Das Innigste das Gott ersann *Ist ein guter Mann.* [25]	The most intimate thing God has devised is a good man.

Now I say it to myself every day and thank God, who has given me the joy to call so good a man my own.

Seventh week [RS]
25 to 31 October

A painful week for Clara; she has not been out except for the concert on Thursday. Some improvement began today. Klärchen, don't get any sicker for me. Besides, the week was one of the quietest. We sent off some of the visitors. Clara was also not allowed to play. And thus for once we plunged into reading, chiefly in Shakespeare, even in Jean Paul (Fibels Leben), with whom Clara becomes better acquainted for the first time. Also I composed a few things:

Two lieder from the Orpheus [annual] of 1841 and by Eichendorff, also the beautiful patriotic one by Nic. Becker.[26]

Letters to Lvov and Liszt have been sent off. The first we expect back from Paris, the latter perhaps for a short while from Hamburg.

Montag from Weimar, a pleasant person and full of the best aspirations, visited us more often; he is spending the winter here.

Thursday brought a beautiful concert (including the Symphony by Schubert that Clara heard for the first time).[27] Elise [List] sang better and also to greater applause. Now one can no longer think of her giving up singing in public.

Friday Dr. Tischendorff left for Paris; he gave me this peculiar compliment: that he was happy not to have met me earlier, since this way the farewell was less painful for him. A refreshing person, however.

This entire week of tribulation the weather was beautiful; this however is always more painful than joyful for those who are sick, but they are mistaken. It is worse to be sick and [have] cloudy skies. Now let yourself be comforted and kissed, my dear Clara, and consider that everything is endurable in a house where love still resides.

Eighth week [CS]
[4–8 November]

The 4th. My indisposition has not improved as yet—my anxiety increases from day to day. I am depressed, and various worries tor-

Marriage Diary I 27

ment me—God grant that my fears will not come true! my great love for Robert makes me torture myself; I want to give him only pleasure, and give him worries. I lie down constantly—what luck that there are books, otherwise I would bury myself completely in my grief.

Last Sunday we had Montag and Lorenz as dinner guests.

Schlegel gave her farewell concert—I did not attend. It seems that also this week will pass by quietly. I'm not allowed to play, also not to go out; occasionally I receive a visit from the Lists, which distracts me somewhat.

Franz Liszt will come soon—only for one day, as he wrote, in order to visit *Mendelssohn* and *Robert* incognito, which he antici- pates will excite him greatly. I look forward to seeing him again!

The 5th. Madame *Friedrich Kistner,* Madame *Friese,* Amalie *Rieffel,* etc., also *Sophie Kaskel,* my former girlfriend, now Count- ess *Baudissin,* visited me. Sophie was very friendly; I wish her well from the heart—the poor thing has endured many love pangs be- fore a husband turned up. But in the end isn't it the *Countess* whom she loves more than her husband? Tenderness did not radi- ate from her eyes, instead there was satisfaction with herself. I should pity her, if I'm not mistaken.

I could not attend today's Gewandhaus concert. Apparently I did not miss much. Elise [List] sang to very little applause; by contrast, *Schloss* had to repeat her aria. God knows what it is with Elise! Robert says that the family is not guided by a lucky star, and it really seems to be like that. I can't say how sorry I feel for her.

A Herr *Kufferath* played the pianoforte rather solidly, as Robert puts it, and for that was rewarded with abundant applause. He is also supposed to have much talent for composition.[28]

Amalie *Rieffel* is thinking about playing very soon, and she came to see me today for some advice. Her playing is as eccentric as her personality. The playing is so restless that it makes one anxious. She has very remarkable dexterity, studies diligently, one hears that; she also has expressiveness once a quiet moment comes over her, which happens rarely to be sure, but she hurries everything so much; she flies over the keyboard in such a way that not one tone is like another, and the touch of the fingers has become peculiarly uneven. I've told her all this, but I don't believe she can ever be cured,—where inwardly she is extraordinarily restless, so also each of her fingers; the individual joints twitch constantly— sometimes I have to laugh, but in general I feel sorry for her, and for that reason I never stop telling her the truth as much and as often as possible, in the hope that it may perhaps do her some good anyhow.

On *the 6th,* Friday, Dr. *Kühne* visited us, with his bride Fräulein *Harkort,* an agreeable pretty girl, and one who seems to me not lacking in spirit, if one may judge by the eyes, in which one can see much fire. I would like to get to know her better, perhaps we might get along well together!—

Elise [List] came to see me to announce her imminent departure, which shocked me quite a bit. As much as I regret that I am now losing my best girlfriends so suddenly, I could not, wanting to be good to her, advise her to sing again once more—her recurring humiliation in the presence of Schloss must not repeat itself, and one could anticipate that. As is the custom among singers, *Schloss* has done her best to suppress her, and by blackening her character has damaged her in the eyes of the public, for which Elise, with her naturalness that allows her to say everything she thinks, has surely given some cause.

These singer intrigues are really *miserable!*—

I feel somewhat better again, and that has woken me from my sadness, which had gained ground significantly—I thought I might never be well again.

Today I will also try to play again.

Marriage Diary I 29

Robert is busily composing lieder and always anew; where indeed do they come from—the sparks!—The last one, "der Schatzgräber" by [Eichendorff] is magnificently conceived, and another pearl in the Book of Songs.

Lvov, adjutant to the emperor of Russia, visited us. He is a spirited, kindly man, and if we ever go to Petersburg we can count on his protection. But he advised us against next winter, since *Liszt* will be there, and one must not try to compete with him. Whomever he does not enchant with his art he will bewitch with his personality—generally, however, both happens. That has long been my concern since, were I really able to give satisfaction with my art, my personality still lacks everything needed to produce success in the world.

Thus I put Petersburg out of my mind for next winter—it causes me conflict. Should I now sit quietly for the entire winter, not earning money, which I could do so easily? Everyone keeps asking why I don't travel—I will fall into total oblivion, and a few years from now, when maybe we will want to make a tour, who knows what other artistic matters people will be occupied with. I want so much to travel this and maybe also next winter, and then to withdraw from the public, live for my home, and give lessons. We can then live without worries—think it over once more very thoroughly, my dear husband.

Lvov plays a Concerto *dramatique* of his own tomorrow before noon in the Gewandhaus. Unfortunately my indisposition still hinders me from taking part in such indulgences. In the meantime I'm supposed to give a lesson to a Madame *Moody,* an Englishwoman—that will not be sufficient compensation.

Sunday the 8th. Today I woke up with much love—on such days (and they are not infrequent) my Robert must put up with many kisses, and he also seems to like that, hm?—Well, occasionally you must let me have a little written conversation with you, because during the whole day I can't get ahold of you often enough.

You may tell me about today's *matinée musicale*—that belongs to the 9th week.

Ninth week [RS]
from 8th to 15th November

During the last week a number of things have changed in our little life and household. The Lists went away on the 9th—to Weimar for the time being; also Agnes Röller, our housekeeper, on the 12th. We were not happy to see either of them leave.

Dear Clara's state of health has improved greatly. Last Monday she went out again for the first time, and also a few times more later on; but you still had to take good care of yourself all the time, little dove.

Our joy with one another is still growing tremendously—and that is good.

Clara is allowed to play the piano only a little these days. The trip to Petersburg is abandoned; maybe we will go to Copenhagen. We've also talked about Paris a lot; we decided to go there later for a longer time. Let's keep to that. First I still would very much like to write a piano concerto and a symphony. I now have enough songs (over 100)—but it is difficult for me to let go. I have also set to music the beautiful "Rheinlied" by Becker, which all Germany is talking about; it came out a few days ago. With that I saw clearly how difficult it is to write singable things for the people.

Lvov departed already Sunday evening. On the same evening the Lists were at our place for the last time, as well as a few friends.

Marriage Diary I 31

The visitors: *Kufferath,* a talented artist; *Friedrich* from Dresden, a sheep trying to seek his fortune with Weinlich; *Schloss;* the little *Rieffel;* the violin genius *Hilf; Lyser* from Dresden; among others.

[CS, in the margin:] Thursday in the Gewandhaus we heard the *A Major Symphony* of *Beethoven, Bennett's* charming Overture to "Waldnymphe," and the *cellist Griebel* from Berlin, whom luck did not favor. The man is very sickly, and thus his playing also lacked a certain uplift, enthusiasm—he played feebly and sluggishly. Schloss pushes herself more to the front all the time, and the way they cheer her on it seems as if she had made the audience completely forget her ugliness.

[RS continues:] Friday night we were at Livia Frege's for a musicale. 1st act of Fidelio [by Beethoven]. Songs by Schubert and Mendelssohn, which Frege sang well. On the whole little of interest.

Saturday night 1st Soiree in the Gewandhaus; Clara was not well enough to attend; I also [was] tired from much work and music.

Clara told me that I seemed different toward Mendelssohn; surely not toward him as an artist—you know that—for years I have contributed so much to promoting him, more than almost anyone else. In the meantime—let's not neglect ourselves too much. Jews remain Jews; first they take a seat ten times for themselves, then comes the Christians' turn. The stones we have helped gather for their Temple of Glory they occasionally throw at us. Therefore do not do too much [for them] is my opinion. We must also do things and work for ourselves. Above all let us now come ever closer to the beauty and truth in art.

Tenth week
[15–22 November]

[CS]

Sunday the 15th. First I must tell you, my dear husband, that I agree with you completely in regard to the above statement, and that I have sometimes, silently, had similar thoughts, but out of great admiration for Mendelssohn's art have again and again adopted the old excessive attentiveness toward him. I will take your advice and not degrade myself too much before him, as I have done so often.

We had *Reuter* and *Hilf* as dinner guests. I'm afraid that the latter will soon regard violin playing as his craft! I don't know whether I'm wrong, but that's how it seemed to me, his behavior is so lacking in artistry.

The Englishwoman has had her 3rd lesson with me today. Nothing more untalented can exist in this world! she is unable to place a single finger on the keyboard naturally, partly because of nervous weakness (which plays a big role with her), partly as the result of poor training, and yet this woman plays—*Moses* Fantasy by *Thalberg, Serenade* by *Liszt,* etc.! ! ! As a person she is quite refined and amiable, and nothing about her reveals the stiffness of the English. Her daughter usually accompanies her and throughout the entire hour sits immobile at the head of the piano-forte. (I receive 2 thalers for the lesson.)

Tuesday the 17th. The "Rheinlied" by Robert is selling very well at *Friese's,* which makes me very happy.

Madame *Friese* often visits me. The woman is a good soul, if only she herself wouldn't mention it so often! She always tells me a lot about Amalie *Rieffel,* about her being in love, about her vanity, about her greed, etc., but is not ill disposed toward her for that, which one really cannot be, at least not I, although there are some

Marriage Diary I   *33*

things about her of which I disapprove—my God! none of us are perfect!—

I have seen little of the *Carls* and I want to withdraw (from her) more and more; she is too rough, too mean a woman, and several times it seemed to me as if she wants to meddle with my household, and I don't like that. She thinks I am much too good to the servant girl, don't exert enough authority in my house, and would really like me to agree with her views, but to that I say no thanks. After all, I consider all external influence on a household to be damaging, but especially in a marriage, and it destroys the unity that the fortune of marriage brings, as we, Robert and I, discover more every day. Would I not have been able to spare myself and Robert many hours of disunity had this tyrant (one can rightly call her that) not been around me? certainly! My intention is firm as a rock; I will live under nobody's influence other than that of my husband, who after all is the only one I live for.

On *Wednesday the 18th* we received the following news from *Graf* in Vienna: my piano, which my father has withheld from me until now, is in Dresden at *Hesse's* and can be redeemed by paying 60 thalers. (He claims to have advanced this amount, which includes freight from Vienna to Leipzig, but I have already paid this out of my own pocket 2 years ago.)[29] On advice of the attorney *Krause* in Dresden, who has accepted our case, Robert for now will deposit the 60 thalers so that the piano will at least no longer be standing in someone else's house, and later it will be determined whether Father even has the right to demand this sum. How happy I will be when I finally have my piano back, which has given me considerable grief. It was kind of *Graf* to write us about it, since Father's intention was that he (*Graf*) should redeem the piano. Sometimes one can barely find one's way out of the countless intrigues that this man instigates. There are calm moments when conciliatory sentiments for my father arise within me, but these are again immediately smothered by a bad move, by a damaging cabal. The man wants to tear even the smallest, weakest sentiment for him out of my heart, and he is beginning to succeed completely.

The Englishwoman came today despite the bad weather. That's a zealous pupil. Today I started her with the little Waltz in *A Minor* by *Chopin*. She will never learn it, as generally she will never learn the shortest exercise—nothing can be done to remedy that anymore.

With Robert I paid visits to the *Harcorts*, the *Baudissins*, he to *Kühne*, I to *Schloss*; I also visited the sick Madame *Meyer*. *Emma* [Meyer] is love itself toward me, and never lets me go without a present, if only a nice pear or apple.

Therese Schumann came to us to announce that soon she would not longer be that, but Madame *Fleischer*. This is a lucky match for her, and both of us hope that it may last forever; it is no trivial matter to bind oneself to a man for one's entire life, when this happens not by inclination but for reasons of good judgment.

This evening passed amid sad thoughts and melancholy tears, which my Robert chased away over and over again, as much as he had brought them about, although completely without his fault. I crab at myself constantly and may not suffice for *him*. Forgive me for that!—

On *Thursday the 19th* the attorney *Krause* spent several hours at our house, mainly to discuss our case concerning my father. I had a small argument with him over *Sophie Kaskels's* (*Baudissin*) playing. I can't stand it when people pass negative judgment on something they don't understand at all.

Emilie *List* wrote me that they want to spend the entire winter in Weimar because of the weak condition of her mother, who is

Marriage Diary I 35

not allowed to undertake the strenuous trip to Paris just now. Elise sang in the theater there to great applause.

Friday (Day of Penance) we were at a musical *matinée* at *Hofmeister's.* The quartet music was bad, but the red wine was supposed to be so much better.

Amalie *Rieffel* played the First Ballade by *Chopin* with fire, only her fingers gave out several times. I maintain that fire and passion may never proceed at the expense of precision, since then it won't bring complete gratification; also I don't like it when the fire consists of an unstoppable haste, which isn't always the case with Amalie but does happen occasionally. That's a fault against which I guard myself incredibly, and which has happened to me very often, especially in the past. Hurrying, e.g., in passages, is a sign of inexperience, when it does not match the character of the piece, perhaps indicated by the composer himself, but then it is *agitato*—something else!—I got into a quarrel with Robert over Amalie, but it soon became very personal and distressing for me. *Tempi passati.*

Saturday the 21st we made our return visit to *Therese* [Schumann]. She seems to be happy, and one cannot blame her for that. She will be in a completely worry-free situation—this and good health surely make for happiness. *Fleischer's* daughters (her future daughters as well) are unpretentious, well-bred girls.

Sunday the 22nd was a restless day, as always the day when one has guests for dinner, even if this is ever so simple. Throughout the entire noon [meal] I always endure a thousand anxieties [asking myself] whether the guests like the taste and [hoping] I don't bring dishonor to my husband. *Madame Friese,* Amalie *Rieffel,* and *Verhulst* were our guests today. After the meal there was much talk about music—*Verhulst* enormously enjoys making musical jokes, but that soon becomes disgusting for others.

Amalie was sad about her fate, that she can't be *me*, that she doesn't position every finger the way *I* do, etc. I tried to console her as much as possible; she, who has learned so much, ought to find such reflections unnecessary—surely her father is much to blame for that, she must have a sad existence with him.

I have now also gotten acquainted with the Kreutzer "Rheinlied" but found it worse than I had expected from the description. Robert's composition is without a doubt the best of all, very popular besides and also easy to remember, as becomes more and more apparent all the time.

Robert has again composed 3 magnificent lieder. The texts are by *Justinus Kerner:* "Lust der Sturmnacht," "Stirb, Lieb' und Freud'!," and "Trost im Gesang." He conceives the texts so beautifully, he grasps them so deeply, as no other composer I know of; no one has a soul like his. Oh! Robert, if only you knew sometimes how happy you make me—indescribable!

Eleventh week [RS]
from the 22nd–29th November

A quiet week, which went by with composing and much loving and kissing. My wife is love, kindness, and unpretentiousness itself. That's what everyone says as well. Health and vigor also are gradually returning to her, and she often opens the piano. What concerns me, I really can't let go of mine—and dear Clara forgive me—so long as I am young and strong, I really want to create and work as long as possible, even if the demons were no longer to compel me.—

A small cycle of Kerner poems is ready; they gave dear Clara pleasure, as well as pain; since she must purchase my love so often with [my] silence and invisibility. Well that's the way it goes in

Marriage Diary I 37

marriages of artists, and if they love each other, that's always good enough.

Few visitors came this week, to Clara an old suitor, Mainberger from Hamburg; to me a singer Bouillon, Hering from Bautzen, frequently Montag and J. Becker, and the little pianist Dörffel, also a musician Hauschild who has made a Gallopage out of my "Rheinlied."[30] The "Rheinlied" generally has brought about much commotion and noise. Friese has prepared a school edition, which we really want to work on with our future children (God willing). How I look forward to that, to the first little song and lullaby. Pst!

Twelfth week [CS]
[30 November–6 December]

The 30th. Monday. My husband surely was right when, while turning this book over to me this week, he said to me, "I am a scoundrel!" I believed it immediately, but as I read further I saw how cunning, incorrigible you are! but I love you anyhow, even with your roguishness. Do you believe me?!—

One more happily married couple in the world. Herr *Voigt* and *Bertha Constantin,* a superior, well-educated girl who was a very intimate friend of Voigt's late wife.[31] Now that happens to be a different sort of happily married couple than we were: they melt in bliss "my little Bertha, my little Carl!" *Eau de cologne, bonbons, etc.* are not missing from the bridegroom's pocket: Bertha coughs—for God's sake give me a *bonbon!* "Here my little Bertha, you poor child!" One can imagine more! But from the bottom of my heart I don't begrudge them their happiness! I for my part thank my God that I did not have a bridegroom like that, indeed that no one other than Robert became my husband.

Ole Bull visited us today. He is an affectionate, spirited man, has much similarity to *Liszt* in his manners. His concert took place this evening; I went there with the greatest expectation and found him to be a highly original, interesting artist, also resembling *Liszt* at times in his playing, but this interest which he awakens is only a momentary one, and the demand for something more solid soon follows. *Lipinski's* or *Vieuxtemps's* playing produced more true enjoyment for me. Unfortunately many of the finest *pp* effects that he (*Ole Bull*) brought eluded me, since I'm not in a position to perceive them on the violin. His entire appearance in private and public is genuinely artistic and surely does not fail to make a good impression on anyone. His wife, a Frenchwoman, was present at the concert, sparkling with diamonds (an adornment rather rarely seen by us in Leipzig) and, what's more, with two big, black, beautiful eyes. Robert thinks, incidentally, that she probably was the most indifferent person in the entire hall. I cannot understand that!—

Eike, Ole Bull's secretary, sang in the concert; little can be said about that, only this much, that after some tramping around in the animal kingdom we discovered that he resembles a spitz.

On *Wednesday, the 2nd of December, 1840,* we went to visit *Ole Bull, Therese Fleischer, Livia Frege,* but had the misfortune (as happens on certain days) to find no one at home except for Madame *Ole Bull* instead of her husband. She is still quite young and really very pretty, but talked to me with such indifference about her imminent separation from her husband (who is traveling to Petersburg) that any attraction she had for me disappeared.

I'm beginning to study regularly again but am not getting any happier about my playing. Something may turn out well at times, but it is only by accident, and thus my playing cannot produce any true enjoyment, since I play anxiously, and this is easily communicated to the listener. This fear of performing for someone

Marriage Diary I 39

often distresses me, but I cannot help myself—sometimes I console myself with the idea that perhaps it stems from bodily weakness as well! I am always exhausted, and the thought saddens me that it may take a long time for me to get my old strength back. I want that for Robert's sake, because it is terrible for a man always to have a lamenting wife around. Moreover, with all this my Robert is so affectionate, and agreeably encouraging, that he almost always chases my troubled thoughts away.

The "Rheinlied" has now lived to see its fifth printing. Robert has sent it to Weimar for 4 male voices; it is supposed to be sung there. He has also set it for orchestra with chorus,[32] which will be sung in the Schützenhaus next Sunday. All of the Rheinlieder are supposed to be performed there, and votes will be collected for the one that has made the best impression. That's an agreeable game for the public, not so for the composers.[33]

Friday the 4th. The concert given yesterday to benefit the widows of musicians can in every regard be called a brilliant one. *Mendelssohn,* who performed his "Lobgesang," was immediately received with enthusiastic applause and a fanfare from the musicians as he made his appearance at the beautifully garlanded podium. The "Lobgesang" is a masterpiece and came across magnificently, only somewhat too tumultuously at times. The most beautiful pieces in it are a duet for 2 sopranos and the chorus in *D major* that follows it, ending in a grandiose pedal point.

The "Jubel-Overture" [by Weber] surely never fails in its effect. After a long absence the Fantasy for Piano with Chorus by *Beethoven* was performed once again, well rehearsed, only not presented with sufficient inwardness by Herr Kufferrath. *Schloss* becomes increasingly boring for me and that was the way she also sang the aria from Titus [by Mozart], which one is almost sick and tired of hearing.

Tonight we spent at *Mendelssohn's*, where *Ole Bull* played 2 quartets by *Mozart* and one of his own, the last one as a solo piece. The first works seemed very boring to me, Robert thinks he played them very monotonously, but the final piece was executed by him in an extraordinary way, and also in its composition struck me as better than the earlier *pieces* of his that I've heard. In his character he is a peculiar mixture of the artistic and inartistic. How does it sound when an artist says, e.g., "One day I play here, another day there, and I do that until I collapse, because I am a poor man and have to earn money!?"—his wife is a disagreeable, cold creature, and hasn't the least bit of the amiability of French women, nor cultivation, it seems.

I was urgently requested by *Mendelssohn* and *Ole Bull* to play, which put me in a very horrible mood, since I had to refuse. Who knows whether I would have remained steadfast, had it not been for the portentous glances of my husband, who incidentally had the complete right not to let me play. One must make oneself somewhat scarce, and besides, by playing right now I would not cover myself with glory, which Robert also knew very well.

Saturday the 5th. Today it's a quarter of a year that we are married—surely the happiest quarter year that I have ever lived. Every day I get up with renewed love for my Robert, and if I sometimes seem to be sad, almost unfriendly, then these are but worries that always originate from love for him. I hope that all quarter years to come shall find us no less fortunate than the one just passed. If something can momentarily dull my happiness, then it is the thought of my father, for whom I feel the greatest pity, that he cannot be witness to our joy, that heaven has denied him a *heart,* and he is insensitive to such happiness as ours. Surely he doesn't have any pleasure right now, and through his behavior has lost not only me but all of his friends as well, not that he had so many of

Marriage Diary I   41

these. That is sad, and even more so for me as I am his daughter. I hope that you, my most intimately beloved Robert, won't bear me a grudge because of that; this childish feeling simply does not let itself be wholly suppressed, and thus you will also forgive me for sometimes having a sad thought about my father.

Well, I see you wrinkling your brow, but a really tender kiss, I think, will make you smile again, and besides, whoever possesses a heart as you do mine can really smile all the time!—Yet it seems to me as though I now would have to ask you, "Are you all right?" I think that a friendly glance shall say yes to my question. My heart is so full that I would like to speak to you longer still, but I've already been prattling long enough, and for that amply plead for forgiveness.

I spent this evening with *Therese Fleischer*—Robert came to pick me up. *Therese* seems very happy, and why shouldn't she be? she really has everything and perhaps has achieved even more than her heart's desire.

Sunday the 6th. quiet day!

Last week I read the "Heart of *Mith-Lothian*" by *Walter Scott*, which engaged all my emotions. The characters portray the personalities so well that they appear before one's eyes, and the course of the action proceeds so naturally that one believes oneself to be totally involved in the reality. I've read nothing for a long time that has excited me as much.

With the closing of this week I beg for your indulgence once more, my dear husband—I couldn't pull my thoughts together very well this week, so many things were actually going around in my mind, my playing above all, which could drive me to despair were it not for you, who always comforts me so lovingly. But I'm still very worried about it, and what will become of me if that does not change?

Thirteenth week [RS]
from 6th–13th December

Much necessary work, which the end of the year always brings, forces me to hurry and be brief today.

Clara is well and affectionate, as of old—I often find her at the piano nearly every day; but she is right, it's the minimum that she allows herself to play so as not to lose some of her dexterity. We must make other arrangements for ourselves later on, so that Clara can play as often as she desires.

I too am busy—the *J. Kerner* Cycle is ready except for a few things, and much in general has wandered into print during the last few days. Don't consider me petty if I record in the diary what I have earned as a composer this year; I've already taken in 240 thalers, outstanding in sold manuscripts 330 thalers, and yet unsold for at least 340 thalers; that really is a handsome amount to live on.

The Rheinlied competition took place on the 6th in the Schützenhaus, where it seems that madness reigned. G. Kunze won the prize. The public's enthusiasm still remains great. Friese sold around 1,500 copies of mine.

Montag from Weimar ate at our house and traveled back to Weimar that evening; a not altogether happily maturing talent, but good and decent in character.

Wednesday a letter arrived from Major Serre with proposals for reconciliation that apparently came from Clara's father himself. What we have to do in response is indicated so clearly that we hardly can waver. There can be no talk of even a merely ostensible relationship between me and him. Clara, however, must not reject it. So that is the way we replied.

Rieffel played in the Thursday concert; Clara takes much interest in her, which pleases me. After the concert we and a few others got together at Friese's, where things proceeded in an un-pretentiously joyous way, really cheerfully.

Saturday with Clara at the Gewandhaus soiree. Mendelssohn played—as only Mendelssohn can play. I heard a trio by Beethoven in *E flat* for the first time; as one gets older "first times" become rarer; it was a festive occasion for body and soul.

Among the strangers were a theologian by trade who nonetheless wants to become a complete musician—Wöhler from Schwerin, and last Sunday an Englishman, Smith, with Verhulst. Clara played, and my Fantasy for Liszt[34] [went] very beautifully.

Ole Bull is still traveling around the vicinity. Agnes [Röller] wrote that she is a bride. Everyone around us is getting married. Happy [are] those who know and love one another, like my Clara and me.

Adieu for today, dear diary; greetings to your reader.

Fourteenth week [CS]
from 14–20th December

The 22nd. This time I'm late, my dear Robert, in turning the diary over to you, but hope to find forgiveness for that since as you already know you cannot accuse me of negligence. I shall write down whatever I can recollect from memory—surely there's much that I've forgotten.

On *the 15th* I was surprised by a visit from Major *von Berge's* wife from Dresden, whom I always esteem and love as a very honest, highly intelligent, but also tenderhearted woman. She was just passing through, and therefore I could enjoy little of her.

On *the 16th* there was a brilliant Gewandhaus concert. The king [Friedrich August II] attended the concert and drew in a lot of people who otherwise don't go to concerts. The Oberon Overture [by Weber], which opened it, made no impression whatsoever on me today, while usually it has always delighted me very much. Mendelssohn played the *A Minor* Sonata, op. 47, by *Beethoven* with David. He played it the way he plays everything—masterfully, full of spirit, but in my opinion without sufficient grandiosity, on the whole too hastily. Could it have been that he did not want to bore the king and thus took the tempi so extraordinarily fast? The violin truly had to fight in order to keep in step with the piano. *Mendelssohn's* "Lobgesang" came at the end. I did not hear much of it, because the yearning to see my Robert was painful.

Mendelssohn was very graciously praised by the king—I don't know anything else as yet!

A talented young composer, Baron *Lövenskjold* from Copenhagen, visited my husband—I haven't met him yet.

Robert was working very diligently this week, but has not felt entirely well since our wedding, which occasionally makes me very sad and worried. We've had to endure much very cold weather these days—my poor husband never could get warm.

For the past week the piano has completely stepped into the background. All the time that Robert was away I spent trying to compose a lied (which was always his wish) and then I finally succeeded to produce *three,* which I want to present to him for Christmas.[35] But they are of no value, only *a very feeble effort,* so I count on Robert's forbearance, and that he will think it was surely done with the best intention, to fulfil this wish as well as all his other wishes. Be gracious, my friend, and be indulgent with this gift, feeble as it is but presented with full love.

I'm thinking of studying diligently again after the holidays—I need that very badly! The sewing and writing has made my fingers stiff, but surely that can be made well again!

I am supremely happy, and becoming more so all the time—if my Robert is [as happy] as I am, then I will wish for nothing fur-

Marriage Diary I 45

ther—because of my love I could sometimes hurt him with my kisses; instead of becoming quieter (as they say one gets to be in a marriage) I become ever more fiery!—my poor injured husband!

Fifteenth week [RS]
from 20–27th December

The Christmas week has just now arrived for me. How much I would like to describe it and how much dear Clara of my heart has delighted and gifted me. Specifically 3 lieder pleased me, in which she is still as enthusiastic as a young girl, and in addition is a much clearer musician than before. We have the cute idea of weaving them in with some of my own and then having them printed. That will result in a booklet truly warmed by love.[36] But in addition I received a lot of other things from Clara, everything well chosen and also useful. The Christmas-tree was a master-piece.

My bestowal of presents came off very poorly by comparison. The best was a present of all of Beethoven's sonatas—[published] by Haslinger in Vienna.

Reuter, Wenzel, and Julius Becker came over later. Clara played a lot—we stayed up until 2 o'clock with music and eating and drinking.

On the 1st holiday Löwenskjold and Helsted, two Danes, musicians, visited us. Clara played a few things for them, also from the Kreisler pieces; she played them [with deep understanding, as though directly] from my soul.

On the 2nd holiday we went to Voigt for dinner, fairly cheerful. This time Clara sat at the head of the table—and again mistakenly, since his mother-in-law should have been there. Thus (unintended) silliness also gets its revenge.

46   The Marriage Diaries of Robert & Clara Schumann

The Englishwoman Mrs. Moody, Clara's student, also had her last lesson that day; I believe they parted as good friends. In the evening we were at Therese's [Fleischer], where for the first time I also observed her husband more carefully. I like him.

For the past week my wife has been giving me beautiful hopes [of pregnancy]. May God protect you.

Sixteenth Week   [CS]
[27 December 1840–2 January 1841]

This week you gave me little, my good Robert, but you are affectionate in each of your words, and have also been that way with your entire personality last week as well as this one.

Robert has described my Christmas joys so quickly that it seems I never had any, and yet I received such generous presents. 3 new (just published) compositions from Robert[37] pleased me very much, but very specially a lied composed for me, "Waldgegend" by *Kerner*, that surely is one of the most beautiful. He had put Henriette's [Reichmann] wedding present (an embroidered representation of *Egmont's* Dream) into a magnificent frame for me, and in addition I found several beautiful gold pieces, which I prefer to such presents, which in the end would have been of no use to me.

Nor did my Robert leave out *Eau de Cologne, soap, etc.*

The 28th. Therese [Fleischer] with her daughters Fräulein *Schloss, Emma Meyer,* and Madame *Schmidt* visited me in the evening. The first ones left early, but thereafter we stayed together for a while yet; Herr *Schmidt* then came as well, and [with] my husband there was assiduous singing, duets, terzets, also [a] gypsy chorus by Robert, which I was extraordinarily pleased to hear for once. Nothing seems to have pleased Robert more that evening than Madame *Schmidt,* who is exceedingly pretty and with whom

Marriage Diary I 47

his own wife may surely not allow herself to be compared. I was besieged with various thoughts that finally made me keep quiet.

Last week I also had a visit from Herr Consul *Schmidt,* who introduced his mother to me, a witty, lively woman.

He sent Robert an English paper *"Athenaeum,"* in which the following appears about both of us, by *Chorley* (who was here in *Moscheles's* company):

> Correspondence from *Nuremberg.*
> *Yet a word more concerning the musical attractions of Leipsig—its being the residence of Rochlitz [who] must not be forgotten, the patriarch of German criticism, and who lived in the hard days, when the* Allgemeine Musikalische Zeitung *had to deal with that comet of audacity and enterprise—Beethoven. The Chevalier's journal is now under other editorship, and has become less venturesome in the cause of the romanticism of to-day, leaving the worship of the Liszts and Berliozes of the newest school of art to its rival the* "Neue Zeitschrift" *whose conductor,* Herr Schumann, *not only critically admires, but creatively emulates, these passionate and dreamy artists; for his compositions, in parts beautiful, symmetrical, and attractive, are confessedly among the most decided expressions of mysticism which have ever been uttered through the medium of the piano. This gentleman, by the way, has a helpmate, artistically of the first value, in his lady— better known in England by her maiden name, Clara Wieck. I know not how otherwise to characterize her treatment of the pianoforte, than by saying, that I have never heard any display so clear of what Uncle Selby would have called the femalities,—rarely a touch more decided, without exaggeration or violence,— rarely a reading of music more masterly, broad, and intelligent. Indeed, if there be a want in Madam Schumann's playing, it is of the daintinesses and coquetries, which are frivolous when coming from a man's fingers, and can hardly be cultivated without enervation of his style.*"[38]

I gladly let myself be accused of this error—I have always detested coquetries while playing the piano; perhaps my father also gave me reasons for that, since he always strove to get me to captivate the public with coquetries in playing and personality. One can certainly do that very easily, but to me it always seemed a dishonorable endeavor, and that I am thoroughly untalented for it.

I'm astonished that the correspondent allowed himself so certain a judgment after hearing me *one time!* whether the verdict is good or bad, it is always an injustice that no connoisseur, much less a nonconnoisseur, may allow himself against an artist. That he is no connoisseur he proves with his opinion of Robert's compositions, which he accuses of *mysticism.* By the way, according to Robert the whole article is written in an attractive style.

New Year's Eve both of us spent unwell at Therese's [Fleischer] and also soon went home, where we then entered the new year, though alone, that much happier with ourselves. We thanked Heaven for letting us finally be united while ending the old one. May you, my most sincerely beloved Robert, only remain well and loving for me, and may it please Heaven to give you ever more happiness through me. Silently I cherished yet another intimate wish, surely yours as well, whose fulfillment would satisfy me more than anything (and you certainly no less).

Oh, my dear Robert, I always want to overwhelm you with good deeds, I want to live only for your pleasure always—are you really completely happy? is there nothing about me, in my essence, that displeases you? oh, tell it to me candidly, I'll surely accept it with complete love!—

The concert on New Year's Day was simply not one of the most brilliant, although rich with beautiful compositions. The Zauberflöte Overture [by Mozart], *C Minor* Symphony [by Beethoven] provided magnificent enjoyment. But during the past winter one also always had the lovely appearances of female singers, and therefore cannot be completely satisfied with Fräulein *Schloss;* today however we did not hear even her, but only choruses sung by the Thomaner [male choir of the Thomas Church], who at times do not cover themselves especially with glory; they sing so mechanically that one wants to scream.

Herr *Hilf* played variations by *Vieuxtemps* and *Tremolo* by *Beriot* with much dexterity, very pretty tone, but terribly indifferently, and even his personality seemed as if he were incapable of any inner excitement. Is no one able to breathe a tiny spark of emotion into this great talent? how is it possible to treat the most impassioned places with the most unshakable calmness? I pity the man, because he surely is very industrious.

A young talent, *Joseph Haindl* from *Würzburg,* gave me much pleasure, although he—played the flute. But he played it exquisitely, with a very pretty presentation, and also looked pretty, interesting. If only he will not disappear, like so many child prodigies! and why does such a gifted talent have to choose the *flute* of all things?

Dr. Reuter gave us a present of 2 very lovely little flowering plants. His attentiveness is always very gratifying—

Nothing about friends pleases me more than small signs of attention, even if these consist of something utterly insignificant, be it only a friendly note. That reminds me of Amalie Rieffel, who hasn't bothered herself about us for weeks, has not sent me, who always has wished her the very best, a single greeting for the new year—such indifference only makes it the more ungratifying.

The last days of this week went by quietly—I was in a very bad state, my Robert as well, whose stubborn cold also plays nasty tricks.

I have not been playing much; I lack strength. But Robert has again composed a very beautiful "Wanderlied" by *Kerner,* and now has completed a book of 12 lieder by *Kerner.*

I've again been somewhat verbose this week—have patience with me, my dear husband.

I would like to prattle to you a bit about my love for you, but when given to excess even the most beautiful things become burdensome, therefore *punctum* for now.

[RS]

A beautiful verse by Goethe:[39]

Was verkürzt [mir] die Zeit?	What shortens time for me?
Thätigkeit.	Activity.
Was macht sie unerträglich lang?	What lengthens it intolerably?
Müßiggang.	Idleness.
Was bringt in Schulden?	What brings in debts?
Harren und Dulden.	Patience and tolerance.
Was macht gewinnen?	What makes a profit?
Nicht lange besinnen.	Not reflecting at length.
Was bringt zu Ehren?	What leads to honor?
Sich wehren!	Defending oneself!

Seventeenth week
from 3rd to 10th January 1841

Throughout this entire period Clara has had to suffer a great deal—from pain, which she gladly tolerates on my account. I have been feeling fairly well. The idea, to bring out an album of lieder with Clara, has given me enthusiasm for work. Thus from Monday to Monday the 11th, 9 lieder from the Liebesfrühling by Rückert[40] were completed in which I think I may again have found a special tone. Now Clara should also compose a few from the Liebesfrühling. Oh, do it, Klärchen!—Otherwise nothing much happened.

Monday the 4th we spent the evening at the young Freges'; it was cordial and musical. Clara played quite beautifully and [Livia]

Marriage Diary I 51

Frege sang also, as always clearly, correctly, and with accomplishment, like a professional and talented singer. At the Thursday concert I unexpectedly met Ole Bull, who is still traveling around in the small capitals. He is enthusiastic about a new violin. A "Historical Symphony" by Spohr that we heard seemed to me unworthy of Spohr.—I often got together with Löwenskjold, the Dane; but I don't like his new things completely.—Finally we also read something *to the end* again: "*Edelstein und Perle*" by Rückert. Now we should get going on the Beethoven sonatas, which I am reading through consecutively and will perhaps discuss in context.[41]

After great coldness the weather is getting milder. Clara has to go outdoors a great deal. Spring, if only you were already here. No matter how old one becomes, the longing for springtime returns again each year. I have many plans; may time bring them to fruition, or just a few of them.—

In conclusion, thank you dear Clara for all the love you always show me, for your patience, your support. Surely everything will turn out for the best.—

Eighteenth week [CS]
[11–16 January]

Saturday the 16th. Not much of interest can be reported about the past week. I spent most of the time being unwell, and only tore myself away one evening, which we spent quite comfortably at *A. Harkort's.* There was no shortage of artists; *Mendelssohn, David, Ole Bull,* and others were there. I had decided in advance not to play, but least of all the *Mendelssohn* Trio, for which I was not at all prepared. Despite that it went better than I myself would have thought, and *Mendelssohn,* who moved me with much pleading to do it, seemed to be satisfied. How often have I actually discovered in myself that enthusiasm raises the artist above himself; how in an ordinary mood one would not have been able to accomplish many of the things for which enthusiasm lends one everything, energy, fire. Fräulein *Schloss* sang various *bravura* arias—why not simple German lieder instead? doesn't one already hear plenty of these Italian flourishes in concerts?

Mendelssohn was very amiable in his conversation—the man really is all life and spirit! *Ole Bull* entertained during the meal, but he talks too much about *nothing* (though not without imagination and vitality). He doesn't let anyone get a word in edgewise, and bores people. Mostly we kept each other company, Robert and I. At parties I always like it best when I can be close to him.

The singer *Hering* visited us one evening. He sang a few of Robert's lieder—unfortunately he no longer has any voice at all. There is really nobody who approaches the ideal that I carry within myself regarding Robert's lieder! *Pauline Garcia* would be the only one, I believe, to grasp them really truthfully—if I only once could hear one of them [sung] by her!—

Because of my indisposition I had to miss the Gewandhaus concert, which created a not insignificant conflict for me because *Mendelssohn* played the G Major Concerto by *Beethoven,* which by Robert's account he performed masterfully (which after all was predictable). I missed a great treat for which I had long yearned.

Several times already I've gotten myself to work on the poems by Rückert that Robert had copied, but it simply won't go at all—I have no talent whatsoever for composition!—

Mendelssohn visited us with an Englishman named *Horsley.* He is an agreeable man, and not at all stiffly British.

Amalie *Rieffel* finally showed up once more—she came to get advice. I told her the truth, what I think of her. Robert no longer wants to know anything at all about her—if she knew that, she wouldn't easily get over the pain.

Marriage Diary I 53

Saturday and Sunday Robert felt very bad, and because of pain in the throat could eat only with difficulty. He was very unhappy about it, since he insists that not being able to eat is the greatest misfortune, and I must agree with him!—Sunday evening already showed some improvement—it tasted superb!—Now I, poorest one, drag myself from one day to the next, get out of bed feeling the way I had lain down. If the cause were not a fortunate one, I would probably lose my patience. What saddens me the most is that I can play so little and am so unenergetic. Now! I think better times will come again, when I can also please you more, my most intimately beloved Robert—until then have patience with me.

Nineteenth week
[17–24 January]

It is contrary to our agreement that I write the book this week, but when a man composes a symphony one really can't expect him to concern himself with other things—thus even his wife must accept herself as set aside! The symphony will soon be finished; although I haven't heard any of it yet, I am endlessly happy that Robert has finally entered the field where, with his great imagination, he belongs; I think that he will also work himself to the point where he will no longer compose anything besides instrumental music.

The past week was fairly rich with musical enjoyments—good ones and bad ones. On Wednesday *Ole Bull* gave another farewell soiree where he showed himself to be a pedantic quartet player, and in the great *A Major* Sonata by *Beethoven* (with *Mendelssohn*) a thoroughly bad musician who knows *Beethoven* only by name but will never understand him. He did himself great damage with this soiree, surely every connoisseur would agree with that.

Thursday the 21st ushered in the historical concerts with *Bach*

54   *The Marriage Diaries of Robert & Clara Schumann*

and *Handel*. There was nothing to complain about the concert other than that there were too many things of beauty. *Mendelssohn* started with the Chromatic *Fantasy and Fugue* by *Bach*. He played it, and also the *Handel* Variations in the second part, with unique beauty, but I can never develop a real friendship with the Fantasy, for me it is a chaos of passages which gave me no musical pleasure.

The *Chaconne* [by Bach] (what does *Chaconne* actually mean?) gave me great pleasure, and David also played it magnificently.

According to Robert the crown of the evening was the *Crucifixus, Resurrexit,* and *Sanctus* from the Great *B Minor* Mass by Bach, which also gave me very great enjoyment. *Handel* doesn't taste all that good after *Bach*—*Bach* stands there too big, too unattainable.

Löwenskjold took leave of us; he went to Copenhagen, where we, I hope, will soon also set our path—what are Robert's thoughts?

The 23rd. Saturday. Today I stood for a third little godchild, *Emma Carl.* I stood with *Dr. Reuter* and Inspector *Seidendörffer* (who incidentally stood as godfather for the 133rd time), and received nice presents from them both. The baptism was held in the Nikolai Church by Preacher *Simon* and indeed it was kept very brief—it lasted barely a quarter of an hour.

Reuter [and] *Wenzel* usually visit us on Sunday, and today the latter also with Herr *Lampadius,* who isn't stupid but horribly tedious. I suspect he is a theologian—he has all the aptitudes of a really philistine pastor.

Twentieth week
[25–30 January]

Today, Monday, Robert pretty well completed his symphony; it seems to have arisen mostly during the night,—my poor Robert

Marriage Diary I

has already spent several sleepness nights because of it. He calls it "Spring Symphony"—tender and poetic, as all his musical ideas are!—a spring poem by [Böttger][42] was the initial impulse for this creation.

Today I visited the *Euterpe* for the first time this winter. This evening I had a mighty desire for music, therefore I also enjoyed it fully, especially during the *A Major* Symphony of *Beethoven*. The performance satisfied me completely. *Verhulst* imitated everything by *Mendelssohn* in the interpretation, each little nuance I would say, which at times doesn't feel altogether acceptable—I can't stand any copies; *Verhulst* is enough of a musician to reflect on the interpretation of such a work himself.

A pretty excursion with my sister-in-law [Therese Fleischer] gave me much pleasure. I spent the rest of the afternoon with her. An argument with her husband made me somewhat hot-blooded—namely, he asserted that *Meyerbeer* is vastly superior to *Weber.* One should really always maintain silence toward a lay person, but my zeal won't easily let me swallow such a stupid opinion.

My state of health now seems to want to improve. What was only a hope for us just a few weeks ago now seems to be turning into certainty—I am really happy!

Tuesday Robert finished his symphony; thus started and finished in 4 days. If only there were an orchestra immediately available!—I must confess to you, my dear husband, I wouldn't have thought you capable of such skill—you always inspire new awe in me!!!—

Livia Frege visited me today with her husband. With closer acquaintance I like both of them ever better. They came to thank Robert for the lieder[43] he sent, about which they spoke with the greatest enthusiasm.

Rieffel also visited me once again—I reproached her for her rude behavior toward me.

Agnes Röller is getting married today *the 28th*. May she find all the happiness she deserves. Pastor Schmidt, her husband, owns one of the nicest parishes in Saxony.

Last week *Voigt* and *Bertha Constantin* also got married, in Schönefeld. The whole day I always thought back to the 12th of September. We were invited to the wedding, but I wasn't well enough to undertake anything at all.

I visited *Madame Schmidt* and found her very pleasant as always but all of her domestic arrangements very confusing—a real comedian's household!—

Robert has started to orchestrate his symphony. According to his description, very beautiful instrumental effects are supposed to occur in it.

Neither of us went to today's subscription concert—I was unwell, and Robert much too busy thinking about his symphony. The entire concert consisted of *Haydn*.

I don't get to play at all nowadays; partly my being unwell prevents it, partly Robert's composing. If only it were possible to resolve the evil of the thin walls; I unlearn everything and because of that might become very melancholic.

For several days Robert has been very cold toward me; although the reason is very gratifying indeed, and no one can be more sincerely interested in everything he undertakes than I, yet this coldness sometimes hurts me who would least deserve it. Forgive me for this complaint, my dear Robert—but once in a while reason must give way to emotion!

On *the 30th, Saturday,* I went for a walk with the *Carls* to *Stötteritz*, which was good for me.

In the evening I went to the quartet, which became very interesting today because of *Mendelssohn's* playing. He played his Trio, which I've wanted to hear by him again for a long time. That was followed by *Beethoven's* magnificent Quartet in *E Flat*,[44] and

Mendelssohn concluded with two of his earlier and two more recent Songs without Words. I know of no performer whose playing makes me feel so good, and one really doesn't know in which *genre* one prefers hearing him, he plays everything equally masterfully. Still, I would have liked to permit myself a few minor criticisms regarding this evening, but I fear, dear Robert, you will immediately lose your temper, and I don't want to anger you, you know that, even though in my naïveté I sometimes do it.

Probst, the biggest raisonneur on God's earth, forced himself on me with his big mouth. He said a lot—including some intelligent things that I had to agree with silently.

At the end of this week my Robert was friendlier to me again, and I was also happy again. It goes in double-quick time with the symphony, Robert is incredibly industrious—and I haven't heard any of it yet!—?—

Next week I will leave the diary to you—now without compassion I demand orderliness. Just write a few words, and it will be more than 10 pages from me. In complete love another kiss for you, my dear composer—as soon as spring arrives I shall crown you with laurels for the Spring Symphony.

Twenty-first week
[31 January–7] February 1841

This week too I still practice patience! I can well understand that the symphony takes precedence, and therefore I won't torment you with the diary, my dear husband. I'll record as briefly as possible what is still in my memory about the past week.

The Gewandhaus concert on Thursday the 4th brought *Mozart.* The *Titus* Overture enchanted me with [its] youthful freshness; *Mendelssohn* played the *D Minor* Concerto and ended especially the last movement with a very beautifully artful cadenza. I was extraordinarily affected by the simplicity of this concerto. I didn't know "Das Veilchen" at all yet, nor generally speaking any of Mozart's lieder, and was completely *en enthousiasme* over them! despite its great simplicity the lied moved me—it made a singular impression on me.[45] The symphony with the fugue at the end went magnificently and the impression of the whole concert was highly satisfying—Mozart makes one feel so uniquely cheerful and at peace, I've already noticed that many times within myself; his operas also have this effect on me.

This week I discharged several ceremonial visits that have lain heavily on my conscience. Madame *David*, Madame *Harkort*, [and] *Mendelssohn's* wife had to be pleased with my visit. Everywhere one hears talk of illness and of the very cold weather—that's all. I met *Mendelssohn* joyously celebrating his birthday, surrounded by presents and congratulations—I modestly added my own.

On the 6th we finally received the news from Berlin of Bargiel's[46] death; it did not surprise us, since we had expected it already every day. He died on the 4th under conditions of the most terrible suffering. It's a blessing for him! he was a thoroughly upright man, and in his sick as well as his healthy days he lived entirely devoted to art, of which he also possessed the most significant knowledge. I hope that as soon as my poor mother has soothed herself a bit from the painful loss, she will be granted a quiet period, which she has long needed; with the chronicity of this illness the woman has depleted herself as well. He was sick for 5 years, during which time my mother had to bear all worries. Heaven grant that she may soon be in a better, more worry-free situation. At such moments of need the thought occasionally obsesses me, "Oh, if only you were rich, and could be helpful at this time!"

Marriage Diary I 59

Today, *Sunday the 7th,* Thalberg arrived and will give a concert for old and sick musicians, which greatly displeases me because I had intended to do just that, only later on. Nevertheless it pleases me greatly to hear *him* again, this monarch of the piano.

At the end of this week I cannot help mentioning my Robert's most affectionate behavior, and to assure him once more that this is my greatest bliss. Does he believe it!?—

Twenty-second week
[8–13 February]

On the 8th, Monday, Thalberg visited us and to my enchantment played beautifully on my pianoforte. There is no technique more perfect, and his keyboard effects must frequently carry the connoisseurs away. He doesn't miss a single note, his runs can be compared to a string of pearls, his octaves are the best I've ever heard. In his concert that evening he enraptured us anew and me really especially with an etude wherein he brought out a wonderful pianistic effect. I must admit, however, that I prefer hearing him in a room, and that I also really like to look at his hands while he plays—he has the most beautiful piano hand. As much as his playing delighted me, I cared little for his compositions, which strike me as very weak compared to earlier ones. It seems to me as if he wanted to imitate Liszt in his fantasies, but for that he lacks Liszt's soaring imagination.

After the concert we had a meal together with *Thalberg, Mendelssohn, David, etc.* in the *Hôtel de Bavière,* where I hadn't been since that unfortunate evening after *Gerke's* concert. Today things were different, and we let ourselves enjoy the champagne better than that time.

On *Tuesday the 9th Thalberg* traveled to Dresden and from

there to Breslau and Warsaw. Soon there will be no city left that he hasn't visited.

On *Wednesday the 10th* when I returned from my walk I found Major *Serre* at the house and was very happy to see him again. Our entire conversation, however, revolved around the reconciliation with Father. He knows far from everything that's happened during the past year, thus he thinks things are simpler than they are. I was supposed to give him a note to take along for Father, whereas at the moment I have taken him to court for restitution of my belongings.[47] Only someone who knows how many tricks this man has up his sleeve can form a true judgment about the whole thing, about the consequences. The good major can't conceive of such a character. Yet he is so excited about this whole thing that he may succeed in forcing Father to restore my things and the piano voluntarily, which would please me without end— thus at least *I* would no longer be in conflict with him.

I again received a letter from Graf—Father is still tormenting him as well with his cabals about the piano—it's enough to drive one to despair!—

The 11th. Beethoven was the Chosen One at the Gewandhaus concert. There's not much to be said about that—nothing that hasn't been said a thousand times. I heard the 9th Symphony for the third time today. The first two movements gratified me greatly, less so the last two, which I haven't understood yet, wherein I can't as yet find the thread.

Herr *Goulomy* (a Russian) played the Violin Concerto in D Major with much dexterity, also energy, but the poetic breath was missing.

A big surprise was furnished by the sudden appearance of *Schröder-Devrient* who happened to be in the hall and filled the gap created by *Schmidt's* indisposition by singing the *Adelaide*. She was received and let go with boundless enthusiasm. I cheered

Marriage Diary I 61

along inwardly, just for having seen her once more, the one I honor so highly, who remains my ideal among dramatic singers.

That Sunday *Pfund* and *Wenzel* ate at our house; after dinner we made music, i.e., Robert played his Spring Symphony, which truly inspires one with gusts of warm spring air, and the rest of us listened. That made me completely well and musical. I'd like to express myself a bit in my own way about the symphony, but I would never finish talking about the tiny buds, the scent of the violets, the fresh green leaves, the birds in the air, all the things one sees living and spinning with the most youthful energy. Don't laugh at me, my dear husband! although I can't express myself poetically, the poetic breath of this work has deeply penetrated my innermost being.

I kiss you at the end of this week with the most affectionate sentiments—not merely on account of your symphony, but also because of the heart from which it sprang.

Twenty-third week [RS]
from 14th–21st February

Now, after five weeks of being silent, back to you, my dear reader. Were I only well enough to describe really beautifully whatever has happened. But of course you know most of it. The symphony gave me many happy hours; it is nearly finished; it will be a complete work only when it has been heard. I am often thankful to the good spirit that allowed me to create so big a work with such ease, in such a short time. The sketch for the entire symphony was finished in 4 days, and that's saying a great deal. Now, however, after many sleepless nights there is also debilitation; I feel the way a young woman must feel who has just delivered a baby—so relieved, happy, and yet sick and in pain.

This too is known to my Clara, and now she snuggles up to me twice as gently, for which I surely will want to repay her later. Indeed, were I to describe all the loving deeds Clara bestowed on me with such a willing heart during this time, I'd never get to the end of it. I would have had to search among millions [to find] someone who gives me as much consideration, as much attention as she does. Now let me kiss you, my good wife whom I love and esteem ever more.

In other respects this period went by relatively quietly and uniformly. We think a lot about spring, and intend then to bounce around outdoors, which both of us need badly. A trip to Teplitz doesn't fit at all into the realm of the impossible.

Perhaps we may also give a concert together. It would be very profitable if I could have the symphony performed yet this year. Clara knows this too, but she is not allowed to decide anything. But now we will soon have to reach a decision and then seize the occasion with energy. A little less modesty wouldn't hurt either of us, I believe, but neither of us are fit for the ordinary life, its treacheries and cunning. But even without these one can always achieve at least something with hard work and by straightforward means. May we leave the rest to our good geniuses.

We have seen only a few *people;* among the strangers Thalberg, Major Serre from Maxen, the young Dane Helsted, A. Böttger the translator of Byron, Schoolmaster Lampadius; more frequently Wenzel and Reuter.

Last Sunday the 21st in the evening we bubbled over a small bottle of champagne; these are joyous hours, sitting like that next to one's wife and enjoying it, while outside it's still wintery and freezing. Nothing can top that, especially after work has been completed and one has the good intention soon to start something new. That's how it was on that evening, and we have already celebrated several like that.

Marriage Diary I 63

Now you, Klärchen, write about the 24th week, so we can get back on the old track.

Twenty-fourth week [CS]
[22–28 February]

My dear Robert has said so many loving and beautiful things about me that I really don't know how to reciprocate, I only want to say this much and have already said it a thousand times, this love really makes me inexpressibly happy. We rejoice in good fortune never known to me before—my father always scoffed at so-called *domestic bliss*. How I pity those who are unfamiliar with it! they are only half alive!—

This week went by fairly quietly. The Gewandhaus presented a boring concert,[48] the weather was horrible, the sky still hangs heavy with snow, and my yearning for springtime grows that much greater.

Robert's little travel plan whirls around in my head and heart—I look forward to it childishly—may it only come true!—

On *Saturday the 27th,* after two years of separation, I finally got my piano back without further ado. I suspect that Major *Serre* brought that about. Great was my joy, but even greater a deep sadness that seized me when I looked at it. The whole wretched past rose up within me so vividly, and I could not ward off a certain sympathy *for* my father. My Robert won't hold it against me—he was so kind and patient while my tears were flowing! Although the piano is somewhat played out, internally and externally it is still beautiful.

Young *Frege* came to see me, to invite us personally to a soiree. He's not at all as stupid a man as so many people would have it—I believe that his wife is partly responsible for this idle gossip, since she always treats him *en bagatelle* in the presence of others, which already has often hurt me. On closer acquaintance, however, *she* is also a fairly pleasant woman.

This week's report is brief, because there hasn't been much worth taking note of. I've been reading a lot, and for the first time a work, *"Notre Dame,"* by Victor Hugo, which disgusts me, however, whenever I think about it. It is full of the frivolous, vulgar, mutilated, improbable—one cannot find a single noble character in the entire work, nothing but the most awful nonsense, which makes one shudder at times. While in the French language it may have been written imaginatively—after all, these sorts of works are only for the French, who love only the shrill and atrocious, but for a healthy German mind such a work is abominable. Robert read it also and felt no better about it than I did.

Our state of health has been bad this week! I have constant headaches and Robert is in a vegetative state—he exerted himself too much with the symphony—it will surely get better again, just don't get depressed my friend!—

March 1841   [RS]
Twenty-fifth week
from 1st to 7th March

The symphony still has been taking much of my time. Now, however, I'm already breathing more freely and can see an end to the work. Also all sorts of hindrances and invitations.

On the 1st to the Harkorts' for dinner, where we had a good time and the company was well selected. In the evening Schloss's concert.

The evening of the 2nd with the young Freges. Big party. Also

Mendelssohn. Clara played, and everyone thought it was exceptional, which always gives me great pleasure.

On the 4th Madame Duflot-Maillard visited Clara. Later we heard her in the concert.

Early on Friday the 6th I went to Mendelssohn with my score. I was anxious to hear his opinion of it. What he said pleased me greatly. He always perceives and hits on the right thing. Remarkably, most of his corrections pertained to places that had been changed, and [he] agreed for the most part with my original sketch. That confirms his exploratory vision. While saying goodbye I let such a stupid word about Clara slip out that it pained me the whole day. In the evening I confessed it to Clara, since I could no longer restrain myself. She was as kind and good all day as she always is when she feels completely well physically.

That day we were joined at dinner by the young Helsted from Copenhagen, who a few days later traveled via Vienna to Italy. We've grown to like him.

This in a great hurry. We are always getting closer to the concert, etc., as will be reported next time.

Twenty-sixth week [CS]
from 8th to 14th March

This week brought various things!

On Monday we attended the last *Euterpe* concert. It ended worthily with *Beethoven's C Minor* Symphony. For the first time in many years I heard *Franchetti* once again, but I felt sorry for her because there's no trace of voice anymore.

On Tuesday *Duflot-Maillard* gave an unfortunate concert in the little Börsensaal. Although the smallest location in all of Leipzig had been selected by Hofmeister, it nevertheless was still too big—

many seats were empty. The singer would have deserved better. She is no longer in her prime, but she has learned a great deal and is better than [many others] I've ever heard, especially with ascending chromatic runs. The *method* she uses is the Italian, but in that hall her recital [was] too animated, exaggerated. There is something captivating about her personality and, as Robert says, something that arouses compassion, and it seems that way to me also. Things would have gone better for her had she not thrown herself into Hofmeister's hands, for he is a dangerous protector.—

Amalie Rieffel played one of Thalberg's Fantasies as soporifically *as possible,* and *Poème d'amour* by Henselt as superficially as possible. Sometimes one wants to assert that when it comes to superficial rushing no one could surpass her. She needs her father!

On Wednesday the 10th *Mendelssohn* visited us and for several hours kept himself busy with Robert and the symphony. He likes it very much, which makes me feel really extraordinarily happy. If all the parts were only written out already! that is going to be an immense amount of work.

Mendelssohn surprised me greatly with the delicate gift of *"Hermann und Dorothea"* by Goethe in a tiny adorable binding. It gave me more pleasure than I could express to him in my embarrassment over this unexpected courtesy of his. But now I have also read it and been amused to the utmost by the beautiful, clean, clear language and the gentle way all the characters appearing in it are treated. Soon I shall read it once more.

We spent the evening of Penance Day (Friday) at *Voigt's.* The *Mendelssohns* were there with an amiable Englishwoman, Miss Horsley, also *David* and others. I played a lot, for which *Mendelssohn's* incessant requests were to blame. He never stops doing that, and thereby often puts me in a quandary. I only want to know whether he really finds my playing enjoyable!? (Here my Robert makes an angry face! Hm?)

Marriage Diary I 67

Several Scottish lieder with *violin* and *cello* by *Beethoven,* sung by Schmidt and accompanied magnificently by *Mendelssohn,* gave me much pleasure.

The dinner was tedious! In his home one can recognize Voigt by thousands of little incompetencies. He put a wreath around *Mendelssohn's* portrait—with the garland down to his nose. The guests were filled with misery by the most boring quartets. The meal lasted until midnight, and we all eagerly gasped for some fresh air.

During the same week we also once had lunch at *Voigt's,* but I returned home feeling hungry—it seems that the housewife had counted on more refined table guests than us, my Robert and I.

We have had a few magnificent spring days this week. Never does one feel more joy in life than on such blissful days, in the sunshine among flowers in the window—then one wants to embrace the whole world.

On *Penance Day* it was half a year that we have been married. How fast gone by, and how happily lived!—If my Robert only maintains such affection for me then no woman could be envied more than I.

Saturday the last quartet soiree took place. The *Quintet in C Major* by *Beethoven* gave me more pleasure than anything else for a long time. *Mendelssohn* did not seem animated while performing the *Prelude* and *Fugue;* anyway, I had been thinking about both [pieces] differently and did not feel pleasantly touched by his performance. I listened to only half of the sonata by *Mozart* [he] played with *David.*

Sunday the 14th. *Dr. Hirsch* with *Reuter* had their noon meal at our house. The first pleases me less and less; everything he says swims around so much on the surface, there is nothing solid about him, and that goes for his singing and playing as well.

Father was here last week! His remarks, heartless as he is, have killed all the feelings for him that had again stirred within me!

Now I cannot consider any reconciliation; must I not be prepared lest every friendly glance might be a trap, so that later he can play his intrigues against me that much more safely? the man really has no conscience whatsoever—won't it ever be aroused?! Regarding the piano, things are also not the way I had first thought. Major *Serre* and our attorney [Krause] have let themselves be bribed with promises, as though after first receiving the 60 thalers he had intended to return them—now the 60 thalers are in his pocket and he makes us the laughingstock—getting them back is out of the question.[49] I have gooseflesh while thinking how things must look in this man's soul. Now I'm supposed to take possession of my belongings—I am eager to know what new sorts of deception *etc.* he has contrived.

I'm practicing incessantly for the concert, and the music copyist works day and night on the symphony. Robert pores over his journal, which right now bores him terribly, as I can well understand considering his constant brooding over music. The poor man!

Next week I request a somewhat longer report from you, my dear spouse—hm? the last one was really too short, as though you did not like making it? Be that as it may, however, we will always remain good friends and love each other sincerely and intimately all the same. Do you agree?

Twenty-seventh week [RS]
from 14th to 21st March 1841

Prospects for the concert look favorable. The day is supposed to be the 27th, and we are bravely working toward that goal. But sometimes the beautiful days anticipating spring have also lured us into the outdoors. With a dear gentle wife things really go

Marriage Diary I 69

smoothly. Honestly, my next symphony shall be named "Clara" and I will portray her in it with flutes, oboes, and harps. What does my Klärchen say to that?

The concerts have now all come to an end, and the only one left is our own. The final one in the Gewandhaus took place last Thursday. Schröder-Devrient sang in it. Clara talked with her a lot—I was wondering what the philosophizing was all about until Clara finally enlightened me. Namely, Schröder-Devrient has offered to be godmother. When you women get together it's just like when we men get together. It amused me. The performance of the lied by Schubert that Schr. sang was my favorite. She is full of surprises! As though she knew all the secrets of the heart! A true actress, who one minute invites herself as godmother and the next could move us to tears with her agonizing tones! But such an artist can never be a housewife, a wife, a mother, and she really isn't any of these.

Clara also got together with her at Brockhaus's. It must have been an interesting evening. I felt like avoiding people and did not go there.

The day before yesterday for dinner at Count Baudissin's with Clara. Sophie [von Baudissin] observes a great deal, which alone is enough to hold me back from getting to know her better. Moreover, she seems to have that sense of clairvoyance and penetration which every Jew and Jewess possesses, even when it comes to music. She also played her own compositions. Clara too. The mother seems to be an excellent woman. The daughter, Philippine, more superficial, but not without cultivation. The count says many things that are pertinent and good. We parted on fairly friendly terms.

Yesterday I received a visit from A. Schmitt from Frankfurt, a demanding individual who thinks too much—half Philistine, half artist. He was very well behaved and said many friendly things.

In the afternoon Mendelssohn, with whom we still negotiated over the concert. He played with Clara a newly arrived concerto by Bach for 2 pianos, then a sonata by Mozart. Love and veneration are the two emotions aroused for him every time one interacts with him. He is also a politician; but that is only a 100th part of his multifaceted personality.

I was happy to hear from Mendelssohn that during the first year of his marriage he kept a diary with his wife similar to ours, but that they later abandoned it.[50] But we don't want to do that.

[CS:] (Certainly not!)

Twenty-eighth week [CS]
from 22 to 29 March

This week went by quietly except for Friday, a day that brought us much joy. Robert's symphony was rehearsed for the first time, and to the delight of everyone present turned out magnificently. It is a masterpiece of invention and execution. *Mendelssohn* was completely delighted and conducted with the greatest affection and attentiveness.

In the afternoon we made a musical promenade to Connewitz—we thought of nothing but the symphony and discussed each one of its beautiful details. Robert seemed happy—I *no less!* every day I become more aware what a treasure of *poetry* resides in him, and, may I say it again, I love him more and more every day—I cannot esteem and honor him sufficiently. Will my dear Robert excuse this little outpouring from my heart—and a kiss added to it?!—

Saturday the 27th *Mendelssohn* brought the Duo[51] composed

Marriage Diary I 71

for my concert. We played it, it displeased him, and he fell into an amusing rage because he had imagined some places would be more beautiful. He played several Songs without Words for us, including a uniquely beautiful folk song. His playing put me in a melancholy mood, I no longer wanted to think about my own [playing]; while this went on I saw Robert beaming with joy, and it was so painful for me to have to feel incapable of ever offering him such playing. Later I felt ashamed by the tears I shed in *Mendelssohn's* presence, but I could not help it—one's heart sometimes just overflows like that!

Sunday I spent the evening at *Mendelssohn's;* we played the Duo again several times—his anger subsided, and a feeling of satisfaction seemed to replace it.—Today I saw him as the father of a family moving around among his charming children, and that made me think a lot about my Robert!!!

Miss Horsley is an amiable Englishwoman and possesses more emotional warmth than I would ever have believed from an Englishwoman. Her little album, which contains quite a lot of autographs, included my name as well.

Robert did not accompany me this evening—he was exhausted and therefore did not feel like it, but would certainly have done well [there].

Next week, the most important one since our wedding, I leave to you my beloved Robert, and I think that you will be gracious in criticising my first *debut* as *Clara Schumann.*

Twenty-ninth week [RS]
from 29th March—to 4th April

On the 31st, concert by the Schumann couple. Happy evening, which we will never forget. My Clara played everything like a master and in an elevated mood, so that everybody was delighted.[52] This day is also one of the most important ones in my artistic career. My wife agreed with that too, and was almost more pleased by the success of the symphony than she was about herself. So then, with God's help let us go forward on this track. The way I feel looks so cheerful right now that I want to bring to light a few other things that ought to gladden our hearts.

In all matters pertaining to our concert Mendelssohn has proven himself again to be a true artist. His empathy for Clara is as genuine as only a heart like his could bring forth. He was also interested in the symphony as sincerely as artists should be with each other and conducted it with utmost care. The following day I called on him and thanked him really sincerely.

I could write down a good many things yet about this week and that evening, about the general admiration that Clara enjoyed, about the enthusiasm that our concert brought out in everyone, so that the whole city speaks of it—but I am pulled toward the new overture that I'm working on—and you, my dear one, will be lenient about my brevity.

Thirtieth week [CS]
From 5th to 11th April 1841

I will have to take much greater recourse to your leniency than you to mine, since this week and its events have almost completely slipped from my memory.

Sunday we ate at the Hôtel de Bavière for lack of a servant girl—I could not longer keep mine. The meal was to our taste, but not the proximity of Madame S[c]hmidt, mother of the English consul S[c]hmidt, who found herself in a deplorable state due to excessive drinking. Her gaze is unsteady, and her mind in a

Marriage Diary I 73

state of terrible excitement. Isn't this vice, which is already loathsome in a man, many times worse in a woman!

In the Thomas Church *Mendelssohn* presented the *Passion* music by *Bach*,[53] for the erection of a monument to the same, as he already did once last year. We had poor seats, heard the music only indistinctly, and therefore left after the first part. In Berlin this music gave me much more gratification, probably partly due to the location, which is completely suitable for such music, while this is certainly not the case in the Thomas Church, [the ceiling of] which is much too high.[54]

On Good Friday *Pohlenz* gave a Mass by *Cherubini* (a magnificent work) in the Paul Church and the Seven [Last] Words of the Savior by *Haydn*,[55] which may well be one of *Haydn's* weaker works; it is monotonous and by no means new and energetic— one is not refreshed by it.

On *Saturday the 10th,* in honor of his brother *Paul, Mendelssohn* presented the Lobgesang, one of his Psalms, and the *E-Flat Major Concerto* by *Bach* for 2 pianos. I didn't like the *Psalm* as much as his other one "[Wie] der Hirsch schreit"—it is terribly thickly orchestrated, calculated more for the size of a church, however, as is also the Lobgesang.—The *Bach* concerto is beautiful, but the double quartet covered the piano voices too much.

Sunday the 1st holiday we ate at the *Fleischers'* at noon; the cuisine was excellent, and had we been the only guests I would have let myself enjoy the meal twice as much. We got to know Professor *Hartenstein* (a highly intelligent man, and pleasant company, it seems to me) and Police Commissioner *Stengel,* a man of determination.

At the end of this week I must allow myself yet another encroachment on the next, which is nearly over while I am writing this. To my great joy, Robert has completed a delicate but cheerful (to use his own expression) sirenlike overture, and now occupies himself with the orchestration, which he pursues with real passion. Inwardly I am really quite happy about it, and wish nothing more than to be able to give him a tiny bit as much pleasure as he gives me. The highest reward for a composer must always be found in his work and in himself, and that is also the case with my Robert, but in no way is he thus completely unreceptive to praise from the masses, and it shouldn't be that way—surely no artist has yet existed for whom the acclaim of the public was a matter of indifference. Everyone who has heard the symphony mentions it with pleasure, and that always makes me feel wonderfully good.

I've been gossiping a bit in my own way—so often you have already forgiven me for that with a gentle smile—why not this time as well!

Thirty-first and thirty-second weeks [RS]
from 11th to 25th April 1841

The beginning of spring in nature—often outdoors with Clara, also at noon—thus once in the Wasserschenke [a tavern]—once in Zweinaundorf—the last time unfortunately in order to chase away a severe hangover that had stuck to me for several days following a revelrous evening. But have also been good and diligent: the Overture in E Major orchestrated in 4 days, a Scherzo and a Finale for Orchestra completely sketched in 3 days. These compositions gave Clara pleasure. An attractive idea pursues me, a symphony for the unveiling of Jean Paul's statue on the 15th of November. But that requires preliminary studies and good helpful inspirations: it shall be called *Sinfonia solemnis*.[56]

A young amiable cavalier, Count Costa, Italian diplomat, visited us; a dilettante of the best kind who also knows Bach's compositions and is said to play the piano really superbly. Clara played

Marriage Diary I 75

for him quite beautifully. Count Baudissin came along, likewise an excellent man and devoted to the arts and to artists. We spent a congenial evening there, the 16th of April. His wife played something by Klengel in Dresden that interested me; Clara [played] among other things the great Fugue in A Minor of Bach from memory in such a way that I was amazed.

A concert for the poor also came limping by on the 22nd; just to get it over with, [it was] also badly attended. Several new things by Rietz from Düsseldorf interested me very much.[57] Wherever one can still find capable people like that, art cannot really be in such bad shape after all.

For months I haven't gotten around to reading anything; I also haven't done much for the journal; it was actually disgusting for me. But I must get myself to overcome this again; one should not treat one's stepchildren without love.

With Clara's health things go as they can, and much better than in the first weeks of our marriage. In her heart she always feels clear and bright and full of love. That I know. And also in mine; one hears that in my music. Occasionally a shadow falls over our happiness, the thought of the hostility of Clara's father, who can never really earn our trust, and that also is something we cannot change. By the way, the personal injury suit against him is now at an end; it brought him 18 days in jail and gave me the satisfaction I owed to myself.

Thirty-third week [CS]
from 25th April to 2nd May

The 25th Sunday we had *Verhulst* and *Fräulein Schloss* at our house for the noon meal. While still at the table we were surprised by the visit of two ladies who did not want to reveal their names—

it was Major *Serre's* wife and Frau von *Berge.* I had not seen the former for a long time! she is always the same kindhearted but most scatterbrained woman, in whose presence one cannot obtain any real peace. Now I would not want to spend 6 weeks with her again as in the past—now, while I am enjoying the most magnificent, calmest life in the presence of my Robert. The major is also like that! He followed on

the 27th with *Krägen* and *Anna* [Bartholdy] and visited us right away. He manipulates incessantly to reconcile us with my father, but approaches it altogether wrong. He insulted my husband a number of times in such a way that he would surely have become his enemy had it not been for the fact that Robert recognizes his friendship for us. This man believes he knows Father through and through, and thus always lets himself be pulled around by the nose by him. He did accomplish one good thing, however—the restitution of my belongings. I can well say that I unpacked them with childish pleasure and thereby found many a thing of value to me. Robert shared my joy wholeheartedly, I could tell by looking at him—the good dear man!

The 28th we ate with the *Serres* (to celebrate the birthday of the major's wife) in the *Hôtel de Pologne,* then went to *Felsche,* and in the evening I played for all of them at home. There were smiles all over *Krägen's* face, which pleased me, because he is difficult to satisfy and earlier, when I was still a child, often distressed me with his criticism—praise I heard from him extremely rarely. He is still the same, indolent, pampered by the major's wife, but by nature a very noble man.

Last Sunday a Madame *Burkhardt* also came to see me with her husband from *Königsberg.* She wanted to give a concert here (she is a singer), but what *Mendelssohn* had already done before I did also—I advised her absolutely against it. She was a pleasant woman, but according to *Mendelssohn* her singing is supposed to be most pedantic—she wanted to make her first *debut* before an audience here. I felt sorry for her, as for all mediocre artists.

Mendelssohn too pleased us with another visit. He will soon be leaving altogether—I doubt that he will return next winter. Major *Serre's* wife did not rest until she had made his acquaintance; she overwhelmed him with compliments—the entire conversation consisted of apologies, flattery, expressions of thanks, and the *point* was—her *album*, which he had to autograph and was then graciously dismissed. These albums could really drive one to despair—everyone, even if he is the most insignificant person in the world of art, must have autographs from the most famous people, and why? maybe because of interest in these people themselves? no! only to brag about it. Sometimes I could really go wild over that.

May 1841

Finally it is here, the beautiful month of May. What a sun, what a sky! These are blissful days, which cheer one's innermost feelings. Nevertheless, for the past week my poor Robert has not been feeling well at all and sometimes worries me—he does too little for himself and depends too much on his good constitution.

We now go walking a great deal, and enjoy the beautiful fresh green all over; even in my tiny little garden the cherry trees bloom, and the young vegetables germinate. It is magnificent!—I work in it occasionally and now and again I also do watering, and all that gives me the greatest pleasure. I truly lack nothing for my happiness, were it not for an occasional melancholic glance to the future, which saddens me—but which my Robert knows how to chase away immediately. This love is really the most beautiful, and every day we get to be more united in heart and soul.

Thirty-fourth week
from 2nd to 9th May

This Sunday we spent most pleasantly in the company of Herr Wenzel and Herr Herrmann in *Halle;* we climbed the *Gebichtenstein,* the Jägersberg, inspected the beautiful ruin [Moritzburg], ate our noon meal in the Kronprinz (which incidentally is very expensive), and in the evening we returned in good shape to Leipzig by steam train, satisfied with the sky, which had favored us with the most magnificent weather. Robert also was feeling better again and now, as I write this, is merry as a lark and mentally alert. For 3 days he has been orchestrating his 2nd great orchestral work—we don't know what to call it yet, it consists of an overture, scherzo, and finale—and again he already has new ideas for a piano fantasy with orchestra that he really ought to hold on to!—The more diligently my Robert pursues art, the less I accomplish therein; heaven knows! there always are hindrances, and as small as our household is, there's always this and that to do, which robs me of time. For several days I have been going shopping—I don't want to betray what I bought, but while doing that I felt quite unusually blissful. May heaven protect me!

3 days ago I began playing scales and exercises again for an hour, so at least I won't unlearn everything, but when it comes to composing there's really nothing left anymore—all poetry has abandoned me.

On *the 6th* Fräulein *Leontine Thun* from *Dorpat,* who has been here already for 2 years, visited me and told me of her wish to study with me. I very much love her personality; she has a determined, independent quality and yet at the same time is so feminine, graceful. I haven't agreed to the lessons yet; first she ought

Marriage Diary I 79

to play for me a few times. It should give me pleasure to be in closer contact with her because she made herself dear to me already the first time we talked.

The 7th. Visits from Madame *Friese* with *Amalie* [Rieffel] and Herr *Elsner* from Russia—a pianist who has had some misfortune; perhaps he might once have amounted to something.

Dünz from Berlin was also here; he wants to go to Vienna, to search for Stegmayer, who is still (already the 4th year) in the process of divorcing his wife [and] from whom one has heard nothing for a long time. I really feel very sorry for the woman!—

Saturday Herr *Veit* from Prague, *Mechetti* from Vienna [and] *Verhulst* with a Frenchman came to see us. I played something by Robert.

On *Sunday the 9th* there was a big dinner party at Hofmeister's to which mostly foreign music publishers were invited. The meal might have been all right had not everything there, glasses, napkins, bottles, pp. pp. [praemissis praemittendis], been so improper. Robert got up hungry from the table—his antipathy was too predominant. Just the opposite was the case that evening at Raimund Härtel's in Lindenau, where we consumed a fine supper, which was good especially for my poor hungry husband. I played a few things before dinner, quartets for male voices were also sung, but not especially well; it is really seldom that one hears a good male quartet!!—both of the Härtels by the way are dear people!

Fräulein *Thun* had her first lesson. She is very talented and has only been lacking good guidance—her playing is very messy, if I may say so.

NB. I forgot to mention the surprise afforded me by the visit of Madame Krägen from Dresden; she was here with Herr and Madame *Paul;* incidentally, I enjoyed her for only a little while; she stayed for too short a time. The Dresdeners don't get much rest in Leipzig, as I've already noticed many times.

Thirty-fifth and thirty-sixth weeks [RS]
from 10th to 22nd May 1841

A May the likes of which I have never experienced before; so warm and delicious. One wants to go away immediately. We always want to do that. But it's so difficult for me to leave my piano, and I always think I'm not sufficiently industrious. Yet I have been for the last 14 days. The *Symphonette*[58] is totally orchestrated; and on top of that a Fantasy for Piano and Orchestra.[59] Now I'm driven to new compositions again, and yet there is enough work to do on the finished ones. Ascension Day was a cheerfully beautiful day for us; I felt so free and light, and so happy near my beloved Clara, who returns each of my glances and handclasps with an intimate one. We were in Connewitz, now a charming resort—Dr. Reuter [came] along—then [we] went into the green forest—the sky was cloudy, but not enough to be disturbing—the birds were singing—we were really happy keeping each other company.

Otherwise little of importance occurred. We had several visitors, Cranz and Schuberth from Hamburg, Mechetti from Vienna, also my brother Carl, to whom I always feel warmly attached, despite his often worrying me so much. Unfortunately he too is already too old to restore to his business that foundation and firmness that it is possible [to give] so easily in one's younger energetic years.

To my great joy I'm now beginning to read scores with Clara; i.e., she plays while I pout my lips or also kiss. Thus it is like a

Marriage Diary I 81

game to get to know the clarinets and horns. And we shall now pursue it daily. We've started with the 2nd Symphony of Beethoven. I really want to know whether Clara is composing; but she must do it for her next concert and I cannot keep from pressing her.

In addition, the kapellmeister Kreutzer and [his] daughter were here; he made a successful appearance and will be engaged here. The girl seems simple and well bred.

Schloss will leave here permanently during the next few days. Also, Mendelssohn seems not to want to return.

Clara's father was here; in his buffoonlike conceit he called my symphony "Opposition Symphony." The man understands so little about creativity that he thinks one does or doesn't do it because of him. But we have to laugh over that word.

Thirty-seventh week [CS]
from 23–30 May

On *the 23rd* we took in a frugal but good midday meal at *Voigt's* once more. They are good people, but simple, especially the wife.

On *the 26th* we went on a very pleasant morning promenade to Gohlis through the Rosenthal. Robert wanted to take this walk once at 3 o'clock in the morning—I myself believe that must be splendid, but for me to take part would be difficult. Morning walks in general, as beautiful as they are, leave one incapable of doing anything serious for the rest of the day, as my poor Robert also noticed disagreeably today, since he mostly had to stay on the sofa. In the evening we went to the theater (the first time again in a year) to hear Fräulein [Cäcilie] *Kreutzer* in *Nachtlager von Granada* [an opera by her father, the composer Konradin Kreutzer].

Both of us heard this opera for the first time and found it more appealing than we had expected; but the music has absolutely no value and is oriented completely to the Viennese taste. We had expected more from Fräulein *Kreutzer;* not only is her voice insignificant, but we also found her technique most defective; every turn, every scale is still clumsy, and thus I don't believe that she will ever accomplish anything of importance. Otherwise her physical appearance is advantageous for the stage, and she herself seems to me to be an unspoiled, well-bred girl. Her younger sister is supposed to be very talented—she strikes us also as having more *spirit* than the older one.

On *Thursday the 27th* we ate at noon at *Dr. Härtel's;* the company was small but pleasant, the meal excellent. Pardon me, my dear husband, for speaking about it, but eating and drinking do play a major role in human life, and even you don't completely condemn the two!

I've gotten to know several Leipzigers who until now were strangers to me: *Gustav Harkort* and his wife, Herr *Lampe* and spouse, *etc.* I saw Amalie Rieffel again after a long interval; I felt sorry for her, I invited her—she turned me down after I had already been waiting for her for half an hour. Why do some people never acquire any manners! and an artist who presents herself openly in public—that is very bad!

Friday. Today was a magnificent day! we ate in *Connewitz,* then went to *Knauthayn* for the tax collector, and returned to Leipzig that evening feeling cheerful and satisfied with ourselves and the heavens. The beautiful girl of Knauthayn who often used to attract Robert, is no longer there—out of the corners of his eyes he searched several times for her window. Now I'd really have to be a tyrant not to let him revel blissfully in old feelings once in a while.

Marriage Diary I

Thirty-eighth week
from 30th May to 6th June

The 31st. The holidays are magnificent! Robert's mind is currently in the greatest activity; yesterday he started another symphony, which is supposed to consist of one movement, but including an *adagio* and a *finale*.

So far I've heard nothing of it, but can see from Robert's work and occasionally hear *D minor* sounding wildly in the distance, so I already know in advance that it is again a work created out of the deepest soul. Heaven really means well with us—Robert could not be happier in his creating than I am when he shows me his works. Do you believe me, my Robert? I would think you could.

June 1841

This month seems to want to be a beautiful one as well; only one day, the 1st, allowed the sun to be pushed aside, but now it asserts its full privilege.

Robert is composing constantly, has already finished 3 movements and I hope he will be ready in time for his birthday. In my opinion, he can look back on the past year and himself with joy! one sees that marriage has not proven to be detrimental after all— so often they say it might kill the spirit, rob it of youthful freshness! but my Robert certainly demonstrates the clearest evidence to the contrary!

On *the 2nd* the singer *Schmidt* visited me with the music director *Seydelmann* from *Breslau*. He is a dried-up, insignificant man, and *Schmidt* the same, although he thinks of himself as a great genius and displays this often enough, with the greatest arrogance.

My piano playing again falls completely by the wayside, as is always the case when Robert composes. Not a single little hour can be found for me the entire day! if only I don't regress too much! The score reading has also stopped again for now, but I hope not for too long!

The composing doesn't want to go at all right now—sometimes I want to beat myself over my stupid head!—

Fräulein Thun comes to me regularly once every week; I make a great effort to bring some solidity to her playing, and to give her the concept of shade and light in playing. There is much to be improved in her technique, here and there even the most basic things. How far a bad teacher can go with a talented student! how many of them are completely destroyed, and the few that remain, how laboriously they push themselves ahead!

Mendelssohn has returned; he will stay this month and then go back to Berlin, where he is spending the next year. But one hopes very strongly that he will conduct a few concerts next winter—I also think that yearning will occasionally drive him to Leipzig, where he is so generally beloved and esteemed, while this can never be the case in Berlin, if only because of the caste consciousness reigning there.

On *the 3rd Mendelssohn* visited us. He is reluctant to leave here, and it is really to be hoped that he will return, since he spoke much about the establishment of a music conservatory here, which seems a good idea to me.

This week I sat down a lot to compose, and finally succeeded with four poems by *Rückert* for my dear Robert.[60] May they satisfy him just a little, then my wish will be fulfilled.

It has been over 3 weeks that I have been waiting for news from my mother, and I suspect that she was not satisfied with our birthday presents—who knows! perhaps she counted on a significant sum of money. But I believe she cannot expect more than we have

Marriage Diary I 85

done—it was beyond our means. As soon as one is married it is a different story in terms of giving money, then one has himself to worry about, and there are so many things that burden a poor father of the family, which soon is what my Robert will ultimately end up being!!!—

Thirty-ninth and fortieth weeks
from 6th to 21st June

Oh, oh! my Robert! soon I may have to write the diary by myself, won't I? How shall I catch up with the 2 weeks that I have partially forgotten! I will at least try.

I will begin with the most beautiful day, the new year that you my dear husband have entered. The weather was horrible on June 8, but our souls lived in the most magnificent sunshine, and thus all went well. Oh, we were very blissful that day, and I devoutly thank God for letting us live so happily through this first June 8 of our marriage, and above all that he created such a dear, excellent human being for me and the world. Don't laugh at me, dear Robert—that would mean pouring cold water on my heart filled with love!—There was little I could give my Robert, but he always kept smiling so amicably because he knew well how affectionately they were given. Four lieder by Rückert gave him much pleasure, and he also treated them so tolerantly that he will even publish them together with several of his own, which makes me very happy.

In the evening came Reuter, Herrmann, and Verhulst, the last two having returned that morning very happy from a trip to Hamburg. We took in a heavy evening meal, but were very cheerful while doing so.

Mendelssohn visited us last week. He played and so did I. Robert showed him his latest compositions, which often forced him to produce an agreeable smile. For the musical supplement [to the journal] he brought along a small Song without Words[61] and played it, also one of his fugues, and, what I like so very much, a folk song without words, one that nobody plays like him, however.

Robert is finished with the new symphony in one movement, i.e., the sketch; he also has started to orchestrate it already, but was again held back from it by other labors, and now will probably complete it only after our little trip. Soon now he will turn the Spring Symphony over to the printer, but first wants to hear it once more.

From Fräulein *Harriet Parish* we received a most friendly invitation, in the name of her brother *Charles* and the Hamburg Musical Association, to the music festival there on July 2,[62] and at the same time the offer of several rooms in her house; furthermore, also accompanying the invitation was one to attend all the concurrent festivities as guests of honor. I really would like to accept for Robert's sake since he doesn't yet know Hamburg, but such an occasion is not suitable for calm enjoyment; one is pushed from one person to the next, and finally is happy to have the whole trip over with; also it is a huge *gêne* [inconvenience] to live with such a family, since one then always has to be considerate to them. We are thinking of taking this trip at some other time (perhaps next winter), when I can also leave the house more calmly than my present condition would permit; this trip would not have been completely without danger to me, therefore *in spe* [let's hope for the future]!

Liszt will be there, and presumably play as well; he has promised to come here next *November* for certain—we look forward to it.

During the summer the days proceed more quietly, thus there is also less to report, which also explains these very sparse [remarks] about the past few weeks. I ask my Robert please to make up for what I may have forgotten!—

Marriage Diary I 87

Forty-first week
from 21 to 27th June

This week the famous *Thorwaldsen* was here for one day. The *Serres* accompanied him here, they shared quarters, and yet I did not see him. *Serre's* clumsy behavior was at fault; he was too provincially egoistic to invite us to meet *Thorwaldsen*, which would have been easy for him; naturally I did not want to intrude, and thus I had to stand back, also during the festival that was given in his honor where *Mendelssohn* played and *Frege* sang, but no one thought about us, which really hurt me tremendously.

Are artists not the first who should be introduced to such a man? and Leipzig really is not all that overflowing with artists to justify passing us by!?—However, I soon got over my resentment, thus *tempi passati!*—

Serre brought us a legal document drawn up by my father in regard to the money belonging to me, which, however ridiculously constructed, could only stir us to laughter. We would have been real fools to agree to such terms, where not 17 groschen, let alone 1,700 thalers, are guaranteed. *Serre* is such a narrow-minded man to present us with something like that.

On the 23rd I gave Fräulein *Thun* the last lesson before her departure for the spa. She was clumsy enough to ask me about the cost of my lessons after I had already told her at her first visit that here in Leipzig I do not give any lessons for money; she behaved even more impolitely when 2 days later she sent me 9 thalers for 9 lessons, which were immediately returned, however. Some people simply have no tact at all. She could have made me happy with a small gift worth less than 9 thalers, and I always would have held fond memories of her.

On *the 26th* we thought of traveling to Dresden, but put it off because Robert had too much work left to do; I also preferred that, since next month I can rely on more stable weather.

Forty-second week
from 27th June to 4th July

Little has happened this week that would be worth noting.

On *the 27th* Pastor *Christner* from Eisleben visited us with his wife. He is a native of Zwickau and an old acquaintance of Robert's. I played a few things for him.

We have to suffer much from the great heat in our lodgings, especially my poor Robert, who sits in his room as if he were in hell.

The 30th. We want to leave tomorrow, but will it really happen!?—The sky seems to want to rebel against that with the gloomiest of clouds.

July 1841

The 1st. Well, today we actually left for Dresden. The journey there by steam train had a profoundly negative effect on me, but having once arrived I forgot this inconvenience and enjoyed the beautiful Elbe bordered by its vineyard hills—it also happened to be a magnificent evening. We checked into the *Hôtel de Saxe* and were stuck into a small dark room there, where on top of everything else we spent a sleepless night, inasmuch as, discounting the bad bed, some chambermaids and servants took pains to keep us awake with their loud conversation.

On *the 2nd* very early we went to *Findlater's* [winery] and from there enjoyed a magnificent view overlooking Dresden, the Elbe, *etc.* Dresden is really too beautiful—how paltry our poor Leipzig seems by comparison!

The longing for the Saxon Alps lured us already this afternoon as far as *Pillnitz*, where we looked at the most attractively situated

Marriage Diary I

castle and then visited the foothills of the Bors Mountains, the Schlossberg with its ruin, from where we could already see the Königstein, Lilienstein, Pfaffenstein, etc. We wanted to await the sunset up there, and did so, but the sun soon concealed itself behind a wall of clouds, and thus we missed the reddish glow of the evening sky, which we had been looking forward to.

The third morning things proceeded to the *Bastei;* the completely clouded sky gradually brightened up, revealing the mountains to us, all in the most beautiful clarity. We got out on the Uttenwald Grund and wandered up to the *Bastei* on foot. It was truly magnificent to stroll among the many differently formed rocks; sometimes they hover over one's head, so that one might be afraid they could come crashing down. I especially had fun looking at the faces into which some of the prominent rocks have been molded! now a friendly one, then again a stern one with a long nose, then a man with a hat on his head, which later will again take a completely different form.

The *Bastei* astonished Robert (I had already visited it once before), but before long, with these precipices on all sides, he became unwell.[63] Neither of us got as far as the railing—one of us always held on to the other. So we soon left, after taking a miserable midday meal, for the Amselgrund. We walked as far as the waterfall, where we rested underneath a small Swiss hut. This gorge is really far more impressive than that of the Uttenwald. I greatly enjoyed the waterfall, but even more the one at the Kuhstall, since it is situated more grandiosely and even more romantically. Here we remained seated for a long time, because a waterfall came down from the sky that was truly the most magnificent. I had been waiting precisely for that in this gorge—I would also have liked some thunder and lightning.—The carriage was waiting for us in *Rathewalde,* just in the nick of time, since we had gotten quite tired indeed. We drove as far as the *Hohnstein* and got out there, but were too tired to do much sightseeing and also were again confronted by horrifying chasms. I also forgot to mention the bridge one has to cross from the *Bastei* into the Amselgrund. It leads over an enormous abyss, and all my limbs were trembling after I had crossed it. In Robert's opinion even the real Alps [of Switzerland] have no bridge this size. I leave it to him to portray the contrasting impressions of these Alps and those of Switzerland.

After passing the dangerous road called "der Ziegenrück" we arrived in Schandau in the evening. This road was constructed by *Napoleon;* in the distance, on top of a mountain, one can also see *Napoleon's* linden tree, the place from where he surveyed his army.

Schandau is charmingly situated on the Elbe, where we even did some rowing that evening. We retired early, after consuming a few delicious trout.

Now my dear Robert may continue, in order to describe the most beautiful day we had, the 4th of July. After all, I must beg your indulgence for my prosaic descriptions of traveling; I certainly feel more poetic than these would lead you to believe, if you did not know me better.

I will always remember this vacation with much pleasure, the first I have taken with my beloved husband.

At the end of this week, a fond, grateful kiss!—

Forty-third week [RS]
from 4th to 11th July

Friday the 9th before noon we came back to Leipzig. The little journey was a fond wish, long cherished. It too, like all travels, will often give us pleasure in the future and in memory. It was

Marriage Diary I 91

especially important for me to see how we would adjust ourselves in a foreign place among strangers. Neither of us are good at quickly becoming acquainted with people we do not know, and thus we tended to cling to each other that much more firmly and found our joy in one another. The region through which we roamed is very much worth seeing. Unfortunately much gets spoiled for me by getting sick, as I always do at great heights, especially when it descends suddenly and steeply. In my imagination the horrible bridge down from the Bastei to the Amselgrund can still frighten me.

The 4th of July, Sunday, was a beautiful sunny day. We left early during the fresh, clean coolness of the morning, drove through the Schandau Valley always along a lively creek to the base of the Kuhstall. At the top we were most magnificently rewarded for our climb. Nature has done wonders here with gigantic cliffs. Switzerland, the real one, really has nothing comparable to offer. And how good breakfast tasted after that; the wife of the driver, a quiet, modest woman, always followed us in the distance and occasionally brought Clara a small bunch of myrtle berries or a strawberry. This morning was our most cheerful. We also crawled up to the height of the cliff, through a narrow crevice not much wider than ourselves. Clara may have uttered a few soft sighs that I did not hear; but then we put everything right again by kissing, proving that Clara is a travel companion just as she is a partner for life, willing, cheerful, considerate, always lovable and loving.

We returned to Schandau in good spirits, took a bath at the spa. On a bad pianoforte that stood there it was possible to bring something forth only with effort. I remembered my earlier musical madness when I would find a piano after a long interval. That was how I would improvise in Switzerland, often into the night. Clara threw herself into a Chopin etude; surely this was the first time something by Chopin was heard in this valley. All of Schandau would have come running had they known *who* was playing there and—beside that been able to be critical. In the inn the trout again tasted most superb. Our faces showed nothing but an aching for *more*.

We departed from Schandau completely content and happy. The best was yet ahead of us: the view from the Königstein fortress, surely among the most beautiful in the country. The sky grew ever clearer and cleaner. Up there I thought a lot about Lühe, an older friend who was imprisoned at Königstein for several years and wrote to me from there nearly every week. Soon the beautiful Saxon Alps were behind us, taking leave of us in the most friendly evening light. We had to give up the nice idea of spending the night in Blasewitz, Naumann's birthplace, because the inn was just having a Sunday dance. Thus we arrived late in Dresden.

Early on Monday the 5th, after breakfast at the attorney Krause's, a relative of mine, we drove by mail coach to Freiberg. A boring trip and very disadvantageous for Clara. But I hope she did not do herself any harm.

In Freiberg we sent for Becker; he was surprised and delighted. In the city, as in Becker's house, things look somewhat disheveled and deserted. We also don't envy Becker his wife, although she may be basically good natured, but otherwise she has everything that could drive a man to despair.

Tuesday morning we made music; Becker's 14-year-old daughter Marie really pleased us and has gotten a solid foundation from her father. Clara also played very nicely. In the afternoon a carriage drive to an attractive amusement resort. Before that, lest I forget the most important thing, we also looked at the outstanding Silbermann organ; the organist preluded and postluded a D minor fugue by Bach in C-sharp minor, which made us laugh a

Marriage Diary I 93

great deal. Clara also played, and soon might well be the most capable player. We are also planning to take organ lessons in Leipzig. I just noticed the end of the book. I close it with love, as I had opened it, yes, with *much warmer* love.

Two

MARRIAGE DIARY II

7 July 1841 – 19 September 1842

Conclusion of the thirty-fourth week [RS]
[7–10 July]

On the 9th of July we returned to Leipzig and joyously greeted our familiar dwelling. We spent only the 7th and 8th in Dresden, hoping to hear Ungher and Moriani, a hope that was not fulfilled. We saw a play[1] in the new theater,[2] which is probably one of the most magnificent in the world; one feels more noble in a beautiful building, although fine artistic judgment could find fault perhaps with some of the interior decoration. But let's get rid of all criticism since so much of beauty remains. We didn't speak with anyone else in Dresden.

Having arrived in Leipzig there was much to be done. We made changes in the apartment because the heat in the room facing the courtyard made me almost completely incapable of working. We talked to Therese [Fleischer] just before her trip to Italy. I was very sorry to have missed the Danish writer *Andersen* who was here and intended to see me. Verhulst soon came by; the recent catastrophe with Dr. Reuter seems to have depressed him somewhat.

I haven't yet thought of composing, of getting back to those compositions that I have not yet completely finished. After not making music for a long time, one is overcome by great timidity about taking the thing up again. Instead I have again experienced pleasant hours with Goethe's "Truth and Poetry" [i.e., *Aus meinem Leben, Dichtung und Wahrheit*] and gotten the most intimate pleasure from this healthy, all-encompassing genius.

Soon the score playing with Clara will also be resumed. We have finished with the symphonies in D major and B-flat major by Beethoven, and four overtures by Mozart, and now are working on the Egmont Overture [by Beethoven]. I'm thinking of establishing a small library of my favorite orchestral pieces, and have already started doing that. Moreover, Clara has been working diligently on several Beethoven sonatas and conceives of them in quite a unique way without compromising the original. That gives me great satisfaction.

For a long time already I have also been thinking about myself and Clara looking more into the older music (before Bach's time). We know only a little bit about the old Italians, Dutch, even Germans. And it really is very necessary for an artist to be able to give an account of the entire history of his art. Surely a good library, which does not exist here, is necessary for that—and, specifically, also collaboration from the human voice. But we certainly don't want to abandon that idea.

What really always remains the most important thing is to be productive. How much I yearn for an opera. I've been thinking of *Calderon,* in whom something for me can perhaps be found, and I've already started with the "Bridge of Mantible"—[3]

Forty-fourth week [CS]
From 11th to 18th July

The 18th. This week I want to make nothing more than a long ———because nothing or very little of interest has occurred. We received several visits from *Heinrich Marschner* and Herr *Goetze*

Marriage Diary II   99

from Copenhagen, a singing teacher who encouraged me enormously to come to Copenhagen. We missed *Marschner;* just that day we had taken a walk to our favorite village, Connewitz. We wanted to visit him the following day, but *Hofmeister,* with whom he was staying, made such a muddle of the arrangements (as he usually does) that we again did not meet. Yesterday he went to Dresden to hear *Ungher* and *Moriani* (about whom the Dresdeners are making a lot of noise), but he will return later. I do regret not having heard at least *Ungher.* They say she may want to end her artistic career in Dresden, but I don't believe it—it would be a rarity for a singer to know the right time to stop!

On *the 17th* Major *Serre* visited us once again, mainly in order immediately to settle our financial affairs with Father; but it didn't work out so easily because one has to be very careful with that man (namely, my father) so that he does not take you by surprise [and] palm off some bad, worthless papers, as he is vigorously trying to do just now. I cannot say just how much I would like to have this thing over with, if this fight would only come to an end. The gulf between us, as big as it already is, just gets bigger all the time, and that is something I really don't want, even though, for Robert's sake, I'm not considering a reconciliation right now. My Robert's love rewards me so highly that I surely live with my entire soul only for him.

This week I have started to play regularly at least 2 hours a day. I play mostly fugues and sonatas by Beethoven, but soon I also want to turn in earnest once more to Robert's compositions. Unfortunately too few hours remain available to me for musical activities, and that also will not improve for the moment—but I'm happy that now I'm playing at least once a day! I go to bed more calmly after having fulfilled this obligation to myself. Robert also seems satisfied, and never fails to be encouraging.

Forty-fifth to forty-seventh weeks [RS]
From 18th July to 8th August

Soon the 52nd! Klärchen, what do you think? Do you still like this marriage! I do—fairly well. We stick together quite courageously and want to be like that always. How much could be said about the past weeks, if I only had enough leisure for diary writing. It still goes most easily in fragments.

First: a lot of visits, good ones and bad ones. C. Decker from Berlin, already familiar, not a pleasing talent—Julius Stern from Berlin, young, ambitious, full of talent—Dütsch from Copenhagen, student of Schneider, also arouses hopes, but already conceited—Hauptman from Kassel, with whom I myself did not speak—Nottebohm from the Rhine, late bloomer, an honest guy nonetheless—organist Hering from Bautzen, not a musician worth envying—Busch from Copenhagen, an old admirer of Clara's, a stiff, tall ass—Mendelssohn, who bade us farewell on the 28th—old Rieffel from Flensburg, a lively man, educated in many things—David with his brother-in-law Liphardt and the music director Grund from Hamburg—Anacker from Freiberg—Professor Röller from Gross Glogau—Flechsig, my dear friend of youth and earlier roommate—Novakovsky from Warsaw, an acquaintance and relative of Chopin's whom I also knew already from early days—finally L. Anger, who brought a book of variations—and Amalie Rieffel, who wants to take lessons from me—

Projects—With true love Clara is practicing much by Beethoven (also by Schu-and-married-man)—she has greatly assisted me in putting my symphony, which is now soon to be published, in good order—moreover, [Clara] reads Goethe's autobiography,

Marriage Diary II 101

she also slices beans if necessary—but music surpasses everything for her and that is a joy for me—

I haven't composed anything new and am still busy with older things—the Symphony in D Minor is nearly finished, the Fantasy in A Minor has been organized and is ready for performance—the same goes for the Symphony in B-flat after just one more rehearsal, which will be held this week—

Now Thomas Moore's "Paradise and the Peri" [*Lalla Rookh*] has made me quite happy—maybe something of beauty can be made of it with music—

There seems to be little that can be used in Calderon, except perhaps the "Bridge of Mantible." I have also read the "Magician" [by Calderón],[4] which Goethe used in connection with Faust.

I was also frequently indisposed. With Clara things are generally going so well that we really have to be thankful. We now look forward joyfully and apprehensively to the coming month. Just have courage, my Clara.—

Forty-eighth and forty-ninth weeks [CS]
From 8 to 22 August

August 9 was a peculiar day! We experienced a hailstorm the likes of which even the oldest people cannot remember. Fearful souls, including myself as well, believed that it might lead to the end of the world. The weather did great damage, just to mention the many thousands of windowpanes it broke! in our own house it smashed 42 panes. Hailstones the size of an egg are supposed to have been found, and not only animals but also several people were killed.

The weather in general is peculiar this summer. June, July, and August, except for a few beautiful days, were cold autumn months—many people heated their rooms. But a beautiful autumn is still being predicted.

Amalie Rieffel had her first lesson with Robert. I really would like to observe him sometime, how he comes across as a teacher!—

The old Rieffel strikes me as a man completely torn with passion; incidentally, in his way of speaking he has much in common with my father. He is most dissatisfied that his Amalie did not become more famous last winter, that not enough was written about her, and that these few lines were cold and indifferent, etc. I'm convinced that Amalie herself is much to blame for this—she is still lacking in *savoir vivre,* on which much unfortunately depends even for an artist.

On *Friday the 13th* Robert's symphony was rehearsed once more in the Gewandhaus, with a few minor changes that he still hit on, which for the most part were also put to good use. How much I enjoyed hearing this beautiful work again! however, under David's direction the ensemble was not *so* good as under Mendelssohn's!—

I also played the Fantasy in *A minor;* but unfortunately in this hall the soloist himself has little satisfaction (in the empty hall, that is), he hears neither himself nor the orchestra. But I played it twice, and found it magnificent! when well-prepared it must give the listener the greatest enjoyment. The piano is interwoven with the orchestra in the most subtle way—one cannot imagine the one without the other. I look forward to playing it in public one day, when it must surely go quite differently than it did in today's rehearsal. Robert enjoyed it nevertheless! he could well have listened to it, and I would have wanted to play it, several times in a row.

Marriage Diary II   *103*

The rehearsal actually was supposed to have been on Saturday, but for the sake of the musicians it was changed to Friday. We had invited Becker from Freiberg to attend, and now this man arrived in the afternoon with *Karl Kraegen* only after the rehearsal was over, which made all of us very angry. The pleasure over the symphony again, as well as over the Fantasy and the playing itself, had excited me so much that I was sick the whole afternoon, and I feel quite badly even now, for which the 4 days of company may be partly to blame, since I couldn't afford to get a single hour's rest. *Krägen* stayed with the young *Serre,* who always reminds me of a young horse. They ate lunch at our house on Saturday and on

Sunday the 15th. Krägen is a good fellow, but has been pampered by Major *Serre's* wife like a little pet; there is no sap and no energy in this man—a major part of his life is devoted to *enjoyment.* His touch at the piano is beautiful, but his playing is as lazy as his imagination. What a pity for him!—

Sunday afternoon I played several sonatas by Beethoven, but neither Becker nor Kraegen found them as enjoyable as such a Beethoven sonata can be. Their cultural expectations have been directed more toward the realm of virtuosity than true music. A fugue by Bach, for example, bores them; they are incapable of appreciating the beauty inherent in the different entrances of the voices with the theme, they cannot follow that at all! I feel sorry for a musician who lacks understanding for this magnificent art. The less I play in public these days, the more I begin to hate all that mechanical virtuosity! Concert pieces like etudes by Henselt, fantasies by Thalberg, Liszt, etc., have become totally repugnant to me, and especially so because of Becker's esteem for them. None of that can provide permanent satisfaction! I will not play any of these things again until I need them for a concert tour; I deplore having to devote time to them now.

104   *The Marriage Diaries of Robert & Clara Schumann*

Robert could barely pay any attention to his guests in these 2 days because he was busy delivering the symphony to the printer, which then finally did happen on

Monday the 16th. How I look forward to the first printed part!—[5]

Robert cannot be any happier about it than I am.

Kraegen left today! here he missed the customary nursing care, someone to bandage his ailing foot, not to mention the gingerbread that the major's wife keeps only for him, etc., etc. —God, how I would feel if I had such a husband!—

On *Tuesday the 17th* we took a walk to *Connewitz* with Becker and ate our lunch outdoors. The day was beautiful, but we were very exhausted—neither Robert nor I can tolerate much commotion, and that always results from having a guest along, even if he is the most intimate friend! just the opposite! especially this one demands the most attention. I played a bit of Robert's symphony for Becker from the score, but he was incapable of following and therefore did not understand it either, which put me in a very angry mood.

On *the 18th* Becker left and thus put us back into our usual state of repose. He is an excellent soul, that cannot be denied, loyally devoted to us, but he's not refined enough to avoid if possible embarrassing his hosts.

I gave him a few lines of congratulations written for my father on his birthday today, and I don't believe it was the wrong time to do so. It seems that our financial affairs are now approaching a satisfactory conclusion, whereby my father (surely, I believe, only on account of cleverness) has complied in a number of things. I'm very happy about it and kiss my dear husband, who has fulfilled my wish to write to my father by giving his permission even before I asked him for it.

For the past 3 days I've been feeling terribly bad! also I can't seem to move from this spot, so that my Robert must really be quite concerned about me.

My most sincere plea to God is this, that He should not take me from Robert just now—that would be the saddest thing I can think of!—I still need much, much time to bestow on Robert all the love that I feel for him—it is indeed completely unlimited!—

NB. I forgot to mention the rehearsal in the Gewandhaus that I attended with Becker and Krägen to listen to *David's* symphony. It is, as was to be expected, cut entirely from the conventional mold; it lacks all individuality, which one cannot even completely deny Reissinger and Kalliwoda (in whose *genre* it is written); in some places it is trivial like *Marschner*. Places such as this:

should never be written by a musician who in other respects is as good as *David*, and there are many places like that.

Fräulein *Haase*, daughter of the horn player from Dresden, rehearsed an aria and did not make an agreeable impression on me! her voice itself is completely muddy, and her training still very defective. A young Dutchman named *Tuyn* gave me far more pleasure with his singing; his voice is not always comforting, but he lets it sound out in a natural way and has had good training; [he] is also, it seems to me, educated as a musician; at times he does some Italianesque sobbing, which I really would want to *eliminate*. He visited us before noon on the 18th with *Verhulst,* and sang a lied of Robert's quite beautifully, also the Adelaide by Beethoven.

On *Thursday the 19th David* came to see us with a cellist, *Lutzau,* from *Riga,* who brought us *Dorn's* greetings. I don't believe that he is a significant artist—at least I've not yet heard his name, and he seems to be too old at this point to make one for himself, but personally he is quite pleasant and seemed to me to have good musical judgment.

On *Saturday the 21st Schlesinger* from Berlin visited me. He is a windbag and enjoys himself especially by producing the most senseless compliments, which he knows how to do for minutes, often uninterruptedly. As friendly and obliging as he was to me all the time, nevertheless I find him most loathsome and disgusting.

Robert made a little overland excursion—the weather was too magnificent!—I'm very sad that I cannot accompany him anymore! but the times will also return when no walking tour was too far for me!—Robert moreover is always so affectionate and considerate, doesn't let me see any expressions of annoyance while I lament in his presence, and thus he greatly eases my situation; it would greatly disturb me if I were to see that my condition produces uncomfortable moments for him.

As far as work is concerned, it doesn't go as easily for me, but that much more so for Robert. He has now put the finishing touches on his Fantasy, here and there he still has taken out a horn or a bassoon, and now while I am writing this he is working on his Overture, Scherzo, and Finale, so that he will soon have this in the clear as well. He regularly schedules the lessons with *Rieffel,* like a conscientious schoolmaster. I also really would like to sign myself up as his student, then I would have the luck of being allowed to play for him more often, for which I would like to envy Rieffel!—But now at the end of the week a really heartfelt kiss, my darling, exceptionally loving husband! Next week, and who knows for how many more, you will have to take over. But I hope that (if God chooses) we will celebrate the anniversary of this book together!

Marriage Diary II 107

On 17th September 1841 [RS]

A new chapter of life has been successfully completed, even if not without worries, so that we must be wholeheartedly thankful to heaven.

On the 1st of September He gave us, through my Clara, a girl. The preceding hours were painful; I will not forget the night before September 1 (a Wednesday). So much stood in danger; once, for *one* minute, it so overwhelmed me that I did not know how to control myself. But then I relied on Clara's strong nature, her love for me—how would I be able to describe all that. 10 minutes to eleven in the morning the little one arrived—accompanied by lightning and thunder, as a storm filled the sky just then. But the first cries—and life again manifested itself to us, brightly and lovingly—we were completely overjoyed with happiness. How proud I am to have a wife who, in addition to her love [and] her art, has also given me such a present. Now the hours flew by with mingled joy and worry. The little one grew from day to day. Clara recovered more and more. Her mother came here from Berlin, and on the 13th of September, Clara's 22nd birthday, we had the baby baptized with the dear name Marie. The mother [Marianne Bargiel], my brother [Carl Schumann], my old landlady Devrient, and Mendelssohn stood as godparents—my brother and Mendelssohn were represented by the bookdealer Barth and [publisher] Raimund Härtel. There was much excitement in the house. Now that the mother has gone back to Berlin it gets to be quieter again. In a few days Clara will be able to go outdoors again, and then new pleasures will always be waiting for us at home; because one can never really tire of looking at one's child. I leave this now mainly to you, my dear Clara, to describe the little life accurately in the diary, how it unfolds ever more each day, she is the first proper honorary member of our union; truly we have always had very good luck, but if anything could have increased and strengthened it even more, then it is this little Marie who shall be the image of you internally one day, as she resembles me externally.

The festivities never ceased at all; on the 12th was our wedding anniversary; on the 13th birthday and child baptism. I was able to give my Clara a little pleasure with the first printed part of my symphony, with the second [symphony], which I had completed in secret, and then with the two published volumes of Rückert lieder [composed] by both of us.[6] What else could I offer her besides my artistic efforts, and how lovingly she participates in those. One thing makes me happy, the awareness that I am still a long way from the goal and must always accomplish even better things, and then the feeling of energy that I can achieve it. So then with courage, my Clara at my side, ever forging ahead.—

We heard Pasta—it was embarrassing—we were glad to get out of the theater. Hardly any traces that she was ever a great artist.

A Dutch tenor, Tuyn, visited us a number of times; the voice is good, but without significant character.—Carl Mayer from Petersburg arrived just at the time of Clara's confinement; unfortunately we did not speak with him, nor with E. Franck from Breslau. All the more Hirschbach from Berlin, the strange fellow with his Mozart profile; he wants to remain here for the winter.

From 13th to 27th September 1841   [CS]

You have described the past few days with such affectionate words, my precious Robert, that I don't know what to add other than that I am very happy to have a child by him who is dearest to me in this world. Each day I think "I cannot love him *more* than that," and yet it seems to me as though I love you more daily! when

Marriage Diary II 109

you yourself are not with me, then Marie, your dear little image, reminds me of you, which really makes me very happy. But such a child also causes worries, especially a first one, whom one doesn't yet know at all how to take proper care of—rightly one calls such a child an anxiety child, since it is truly that! I observe every movement of my little one with a feeling of anxiety and joy. Now things are going well with little Marie, but it was high time for us to provide the child with a different wet nurse, lest it were to starve half to death. As for my state of health, it is quite good now and extraordinary considering the brief time since my confinement. I take a walk daily for at least an hour with my beloved Robert, and thank God that He has let me stay on this earth, where I live so happily.

My birthday was a day filled from morning to night with enjoyment and happiness. Robert surprised me with so many things, his completed *D Minor* Symphony, the first printed part of the *B-Flat Major* Symphony, and most of all with the published *Rückert* lieder, wherein a few of my feeble productions also appear. I had no inkling of this surprise. Moreover, on this so richly laden table there was no lack of products such as soap, *eau de cologne*, etc., for which a woman's heart also craves once in a while. A beautiful present for me was the score of *Don Juan* [by Mozart] in which I play diligently; it gives one true pleasure to read it because it is so beautifully engraved, and now this music, interesting from one note to the next!—I squeeze your hand once more, my Robert, for all the pleasure you have given and always give me.

The presence of Mother seems like a dream to me! unfortunately she only stayed for such a short time that we could not completely talk things out. Incidentally, I feel very reassured about her situation; people in Berlin take care of her most graciously, she has to give lessons from morning to night, and what is most important, she is well physically and also finds herself so happy in her small apartment, with a little garden and with her children, that I'm very glad about it. God never really abandons a person! as proven again by my mother! during the most deperate moments after her husband's death, without any money, He stirred the conscience of people who helped my mother bear all of her suffering so easily. One must never lose faith!—

On *the 25th* the wife of *Dr. Frege,* who had just come back from her bathing trip, came to see me; she missed me. I visited her on the 27th but found her still very saddened by the loss of her only child.[7] Such a loss certainly is terrible, but easier to bear when people (husband and wife) love each other tenderly, where mutual love provides consolation, where each one makes an effort to find distractions for the other, but when that is not the case such a tragedy is twice as awful!—It gives my soul the deepest pain to think about it and especially about *Doctor Frege,* who is said to be completely disconsolate and despondent.

On *the 28th* we took our first outing in the country, to Connewitz by coach, but we walked back. It was a beautiful day and we were quietly happy.

I notice just now that I have run into your week—a sign that I am out of material.

About my educating of little Marie, dear Robert, not many results can be shown as yet; so far the best result is that she drinks *comme il faut* and that she sleeps. Soon I hope she will learn to smile at you, the first sign of comprehension!—incidentally, even now she sometimes looks around in a fairly intelligent way.

From 27th September–24th October 1841 [RS]

Things are going fairly well in the Schumann house. The little one is already beginning to smile, the housewife is the old dear

Marriage Diary II   *111*

one, and only the head of the household is sometimes in a dark mood. Why? He doesn't know it himself; he ought to be content to have such a wife and child, and yet often he doesn't show it at all and makes his wife sad. You know what often makes me wild and angry, the thought of your father. Let me keep quiet about that. Often it is also dissatisfaction with myself, with my literary and artistic circumstances. So don't be angry with me, dear Clara. An artist's heart is always in a certain commotion, it alway drives him restlessly onward. But then again there are also more peaceful hours, and we have already spent so many beautiful ones together. Nor have the last weeks been entirely unproductive; a little symphony in C minor is almost completed in my head,[8] the corrections for the one in B-flat major have all been delivered, and a few other things. Clara also has finished a small composition[9] that exudes a rather nice quality; she is now allowed to play regularly again; but of course as the artist she must sacrifice many an hour on behalf of the mother.

Incidentally, our little angel is already beginning to respond to music; whenever she is rather restless, Clara plays for her, which pacifies her immediately and puts her to sleep.

Our nursery trip to Sittel was a tragic story and it will long remain in our memory; instead of 8 in the evening we returned after 1 in the morning in the blackest night; there were terrors upon terrors, which a single ray of sunshine could immediately have chased away. Dr. Reuter was with us.

The subscription concerts began on the 3rd—they have to be held without Mendelssohn maintaining them at a high standard—but beautiful evenings remain nonetheless, and if ever an audience has interest and reverence for music it is the Leipzigers; they sit more attentively and quietly than in church.

An Italian violinist, Sivori, had success; he also visited us; a quiet, unpretentious man with whom unfortunately it was impossible to converse, since he doesn't speak German. Meerti doesn't please as she did earlier; they say of her that she is no *longer the one*. Tuyn is supposed to make dreadful faces while singing, which is why the ladies are not especially fond of him: they always sing boring stuff.

Among the visitors there were also Streicher from Vienna, the young Dütsch from Copenhagen, and a G. Wöhler; we always sent most of them away.

Julius Becker, a kind, gentle person who always supports me loyally, seems to be afflicted with incurable consumption; his loss would sadden me greatly.

We also played the organ once in St. John's Church; an awful thing to remember because we did not handle it with any accomplishment, and in the Bach fugues Clara could never get past the second entrance, as though she were standing at a wide stream [i.e., *Bach*]—but we want to try it again soon; the instrument really is just too magnificent.

On the 17th we had Verhulst and Reuter over for dinner; we were quite cheerful. On the 20th there was a fire in our vicinity; but we were able to view it calmly.—

Now, Clara, give me your hand if you please and a kiss. You surely are and always will be my dearest—you know that of course.—

From 24th October to 14th November 1841   [CS]

The diary looks at me quite like a stranger, I haven't written anything in it for so long, and even now there is only little of any consequence.

On *the 24th* we had *Böttger, Hirschbach* (a sad genius), and

Wenzel with us for dinner. There was much drinking and much music making; it may well have been the first time for years that I've played Robert's *F-Sharp Minor* Sonata—it delighted me anew! I consider it one of Robert's most magnificent works.

On *the 25th* there was a small party at *David's*. Meerti (a dear girl) sang, *Tuyn* as well, and *David* played a little sonata by *Beethoven G major* with me, after I had played several solos—*Diversions* by *Bennett,* the performance of which greatly satisfied Robert, which made me quite happy—I so rarely get any praise from him!

They have asked me to play in one of the Gewandhaus concerts; Robert has accepted it, but only after my own concert in November is over. I wish the time were here! I haven't gotten my old strength back yet, and thus am quite afraid of that day.

The 28th was the 4th subscription concert. Neither of us attended the third one because it was of little interest, and father, mother, and child did not feel well. Today's concert also did not have especially much to offer. An old little symphony by Haydn came at the beginning, *Tuyn* sang an aria by *Weber* with Italian feelings—intolerably sweet! *Röckel,* an inexperienced pianist, played Oberon's "Magic Horn" [by Hummel] but without any magic, and after that a fantasy composed by himself—a *non plus ultra* of fantasy*less*ness. He visited us, but we did not see him; he had already been here for nearly a week before coming to our house, I believe he just isn't modest. The *finale* from *Idomeneo* [by Mozart] was probably the high point of the concert. The *Melusine* by *Mendelssohn* is not exactly my favorite among *Mendelssohn's* overtures.

We paid *Meerti* a return visit. I liked the mother and daughter very much, if only she sang better—I had rather big expectations of her and found myself minimally satisfied; also, she sings so little that is good, and just that not well.

On *Saturday the 30th* we ate once again in Connewitz. I'm

always quite happy during such outings with my Robert; then I have him all to myself, and that's the way I like it. I had several unkind days in which I tormented my poor husband quite a lot— I thought he no longer loved me as much as the first year! He had some things on his mind that were annoying him (I'm well aware of that) and I was very irritable, consequently I gave myself some dreary hours.

But now everything is well again—Robert is affectionate and I am happy. To our joy Marie grows daily, physically and mentally— she seems to want to resemble the Papa in everything except for the little hands with the long piano fingers, which one cannot well dispute as inheritance from the mother.

On *Sunday the 31st* we again had dinner guests. Herr and Madame *Voigt* and *Amalie Rieffel,* with whom Robert had some fun, she[10]

At the Meyers' that evening, the *Carl* vixen insulted me in such a mean way that I decided to withdraw altogether. Nobody, not even the most peaceful person, can get along with that woman for long, and *he* is weaker than a woman.

From time to time we still have magnificent days, which we then also make use of. Thus on the *3rd of November* we went to *Möckern* for lunch and found ourselves quite content there.

Robert is always very busy, a good example for the wife!—

Meerti visited me with her mother. I'm really in love with them both!

On *the 4th* was the 5th subscription concert. Except for the symphony by *Schubert* and the overture by *Rietz* there was nothing for good ears. Meerti and Tuyn sang a duet from *Zemire und Azor* by Spohr in a very mediocre way. There was neither a spark of inwardness nor passion to be found—the audience remained *cold.*

Sivori played once more, as always, extraordinarily clever little tricks.

My playing is going *badly!* I have no strength, pain in the fin-

Marriage Diary II 115

gers, and thus inwardly it doesn't look very agreeable. The day of the concert in Weimar approaches steadily, and now I'm supposed to play here as well, and can't do anything properly!

Hirschbach had a symphony rehearsal, also a quartet at his home, but left everyone cold. All feel sorry for him because his talent is not supposed to be overlooked, but at this point he seems to have learned too little and is too immodest to believe this. Robert has often told him that already, but it usually results in dissension.

On *the 7th* we had our noon meal at the *Voigts'*, drank champagne, and made much music. I played the sonata by *Mendelssohn* for cello and piano with *Wittmann,* as well as the one in *A major* by *Beethoven.* Playing the one by *Mendelssohn* gave me especially great pleasure.—*Amalie* [Rieffel] let us hear a few things by Robert and *Mendelssohn.*

Monday evening with *Meerti* I sang through a few songs by Robert, in order to make a selection for my concert. But only a German heart that can feel intimately is appropriate for German lieder. I like *Meerti's* voice very much, however, especially in the middle range.

Verhulst loves *Meerti* and has asked me to find out whether there is any reciprocal love. What others have too much of, *Meerti* has too little—good sense. She is beside herself to find that she is criticized in Robert's newspaper! she can't understand that, because she is in good standing with us and is supposed to sing in my concert, *etc.* It would be smarter for her not to let any anger be noticed; there is an arrogance in that which I would not have expected in this likeable exterior.

November has revealed itself for several days in all its unfriendliness. I want to compare myself with it, that's how unkind I find myself. My dear Robert must really have patience! *Marie* grows visibly—she is our joy.

Wednesday the 10th. Visit from the *music director Müller* of *Ru-*

dolstadt. I played a few things—I believe he didn't really know what it was all about.

The Gewandhaus concert was on Saturday [instead of Thursday] this time, and at the conductor's podium stood—*Mendelssohn;* there was no lack of *bravos,* and the ladies may well have been the happiest, sitting with open mouths throughout the entire concert and behaving as if they hadn't seen any conducting in their lives. I certainly esteem *Mendelssohn* highly, but this shallow idolatry, as happens with a large part of the local public, is unbearable to me.

The *A Major Symphony* [by Beethoven] went splendidly! One did notice the conductor, who disseminated soul over the whole thing.

Meerti pleases less all the time, and *Tuyn* excites noticeable discomfort among the public. I pity both of them! Tuyn did learn something, and it is only his unpleasant *voice* and pronunciation of German that spoils his career.

On Sunday *Mendelssohn* came to visit his little godchild [Marie Schumann] and seemed to like her; indeed she is just too adorable—as soft and white as alabaster!—

Mendelssohn was happy to have turned his back once more on Berlin, which he hates. Mother should hear that![11]—Dear husband, forgive the little silliness at the end of the week.

From 14th November to 1st December 1841 [RS]

From my brief notes about the preceding weeks I still find the following:

27 October "Tragödie" by Heine, composed for various voices with orchestra (my first attempt at vocal composition with or-

chestra)[12]—Kapellmeister Pott from Oldenburg—7 November dinner at Voigts with Rieffel and Wittman—sonatas for piano and cello by Beethoven in A major and by Mendelssohn—Wittmann also sings very pleasantly and like a real musician—Early on the 8th of November a sad quartet at Hirschbach's—all hope seems to have abandoned him—he wants to give up music completely—on the 10th, a day of joy because the symphony [B-flat major] was completed—

On the 14th a small Jean Paul Festival in the Stadt Hamburg [a hotel]. In the morning Mendelssohn came to see Clara, at noon Wenzel, Reuter, and Julius Becker at our house for dinner.

On the 15th performance of my symphony [B-flat major] at the Euterpe—somewhat hasty performance—the following Wednesday Verhulst rehearsed his first symphony, which demonstrates everywhere his fine lively striving, as well as his sense of harmony, gracefulness, and form.

Verhulst and Mendelssohn were at our house for the noon meal; the time flew by only too fast. Every word of Mendelssohn's would be worth recording. After the meal he also played several of his *Variations serieuses;* but his hands and our heads seemed heavy. Mendelssohn too has finished a new symphony.[13] I may be partly to blame that they are all writing symphonies now; but it is a nice reward for my work if it stimulates, as it really has stimulated the local talents.

Clara practiced a lot for the Weimar trip, which would have deserved a special page in our diary if new impressions had not already suppressed the memory of it somewhat. We left on the 18th—the first snow of the year was falling—overnight stay in Naumburg—on the 19th the sky cleared up—walking tour with Clara starting in Eckartsberga—arrival in Weimar at 4 o'clock— Chelard came to meet us immediately—his relationship to the other musicians was soon cleared up for us—he is completely excluded—everyone pecks at him, like the jackdaws at the top of a steeple—we don't know him well enough, even as a musician, to pass judgment on that. But we felt sorry for him. Gradually the other acquaintances arrived—Lobe, Montag, Götze, Bürck, etc.—Saturday morning rehearsal in the theater—the orchestra treated us very cordially (Clara was playing for the foundation)—in detail the symphony went superbly; Chelard doesn't seem to be a conductor for a German orchestra—what's required there, to be rude and to have learned something. Genast's acquaintance gave us pleasure—we also spoke with Sabine Heinefetter. From Leipzig there also was Queisser.

Sunday morning visits in a government carriage to Herr von Spiegel, Frau von Pogwisch, Genasts, Eberwein, Götze, Frau von Göthe—we were received everywhere in quite a friendly way—in the evening concert in the theater—Clara played superbly, the Capriccio by Mendelssohn and Fantasy by Thalberg—the symphony went and sounded better than I would have expected—considering that they were Weimarians they were very generous with applause—the court was in attendance—We remained together for quite some time yet after the concert (let's not forget the bailiff Petersilie [parsley], likewise Keferstein, who had come to the concert)—

Monday evening at Lobe's house—much music—trio by Mendelssohn—lieder by me, which Götze sang quite beautifully—noon at Frau von Pogwisch's in pleasantly elegant company—I sat next to Ulrike von Pogwisch, an interesting person, and Frau von Gross (Amalie Winter)—the brothers Röckel were there also—

Tuesday evening at Genasts' very cheerful—pretty music—Strohmeyer (the old bass who had bored us already at Lobe's)—Civil counselor Schmidt, a very cultivated man—Frau von Heygendorff—we also danced, I with my Clara for the first time again as a married couple—home late at night—

Marriage Diary II 119

Wednesday evening "Wasserträger" by Cherubini in the theater—Genast was magnificent—the music always remains fresh—we were completely saturated—

On Thursday the 25th in the evening, concert in the castle—the court very friendly toward Clara—a singer Pauline Lang from Karlsruhe—Liszt had arrived—great joy—we met him at our inn—the champagne flowed like a stream—he was very affectionate and cordial. We stayed there until Friday because of him; there was great excitement. We also got to know Prince Lichnowsky, a noble adventurer. Liszt also played a few things—one can recognize him even behind closed doors—the assessment of him is confirmed. We ate lunch together.

The evening was one of the silliest and most tedious. Liszt had been invited to court, but also wanted to go to Lobe's, who had asked a sizable group of people to get together. For four hours the company now tormented itself most horribly while waiting for Liszt—he finally arrived at 11:30—that same night we returned to Leipzig. Liszt had given us his promise to play at our concert—for which he also kept his word, as he then showed himself to be an affectionate person and friend for us in everything.

On the 27th toward evening we arrived in Leipzig. Now you write, my dear wife, and with it don't forget to say a kind word to me, your friend and life's companion

Tuesday the 14th December   Robert

From 1st to 31st December   [CS]

I don't know where to start, there is so much to catch up with—but I am now determined that with the new year the diary has to

120   *The Marriage Diaries of Robert & Clara Schumann*

be delivered properly, at least every 2 weeks, and surely my dear husband is in agreement!?

Now, I will write what I know, you will pardon me for what I forget—it is a chore not to forget anything about the events of this month. I shall take the days sequentially, perhaps things will go best that way.

On *the 1st Liszt* arrived here from Weimar, and in the afternoon we rehearsed the Hexameron[14] together. This is a terribly brilliant piece, there may be nothing else that surpasses it. We were happy to see Liszt once again within our four walls, and to be together while enjoying his presence (the previous time we were only engaged to be married).

On *Thursday the 2nd* we gave a *dinée* [sic] in his honor—my first major *debut* as a housewife. *The Freges, Härtels, Davids* among others were our guests, and *Liszt* livened the whole thing up with his clever conversation and his amiability; he also played a bit—enough to demonstrate his mastery of the *pianoforte,* which he commands as no one else surely does. *Prince Lichnowsky* came across as a capricious little woman, afflicted with all the virtues and vices of such a person. Besides, he is not without spirit, which his books (about what?) are also supposed to prove.

On *the 3rd Liszt* went to Dresden—I wanted to use the time to practice for my concert, but a *demon* must have conspired to oppose that, because I pricked my finger and wasn't allowed to play.

On *Sunday the 5th Liszt* returned in order to play the *duo* with me on *Monday the 6th.* One can imagine how the public reacted to his attention toward us. It created a sensation, and we had to repeat one part of it. I was not satisfied, even very unhappy that evening and the following days, because Robert was not very content with my playing; also, I was angry that Robert's symphonies[15] were not performed especially well, and there were many little fa-

Marriage Diary II   *121*

talities generally, with carriage, forgotten notes, shaky chair while playing, restlessness in Liszt's presence, *etc. etc.* There was a combination of too many good things—*Liszt,* a monstrously full hall (900 people)—for something disagreeable not to have disturbed my enjoyment of it.

During the intermission *Liszt* was attentive enough to bring me a bouquet of flowers, which was accepted very amiably by the audience. They greeted my first appearance with general applause, which increased during the concert, although, as Robert said, I did not play as well as on many other occasions—I too must admit that!—

We showed *Liszt* our pleasure over his kindness to us with a present, a beautiful silver goblet with both our names on it, which he found when he returned once more from Dresden to give his own concert, which he finally let himself be persuaded to do.

After the concert *Liszt* gave an exquisitely fine supper—beginning with oysters and *trout.* We were both tired, and soon left; the others may have reveled for quite some time. Another morning we found *Liszt* lying in bed, where he remained the whole day, until *Wednesday the 8th,* when he went back to Dresden.

In the evening we were at the Voigts, together with people who suited us as little as we suited them—I'm arrogant enough to believe that Voigt invited us to lend interest to his *soirée.*

On *Thursday the 9th* we were invited to a brilliant *dinée* [*sic*] at *Schletter's.* Few princes in Germany could match him in silver and gold. It was a large party, but not at all formal, and while *Schletter* is a man without much spirit it seems to me he has feelings. I rather like him.

This concert in the evening may well have been the most boring this year. Hermann's interminable symphony[16] aroused general displeasure; I felt very sorry because it is well worked out and surely evidence of a thoughtful musician, but it is dry and unappealing and long, as a piece has rarely seemed to me. It combines everything to drive an audience to the greatest despair. The brothers Stahlknecht with their *Duos*[17] might have been more appropriate in a tavern—somewhat harsh, but true! The *cellist* however seems not untalented.

On *Sunday the 12th David* gave a *dinée* [*sic*] for *Liszt* to which we were also invited. After the meal he tried out the Septet by Hummel, which he plays exceptionally well, although here and there one perhaps wished some places to be played differently. But what artist in the world would be able to please everyone! *Liszt* may play as he wants, it is always spirited, even if tasteless at times, of which one can accuse his compositions especially; I can't call them anything but abominable—a chaos of dissonances, the shrillest, a ceaseless murmuring in the deepest bass combined with the highest treble, boring introductions, *etc*. As a composer I could almost hate him. But as a player in his concert on the 13th he astonished me extremely and especially in the *Don Juan* Fantasy, which he played rapturously—his performance of the champagne aria will remain unforgettable for me, this wantonness, the joy with which he played it was unique! one saw *Don Juan* in front of the champagne corks popping, in his complete dissoluteness, as only Mozart could have imagined him. After the concert we had dinner together in the evening at *Heinrich Brockhaus's*—there wasn't much to be done with *Liszt*, since 2 ladies had taken possession of him. I'm convinced that women generally are at fault when *Liszt* sometimes shows himself to be very arrogant, since they pay court to him everywhere in ways that I detest, which I also find highly indecent. I worship him too, but even veneration must have a limit. I'm gossiping, isn't that true dear Robert, pardon! give me a slap.—

On *Thursday the 16th Liszt* played for the last time, the *E-flat* concerto by *Beethoven* masterfully, but then the *Robert*-Fantasy in

Marriage Diary II

terrible taste, and afterward also the *Galopp* [*sic*]. He seemed tired out, which with his life-style is not surprising—he didn't arrive from Halle, where he had caroused all night, until early in the morning, and still held 3 rehearsals before noon.

NB. At *Liszt's* concert we played the Hexameron once more, creating the same sensation as the first time.

On *Friday* we gave a little soiree—our guests were selected. Only these days did I get to know Madame Ungher-Sabatier, and today I also heard her; although with a hoarse voice, still she really affected me most deeply, as singing rarely does—I don't know whether it was my doing, I had to cry in a way that seldom happens to me with music. Her personality is most lovable, modest, and unpretentious, which hasn't happened to me with a singer except for *Pauline Garcia*. Her husband [François Sabatier] seemed very quiet to me. *Madame Schubert* from Dresden and Herr *Schober* from Vienna were here with them; *Schober* is supposed to be a very imaginative man! earlier he made a name for himself as the poet of many lieder composed by *F. Schubert*. *Liszt,* as always, arrived very late! He seems to love keeping people waiting for him, which I don't like. In general he strikes me as a spoiled child, kindhearted, imperious, amiable, arrogant, noble, and generous, often harsh toward others—a peculiar mixture of characteristics. But we have gotten to be very fond of him, and also he has always shown himself most friendly toward us. We did feel sorry when he left—who knows when we will see him again!—I wouldn't be surprised were he to go soon to America. He left here on

the 18th for Halle. We were supposed to accompany him that far, but were yearning too much for peace and quiet. Liszt's whole way of being and doing things is not suited to letting anyone have a moment's rest. After his departure the Christmas commotion started up again, the running and buying, and thus we haven't had any peace as yet. That is how the days up to the 24th passed by. I tried to compose something for Robert, and look here, it worked! I was really delighted to complete a first and second sonata movement,[18] which then also did not fail to serve its purpose, namely to prepare a little surprise for my husband. But he too gave me and my little Marie a charming lullaby[19] that he had composed only on Christmas afternoon.

It was a beautiful Christmas, even more beautiful than the last one. What at that time we had hoped for, now had materialized— our little Marie could share our joy, even if it was only on account of all the candles. It gave me endless pleasure also to light a small [Christmas] tree for her, and in addition to bestow a few small things like little dolls, little cats, *etc.* We are really very happy, isn't that true my dear Robert? I think you will say yes, and give me a kiss.

Wenzel, Reuter, J. Becker, and *Lorenz* spent the evening with us; we were quite cheerful.

Moreover, Robert had given me presents in great abundance, and what pleased me especially were the works of *Byron,* the last volume of which is dedicated to him by the translator [Adolf Bött-ger], and the start of an inheritance for Marie consisting of an old ring of his mother's and several coins. Such a present I find very nice for children, it instills in them a certain reverence for their forebears, and always remains for them a valuable way of remembering them, as well as their parents.

Thank you once more, my good one, for all your love!—

On the second holiday we went to the Gewandhaus ball with the *Fleischers*—it was the first and perhaps also the last that we attended. We were happy after we had endured this pleasure.

On *the 28th David* arrived and urgently begged me to play in the New Year's concert—I accepted, even though the piano had been resting for 3 weeks, and in addition I even decided to prepare the *G Minor* Concerto by *Mendelssohn* for it. You, dear husband,

Marriage Diary II 125

may describe how this turned out—it no longer belongs to this month, and I have enough for now!

New Year's Eve we celebrated with champagne, but I only half-way since of course it was the night before the concert.

The midnight kiss was tender, no less than the New Year's kiss, and I hope that also in this year we will remain devoted in most sincere love.

Notes from the 1st of January 1842 [RS]
to the 18th of February

January 1. At the Gewandhaus concert Clara received with great enthusiasm.[20]

Work on the text of the Peri—present from the king [Friedrich August II of Saxony]—[21]

January 11. Quartet, in which Clara played—Count Reuss returned from England—my nice complimenting of Dr. Kühne.

January 12. Bennett's arrival.

January 13. New symphony by Spohr, most interesting.[22]

— 14. Dinner at Voigt's with Bennett. Sleigh ride to Connewitz.

— 15. Clara has finished her sonata[23]—Marie to our joy always well and cheerful.

— 16. Bennett & Böttger for dinner.

— 17. Meerti's (farewell) concert. Started an arrangement for pianoforte of the symphony [B-flat major][24]—terrible days and torment over it—

— 18. Soirée at R. Härtel's—

— 24. Concert by Verhulst. Pianist Krause!—

— 27. Shaw in concert for the first time.

28. Evening meal at Dr. Härtel's—

29. With Clara in the *Hôtel* de Bavière at Bennett's table for dinner—

30. At the Voigts for dinner—some music—Bennett—

31. Tuyn's farewell concert—Krause! I almost always unwell—read "Blasedow" by Gutzkow—read much in Mozart's symphonies—came to know many new ones—

February

3. At F. Brockhaus's for dinner—pianist Krüger from Stuttgart—

7. Hermann, Willkomm & Marggraf at dinner—Since then almost always in poor health, until today, the day of our departure, the 18th.

Parish Alvars, Remmers.

On the 14th, farewell from Bennett, who again [went] to Berlin.

Trip to Bremen and Hamburg
until our separation in Hamburg the 10th of March

Leipzig, the 14 of March

That I may perhaps drive my melancholia away somewhat by remembering the last weeks I have spent with Clara. It was really one of the most stupid things for me to let you leave me. I feel it ever more. May God guide you happily back to me. In the meantime I will watch over our little one.

The separation has again made our singularly difficult situation really palpable to me. Shall I then neglect my talent in order to serve as your companion on trips? And you, should you therefore leave your talent unused, because I simply am chained to my

Marriage Diary II

journal and the piano? Now, when you are young and fresh with energy? We have hit on a way out. You took a female companion for yourself, I returned to the child and to my work. But what will *the world* say? Thus I torture myself with thoughts. Yes, it is absolutely necessary that we find the means to use and develop both of our talents side by side.

I have America in mind. A horrible decision. But I firmly believe it would have its rewards. We must decide before the end of April. The thought of America appeared during the trip—on a beautiful day—out of a healthy mood. I felt so fresh and enterprising that morning—the proximity of Bremen, which is like a close relative to America, probably did it as well. We pondered it. There is so little which ties us down here. Only the thought of Marie, whom we would have to leave behind, was terrible. But of course it would be best for her too, for the security of her future. I suppose we could also travel in Germany. But what comes of that? Whatever Clara earns I would lose in income and time. So we prefer to embark for two years on a major plan of our life which, if it turns out successfully, would give security for the rest of our lives. And after that I could devote myself completely to my art, which is my sole, most yearned-for wish. May You, who until now has united and led us, also guide our further steps.—

On the 18th of February in the afternoon we left on our trip—I still very unwell; but the air refreshed me. Clara was well; but the pain of having to separate herself from Marie was sometimes visible in her eyes.

At 6 o'clock we arrived in Magdeburg. I saw the cathedral only in the roughest outline, because the fog was so heavy. The trip to Braunschweig generally not very comfortable—the roads unbelievably bad.

On Saturday the 19th arrival in Braunschweig. The mix-up over inns was funny enough; namely, we expected to reside in the inn next door to us. Young Griepenkerl soon arrived. An extremely attractive person, whose eyes and lips radiate wit and spirit. He invited us to his father's, where we met concertmaster Müller and Frau von Bülow. The old man is an enthusiastic Bachian; we communicated quite well. He also showed me compositions by Friedemann Bach: polonaises that seemed very interesting to me. Clara played a few things—to her agony—since the piano was totally disabled. From that we learned the good lesson not to perform on poor instruments. Preferably myself, since I don't do it on any.

On *Sunday the 20th* the sky cleared up gradually to be most beautiful. It was here that the thoughts of America awoke for the first time, which then occupied us constantly during the following days. Shortly after the awakening of the idea, a sheet of paper fell into my hands at the inn, with a poem that made me really sad. It spoke of a youth who also was seeking a foreign continent, and there, betrayed in his hopes, plunged into the sea with his lyre. That it was a youth compensated somewhat for the bad omen. Clara read the poem as well and seemed to reflect on it.

We traveled past Hildesheim, quickly through Hanover, where we had no desire to stay. Clara already knows all of these towns from earlier. A night's rest at Neustadt in a very good inn. We were in a really good mood; we drank a small bottle of champagne.

On *Monday the 21st,* the trip on to Bremen in clear weather of no particular interest—the region is completely dreary—all sorts of swamps and unkempt woods—evening arrival in Bremen— Töpken and Eggers arrived immediately. Cordial reception.

Tuesday the 22nd. In the morning visits to various people: Madame Sengstake (sister of Grund), the Schmidts, the old Riem, the young Klugkist. Riem is the most interesting musical acquaintance in Bremen; he seems to have carried ideals within himself that he never attains—and perhaps [he is] not completely satisfied with the world, which granted him no recognition. He had studied my symphony thoroughly and well.—the Schmidts we had already known: the woman is wilted, but still quite tolerable.—Klugkist I had gotten to know already in Heidelberg: a worthwhile person, perhaps somewhat conceited.—We ate our midday meal at the Eggers'—a couple that seems to devote itself completely to artists. Töpken, a dear old acquaintance, was visibly happy about our presence.—Museum, a casino with a large reading room.—In the evening we spent a few cheerful hours in the *Rathskeller.* One cannot feel much more at ease than within those booths, with Rhine wine and close to affectionate people. I could have stayed down there much longer. But the 23rd required clear heads.

On *Wednesday the 23rd,* early rehearsal in the beautiful concert hall. An orchestra that plays well together and is strong. The piano from Härtels, which they had sent to Bremen for Clara's sake, unfortunately did not turn out well, also not in the evening. Fräulein Caroline Quenstädt from Braunschweig, who sings the way she looks, i.e., fresh and healthy, sang "Widmung" from the *Myrthen.* In the evening the symphony went better than I would have thought after *one* rehearsal. The Bremeners are stingy with applause; the gathering generally has more the character of a closed society.[25] Clara exerted herself to play beautifully on the toneless piano.[26] After the concert a little supper at the clubhouse. Everything quite friendly and decent. Old Riem gave many toasts.

On *Thursday the 24th* at 1 [o'clock] to Oldenburg in magnificent weather.—we stayed at Pott's, who had sent his servant to meet us. His wife, a Viennese, makes you think; she is polite, musical, soft, but lively while speaking, an odd creature. He is said to be a rogue and complete man of the court. He had invited an aristocratic gathering to his home for the evening. Clara played a lot and superbly. Herr von Beaulieu, fine and courteous in his behavior, showed himself the next day without manners toward me. A disagreeable story—this one. A warning for similar cases.—A Herr von Wedderkopp, cultivated, intelligent man.

On *Friday the 25th* Pott played a few things for me, also with his wife the A Minor Sonata by Beethoven—he reminds one a lot of Lipinsky, whom he barely knows, however. In the evening, concert in the theater, surely one of the shortest the world has ever heard.[27] The audience left as if in a dream.

After the concert the letter of the above-mentioned Beaulieu. Quarrel and excitement. I must testify on behalf of my Clara that her behavior was exemplary through it all.

On *Saturday the 26th,* adjustment of differences at my expense—it happened because of my kindhearted weakness, because I simply cannot tolerate strife and dissension—well, Clara had driven to court and came back pleased by her reception. But the thought of my unworthy position in such cases did not let me experience any pleasure. We returned to Bremen yet [that evening].

On *Sunday the 27th* at dinner Molique, who wants to go to Holland and England. In the evening, company at Eggers. Clara played the Trio by Mendelssohn with Eggers and Klugkist, and a few other things as well. Our great fatigue.

Monday the 28th—Rakemann's brother put in an appearance; he looks *à la Liszt.* In Madame Schmidt I found a darling; we rehearsed the lieder with her that she is supposed to sing in the evening. Billiards with Molique. Evening soirée and refined audience. My poor Klärchen could not get away from the piano. After the Fugue in E Major by Mendelssohn I was so distracted that I joined the applause vigorously, so beautifully had Clara been playing. Dr. Engelken, psychiatrist, already known [to me] from

Marriage Diary II 131

Heidelberg. Elise Müller, a peculiar person it seems. Exchanged a few words with her. After the soirée a small supper at our place. Riem, the Eggers, the Schmidts, Töpken. Very cheerful. We waited for little Marie's half-year birthday on the 1st of March.

On *Tuesday the 1st of March,* natural history collection in the museum—coffee at the Eggers'—farewell from him and Töpken—departure at 6 o'clock for Harburg in a stormy night—

On *Wednesday the 2nd of March,* departure early at 7 o'clock with the steamboat for Hamburg, which one can already see in the distance—bad weather. Clara walked around a lot on the deck. Arrival in the port at 9 o'clock—a new sight for me. Avé-Lallemant expected us. We stayed in the St. Petersburg [Hotel]. Cranz and Schuberth, two antipodes. In the evening for a while at the quartet of Hafner, Sack, etc. Then to the theater: "The Two Foxes" by Mehul—delicious opera. Krebs conducted well, but with many gestures and grimaces. As we stepped into the theater the flutist (Canthal) was just practicing a solo from my symphony, which I found amusing.

On *Thursday the 3rd of March* in the morning I visited Grund and went through my symphony with him; Grund is a truly musical soul. That the giving of so many lessons has not killed him must be admired. He also composes well and later showed me an opera.

From Grund's to the rehearsal. The musicians made a great effort and played the symphony energetically. I found all of Grund's remarks sensible. Concertmaster Lindenau. In the evening concert of the Liedertafel by H. Schäffer in the Apollo hall. Clara in the meantime was at Cranz's, where I went later as well. There is something very comic about Cranz's contradictory spirit. The daughter seems peculiar.

On *Friday the 4th of March* in the morning I visited Ole Bull, who nearly crawls with politeness but always has something that is attractive. Riefstahl from Frankfurt I'd already known earlier; we drove to the harbor with him and Lallemant. Clara was very much afraid of it. We boarded a ship that had just arrived from *Rio*. The ship's crew was very helpful about it. They accepted no tips. For dinner at Lallemant's, who has an agreeable, well-educated wife, as he is himself. Moreover, in Hamburg everyone attacks and insults each other; can anything proper come of that.

Very exhausted we still went to Dr. Abendroth for an evening party, where Hafner, etc., played quartet.

The main rehearsal at 1:30 P.M. went very successfully. Christern, who wanted to listen, was expelled out the door by Grund, as demanded by the orchestra. The musicians hissed him. So much for harmony.

On *Saturday the 5th of March* to our surprise Ulex showed up in the morning. He told us the story of his marriage; to some extent it resembled our own, only that we carried it out honestly. Ulex had gotten married in England; the bride followed later by herself. We got to know her later and Clara liked her. E. Marxsen also visited us; his Jewish physiognomy disgusted me.

Philharmonic concert in the evening. It started with the symphony, which was presented very well. Clara played with great care at first (the Concertstück [by Weber]), but the other pieces[28] without enthusiasm, because the instrument didn't want to produce anything. The audience was courteous and very attentive. The Parish family literally encircled Clara. After the concert to Schuberth for oysters. We heard nasty stories about Ole Bull.

On *Sunday the 6th of March* in the morning with Lallemant to an oyster bar—before that a crowd of visitors at our place: Dr. Busch, Colonel Stockfleth, Fräulein Stahl from Stockholm, the Schuberths, the Cranzes, Riefstahl, Fräulein Lilli Bernhard, etc. etc.

At 3 o'clock we drove to Parish's estate two hours from Ham-

Marriage Diary II 133

burg—We had the carriage stop at Klopstock's grave (in Ottensen).

The weather was marvelous. Beautiful view from the Parishes'. The daughter Harriett a dear modest girl; we played from the Passion by Bach, she revels in it. Then a most elegant dinner. Old Parish, a philosophizing person and businessman, who nearly talked my head off. At 11 o'clock we drove back into town.—

After long hesitation the trip to Copenhagen was decided on.

On *Monday the 7th* we took a walk to Altona with Otten [and the] Lallemants, before that to the Michaelis Church with its wonderful organ. The organist behaved well, but didn't know very much and played unworthy compositions. Then to Hutmann's with a view over the Elbe and oysters. For the midday meal we had invited Grund, with whom we spent a couple of cheerful hours. Symphony by F. von Roda in Braunschweig, which interested me.[29] I mixed too many drinks in a muddle on this day. The stolen cigars and suspicion of Ulex.

Tuesday the 8th feeling badly. Looked at the new Stock Exchange, the most beautiful building in Hamburg.[30] In the evening the Lallemants and Lilli Bernhard. Much music making. Clara was really full of music and played and sang in one breath.

On *Wednesday the 9th,* concert by Sack, in which Clara played, then for oysters at Grund's. The night, our last one before the separation, was horrible for us. Below us in a cellar bar (we were living *parterre*) there was the most terrible noise and yelling until 4 A.M.

Thursday the 10th, the sad day. Marie Garlichs [Clara's travel companion to Denmark] arrived. At 10 o'clock we said farewell.—

The 30th of March

Quiet Easter—without Clara—what will those of the future only be like!

The little one is lovely and completely healthy. In three weeks at the latest we await the return of the housewife. She writes diligently from Copenhagen.

End of May 1842 [CS]

It's a major task to recall 2 whole months from one's memory, on top of that, two that were as eventful as those just past—therefore be tolerant my Robert with a defective report, the only way I can deliver it just now.

"From the day of our separation to that of meeting again!"

Thursday the 10th of March was the most terrible day in our marriage so far—we separated, and to me it seemed as if I would never see him again. The trip to *Kiel* proceeded with sobbing, lamenting.—I cannot describe how unhappy I felt, in addition my companion, Marie Garlichs, although a dear girl, was incapable of understanding my pain. We arrived in *Kiel* in the evening, and then I immediately went to do some concert errands, which I should have spared myself, because by noon

the 11th I was so sick that a concert was no longer to be considered. I still tried to pull myself together one hour before the concert, but all strength had left me, and the pain was now even more intense. The assembled audience was sent away, and I—paid the expenses, 47 marks, out of my own purse—fine start!—

Saturday the 12th was a day of new suffering. I wanted to go to Copenhagen by steamboat, but the heavens were against it, the storm increased to an unusual intensity, and I—remained in Kiel. I was supposed to wait a week for the next steamboat; should I spent them being idle? I traveled

Sunday the 13th to Lübeck on country roads, with the most

intense rain and howling of the wind, was thrown from one pot-hole into another; my body was still in a cramp and only got worse with these blows, in addition the anxiety, the yearning for my Rob-ert,—wasn't that enough to lose courage? but I had to endure a full week of tribulation before I arrived at the goal.

I came to Lübeck, but had to leave without accomplishing any-thing. The duke of Schwerin had died, and thus his opera com-pany had gone to Lübeck. A theater production was quite an event for Lübeck—they had sold out every evening—what ought I to do there? rather than giving a concert in an empty house, I pre-ferred to leave.

On *Monday the 14th* I paid several visits, found everyone sick except for the Avés, who were very friendly to me; in the evening I went to the theater, heard *Riefstahl* play in a fairly mediocre way, and on

Tuesday the 15th I traveled to Hamburg; I thought I could per-haps play in the theater there some time. It was a dreary day, that one, my oppressed heart dissolved in tears that flowed unceasingly. In the afternoon we arrived in Hamburg.—Playing was out of the question, just before Easter, no person wanted to have anything to do with music.

Cranz was the first one I visited; he was shocked to see me, believing I was in Copenhagen. I didn't want to let him notice anything about my distress, but who can be held responsible for his emotions—[I] really cried my eyes out there. My friends were astonished that despite all the mishaps I still wanted to go to Co-penhagen, and several times my courage did sink; I thought heaven had sent me all this unpleasantness in order to divert me from my plan, but the thought of Robert, the wish also for once to contribute a little something to him with my talent, then the happy reunion after a successfully completed tour—that encour-aged me again, although one probably couldn't see it, because the grief didn't leave me for a minute, to which was added that I received no news from Robert, who of course thought I was already in Copenhagen; for nearly two weeks I knew nothing about the child—oh, it was enough to drive one to despair!—

In the evening I went to the theater in order to distract myself, but mainly to provide enjoyment for *Marie* [Garlichs], who up to now had experienced only unpleasantness because of me. *Madame Cranz* accompanied us.

Wednesday the 16th we spent quietly—I, submerged in grief. For the first two weeks of our separation I was often so empty of thoughts that it made me shudder. I was always saying something different from what I had intended, and whenever someone asked me about you, my dear Robert, then that was the end—my voice choked—thank God that this condition did not last long!—[31]

Thursday the 17th we spent at the Avés, ate there and I played in the evening, *Beethoven* sonatas almost exclusively. *Otten* and *Avé* were happy!—[32]

Friday evening I left for Kiel and stayed there, on

Saturday the 19th, with the music director *Graedener,* kind people. [Frau] *Graedener* is a gentle woman—I think I could get to like her. But much less so Madame *Schlossbauer,* a conceited, uneducated, and most rude woman. She took it upon herself to let me know right away what people—only the nasty socialites, of course!—have been saying about me, that I did not give the concert.

In the evening I finally boarded the magnificent ship "Christian the Eighth" that I had dreaded for so long. The *Graedeners* had brought me on board—it's fortunate that Robert had not postponed our separation up to this point. I was feeling awful as we pushed off from shore—how I was sobbing for Robert, for the little one, and I almost believed that I would never again step on solid ground—a fear that probably seizes everyone who has never

Marriage Diary II   137

traveled by sea. The voyage was fairly calm, we did not become seasick, although I was not far from it; one is overcome by a disagreeable unease caused by the incessant rocking, and the nausea does not disappear until one arrives on land, but we still felt the rocking for one whole day.

On *Sunday* noon we arrived in Copenhagen; *Olsen* and yet others came on board the ship from a small boat to receive me, and from that moment on I was in safe hands—*Olsen* took care of me in a way that no man could have surpassed. He had reserved rooms for us in the *Hôtel Royal,* and there we found agreeable hosts, Germans, who for the entire 4 weeks of my stay anticipated all of my needs—of course I had to pay plenty.

On the same evening Madame *Tutein* still came to visit me, an eccentric but talented woman. She received me in a very friendly way.[33]

On *Monday the 21st,* after a most invigorating night's rest, there was much turmoil. I paid many visits, received many, and was living so to speak a life of pleasure and revelry—but I lacked what I wanted most, and amid all the applause, enjoyment, I really could not be cheerful until the last 3–4 days, when my departure was settled.

I would have to write many pages yet were I to describe each day in detail, therefore just a few notes about the friends who have become dear to me, and then a brief note about my doings and activities on each day.

Madame Tutein and Madame *Hartmann* were my dearest female friends. Both seemed to like me quite well—each in a different way. The first loved me because it flattered her vanity to show herself as my protectress; this vanity outweighed all feelings of envy, she subordinated her talent completely to mine, she exalted me publicly in front of everyone at her own expense (since in Copenhagen she is considered a great pianist), why? she took pride in being counted as a friend of mine! incidentally I believe that she really does have a tiny bit of true affection for me.

Her talent is a significant one, her education (namely, musical) superficial. She has an exceptionally good memory, plays mostly by ear, but *what* does she play? only what happens to catch the eyes and ears—vanity again!—otherwise she is amiable, extensively educated, fiery, somewhat affected, but easy to take, thus I also enjoyed going to see her. Her children also played a role: the eldest son reveled in me, no less than the eldest daughter, and both competed in their attentiveness to me—one rose from my hand rewarded them generously.

Madame Hartmann loved me (I am arrogant enough to believe) for my own sake. She supplied me with everything good that could possibly be imagined, she sent me wine and fruits, she spoke with me about Robert and the child, she literally nursed me, I almost want to say that sometimes she gave me pain with all her love. But none of this did she do in front of other people, rather in her home when I was alone with her; in public no one saw her at my side, she always withdrew modestly. Of course something also tied me especially to both of these people; they were tenderly affectionate with each other, and thus they were the only ones who completely understood my feelings. He too is a dear, fine man, highly talented, and this really is the sort of couple one does not find easily.

Stage, the *director* at the theater, and *Olsen* were the two concert arrangers who proved to be devoted friends to me. The wife of the first one is a dear but spoiled creature; she is a singer at the theater, but 3rd rate, which she is probably aware of—this torments both of them; he coddles her like a child.

Among the most interesting acquaintances belong Professor *Hejberg* and his wife, the poet *Andersen,* and Professor *Weyse.* The first of these reveals nothing outwardly of what he may harbor within himself—he is known as the leading Danish writer. Madame *Hejberg* not only wants to be considered the leading Danish actress, but surely also to make a success in Germany, if she could speak the language adequately. She is one of the most delightful theatrical phenomena I have seen, and as such unforgettable for me; but with that she unites a delightful quality, is very pretty, interesting, and also her personality *itself* would be suited to make me like her. I saw both of them less frequently than I would have wanted—I just was too much in demand.

Andersen has a poetic, childlike soul, is still rather young, but very ugly, along with being vain and egoistic—nevertheless I liked him well, and it was interesting and worthwhile for me to get to know him. In any case, his virtues far outweigh his weaknesses.

Professor *Weyse's* acquaintance was also interesting for me, although after getting to know him better I lost much of the admiration I had held for him. He is a most narrow-minded, egoistic musician, considers himself to be misunderstood, and despises (this may be expressed somewhat harshly) all of his contemporaries, except for *Haydn*, whom he does grant something of value. *Bach* is artful, but not beautiful; *Beethoven* has never written anything that is completely beautiful, *Mozart* will just do, *Mendelssohn* is a copy of *Bach*—those approximately are his views, by which he condemns himself.

In addition to the above-named families I often visited Frau von *Zahrtmann née Donner* from Altona, a dear and cultivated lady; also Madame *Paulli,* wife of the minister in residence; Madame *Loose,* a good old but coquettish woman—a young coquette is horrible enough, an old one completely so.

Except for the Swedish consul *Ewerlöf* and his family I met no one I did not like. They were unkind in a way that has seldom happened to me.

So these were just about my main acquaintances, the others I will merely jot down.

On *Tuesday the 22nd,* visits from *Hejberg, Andersen* (both ene-mies at heart—they met many times at my place, and once even [exchanged] their cards, which made me laugh), *Stage, Baroness* (better called *Blabbermouthess*) *Löwensciold* with her unmarried daughter, *Gade, Courländer, Rudolph Willmers,* among others. The last elegantly made up in the French manner, a disgusting appear-ance in my opinion. *Courländer* is supposed to be talented—I did not hear him.

In the evening at the *Hejbergs* with the attorney *Bunsen*—a very smart man.[34]

On *Wednesday the 23rd,* dinner at Madame *Tutein's,* before that visits to Frau von Zahrtmann, ladies-in-waiting *Elise von Pechlin* [and] Frau von *Waltersdorff,* Court Marshal von *Blücher-Altona.*

A small pleasant gathering at Madame *Tutein's*—I played—Madame *Tutein* was on fire over the *A Minor* Waltz by *Chopin,* which I had to play for her four times consecutively.

Visit from Herr von *Levetzau,* one of my influential protectors, a most friendly, captivating man.[35]

On *Thursday the 24th,* dinner at Madame *Loose's*—neighbor at the table *Weyse;* moreover, a large party.

On *Good Friday the 25th* we looked at the Frauenkirche, a beautiful building in the newer style. Thorwaldsen's 12 apostles in marble, famous masterworks. I understand too little about such art to pass judgment, but in that same church I was delighted by a kneeling angel, holding a baptismal font, which was charm-ingly constructed.

In the evening in the same church I heard sacred music by old Italians. I've never heard such a miserable performance.[36]

On *Saturday the 26th,* evening at Madame *Tutein's.* Much mu-sic! Both of us played. I had a significant quarrel with Madame *Tutein.* She raved about an Italian opera troupe currently per-

Marriage Diary II   *141*

forming in Copenhagen that belongs to the worst I've ever known; furthermore, she is enthusiastic about *Bellini, Donizetti*—one may be able to accept that coming from a lay person, but not from a musician who wants to be thought of as one. If it is performed magnificently I would, in the worst case, listen to such an opera, but the way they sang it, one simply cannot tolerate that—and this woman raves about it—I was completely beside myself! Later I found it better to remain silent on this point—that way I suffered the least.[37]

On *Sunday the 27th* in the evening, pleasant company at Minister *Paulli's*. Madame *Tutein* played mazurkas by *Courländer*, after she had first played several by *Chopin* (again a sign of poor taste),—I also played a few little things.[38]

Monday the 28th is marked in my diary as a very gloomy day. Robert wrote sadly, full of despair—I cried a lot.

In the afternoon we visited the Rosenburg Garden and the court gardener *Petersen*, who during my stay in Copenhagen always supplied me with the freshest, most beautiful flowers, which gave me much joy. In the evening Italian opera[39]—not worth criticizing! the audience in ecstasy.

On *Tuesday the 29th*, visit from the *Hejbergs*. For dinner at the *Hartmanns* with the attorney *Bunsen*.

In the evening ballet by the ballet master *Bournonville*, "Napoli"[40]—very pretty; with few contrivances he accomplishes the unbelievable; the stage is much too small for ballet.[41]

On *Wednesday the 30th* for dinner at Captain *Zahrtmann's*— small party—the hosts amiable and refined.[42]

On *Thursday the 31st* in Madam *Tutein's* company we looked at the Nordic Museum. I found some things of interest, many things boring.

In the evening we spent a cheerful evening at the *Stages'*. *Andersen*, the *Lüders, Gade, Faaborg*, [and] the *Bournonville* family made up the biggest part of the company. *Bournonville*, already mentioned above as ballet master, is an outstanding man; not only is he a master in his art, but he is also a good musician, plays the piano nicely, sings prettily (he sang many Swedish and Danish folk songs), and is a fine, amiable gentleman, scientifically educated, *etc.* His wife is as soft-hearted a woman as I have rarely seen—charmingly graceful.

They had only a square piano, but I played a lot because I saw that it gave the whole group pleasure for me to do so.

April 1842

On *the 1st* I was really properly misled! I was invited to Consul *Ewerlöf's*, and had been told that this family would be a pleasant acquaintance for me. The reception taught me differently! They were most unpleasant—after one hour I withdrew—for the first and the last time.[43]

Saturday the 2nd I spent at Madam *Tutein's*.[44]

On *Sunday the 3rd* I finally gave my first concert in the Royal Theater. Full house—big celebration! several requests for encores, *da capos*, good return (surplus of 228 after deducting the cost of 159 thaler *courants*), instrument fairly good—lent by *Waagepetersen*, a pleasant young man. His father had recently died and earlier had led the main musical house of Copenhagen. During the rehearsal I had various nasty accidents with instruments before I decided on the one just mentioned.

The court also attended the concert, except for the king and queen. Etiquette demands that the court does not attend a concert before the artist has played at court. So many unfortunate incidents had accumulated that it was not possible to play at court until now.

Marriage Diary II 143

On *Monday the 4th,* evening at the *Hartmanns.*[45]

On *Tuesday the 5th,* court concert with orchestra. The king and the queen are kind, the latter can be considered beautiful, although they have already been married for 26 years. Both of them gave me a most honorable reception.

On *Wednesday the 6th* I played at the society's concert. I received an honorarium of 70 *gold thalers.* That evening became very difficult for me, because the Härtel instrument that I had received only the day before from Hamburg seemed terribly heavy to me after I had again gotten used to German instruments. No one in the audience noticed it.

The Song of Praise by *Mendelssohn* went well, considering the circumstances. Four rehearsals had been held, each by a different person, the performance by yet another—what can come of that?—the musicians here are pure mechanics—maybe a capable kapellmeister could put an end to this monstrosity.

Visits from Fräulein *Abrahams* with bridegroom, councillor of commerce—*Andersen* often visits me—he is very infatuated!

Thursday the 7th was a day for writing, I also received a letter from my dear husband. That was always a blessing for me, such a letter! customarily I have received one of them on the day of the concert as well—then I obviously could only play well.

In the evening we drove to the sea. The setting sun presented a magnificent spectacle, and its rays illuminated the horizon with its many ships. How I longed to have my Robert here for such moments. Such natural beauties are unknown to us at home— for me nothing is more sublime than the sea. It gave me the greatest pleasure to discover the sea colored differently each day, green, light blue, black as iron were the most frequent colors in which it played.

After this drive in the *Hartmanns'* small carriage we spent the whole evening with them—new acquaintance, *Hornemann,* a musician I believe. With great charm the children of Hartmann presented me with a small silver goblet for little Marie, which gave me great pleasure.

On *Friday the 8th*, a chilly carriage drive to *Friedrichsberg* with *Olsen*. I was very disagreeable, the good *Olsen* very patient!—Was it so unnatural for me to be like that? Far from my own, always having to be among people, not a moment's rest even when I get home, that sometimes got to be too much for me, and thus my dearest friends, in front of whom I did not feel embarrassed, had to suffer on account of it. Olsen occasionally sobbed, "You better not come back to see us without your Robert!"

Midday meal at the home of the old gentleman *Tutein,* who, despite his age of 84 years, still presides over a household and plays the agreeable host.

In the evening to a ball at the home of Princess *Juliane* [von Hessen] *Philippsthal,* who had invited me personally to attend. I had planned *not* to dance, but what human being is without vanity; when two princes came over I did dance two dances—they were Prince von *Glücksburg* and Prince von *Hessen,* two nice little fellows—both of them are very young yet.

The king and the queen spoke with me and expressed the pleasure they would anticipate from my second concert.[46]

On *Saturday the 9th,* walking excursion to the "Long Line" [a path around the walls of the seventeenth-century castle in Frederikshavn]. The two princes mentioned above met us and went with us a major part of the way, which led to much gossip in the very provincial Copenhagen.

In the evening we went to Frau *Zahrtmann,* who seemed increasingly kind to me.[47]

On *Sunday the 10th,* second concert in the Royal Theater; full house again, much applause, calls for an encore, *da capo, etc. etc.*

Surplus after deduction of expenses of 114 thalers, 10 groschen = 316 [thalers], 21 [groschen].

Marriage Diary II 145

From the king I received 120 for his loge at both concerts, and 150 thalers as honorarium for the court concert.

Also today Robert sent me a letter full of love again.

On *Monday the 11th,* drive to the Tiergarten with Madam *Loose,* where I saw the most beautiful forest of beech trees—at home one does not know these trees at all in the splendor with which they can be found in Denmark. The entire outing was charming, the route always went along the sea, the day was magnificent, in the Tiergarten stags and deer leapt about even though it was early in the season. How often I wished to have you nearby, my Robert!—After the outing we ate at Madame *Loose's,* also spent the evening there.

On *Tuesday the 12th Anderson* led us to the *Christiansburg* Castle in order to look at some of *Thorwaldsen's* work.

In Copenhagen *Thorwaldsen* is revered as a king, and he is one! in addition to the many works of art that he has given the city, he has also contributed much money for buildings; the *Thorwaldsen Museum* that is just being constructed will serve the sole purpose of housing his own works. He himself has given about 100,000 thalers for it. I really regret his absence very much, because it would have been of the greatest interest to me to get to know him, who in person is also supposed to be a most outstanding man.

On the same morning we went yet to see a frigate that was supposed to go to the Mediterranean in May.[48] It held 40 cannons, 60,000 [pounds] of cannonballs, thus was really rather large. Herr *Shmidt,* a young amiable naval officer, accompanied us. At noon at the *Hartmanns',* in the evening home at last.

Throughout my entire stay in Copenhagen I always had to tolerate grief and anxiety concerning my fingers, which were constantly inflamed from much playing. Fortunately it did not hinder me at any concert, although I endured especially the last concert with much pain.[49]

On *Wednesday the 13th* to the gallery—the worst I've ever seen.

It is more like an institute that accepts works by young beginners in order to encourage them, while in other places an art gallery shows only works that are excellent.

On *Thursday the 14th,* my third and last concert. Surplus after deduction of expenses of 75 thalers = 196 thalers, 4 groschen. I played many things in this concert[50] and had an exquisite and fine audience, if not a large one, for which mainly the currently unfavorable time, because people are moving into new quarters, may primarily have been responsible. The pianoforte sounded magnificent, and I believe I played especially well that evening.

Nobody from court enters the hall;[51] the two princes, however, were there.

On *Friday the 15th,* Rosenburg Castle, the residence of the former regents of Denmark. Highly interesting on the outside as well as the inside. Old *Weyse* accompanied us with *Olsen.* In the evening we once more saw the charming ballet *"Napoli"* already mentioned, and went afterward to the festivities of Herr *Carstensen* at the racetrack, which holds 4,000 people. This gentleman is editor of the paper *"Figaro,"* one of the most widely read, and each year gives a number of festivals for his subscribers, in the summer in the Rosenburg Garden, in the winter in the racetrack hall, where from 9–12 o'clock (at night) there is music making, all kinds of refreshments are to be had, and the hall is illuminated to utmost brilliance. This repeats itself for 3 consecutive nights; the first night his subscribers receive free tickets; anyone who pays, however, can be admitted. I have never seen such a brilliant festival, only that a few thousand Viennese and Parisians were missing from the hall.

On *Saturday the 16th* I played once more in the queen's chambers, where a very small party had gathered. She was most pleasant, and gracious enough to cut a few flowers for me herself from her little winter garden and to present them with a few very kind

Marriage Diary II   147

words.[52] Before going there I saw *Hejberg* as *Preciosa*[53]—I can't recall anything so enchanting in a long time! this music and these scenes of charm and loveliness—no one could be left cold by that.

On *Sunday the 17th* I made my last public appearance. I played yet another piece at a charity concert in the Royal Theater, and was greeted by the audience with the greatest enthusiasm—called back after the end of the piece. I was in a very tender mood! reluctantly I took leave of the city where so much love had been shown me, and where I received so much honor at all times, but the thought of my loved ones at home immediately drove away all sadness, which then turned into the most joyful hope.

Monday the 18th was finally the day of my departure, a day full of restlessness. In the morning I still had a private audience with the queen, who gave me a diamond brooch and in a very friendly way invited me to come back soon.[54]

We departed at 6 o'clock in the evening—again on the *Christian the 8th,* which I was able to trust at last. The *Tuteins,* the *Hartmanns, Olsen,* and some others took us on board and stayed until the boat's departure. Emotions of various kind rose up within me, but I do not want to dissect them, everyone could well imagine what they were. The voyage was heavenly, no question of any commotion of the boat. We lay at anchor for 10 hours because of the fog, but in the morning we saw the most delightful sunrise just as we were passing *Möhen* Island. In the vicinity of *Kiel* rockets were released; the moon was shining in full glow, so that one could clearly recognize the beautiful shorelines formed by the Kiel harbor; finally at 9 o'clock we arrived at that very place, where the *Graedeners* and *Schlossbauer* were already waiting for me and brought me to the *Stadt Lübeck,* where I found an altogether lovely room waiting for me, with a bit of a view over the water.

Wednesday the 20th was my concert in the theater. Much applause—few people. Kiel is just too small, and the auditorium too big. But after deducting the expense of 40 thalers, there remained 74 thalers for me.

On *Thursday the 21st,* drive to *Knoop* with the *Graedeners* and the *Schlossbauers* in order for once to look at the ships going through the locks, which I've never seen before.

Evening departure for Hamburg.

Friday morning arrival there, accommodations at the old Stadt London. Various changes of plans awaited me: nothing could come of the concert, since people have already left for the country; I couldn't go to *Cranz's*—he had insulted us by [sending] slanderous news to Leipzig.[55]

In the evening we went to *Müller's* quartet, which after a long time gave me great satisfaction.

On *Saturday the 23rd* we spent the afternoon at the *Müllers'* again and the noon and evening at *Otten's.* For those few days I felt very unwell, and yearning seized me with great intensity.

Sunday we separated, *Marie Garlichs* to Bremen, I to Magdeburg. We had gotten along quite well together, but I could feel no greater intimate affection for her, even if she was a dear good girl.[56]

I departed by steamboat at 7 o'clock in the morning—*Cranz* also wanted to take this boat, but oh what fate! he rushed there just as the boat was leaving. Under the circumstances that had thus occurred, I was very happy about this coincidence. I had pleasant company, but only men, which sometimes did become oppressive for me. It took [us] two whole days before we finally arrived

Monday evening in Magdeburg. Still a malicious demon wanted us to miss each other; Robert drove to the pier, I to the inn, but I did not wait there long before Robert opened his arms, into which I flew immediately. That was a delight, a bliss that

Marriage Diary II 149

seemed quite enormous to me! how we thanked God, who now has brought us, so happy, so healthy, back together again![57] We spent the night in Magdeburg and traveled on

Tuesday the 26th to Leipzig, where *Marie,* that dear delightful child, received us. Such a reunion does compensate for all the endured pains of yearning—Robert too seemed very happy, and then led me home, where I found everything garlanded; furthermore, Robert had given me a beautiful rug; but the most beautiful was the affectionate look, which I now could receive again, and the little red cheeks of my little angel, which I could kiss again.

I had a gross income of 1,155 thalers for the past interval of 7 weeks, but there remained no more than 100 louis d'or[58] after deducting all expenses, which were not insignificant according to [my notes].

[RS, in the margin:]
Now there will be better days again.

The 29th. In the morning Carl [Schumann] from Schneeberg. In the Rosenthal [park] Mendelssohn, who gave Carl a flower.

May 1842 [CS]

On *Monday the 2nd Ernst,* whom I had not yet heard, gave a concert. I liked him very much, but I did not feel myself enraptured— unfortunately he played only his own compositions, which, although they are pretty as concert pieces, become intolerable when [played] one after another.

After the concert we had supper at *Heinrich Brockhaus's.*

[RS, in the margin:] Dr. Jahn from Kiel.

[CS]

Wednesday the 4th Emilie Horlbeck, who is a good girl and had taken good care of my house, returned to Adorf.

Ernst ate at noon at [our house], and after the meal played the *A* [Major] *Sonata* by *Beethoven* with me, very beautifully.

On *Saturday the 7th Olsen* from Copenhagen surprised us, which really made me happy. In the evening he came to our house.

On *Sunday the 8th* we received terrible newspaper reports from Hamburg, of which one third has burned down.[59] Nothing is left of the beautiful old Jungfernstieg with its Stadt London, Streits Hôtel, *Heine's* magnificent house, etc.—it's a terrible disaster.

On the same day a terrible accident also happened on the train between Paris and Versailles, where 3 cars completely burned with all the people they contained, and in addition many were injured, 12 people went insane because of the shock—the unfortunate events continue to coincide! Now we receive news of big fires almost daily.

[RS, in the margin:] *the 9th:* to Gohlis with Clara—saw Schiller's house.[60]

The 10th: Hurried conversation with A. B. Marx and C. F. Becker.

[CS]

On *Wednesday the 11th Olsen* ate lunch at our place, and then drove with us to Connewitz.

On *Saturday the 14th* he left again, with many letters from me to Copenhagen.

Marriage Diary II 151

On *Wednesday the 18th* we made a lovely excursion to Wa[h]-ren, Königseiche, and Möckern—our first one again.

[RS, in the margin:] In the evening Bohrer from Stuttgard *[sic]*.

[CS]

On *Thursday the 19th,* the wet nurse left, the child was weaned. It seems that a blessing from God rests on the child. She tolerated it really perfectly, lost no weight whatsoever, and until now has always remained the happy friendly child.

[RS, in the margin:] On *the 19th* the dinner story with Bohrer.

[CS]

On *Saturday the 21st* we, *David,* I, and the orchestra gave a concert for the benefit of the victims of the Hamburg fire. It was fairly well attended, but the heat was terrible. Yet 100 thalers are supposed to have been left over.

Now I don't know of anything more to report for this month, except that we have adjusted ourselves together again fairly well, and belong to each other in old love. Our child is our joy, our mutual love, our *jewel*.

[RS, in the margin:] Truhn. Count Lichnowsky. Riefstahl. Bogenhard from Hildburghausen.

The 27th Bohrer really for dinner—boring fellow—E. Methfessel from Switzerland.

June 1842 [CS]

The 28th of June [RS]

Our little one gives us indescribable pleasure; she grows daily and shows a good-natured personality with great vitality. Now the first tooth is also in place. Clara's happiness about this and about the whole child is mine as well. The entire June was a kind month except for some days and nights of revelry.

Yet I was also industrious, in a new sort of way, and have almost completely finished making and also writing down two quartets for violins, etc., in A minor and F major. Also working a great deal on my journal.[61]

Clara is playing little, except from quartets by Haydn and Mozart that we took up consecutively at the piano, and has also composed two lieder for me for my birthday, the most successful she has ever written up to now.[62] On this day, the 8th of June, she gave me as always a large number of beautiful things, and above all [gave] the little one a wreath. But I was melancholy and unwell on that day. In the evening we cheered ourselves up; several acquaintances were there, and much wine flowed into grateful throats. Yet the best thing after that was music, which Clara gave us as yet.

[CS, in the margin:] During that night Marie got her first tooth—the second one soon followed.

[RS]

Otherwise nothing exceptional happened in June. The weather is peculiar because of its continuous beauty and warmth for 10

Marriage Diary II 153

weeks. I have moved out of my sweat box, and am happy in the small front room that my Clara has arranged most comfortably for me.

On the 15th we had a great joy. We had sent our lieder to Rückert, who responded to us with a masterful poem. (My dear wife might well be able to transcribe it into the diary!).

Also, we often stroll around in our little garden. Generally speaking, I like it in my Inselstrasse,[63] so that I have no desire for other places at all. But Clara has a great desire to travel, and we really would like to go to Salzburg for the 4th of September, where Mozart's monument will be dedicated.

On St. John's Day, the 24th, we made a very cheerful excursion to Connewitz—Marie's first trip—there I sometimes think about my dear parents, that they were unable to share this joy. Clara had decorated Schuncke's portrait that day with a garland.[64] He too could still be alive! Now enough for today.

July 1842   [CS]

If I could only learn to do what you do, my dear Robert, to say much with few words! but unfortunately it's the opposite with me, no matter how much I try, if not to be your equal (for that would be impossible for my small mind), at least to resemble you a little bit.

Accept a kiss for your last report, and for your love to me and our little Marie in every one of your words—you cannot imagine how well that makes me feel, how happy it makes me. But rather

The Marriage Diaries of Robert & Clara Schumann

than reveling in words, on with the thing that is most important,
to fulfill your wish and transcribe Rückert's beautiful poem,[65]
which I do with real pleasure.

Friedrich Rückert

to

Robert and *Clara Schumann*

in Leipzig, in thanks

for their musical composition of his

Liebesfrühling

Lang ist's, lang,	Long it's been, long,
Seit ich meinen Liebesfrühling	Since I've sung my love's spring
sang,	song,
Aus Herzensdrang,	From the craving of my heart,
Wie er entsprang,	Whence it had sprung,
Verklang in Einsamkeit der Klang.	The sound faded away in solitude.
Zwanzig Jahr	Twenty years it's been
Wurden's, da hört' ich hier und dar	When finally I could hear
Der Vogelschaar	Birds flocking distant and near
Einen, der klar	One of them whistled
Pfiff einen Ton, der dorther war.	A tone bright and clear.
Und nun gar	And now at last
Kommt im einundzwanzigsten Jahr	In the twenty-first year
Ein Vogelpaar,	There comes a pair of birds
Macht erst mir klar,	That finally makes it clear
Daß nicht ein Ton verloren war.	That not a single tone was lost.
Meine Lieder	My songs
Singt ihr wieder	You're singing again,
Mein Empfinden	My sensibility
Klingt ihr wieder,	Resounds in your activity,
Mein Gefühl	As you give wings again,
Beschwingt ihr wieder,	To my emotions.
Meinen Frühling	My spring
Bringt ihr wieder	You return to me,

Marriage Diary II

Mich, wie schön,	How beautiful it is
Verjüngt ihr wieder	To be made young again:
Nehmt meinen Dank, wenn euch die Welt,	Accept my thanks, even if the world withholds
Wie mir einst, ihren vorenthält!	Its gratitude, as it once did from me!
Und werdet ihr den Dank erlangen,	And should thanks ever come your way,
So hab' ich meinen mitempfangen.	Then I will share it, if I may.

On *the 3rd* at City Councillor *Fleischer's* the engagement of his eldest daughter *Agnes* was celebrated, to which we were also invited. The bridegroom was a university friend of Robert's [Moritz Semmel], and they had not seen each other for a long time—thus a double surprise occurred.

In the evening I went to the theater with the aunt [Emilie Carl]: "Son of the Wilderness" by *Halm* (Count *Münch* von *Bellinghausen*), the *Rettichs* as guest artists. The dialogue in this piece is very beautiful, even if the characters are not always beautiful—sometimes the contrasts are presented very glaringly. Not much can be said about the acting of the couple—she is an excellent woman, *he* less so, which I noticed especially in [Don] *Carlos* [by Schiller], in which he couldn't in the least equal *Emil Devrient* as *Marquis* [de] *Posa*.

On *Tuesday the 5th* by coincidence I came to the theater again for *Iphigenia* by *Goethe;* I saw only 3 acts, but in this role *Rettich* seemed outstanding to me, her noble voice contributing a great deal to that.

In the afternoon I visited [Livia] *Frege*.

On *Thursday the 7th* in the evening, music at *Dr. Petschke's* home, in honor of *Marschner*. I played his trio, which seemed very flat to me, similarly several of his lieder, sung by his wife. [Livia] *Frege* sang several of my husband's; heavens, what a difference! Robert, the gentle mood, the nobility in every measure, always

156 *The Marriage Diaries of Robert & Clara Schumann*

distinctive, where nothing trivial can be tolerated, and *Marschner,* such raw passion, full of platitudes, trivial, and not even fresh anymore! He shouldn't have written anything more after his *Templar, Vampire,* and [Hans] *Heiling.*

On *Friday the 8th* pretty much the same evening repeated itself at the *Freges'.* She [Livia] sang a whole book of *Marschner's* lieder at sight, which was astonishing. Few singers will be able to equal her in that.

[RS, in the margin:] On *the 8th* Etienne Soubre, the prizewinning Belgian composer, brought me a letter from Fétis. Soubre [is] a very captivating young man.

[CS]

On *Monday the 11th Marschner* was at our house, but without his wife, who was ill. I was in a very bad mood that night, to which *Marschner* contributed a lot, because with his daughter he had brought a thirteenth person to our table, so that we had to divide the company between two tables. This particular superstition about thirteen at the table is still very widespread, and no one likes to challenge it.

There was singing again, and I also played a sonata by *Beethoven.*

[RS, in the margin:] On the 12th a young, pretty-looking organist, *Homeyer,* from Westphalia.

On the 18th a young Viennese composer, *Füchs,* and the librettist *O. Prechtler.*

[CS]

On *Tuesday the 19th* Woldemar and Eugen *Bargiel* came from Berlin to spend their vacation in Leipzig. Both of them stayed

Marriage Diary II

with me. They are a pair of well-behaved boys, I especially love the younger one, *Eugen,* who has a sincere, kindhearted personality; the older one completely resembles his father, whom, to be honest, I would never have been able to like, although I have esteemed him highly for his many virtues. I've always had a secret dread of him, which *my father* instilled in me against him already as a child (when I went to Berlin for the first time).[66]

[RS, in the margin:] On the 22nd finished writing down my 3 quartets. In the evening Lampadius with wife, and Julius Becker for supper at our house. Read Immermann's delightful Münchhausen.

[CS]

On *Monday the 25th* we drove to Connewitz and spent a few hours there in a somewhat boring way—we were neither happy nor sad!—

On *Tuesday the 26th* we took a walk with the boys into the Rosenthal—at Kintschi we made a small stop. When we got home Spohr had been there with his wife and daughter; he was traveling through, so that we did not see him at all, which I regretted very much.

NB. On *Sunday the 24th* we played [a] trio by Spohr at the *Voigts'.* The last two movements attracted me especially; one recognizes the master throughout, only that it seems to me there is often a lack of freshness.

For the first time I also played some sonatas by *Bach* today with *David.* I cannot yet render a judgment, because one has to play these things often in order to get to like them. It was very apparent to me that *David* played all continuous figures staccato—would *Bach* really have wanted it that way? I suspect that *Mendelssohn* surely played them that way, since David does not do things that way on his own, so it interests me even more whether that really is correct!—

On *Wednesday the 27th* we walked to Lützschena and back. It was a pretty walk, only the place itself was very unsightly, poor service, bad food, many flies, *etc. etc.* We had the two boys with us.

On *Thursday the 28th* I introduced the boys to the old wife of Finance Councillor *Frege,* who had known them from earlier times and was very happy to see them again so grown up. Also, she presented them with signet rings. *Dr. Frege's wife* visited me on *Friday the 29th* in the afternoon, in order to say adieu to me; she will be traveling along the Rhine. Everyone is traveling, for 2 months we have *wanted* it also—maybe it will happen soon, or not at all! I feel impelled to go out into the mountains, and yet it gets to be so difficult for me to abandon the little one, to leave her in the hands of servants. Were it up to me I'd take her with me, even though I would have to take care of her she would give me considerable pleasure. But I accommodate myself as you, dear husband, wish it, and thus nothing is lacking, except a decision.

Today we were alone together for several hours, Livia Frege and I. For some time I have been coming to like her more and more, and she completely overcame my prejudices against her today, when she showed a friendly trust in me and awoke my innermost sympathy. She does not live a happy life, nor a happy marriage, can there be anything more terrible? her mother-in-law is certainly to blame for much of it, and that could make me hate this woman whom I had always liked so much.

I cannot describe what an indelible impression her fate has made on me, already when she lost her child, and even more so now that she has let me look into her hopeless inner world. But that is expressed only in this book, which of course exists only for the two of us; I know how to honor a confidence like that.

Marriage Diary II 159

It was also today that the two boys left—the 12 days flitted by, like a dream! If only Mother could come here, I wish so longingly for that.

One evening Robert brought the *music director Kossmaly* along, whereupon to their heart's content the assembled literary gentlemen drank good wine to the welfare of the new journal!

Robert has been very busy, completed 3 quartets, but I did very little, did not play at all, despite my intending so often to do so. But as soon as I will come back from the trip, a serious course of studies should begin again. Then we will also hear the quartets sometime, which I look forward to very much; they must be quite delightful, according to what I've occasionally overheard. *Lampadius,* who with his newly married bride spent an evening at our house, let us drink to the health of these 3 *children,* barely born and already completed and beautiful.

August 1842   [RS]
Excursion to Bohemia
From 6th–22nd August

The trip was short, but perhaps the most beautiful and cheerful that I have ever made with Clara.

Favored by the most beautiful weather, which accompanied us on the entire trip, we drove

Saturday on the 6th, with joyful courage, by steam train to Dresden. The only interesting event on the trip was a tragicomic situation, when a Frenchman missed the departure of the steam train, and as he saw it leaving tried, screaming, to break through the assembled crowd.

In Dresden the music-seller Paul and his wife, who had reserved lodgings for us, awaited us. Soon Clara's brother Alwin showed up too; he is supposed to be industrious on his violin, but showed every sign of a future conceited fool and egoist, so that we were happy to be rid of him. We still had time to go to the Brühlische Terasse, where we met Becker from Freiberg, who as usual greeted us with reproaches, as Clara quite correctly observed. The proximity of the old man [Wieck], who naturally first wanted to know every step we took, made our stay embarrassing and uncanny the whole time.

On the Terasse I also met the chamber musician Horak, who in quite a lively way brought back to my mind an old dear memory of my youth in Zwickau, where I let myself be heard in a concert of his. Great expectations were placed on me, as I again noticed from the conversation with him; they have so far been only partly fulfilled; it again occurred to me how much there still is left for me to do.

On *Sunday the 7th* in the morning we visited the art exhibit.[67] Many outstanding paintings captivated us there, above all the "two Leonoras" by Sohn, a number of Italian genre paintings by Lindau, several landscapes by Dahl, then the Javanese Bull Hunters by Prince Saleh, and his portraits of Major Serre and his wife. Also, the replica of the Veitskirche in Prague done by a woodcarver from Erfurt made the impression of perfection and mastery.

In the Catholic [Hof]Kirche we heard a good-sounding mass by Reissiger. But the large crowd takes away all enjoyment. We spoke briefly with old Mieksch, Clara's former singing teacher.

Then we visited Schröder-Devrient, at whose place we also met Fräulein von Hagn. Those few moments will remain unforgettable to me. The natural freshness and graciousness as well as sturdiness of Schröder has no equal. She conversed with us in the most amusing way, namely about Liszt, and imitated him in the most ridiculing way, whereby she then teased Hagn, who is sup-

Marriage Diary II 161

posed to be one of Liszt's greatest fans if not more.[68] We laughed a great deal. Among pianists she considers Mendelssohn, Henselt, and Clara the greatest; Liszt counts as a mere caricature for her. We parted from each other in the most friendly way. Clara also paid much attention to Schröder's room; it really is charming and resembles more the summer house in an Oriental harem.

At noon we had a meal at the Linke'schen Bad with Becker, of whom it was most impolite, when we then went to the Vogelwiese, to remain behind because Clara's father was there, to whom Becker probably wanted to show his neutrality. On the one hand we are obligated to Becker for his earlier, very friendly efforts on behalf of our union, on the other hand he really isn't important enough for us to pick a quarrel with him because of such an oversight. So we let it go at that.

Evening at the theater: "Adèle de Foix" by Reissiger, which has much that is of merit but also weak, and is tiring in the end.[69] All German opera composers get shipwrecked by trying to please the public; they want to do the right thing by everyone, and thus nothing right ever comes of it. One pays no respect to those who would always approach us with open arms.

Tischatschek's voice still is always enchanting; his acting by contrast is crude and disrespectful. Schröder just did what she could; she had explained to us already in the morning that she does not like to sing in this opera—despite all her efforts the result would be so minimal.

On *Monday the 8th* at Paul's I met Reissiger, who, as he said, did not participate at all in the choral festival.[70] In the meantime Clara was at Madame Krägen's, where malicious gossiping again had taken place, over which I then had to expectorate fairly violently. That too was easily forgotten because of the beautiful day [and] the bustling of people who wanted to witness the singers' departure. Incidentally, the 30,000 people found themselves most badly cheated. The arrangement lacked all organization and all polish. And in addition we had to wait for 2 hours on a sandy plain in burning heat. Nicer was the evening in Loschwitz and Blasewitz, where we had driven via the "White Stag." The colorful life on and along the Elbe, the fragrant evening breeze over the whole landscape, intermingled with cheerful music, the shooting and noise everywhere—all this provided a picture of life and the joy of living as I have seldom seen it. Here we also heard Mendelssohn's "Wer hat dich du schöner Wald" sung very well.

The joy was followed again by anger, this time over my wife, who otherwise is so good and loving. But we don't want to think about it any further.

On *Tuesday the 9th* in the morning we had a fairly lively breakfast with Paul, Becker, and Reissiger. Various things were discussed and touched on. Reissiger also told us about the duel with pistols that Banck has been contemplating against the old man [Wieck]. They seem to make a lot of fun over the thing in Dresden.

In the evening young Kirchner arrived, a significant talent, whom I have always treated with great consideration for seeking advice from me. I always think Heaven will always help those who are truly talented, and I also consoled him in regard to this. We looked at the art exhibit once more, then toward evening went with the Pauls to the Feldschlösschen to wait for the return of the singers, which was again very poorly organized, however. A young pianist, Blassmann, paid me a compliment; he seems to be a worthy counterpart of Alwin [Wieck].

We spoke in passing with Tischatschek and Pohlenz from Leipzig.

On *Wednesday the 10th* to Teplitz by cab, always in wonderfully beautiful weather. The way there always has variety and things of interest; approaching Teplitz the countryside becomes really

Marriage Diary II 163

magnificent. In Peterswald Clara met a Copenhagen acquaintance. We arrived in Teplitz during a beautiful time of day, had time to see the Schlossgarten and walked over the mountains and then to bed. This day is the anniversary of the death of my good father, about whom I have often been thinking; he was often in Teplitz; if only he could also have seen us here together.

On Thursday morning we climbed the Schlossberg. It was very exerting for Clara, also myself. The reward up there is great, however.

On returning to the city we saw the duke of Bordeaux and later [the Duchess de] Berry as well. The great heat kept us at home in the afternoon; but toward evening we walked to Thurn, a pretty wooded area with a coffeehouse. A band of musicians made up of small children, properly uniformed, gave me much pleasure.

On the way home while having dinner we met a man from Leipzig, J. Hammer, a talented writer. Later we had a nice intermezzo in a pastry shop, where we heard music being played. Unfortunately Clara was soon recognized; she played the Variations by Henselt. A silly music director from Berlin had told her "she shouldn't be afraid, because only amateurs would be listening."

Friday the 12th will remain unforgettable for me; we drove to the Milischauer [mountain] in the company of, as it seemed, a natural scientist with two cute boys. The drive to the foot of the mountain is already very rewarding; the road goes through charming areas and distant views.

The ascent took place in already great heat and demanded much from me. Today Clara was more vigorous than I, which pleased and angered me; because the husband really doesn't like being always 20 paces behind the wife. Finally it was climbed. Up there one is addressed by pretty mottos, and the comfortable facilities provide shelter against storms and heat. And then the magnificent panorama! One is even supposed to see beyond Prague. But up on a mountain I prefer not to be slurping too much over just the details, I prefer to let the whole thing flow into me. Then one appreciates God's beautiful world. I could easily have wanted to stay up there for a week. The Schlossberg lies at one's feet like a molehill. That's the way it also is in life and in art. Only when one is on greater mountains does one recognize the insignificance of those that have been surmounted, and if only yesterday one imagined himself to be standing high, then on the following day one feels how with exertion and effort he can get even higher. Around 5 o'clock we left the beautiful giant mountain, which continued beckoning to us for a long time and finally shrouded itself in complete darkness.

Saturday the 13th was rather boring for us. The most interesting was a visit from one of Ernestine's [von Zedtwitz] acquaintances, Pielsticker von Mühlburg. He didn't know Clara at first, and wanted to make her think that he had heard her on Thursday until the thing was then cleared up. In the evening past eight o'clock we drove to Karlsbad by stagecoach. It would be worth taking the way during daytime. I remember it from 1825, when I did this on foot. Much of it was still in my memory, namely, Reichau and Engelhaus before Carlsbad, the beautiful cliff ruin.

In Carlsbad, where as an 8-year-old boy I had spent many weeks with my mother, I remembered all of my old beloved places. But nothing much has changed. We lived very comfortably in the Goldnen Schild [Hotel], drank champagne at noon, and not without good reason; since in 1837 on that very day I had received Clara's *yes* reply in a little secret letter,[71] to which she has not been disloyal so far. Labitzky, the dance composer, accompanied our thoughts with cheerful music.

In the evening we had time for a solitary walk to the Posthof, where I had been so often earlier, holding my mother's hand.

Monday the 15th endeared itself to us with two beautiful excursions, to the Kreutzberg and to Elbogen. In the morning at the fountain we met Fischhof from Vienna and Dr. Franck from Breslau (the 4th of the brothers, whom I know). Climbing the Kreutzberg is like child's play; too bad that to the north the mountain is overgrown and one has only the one view toward Carlsbad. Clara remarked quite correctly: Carlsbad resembles the sort of children's toy village that one gets as a present for Christmas. I compared the whole thing, namely the way it was illuminated by the moon one night, to such a Christmas present. After we had refreshed ourselves up there, and returned to the town, we looked for the Parishes, mother and daughter, who received us very cordially and immediately invited us on a drive to Elbogen, for which we must be very thankful to them. At noon we ate together with Fischhof, while consuming much champagne. Fischhof, a Jew, smart and political, can also be very pleasant, even comfortable.

So, from there off to Elbogen, which I now want to describe right away, surely the most delightful excursion around Carlsbad. Clara was completely enchanted, and so was I. In addition, very nice conversation with the Parishes, both most highly cultivated and, as usual in an unfamiliar place, less ceremonial perhaps than at home. The last word, "ceremonial," doesn't apply at all to the daughter, however; her clean, clear eyes must be mirrors of a beautiful heart. In addition she understands much about music and makes fine and reasonable judgments. I have to record what she said about Clara: "what she liked so much about Clara was that she pursues art *more like a dilettant.*" These words contain as fine a compliment as the opposite, if one says about [Harriet] Parish that she pursues art like an artist—which I've always wanted to tell her, if it would not have been much ruder than her remark. We drove back in twilight and parted most cordially.—

On *Tuesday the 16th,* set off in good time for Marienbad. The pretty way through the valley to Hammer is soon followed by a completely uninteresting one almost to Marienbad. We arrived there toward 2 o'clock. It is situated in a bigger valley than Carlsbad and in general is more friendly and mild. The entire town really is like a park enclosed by houses. Everything still looks new and newly washed. That also makes the people look different.

We knew that Major Serre's wife was there and toward evening found her by accident at the spa. A curiously distracted woman, who may nevertheless be kindhearted, but not lacking intelligence and wit.

In the evening she had invited a small musical group to get together, where the daughter of the pharmacist also sang our lieder for us, which Clara accompanied for her. A clergyman from Pilsen who heard Clara for the first time seems to have been the most greedy of the listeners. He couldn't get enough. The company also wanted to hear something of my compositions, whereupon Clara then said she couldn't play any of them. This caused an exchange of words between us yet that night, which was gentle enough and in which Clara certainly did not misunderstand me.

In the Neptune Inn we received good service because the owner, an educated, pleasant man, knew Clara and, as he often assured us, considered it the greatest honor to wait on her.

Wednesday the 17th began under a good omen. The weather never stopped being the same. The mornings were always wonderful, the evenings no less so, the nights with millions of stars. We had heard that Prince Metternich was supposed to be in Königswart and made an excursion there, partly for seeing Königswart itself, but even more to see the great diplomat. The road there is rather uniform. The entire region is very hilly and very well suited for parks. On first entering the district of Königswart, the entire region assumes a more friendly, kindly character. Soon

Marriage Diary II 167

the beautiful castle appeared before us, less in a palatial style than built comfortably, tastefully. Flags had been planted on the two end towers of the castle, as a sign that the count was there. We stayed at the inn, which, as if in mockery, is located opposite the castle. Because dirtier interior accommodations cannot well be imagined. A walk through the gardens (they are not a park) gave me great pleasure. Clara less so, for today was her day on which everything seemed to anger her—who knows why—human beings often are simply capricious despite the most beautiful, bluest sky overhead and the most delightful surroundings. It was very quiet in the garden, we encountered only a young boy with his tutor, the former was probably a prince.

The great drought, which reigns over the whole world this year, seems also to have robbed the garden of its main treasures. But the weather was so delightful that there was plenty left for the heart and eyes. Notable is the obelisk on one of the garden hills, which was placed there by Prince Metternich for Emperor Franz. It is quite tall. A golden globe, guarded by an eagle with outspread wings, rests at the tip. At the base lies one lion that is asleep and one that is awake. It is a joke among the Austrians that the former is the emperor, the latter Prince Metternich. If one stands in front of them at the entrance of the castle, then the globe with the eagle seems to be poised right on top of the castle itself, which perhaps was flattery on the architect's part. From the hill where the obelisk is located, one has a view down to the whole garden with the castle; on the other one can see quite far into the distant land. The distance was shrouded in fragrant blue. All of this gives the impression, but more a comforting than an intimidating one, that a mighty, fortunate person must live around here.

Now we had ourselves announced to the prince. A porter and another servant soon took us to a higher official, to whom I gave

Clara's card. He summoned us after a quarter of an hour, which we spent in the garden. When we went back, it took a few seconds and we stood in the count's salon. My heart pounded a bit. I thought of the words of Goethe who said somewhere: for him Prince Metternich had always shown himself to be a gracious gentleman.[72] If that was what Goethe said, then I, a poor musician, was surely permitted to have a pounding heart. Soon he stood before us. But the first words from his mouth soon completely chased away all anxiety. He received Clara in a most gracious, almost friendly and intimate way, also asked sympathetically about me, so that he led the entire conversation almost completely by himself. Of Donizetti he said "that he had given him a brilliant opera,[73] and that the emperor had appointed him kapellmeister (because he was an Austrian subject, a native of Bergamo), that there is a motif in this opera which like Rossini's *Tanti palpiti* will soon be a popular tune, that Donizetti, still so young, had already written his 76th opera." Then he inquired about the conditions of music in Leipzig, about Clara's trip to Denmark, etc. When we spoke about the gardens surrounding Königswart, he said "that he does not like being *fenced-in;* nature has already done everything, he had parceled it only here and there, etc. etc." In parting he still promised us a good reception in Vienna if we go there, and in saying farewell he gave me his hand, which I was too embarrassed to accept. Thus we left him, enriched, uplifted, and strengthened for life by a few unforgettable minutes. The benevolence of a powerful person reminds the one who shares it of the common bond that embraces everyone. One feels renewed courage in facing life, new desire for pressing forward in order to come closer to the worthiest ones on this earth. That was the effect of those minutes, at least on me. The tone of that man's voice, the halo that hovers over so celebrated a head, sort of hypnotized me, so that only an outline of his external appearance

Marriage Diary II

stood before my eyes. Yet I still remember the large, intelligent eyes, the firm, vigorous gait, and above all just that clear, distinct voice, which may be what every great man possesses.

We also looked at the collections in the castle, about which books could well be written, but only in the greatest hurry. Among many noteworthy things we were shown: Ziska's mace[74] (or sword, I don't know exactly); Ypsilanti's dagger; the lavoir of Napoleon, presented to the prince by the duke of Reichstadt; the canes of the Duke of Reichstadt and of Talleyrand; the ring of Sobieski; cocarde and hair of Napoleon; hair and the house cap of Emperor Franz; a Spanish costume of Don Carlos, who was shown as *pretender to the throne* of Spain; a small landscape by Pedro II, a present for the prince; a portrait of Dom Sebastian; as well as many gifts from the pope, from the sultan, from Meh[e]med Ali, namely, two 2–3,000-year-old mummies from the latter (a king and a queen), many Chinese things, etc. The coin collection is supposed to be outstanding and complete. How sad that we had to fly by everything so fast.

Yet the chapel of the castle demanded our attention; it is an image of the prince himself and so welcoming that one immediately wants to pray. The most valuable things there are the altar with Hadrian's tomb, then the skeleton of [a holy boy] Boniface, a gift from the pope.[75] The manuscript of a title to this gift hangs on the door to the church. Several well-selected portraits decorate the chapel's gallery, among others a Titian, a Lucas Cranach.

Toward 1 o'clock we drove back to Marienbad. Toward evening we visited Major Serre's wife again, where we met Klengel from Dresden and a young musician, Schlesinger, from Marienbad. Things were cheerful, ladies and gentlemen smoked Spanish cigars, and then there was some music making. Clara played with truly musical intelligence the *Novellet,* among other things; Klengel played something too, but with much anxiety just like

L[udwig] Berger, whose fellow student he was at Clementi's. In the evening the young Schlesinger came to visit me in the hotel, a pretty, gentle person who radiates music from his eyes. He wants to come to Leipzig.

This highly interesting day was followed by a boring one,

Thursday the 18th, on which we traveled back to Carlsbad in a miserable mail coach and in miserable company and also saw and heard nothing of importance there.

On *Friday the 19th* we drove to Schneeberg. The road there is richly varied. A strange sort of intermezzo happened to us at the border in Wildenthal because of the stupidity of our Bohemian coachman. Toward 5 o'clock we were in Schneeberg. The first familiar face was my old friend *Röller.* Then Carl and Pauline [Schumann] arrived, who received us heartily.

On *Saturday the 20th,* Deacon Körner and many others at lunch, then a wonderfully pretty trip to Stein and the Prinzen-höhle.[76]

On *Sunday the 21st* in the morning, music at Judge Kasten's. At 4 o'clock departure for Zwickau, which lay before us in the most beautiful sunshine. Carl's son, a beautiful, spirited lad—Rascher's wedding—There is so much to report—but the book is coming to an end—in it yet a kiss, dear travel companion, at the end of the trip on Monday, when we arrived in Leipzig in the morning at 7 o'clock and found our little Marie well and in good health.

[CS]

To read Robert's report was a double enjoyment for me; the report itself interesting enough in addition the memory of our beautiful journey!—But even at home I find myself quite *con amore* again;

Marriage Diary II 171

that wasn't the way it went for my dear Robert, who seemingly would have preferred to take another excursion immediately.

On *the 26th Tomaschek* from *Vienna* visited me, a good but rather silly Austrian.

There is nothing of further interest to report this month, therefore directly to

September,

when our dear child was born. We cheerfully celebrated her birthday, but the joy soon had to be followed by grief. On the very same day the child became very dangerously ill with cramps [an infection] of the teeth and jaw. We were at Lampadius's that evening, but were soon called home, where the poor child lay unconscious. This sight was heartrending, to see a small dear creature suffering like that. Robert was in despair and doubted that the little one would recover—I was governed by too much concern for her, as for him, to be able to arrive at any particular emotion—I did not lose hope, however! But it did not last long and there was help from Heaven—thanks be to Him for preserving our jewel. She is still very sick today,

the 5th, but out of any danger. I had always loved my child inexpressibly, but now I feel as if she were given to me anew once more—one can never sufficiently appreciate such a possession, one truly feels this for the first time when one has been close to losing it, as was really the case for us!—

My dear Robert gave little Marie a really nice and thoughtful present, a diary in which he had described her first year of life,[77] and a small silver savings box into which he put the money that was in the purse I'd given him when he went to Vienna. In addition she received a few other small items, also a little dress from her godmother, Madame Devrient, and from Mother little baskets, stockings, and several small things and a letter that found its place in the diary of our little debutante.

On *the 6th* Mother finally came from Berlin to stay with us for two weeks, which has long been my wish. She always remains the same enthusiastic, cheerful, and agile woman, and is remarkably well preserved despite all the suffering that she has gone through and has to go through even now. She was very happy about little Marie, although she was still very sick, which only changed during the last days of mother's presence here.

On *the 11th* we went to the concert in the *Hôtel de Pologne* that *Härtel* gave for victims of the Oschatz fire. The best thing about it was its worthy cause. After the concert we ate there, but by accident got into a group that Härtel had invited, which angered and amused us.

On *Sunday the 12th* we celebrated our wedding anniversary simply with a glass of wine. Two happy years have passed—may there be many like that to follow.

The 13th was a day filled with gladness and joy. My Robert surprised me with many things, but what gave me the greatest pleasure was the present of his 3 quartets, which he had *David, Wittmann,* and others play for me that very same evening. That was a great delight for me! these compositions, this performance, and all that magnificence because of my Robert! my veneration of his genius, his mind, indeed of the whole composer increases with each work! I cannot say anything about the quartets except that they delighted me in even the finest detail. Everything there is new, along with being clear, well worked out, and always appropriate for a quartet, but what is my judgment worth? accept my most heartfelt kiss, of which I would like to give you a thousand for the pleasure you gave me today.

In addition there was no lack of abundant presents, Robert always gives me much too much, which I don't deserve at all. Mother also gave me a most charming little basket, and Heaven made my little Marie come to me well and merrily with a little garland. The dear little child seemed to be enjoying it herself, because she laughed like the rosebuds that she was wearing.

On *Wednesday the 15th* we got the news that *Henselt* would come here, but only for one day. He arrived on

Sunday the 18th after we had twice waited for him in vain. *Serre, Kraegen,* and his wife (Henselt's wife) accompanied him. They ate lunch at our house, and in the evening he played at Lindenau at Härtel's for a small circle of connoisseurs. He delighted me as formerly with his imposing yet tender playing; his delivery is beautiful and natural, in general I think the whole man is emotion. As a composer, however, he has made no progress, all the melodies he already had earlier, only fresher [then], and the form is always the same. As magnificent as his playing is, each tone so precise, I do believe that with much mechanical exercise his touch has lost delicacy. He doesn't seem able to play really delicately, poetically, at such places a certain stiffness can always be seen and heard. Pity, that he has buried himself in Petersburg, where his talent, while not destroyed, does suffer from giving lessons. Incidentally, he again discouraged me with his playing, as he did 6 years ago, but then also fired it up. I've been inexcusably lazy with piano playing recently, but I want to make amends for all of that as much as I possibly can.

On *Monday the 19th* everyone left; the *Henselts,* Mother, Krägen, Serre, *etc.* We took them to the railway station. Mother traveled with the first [i.e., the Henselts] to Berlin.

NB I still forgot to mention Madame *Henselt,* who seems to be a pleasant and above all an intelligent woman. *Henselt* also really had to have one like that, in order to do as well in Petersburg as is the case. He receives 1 louis d'or for a lesson, of which he gives nine a day. He strongly encouraged me to come there, which will also eventually happen sometime.

Brief was the pleasure of seeing *Henselt* at our house, but he promised us a longer stay next year. As brief as his stay was, I did really come to like him, because he seems far more comfortable and natural to me than years ago.

Calm has now set in for us! I will use it to live really calmly again for my art and my two dear ones.

Just now I notice that I have continued this book beyond the end of the second year of our marriage, and now have to start a new one in the middle of the month. Pardon the hastiness, my dear one!—

[RS]

Of visitors from other places I still find in my notes: the pianist *Voss* from Mecklenburg, Walter von *Göthe, Hauptmann* from Cassel now employed here as cantor at the Thomas School.

Three

MARRIAGE
DIARY III

20 September 1842 – 31 May 1844

Diary of   [CS]
Robert and Clara Schumann
from 20 September 1842 on

As far as our external life is concerned, the last week of the month of September went by very quietly, but thus my Robert worked more with his mind! he has almost finished a quintet which, according to what I have overheard, again seems to me magnificent—a work filled with energy and freshness!—

I hope very much to play it here in public yet this winter.[1]

On *the 29th* the *music director Schulze* from Zwickau came to our house with a very talented daughter, whom he wants to make into a singer, or rather in his opinion has done so already. She is only 16 years old, thus cannot have a firm voice, so of course one cannot know in advance how it will turn out; but she is very musical, plays the piano nicely, and thus there is much to be hoped for.

I have been fairly industrious at the piano, and want to continue to be, otherwise it will retrogress, if not with my internal music, then with my fingers.

Now your month arrives, my dear husband—I look forward to read the way you put things again, which for me is really the most beautiful and most affectionate.

September 1842   [RS]

About September I still have to report that on the 29th David played my quartets for Mendelssohn, who passed through here after his Switzerland journey.[2] The only ones present were Hauptmann, who now [is] cantor at the Thomas School, and Verhulst; a small but good audience, on which the music did seem to have an effect. Mendelssohn told me later while leaving that he cannot really explain to me how much he likes my music. That made me very happy; since I consider Mendelssohn the best critic; of all living musicians he has the clearest vision.

October started to be busy right away. Clara played in the 1st subscription concert, which Mendelssohn conducted, and that always produces unrest. She played well and beautifully as always. It often worries me that I frequently inhibit Clara in her practicing, since she does not wish to disturb me while composing. Because I know quite well that the artist who appears in public, even if he is the greatest, can never completely neglect certain mechanical exercises that must always keep the fingers mobile, so to speak. And my dear artiste often lacks time for that. As far as deeper musical development is concerned, Clara surely has not been standing still, on the contrary has made progress; of course she lives completely immersed only in good music, and thus her playing now is certainly even healthier and at the same time more spiritual and gentle than before. But to elevate this mechanical security to infallibility, so to speak, for that she sometimes lacks time nowadays, and I am responsible for that and yet cannot change it. But Clara does recognize that I have to nurture a talent, and that I am full of the most beautiful energy right now and still do have to make use of my youth. It is only like that in the marriages of artists; everything cannot go on simultaneously, and the main thing of course is always the happiness that remains, and we really are most fortunate to have each other, and understand each other, understand so well, and love each other with our whole heart.

I've also been industrious again; a quintet in E-flat major is at

Marriage Diary III

the copyist, and I've finished something else, at least in my mind, which I may not reveal to you as yet however. The 3 quartets I've sold to the Härtels—and thus things always move ahead.

We had a few nice visits, in addition to *Pott* from Oldenburg and Dr. *Kahlert* from Breslau, also Fräulein *Lichtenstein* and her parents from Berlin. For the concert that Clara played in, Madame *Parish* and her daughter Harriet also came over from Dresden and showed themselves to be friendly and sympathetic as always.

After that, Colonel *Stockfleth* from Hamburg, the singer *Tuyn* from Amsterdam, the young talent *Kirchner,* and many others were there whom we have often refused to receive. Clara's brother Gustav [Wieck] surprised us as well; he seems to be an honest fellow, and more kindhearted than Alwin.

Likewise Frau von *Ridderstolp* from Stockholm, a sensible, cultivated woman. The [singer] *Schloss* spent an evening with us.

The second half of the month I spent being quite sleepless. The music had excited me too much. Now I'm back in good shape.

We spent one evening at Lampadius's, who has a pretty, robust woman as his wife. One noon in Dölitz at Madame Harkort's, where Dr. Kühne and his wife also are staying.

Marie is completely recovered again, and to our joy grows from one day to the next; she manifests a cheerful disposition and is always full of joy and life.

The twilight surprises me. My eyes hurt. Kiss them for me, dear good wife!—

November 1842 [CS]

An indescribable sadness has fallen over me the last few days—I think you don't love me anymore as you did, I often feel so clearly that I cannot suffice for you, and when you are gentle, then I sometimes attribute that to your good heart, which does not want to hurt me. Many sad thoughts about the future, which often don't leave me for days on end, which I cannot dispel at all, are now added to this grief, so that you must be tolerant with me occasionally. Oh, Robert! if you only knew how I am always so full of love within myself, how I want to wait on you hand and foot, to show life to you in only its rosiest colors, how I love you so infinitely! all my worries are only for you, of course; my most terrible thought is that you should have to work for money, because that simply cannot make you happy, and yet if you do not let me work as well, if you cut off every means for me to earn something, I see no other way out. I would gladly earn money however, to create a life for you that is entirely dedicated to your art; it pains me most deeply when I have to ask you for money, and you give me what you have earned; I often feel as if this must rob your life of all poetry. You are so much of an artist in the true sense of the word, all of your creating and striving is for me something so tender, poetic, I want to say holy, that I gladly want to protect you from all the prosaic things that simply cannot be avoided in married life; it wounds me to have to tear you so often from your beautiful dreams. Forgive me for pouring my heart out, my good Robert, but this is by no means all that weighs on my heart concerning you. Give me a kiss [to show] that you are not angry with me, and if you can, then just never stop loving me a little, your love is my life.

On *the 3rd of November* Robert's *B-Flat Major* Symphony was performed in the Gewandhaus and gave every connoisseur renewed pleasure. It went well and again received much applause, but no one of course can perceive the supreme happiness with which I listen to such a composition by my Robert!

On *the 1st Verhulst* was at our house once more for dinner before his departure, and after a long struggle he finally left for Holland on *the 2nd.*

Marriage Diary III 181

On *the 10th Mendelssohn* visited us, and thus I had to do a lot of playing. *Mendelssohn* was very affectionate and transported me into a musical fire with his appreciation of my playing, which I had to pay for dearly; the next day I was so unwell that I could not receive the visit of *Schröder-Devrient,* couldn't join her at *Brockhaus's* on the *13th,* and also had to miss the Gewandhaus concert that same evening. I was very sad about it.

The 15th. Robert has also been very ill for several days, and scared me at first—the typhus epidemic is just too prevalent, for several days I was afraid of setting foot on the street.

On *the 16th* I saw Döring in two comedies[3] and found him excellent! Despite that, I was angry to have spent my money. A comedy never completely satisfies me; I always feel as if I've seen something that isn't substantial, isn't complete.

On *the 18th Mendelssohn* came to our house again, was very delighted with Robert's *nouveautées* library, had much to say, and shared with us his serious plan for establishing a sort of music conservatory here, in which *David, Pohlenz, etc.,* and also Robert shall obtain a regular position. Robert is very satisfied with it— for me the whole plan, or rather its implementation, isn't yet completely clear.

The 21st. Concert for the musicians. *Mendelssohn* played, together with me, *Moscheles's E-Flat Major Sonata for 4 Hands;* in addition, among many things of interest that were given was *Beethoven's* incidental music for "Egmont" [by Goethe] with *Mosengeil's* text (well recited by Madame *Dessoir*). I cannot describe the impression that this music made on me today! already the first song by Clärchen, "die Trommel gerührt," wanted to tear my heart out, I had to sob like a child—I don't know everything that passed through my mind, but never has this music (I've already heard it several times before) affected me as deeply as today.

The 24th. Subscription concert. One does notice that *Mendelssohn* stands at the pinnacle; now we really hear good vocal music as well. Finales, terzettos, *etc.* Today it was the finale from *Così fan tutte,* which enchanted me—dear Mozart! he must have meant well with the world, he does the heart so good, and never have I heard anything by him that did not put me in a cheerful mood, and that surely happens to everyone who understands him.

Eroica by *Beethoven* closed the concert. Today I found the march the most beautiful, sublime, grand, as always all of *Beethoven.* I have certain feelings for both of these two great masters, *Beethoven* and *Mozart. Mozart* I love really tenderly, but *Beethoven* I worship like a god who always remains distant to us, however, who never becomes one of us. Now Robert will think, "My wife is a little goose, she wants to be poetic but is so dull." You're right, my darling! it would be good if heaven had only given me a little bit as much intelligence and soul as I have feeling for everything beautiful and noble.

The 26th. Concert by the old *Sophie Schröder,* with the assistance of her daughter [Wilhelmine Schröder-Devrient] and *Tichatscheck,* and in addition *Mendelssohn.* The old 65-year-old woman conquered everyone; never have we heard such declaiming, but also never has a declamation so agitated the entire audience as this one. "Die Glocke" by Schiller was the last thing she recited—the people cheered. *Devrient* and *Tichatscheck* had chosen arias from *Rienzi* by *Wagner*[4] that did not make any impression at all, and only at the end was *Devrient* with a few lieder able to regain her usual justice and appreciation by the audience. *Mendelssohn* played his *D Minor* Concerto, but was not energetic, as one could see most clearly in the cadenza, which did not emerge from *Mendelssohn* the way we usually know him.

On *the 28th Doehler* gave a concert before a very small audience, and did not satisfy even it at all. He played in such a flat way, so lacking in spirit and soul, and the whole man is so dreary and superficial that one doesn't care to remember him. When he

Marriage Diary III 183

was here 7 years ago he may well have played better, but ever a feeble light, he has now collapsed into himself.

The 29th. Visit from *Devrient*—as always charmingly kind-hearted! if only she did not always have such a collection of admirers following her. One of them[5] she really wants to marry now—incidentally it's quite possible that for her it's only a joke.

In the evening we rehearsed for the first time the quintet Robert has just now completed, which is a magnificent work, and also extremely *brilliant* and effective. It didn't yet go the way Robert probably intended, but I think it should improve later on and already look forward to the next time I shall hear it.

Robert also had the First Quartet played, in order to listen to it once more before delivering it to the printer. It delighted me indescribably, and only now do I begin to find any enjoyment from quartet music, since up to now, I must admit openly, this music generally bored me, I couldn't discover the beauty in it.

On *the 30th Hesse* from *Breslau* visited us; I played a few things, *he* nothing. He is here to perform his symphony.

This month ended with a disagreeable incident involving our maid whom we had to part with immediately, because she has robbed us most shamefully. Thus pleasure and pain, poetry and prose, constantly alternate in our life. But along with everything I really love my Robert, always right out of the depth of my soul, and this poetry does remain eternal!—

On the 17th of February 1843				[RS]

Clara is in Dresden, to visit her relatives. Her father's disposition has suddenly changed,[6] and I am happy in my Clara's soul. Because parents remain parents and one only has them once.

The past months in general were eventful. Whatever life brings in the way of small sorrows will soon be drowned out by music. Thus we have often been quite happy along with various worries about our domestic life. Because we spend more than we earn. But hope looms even in this respect. The founding of the conservatory will surely be profitable for us as well; also as a musician I look forward to its beginning. It will surely be a support for good music and a significant influence on the whole education of German youth. Currently employed as teachers are Mendelssohn, David, Hauptmann, Pohlenz, Becker, and I. Later on Clara probably will be as well, when they, as they say, can offer her a proper [salary].

I have spent many intimate hours with Mendelssohn; all the external honors that have come his way only make him more accessible, more modest. He also may well feel that he is now at the peak of his fame, that he can hardly ascend any higher. Therefore I've occasionally sensed a trace of mourning in him, which he never had before. How happy I am to belong to the beautiful blossoming times that we now have. Everywhere there is a stirring for the good in music; the participation of the public is extraordinary; much will yet come from here.

The public is also beginning to be interested in my work. I noticed this with pleasure in a *matinée* that we gave privately.[7] We must save the announcement. We made many friends on this occasion. Clara was a hostess and played incomparably well.

In the last months I have been working [on] a quartet for pianoforte with violin, etc.; a trio for pianoforte, violin, and violoncello; and finally variations for 2 pianofortes, 2 violoncellos, and horn.[8] The first two I wanted to give to my Clara as a present for Christmas, but was not able to finish the trio completely, and because of working too much I had come down with a nervous weakness that scared us. But heaven has protected me, and Clara's most affectionate care has given me comfort.

Clara has written a series of smaller pieces,[9] more delicate and richly musical in their invention than she's ever achieved before. But having children and a husband who constantly improvises does not fit together with composing. She lacks the ongoing exercise, and that often bothers me, because many a heart-felt thought thus gets lost that she does not manage to execute. Clara herself knows her primary occupation to be a mother, however, so that I believe she is happy under these conditions, which just simply cannot be changed.

Marie grows from one day to the next. A dear child, our greatest joy. Speech progresses only slowly. But Christmas already gave her great pleasure.

We had a visit from Elise List, before and after Christmas. The second time she was different from when she had left the first time. It's her good fortune that she had understood that she lacks what is most important for art—a warm heart that can sacrifice everything to art. It's a shame about the beautiful voice; but that appears to come only from the throat. With her, intellect predominates completely. So now she's given up on being a singer, with great pain I believe. But it is to her advantage.

Of other visitors there have been a lot since November: *Hesse* from Breslau, the pianist *Voss* from Strelitz, Madame and Fräulein *Parish* from Hamburg, for whom we once gave a musical evening, *Helsted* from Copenhagen, the pianist *Schulhoff* from Prague, the composer *von Alvensleben,* the composer *Schladebach* from Stettin, Madame *Goldschmidt* from Hamburg with a talented boy, *Nauenburg* from Halle, *Kittl* from Prague, an acquaintance of Mendelssohn's from *Java,* the organist *Franz* from Halle, an interesting and modest musician, and finally *Berlioz*.

If only I had the time to talk in greater detail about some things; but I progressively lose my facility in writing letters of the alphabet—I always want to write only music.

Berlioz, of course, was the most interesting for me. I saw him for the first time in a Euterpe concert. A friendly encounter. The following day, the 31st of January, was the 1st rehearsal. He conducts extremely well. Much that is intolerable in his music, but certainly extraordinarily imaginative, even full of genius. He often strikes me like the powerless King Lear himself.[10] A trace of weakness is even noticeable in his otherwise distinguished face; it's around the mouth and chin. For sure, Paris has spoiled him, also the dissolute life of young people there. He now travels with a Mlle. *Recio* who apparently is more than his concert singer.[11] Unfortunately he doesn't speak German at all and thus we didn't talk much. I had imagined him to be a livelier, more temperamental person. There is something hearty in his laughter. Otherwise he is a Frenchman, drinks wine only with water, and eats stewed fruit.

I had an interesting evening at the Voigts'. Unfortunately, Clara was so indisposed that she couldn't go there, and thus Mendelssohn played the quintet at sight, making my heart laugh inside my body. Another evening we spent at Äckerlein's [vault], a prenuptial celebration for the wedding of Agnes Fleischer and Moritz Semmel, the brother of Therese [Fleischer].[12]

Hirschbach gave a soiree, but is unable to arouse any response. He still lacks the fundamentals of art too much; he resembles Berlioz.

On the 13th of January a letter from the old man [Wieck] in Dresden arrived unexpectedly; later he himself.

I trust that my Clara will return happily tonight.

[CS]

The 18th. I want to report a few other things yet about my stay in Dresden, above all that I was with you always and every minute,

Marriage Diary III 187

and only the thought that it makes my father happy to have me with him—a pleasure he has long done without, it's surely his own fault—could induce me to stay there so long. Incidentally, all these days went by very restlessly; Father always busy with pupils, above all with *Marie* [Wieck], an affectionate, interesting child, and *Alwin* [Wieck], who seems to be turning into quite a capable person. *Marie* plays most delightfully, but what always bothered me about her playing is the displeasure that seems to sound in every tone; yet I'm supposed to have done it that way too, and now can well imagine how terrible that may have been for father at times. *Alwin* was very diligent, but his playing lacks purity and delicacy; he plays the way he often is as yet, *roughly,* with the exception of only one piece, the *Elegy* by *Ernst,* which father made him study. That he has sometimes played in public happened without father's permission, because he knows quite well that Alwin is still far from being ready to step before the public. *Marie,* however, is soon supposed to appear publicly—it's the same for her as for me in childhood—she has no fear of playing, only of curtsying. By the way, Alwin also plays the piano quite prettily. The two little girls [Marie and Cäcilie Wieck] I've really taken to heart, they're a dear couple of children—also the mother [Clementine Wieck] behaved as sincerely as she possibly can, since there is a certain coldness in the entire *Fechtner* family. Father was, as one can well imagine, excessively affectionate and friendly toward me—heaven be praised that it went that way. Robert was so gentle and dear toward me during the entire time, once again showed me his beautiful, noble heart so clearly, that had I never loved him, I would have to now—but of course I've long been familar with that heart down to its deepest depths. I love you unspeakably, my Robert, and you will have to hear that often yet!—

On *the 12th* I finally saw 2 acts of the great *Rienzi* [by Wagner], which has driven all of Dresden crazy.[13] I cannot pronounce a judgment about the details after one hearing, but it made an impression on me that I would not seek to have a second time. My entire reaction was *displeasure*, more I cannot say. The same feeling repeated itself when I got to know *Wagner* personally; a man who never stops talking about himself, is most arrogant, and constantly laughs in a whining tone.

On *the 13th* I took *Marie* [Wieck] to see *Präziosa* [by Weber], but the performance was far worse than what one could have found in a provincial town.

On *the 14th* Father had invited a party of connoisseurs to hear Robert's quintet, which we then actually played twice in a row. *Schubert, Kummer,* and two others accompanied me, so that it was a pleasure—I wish Robert had heard it. The quintet did not lack its effectiveness, but rather enchanted the entire group of listeners. Father is now aflame for Robert's compositions.

On *the 15th* we played the quintet once more at *Serre's* because of some musical ladies—Frau *von Lüttichau,* Countess *Benckendorff,* and still others. The gentlemen played less well, they were dead tired because of rehearsals for *Berlioz's* second concert.

In the evening I enjoyed myself with *Freischütz* [by Weber], which I had not seen since my childhood. *Devrient* was great as always, and *Tichatscheck* warmed one's heart with his melting voice.

The 16th was dedicated to my family, and the *17th* led me back into the arms of my Robert, who was probably also a bit happy to have his old one again. *Marie* [Schumann] had been unwell the entire time, but soon improved, and seemed to recognize me again joyfully. Robert thinks she missed me. How gratifying it is already to feel loved by such a tiny creature!—

Madame Lallemant asked me so fervently to give her daughter lessons that I've decided to do that and started with the first lesson on *the 20th.*

For 3 days I was really very unwell, most likely as a result of the

Marriage Diary III

189

many kinds of excitement in Dresden. I had to miss the concert for the poor on the *23rd,* which I regretted mainly because of the *Offertorium* by *Berlioz,* which is supposed to make an extraordinary impression.

On *the 27th* for *Berlioz's* sake we played the quintet by Robert at our house, also Robert had 2 quartets played for him; he [Berlioz] was unwell, nevertheless he could have behaved more friendly and sincerely if it were art that inspires his soul. He is cold, indifferent, peevish, not the sort of artist I love,—I cannot help myself. Robert is of a different opinion and has taken him completely to heart, which I cannot understand. As far as his music is concerned, there I do agree with Robert; it is full of interest and imagination, although I simply cannot conceal that this is not music that gives me pleasure, and I do not yearn for *more.* Forgive me, my Robert, but why shouldn't I say what's in my heart.

Parish Alvars gave a well-attended concert with the *Levys;* I was not there.

The household gave me much unpleasantness this month, I often had to change nursemaids and had much trouble. Those are the dark sides, and it has to be that way! I do have enough happiness with my Robert and child.

March 1843

The 2nd. Gewandhaus concert. A symphony by *Gade*[14] interested us the most, although it did not entirely fulfill our expectations. The *scherzo* is probably the most original of the whole thing, in the rest there is a great deal of *Schubert,* few of his own thoughts; every movement turns on just one idea, which gets to be tiresome. I believe *Gade* will soon be finished; his talent seems to stretch only as far as one particular *genre,* but he must soon be exhausted, since the Nordic national character (the *genre* I'm referring to) quickly becomes *monotonous*, just like all national music.

The 9th was the 100-year jubilee of the Gewandhaus concerts, where compositions by the chief conductors of the concerts for the past 100 years were performed consecutively; inconceivably, *Schulz, Pohlenz,* and one other (I've forgotten the name) were completely ignored. After the concert the Gewandhaus administration gave a banquet for the orchestra members and many other musicians; there was no lack of toasts, but *Pohlenz,* who had conducted the concerts for 10 years, was overlooked here as well—unfortunately, this inexcusable error had the most deplorable consequences—the insult brought *Pohlenz* a quick death, the other day he was found dead in bed as the result of a stroke. There was great sympathy, the entire city was moved by it; *Pohlenz* had many friends, since he was of excellent character and never seems to have done harm to anyone. Now everyone picks on the administration, *Mendelssohn* and *David*—the latter surely without justification. The administration (*Schleinitz* primarily) for once did deserve such a reprimand.

On *the 13th* a great number of friends accompanied *Pohlenz's* body to the graveyard—Robert also went with them.

In the afternoon at Härtel's we tried out Robert's exceptionally charming variations for 2 pianofortes, 2 violoncellos, and one horn. It went fairly well after playing through several times but the sound was by far not gentle enough,—while I feel how Robert had imagined it, one cannot expect that of others; even *Mendelssohn* approached the whole thing much too physically for my taste.[15]

Robert has now started his oratorio "Paradise and the Peri," and it progresses rapidly. He has already played the first part of it for me from the sketches, and I think it is the most magnificent thing he has ever written; but he works on it body and soul, with a glow-

Marriage Diary III 191

ing heat that sometimes makes me fear it might do him harm, and yet it also makes me happy; then again I think it must also please God that a person creates something so noble, and therefore He will protect my Robert!—

On *the 17th* Father came here for a few days, where we then made several afternoon excursions, as in the old days.

On *the 22nd* he left. In the afternoon we went to a *dinée* [sic] at *Schletter's*—unfortunately I had to leave the table, sitting too long isn't good for me right now. For me *Schletter* just doesn't really fit into all that luxury—he is all right, but exceedingly materialistic and as a representative of the Leipziger *haute volée* just doesn't have sufficient refinement.

The 23rd. Visit of a boring, gossipy Silesian named[16]

The 27th was the great day that was supposed to decide the fate of many musical talents. The conservatory will now begin in earnest; the auditions were difficult days for the teachers, although many interesting, even ridiculous things happened to them as well. Altogether many real talents came to light, most of whom requested scholarships.[17]

In the evening was the *Requiem* by *Mozart* honoring *Pohlenz's* widow. I wasn't there, also missed the two last Gewandhaus concerts—I no longer like to be with people right now, the pressure I must inflict on myself due to my pregnancy makes me sick.

On *the 26th Emma Meyer* and [Albert] *Leppoc* had a wedding shower; I attended for an hour, to demonstrate my friendship for her. How I hate such festivities! I find it much more fitting to hold such a celebration only among one's own family and a few dear friends. On such occasions I always think back on our own wedding eve and engagement day with twice as much joy—so few of us were together and yet we were so happy and inwardly most joyful. Just the formality that goes with such a big party, along with the ceremonies, the speeches about themselves that the bridal couple has to put up with, the fatigue that must follow it, all that and much more really cannot allow them to have any joyous feelings. But of course not everyone feels the way we do, it may well make many a girl happy to see herself once as the queen of a festival; not all marriages are bonded by such intimate love and devotion for one another as is ours—for us, of course, any external interference would only have been disturbing. But enough about this matter! when I get onto this theme, I can't find an end because of my happiness. I did not go to the wedding—I was afraid of the Jewish ceremonies, which I could not have witnessed without displeasure.

Marie has been quite sick for several days, and I feel terribly sorry for the poor child, who can't even say what's wrong with her. I hope this will soon be over!—

April 1843

Robert completed the first part of his *Peri* at the end of last month, and soon now will proceed to the second; unfortunately, the nasty journal has already kept him from everything for a week, which puts him in a really bad mood—why am I not a writer? how much I could help him, more than I ever could with my piano playing. Nowadays I barely play at all; during the day it's impossible because it disturbs Robert, and in the evening I'm always too tired for it, and my condition just makes the playing too difficult.

On *the 5th* Robert began giving lessons at the conservatory— I have no idea how one can teach 6 students at the same time.

In the evening we played Robert's *E-Flat Major Quartet* for the first time at our house, and again I was really enchanted by this beautiful work, which is so youthful and fresh, as if it were his first.

On *the 18th* the most boring of all boring people, [Carl] *Kloss*

Marriage Diary III   193

from [Eperjes], gave an organ concert that simply wasn't very edi-
fying. But much more so was a concert for the *Bach* monument
that *Mendelssohn* gave on the morning of the 23rd in the Gewandhaus. He himself played the *D Minor* Concerto by *Bach* with
customary and yet always surprising mastery. In addition we heard
many beautiful works of *Bach*, which constituted the entire program.[18] After the concert the monument in front of the Thomas
School was unveiled, and surprised us with its good taste—simple
and yet worthy of the old *Bach;* his head in a niche actually appears friendly, in addition, on three sides there are thoughtful *bas-
reliefs* designed by *Bendemann* (who himself came from Dresden
for this festival) and executed by the sculptor [Knaur]. Various
speeches were given, of which one did not understand much, however, as usual on such occasions. After this ceremony *Mendelssohn,* in honor of *Bach's* only surviving grandson (he himself, a
very old man, had come from Berlin with his family), organized a
luncheon in the *Hôtel de Bavière* attended almost exclusively by
artists. I myself dared to participate in this whole ceremony, and
made it through to the end.

On *the 24th* we were about to hear Sabine *Heinefetter* in *Fidelio*
[by Beethoven], but the rest of the mediocre cast and therefore
the two-thaler *entrée* scared us away, and we cautiously went back
to our house.

On *the 25th* I had a difficult hour, but really only one, until the
second little daughter [Elise Schumann] appeared at 9:30, after
which all pain was forgotten. This time it went easier than the first
time; also, considering the circumstances, I was exceptionally well
throughout the entire confinement, and could breathe fresh air
already on the 11th day. I was amused that our little daughter was
born on the same morning as the youngest princess of England,[19]
only the little princess a few hours earlier, which is also quite appropriate.

I had especially wished for a boy for myself and Robert, and surely my Robert was inwardly disappointed that it didn't turn out that way, but he is too good not to like this child as well, if only for my sake, and of course we are still young, in due time heaven will give him a boy who will cheer his paternal heart.

At the end of this month I have yet to mention a few domestic annoyances that were more unusual than the customary daily ones. We suddenly had to discharge our cook because of *malice* and rudeness; soon after her departure we discovered the loss of 50 bottles of wine from the cellar, which seemed to be forcefully broken into, and so many other thefts were soon discovered that we realized we had been dealing with a cunning thief. In addition the embezzlement of money was discovered, and thus the girl was arrested on orders of the court. Nothing has been decided so far, but in any case the girl may not remain here.

We had various visitors. *Herr* and *Madame Wartel* from *Paris* wanted to give a concert, but the season is too advanced and so they left. Herr *Wartel* is *supposed* to sing especially Schubert's lieder very beautifully—I suspect in the French manner, which I cannot find beautiful at all. Madame *Wartel* is supposed to play the piano prettily, and has a dear, pleasant exterior.[20]

Robert has completed the second part of the *Peri*, but has not told me much about it. I look forward immensely to the performance in the fall, where I will once again luxuriate in my Robert's music, which is really like no other that I know. And now give me a kiss my darling, even if you don't agree with what I have said.

May 1843

Our poor diary would like to request that you soon finish the *Peri*, since its interest completely disappears when you don't write in it.

On *the 7th* we let our youngest little daughter be baptized, and

Marriage Diary III 195

gave her the name Elisa; godparents were my aunt [Emilie] *Carl* with Herr *Robert Friese,* the wife (Robert's sister-in-law) of City Councillor *Fleischer,* with the businessman Herr *Voigt* and my father; the latter, however, merely inscribed in the church register.

On *the 9th* the violinist *Bazzini* visited us, an unassuming, modest artist, and *Sigmund Goldschmidt,* a pianist but an unpleasant one. He played several times in Robert's room—the poor instrument groaned and we did too; in addition, he himself is a boring person who isn't one bit of an artist.

On *the 13th,* concert by *Bazzini,* who is a great artist. Robert and I were in agreement that we haven't heard such a great as well as satisfying violinist for a long time. His technique is eminent, his tone extraordinarily gentle and beautiful, his performance so natural, so youthfully inspired, and his compositions, while not exactly very deep, still better than many by the newer virtuosos. Robert has written quite nicely about him in the journal.[21]

He didn't have much of an audience, and those who were there did not know how to appreciate him. *David* and *Mendelssohn* did not treat him very nicely—how intrinsically nasty envy is, and even how much nastier with an artist like *Mendelssohn.*

On *the 19th* Father arrived with his entire family. My brother Alwin had already cleared out secretly a few weeks earlier, which saddened me, because I'm convinced that he cannot make much progress in this world with his violin. So now he sits here and acquires debts, and incidentally is not a likable person at all, which makes it more difficult for him to earn a living. Although Father has not deprived him of his support, he has proposed a trial year before he can again make any demand for that. He wants to prove that he can exist without his father and only through his violin (Father wanted to make him into a piano teacher,[22] which actually was the reason that led to all kinds of squabbling). I worry about him, and that makes my heart quite heavy.

I haven't seen much of father, he was busy from morning to night with instruments and with *Marie*, who had to try them all out. I am so accustomed to a beautiful, peaceful life with my Robert that I couldn't stand 4 weeks of being around Father anymore. This terrible unrest, this restlessness of the mind as well as the body, lets neither him nor his environment get any calm enjoyment of life.

My sister *Marie* played a few things for me; she plays prettily, but all of it still sounds terribly pedantic, which considering that she is a child cannot be otherwise. True emotion, the deepest sensibility, awakens only with love; that I claim since I have experienced it for myself.

A young pianist from Italy, *Angelo Russo,* was here, but because of the advanced season was unable to have a concert. He visited Robert, but did not get him to like him, because he showed himself to be arrogant and ignorant. His playing, according to Father, is supposed to be most mediocre.

On *the 25th,* Ascension Day, Robert completed the sketch for the third and last part of the *Peri* and delighted me with it; the music is as heavenly as the text! what a treasure of emotion and poetry there is in it, in the music as well as the text!

On *the 28th* Robert began to orchestrate the 3rd part,—a lot of work yet. If only he wouldn't have to strain his eyes so very much with it, that often makes me really very anxious!—

Father left yesterday; Mother was here with me several times with the sisters, who were happy with our little darling Marie. She is now starting to talk, and is our greatest pleasure. *Elisa* now is still vegetating in the stupid first three months, but grows, to our joy, and is a strong, healthy child. She doesn't create as much trouble or worry for me as did *Marie* during the first three months.

The 29th. my brother [Alwin Wieck] has received an appoint-

Marriage Diary III   197

ment in the orchestra of *Reval* [now Tallinn, Estonia] —a stone is lifted from my heart. I've worried more about his existence than he himself.

June 1843   [RS]
On 28th June 1843

During the interval that I wrote nothing in the diary, much has happened and been created. On the 25th of April, at 20 minutes past 9 o'clock in the morning, my dear Clara gave birth to a little girl, whom at the baptism we named Elisa. Her development progresses more slowly than with Marie, and I also believe that the child does not hear well. But one must be patient and thankful for eveything that God brings.

On the *16th of June* my "Peri" was completely finished after many days of strenuous work. That was a great pleasure for the Schumann couple. Except for several oratorios by Löwe, that mostly have a didactic aftertaste, however, I know nothing like it in music. I don't like to write and speak about my own works; my wish is that they may have good effects in the world and assure me a loving remembrance from my children. In the winter I hope to perform it and then will also try myself out in conducting for the first time.

The conservatory gives all of us work and worry; but also pleasure. I've taken on piano teaching only *ad interim* and later on will create a different position for myself. The number of students, etc., amounts to just 40 right now.

The Peri and somewhat the conservatory have thus laid claim to all of my time in the past three months. Little was left over for other things.

On my (33rd) birthday, the 8th of June, Clara as always gave me presents.[23] The reason for her melancholy, as I perceived it that day and the following ones, I know quite well; she would like to overwhelm her family with gifts; but all good fortune cannot come at the same time, and we want to thankfully acknowledge what we have: talent, health, children that grow well, a magnificent attachment—that is also something and cannot be compensated for with wealth. But of course we must also think about it and about the security of my existence, and surely that will come also.

To our joy Clara's mother surprised us on the *8th of June;* she stayed for only three days. Marie is still talking about her. The child gives us much joy: she shows an unusually quick mind and a gentle, affectionate heart.

I started the Peri on the *23rd of February;* so I was finished in not quite four months and must really give myself credit for my diligence.

Visitors who were at our house: *Berlioz,* about whom Clara has written already; Gebhard *von Alvensleben,* who gave a musical matinee; Madame *Hensel,* Mendelssohn's sister, whose eyes radiate soul and depth; *L. Huth,* who God only knows how has become kapellmeister in Sondershausen. The director *Schadow* from Düsseldorf we saw briefly; also *Bendemann.* Baron von *Haugk* from here, an enthusiastic music lover, at whose house we reveled a long night away. *Kloss,* the restless, uncomfortable one. The *Wartel* couple from Paris. Sabine *Heinefetter. Bazzini. S. Goldschmidt* from Prague, *Netzer* from Vienna—two of the most boring people. *Russo,* a stupid Jewish boy. The music teacher *Adam* from Dresden. A. *Bürck* from Weimar. J. *Rietz* from Düsseldorf, the most interesting visit for a long time, a true artist it seems to me. The kapellmeister *Gläser* from Copenhagen and Madame *Simonsen. A. von Villers.* Also Frege has returned from her Italian trip.

The 21st, the longest day of the year, I spent quite intimately

Marriage Diary III

199

at Mendelssohn's with a bottle of wine; we really got everything out in the open, and I left him as always feeling refreshed.

Clara is now putting her lieder[24] and many piano compositions in order. She always wants to make progress; but on the right *Marie* hangs onto her dress, Elise also makes work, and the husband sits absorbed in Peri thoughts. So then, through joy and sorrow ever forward, my Clara, and love me always, as you have always loved me.—

July and August 1843   [CS]

These two months had few interesting events; the most interesting were the visits of the *Viardots* and of *Doctor Krüger* from *Emden,* who is a bright man and a capable musician, especially on the organ, which by the way he learned in 3 years. He spent much time with us, and Robert and he established a mutual affinity for each other. On *the 13th of July* we accompanied him as far as *Halle*—he then drove further to Berlin and back home under the yoke of a schoolteacher.

From Halle we made an excursion with the song composer *Franz* to the bathing resort (!) *Ober-Roeblingen,* which actually lies on a beautiful blue lake[25] in which swimming is magnificent; we found a few Leipzigers there, but besides that the region is so unattractive that one can enjoy being there for only one day. We returned to Halle in the evening and on

the 14th took a most delightful tour on the water with *Franz* and a male quartet; this excursion was the most beautiful on our trip.

Franz is a great favorite of Robert's, therefore I also want to be discreet with my opinion of him.

At the *end of July* I finally saw my dear Pauline (*Viardot*) again, and found her as always the old, most kind, and most genial of all female artists. She spent only 2 days with us, and we also liked him [Louis Viardot] very much. He doesn't seem like a typical Frenchman to me—much more serious and solid and affectionate toward Pauline, who is exactly the same toward him. Pauline has made significant progress as a virtuosa, as she demonstrated in the concert she gave on *August 19,* yet her choice of pieces did not appeal to us and Robert occasionally found something *not noble* in her voice (whose range is 3 full octaves, equally strong.) A pity that such a thoroughly musical creature as Pauline, who certainly has the sense for really good music, completely sacrifices her taste to the public, and thus follows in the footsteps of all the ordinary Italians.—At our house she sang a Spanish and an Arabic romance for us, which interested me the most; she makes an extraordinary impression with the power of her voice, and I've never yet heard a woman's voice like that. Her concert was very well attended and the audience enthusiastic, only disturbed in the middle of the concert by a fire alarm. I played the *D Minor Sonata* by *Beethoven* and with *Mendelssohn* Robert's very charming Duo (*Andante with variations*—formerly accompanied by two celli and a horn, but now set only for two pianos because of the difficulty of performance), which also was well liked and would have been liked even better if the fire alarm hadn't caused the audience to miss a little of the musical conception and calm, which is exactly what is needed for responding to such an intimate, tender-hearted piece. This piece was gratifying after all the interminable coloratura flourishes that just are not music.

On *the 20th* Pauline left after giving me a beautiful shawl and taking one of my old ones in exchange. *Mendelssohn* was indignant that Pauline did not even thank him for all his efforts, but surely that did not happen with any malice on her part—her head and heart were already in Paris.

Marriage Diary III

On *the 1st of August* Father also came here again and visited me one evening, when I had to play for him. *Marie* [Wieck] came along as well. He also reimbursed us 50 thalers for the Graf piano, which I would have preferred not to accept, but of course Robert had already given it out of his pocket in the first place!

I have received good news about Alwin [Wieck] from *Helsinki,* where he arrived after a cruise of 14 days,—he seems to be earning money! of course one must wait to hear what follows.

At the end of July I started to do the piano arrangement of the "*Peri*"—a job that gives me great satisfaction.

Professor Fischof from *Vienna* visited us here and had dinner at our house on *the 27th;* it is pleasant to converse with him, only he just talks so much about *himself.*

Otherwise we just lived rather quietly for ourselves; I gave quite a few lessons; twelve to Frau *von Hagemeister,* a *Polish* woman who did not want to learn anything but plays the most difficult things with a dreadful touch. She left at the end of August. A Scottish woman from *Edinburgh* arrived here in order to obtain piano instruction from me; she started the *25th of August*—plays rather prettily, diligent and solid.

Our children have continually been well; little Elise becomes prettier and more intelligent from day to day—there is something really gentle and easygoing in her gestures.

Our marital life together has as always been affectionate and happy, except for a few little storms, which incidentally were my fault, that have passed, however. I worry about our future, want now, while we are young, to earn money, to accumulate a small amount of capital, while Robert is of a different opinion and cannot make up his mind about that. But he has calmed me down by promising that next winter we will certainly undertake something big.

I have often made you sad already, my good Robert, with this worry of mine, but surely it always occurred with a very heavy heart and after much conflict. If I didn't love you so inexpressibly, I wouldn't worry myself so greatly, but thus my highest pleasure consists of the thought of seeing you live completely for your art and without any mundane worries, and this I must finally accomplish if I am to be satisfied and happy.

Let me kiss you, my most intimately beloved Robert, and do believe that in joy and sorrow my love for you will always remain endless.

The 21st of November 1843   [RS]

Clara is still in Dresden, where she gave a concert last night; it seems so quiet and desolate in the house when she isn't there. Then I reach for you, dear diary; much joy and sorrow spans the time since I have written anything in it. But words and letters are difficult for me, and in fifteen minutes at the piano I can express more than when I write whole pages. Therefore only about the external life, and what it has brought. The most important thing recently was a proposal from the Härtels to take over the editing of their journal.[26] I haven't yet decided the matter; as happily as this can turn out, I nevertheless would sometimes think to myself, "Shall I then never be able to live entirely in my beloved art?" If Heaven would only grant me this favor for once—and while I am still young. Because the blossoms of youth will disappear and learning will always be more difficult in old age.

Otherwise almost everything for the last months has revolved around the *Peri,* and my Clara surely thought me to be an egotist sometimes, when I only mentioned it. But thoughts of a more serious kind attach themselves to this work, for which, if I were to tell you all of them, you surely would not judge me adversely.

Marriage Diary III 203

With great sacrifice and love Clara has prepared the piano arrangement of the *Peri,* and externally I have thanked her only a little for that; but I can appreciate her effort and love and I have often felt moved and have turned away when I saw her working so eagerly at the piano.

Now the 1st performance will take place on the 4th of December, if all goes well. I have also tried being a conductor and can see that I have a knack for that. My nearsightedness handicaps me the most, and later I will surely have to obtain glasses.

Incidentally I haven't been composing at all because of the Peri work. But a couple of opera plans occupied me very much: "The Veiled Prophet of Khorassan" from Lalla Rookh [by Thomas Moore], and "Till Eulenspiegel," which I have already outlined for myself.[27] The next thing shall be an opera, and I'm fired up about it.

Published during this time were a book of lieder, "Frauenliebe," by Chamisso, and the Quintet; soon the Variations for 2 Pianos, the big Heine Lieder Cycle, a book of Ballades, and a Quartet for piano will come out: by Clara a book of very intimate lieder.

Clara has already reported about the months of July and August; from several notes I remember as yet: in August: visit by *Anacker* from Freiberg, whom I got to know for the 1st time; lively man with expressive head, whose eyes manifest determination and efficiency. By *L. Anger,* who has now become the organist in Lüneburg; a former walking companion of mine; inferior talent and full of vanity, but not without worthwhile qualities. Often played billiards with *Mendelssohn. Franz* from Halle and his love story;[28] a significant character.

On the *1st of September* happily celebrated Marie's 2nd birthday.

Recently she was disfigured by a nasty skin rash; but it has already improved. Elise grows more lovable from day to day.

On the *4th of September Landsberg* from Rome, whom I had already met earlier. On the 5th *Julius Miller,* the well-known old tenor, a dangerous schemer I believe.

On *the 7th* Clara left with Marie for several days to visit her mother in Berlin; during that time I went on a walking tour with Julius Becker to the Col[l]mberg, etc., in magnificent weather; there was a peculiar melancholic attraction not to have one's dear wife along and yet to know that one is loved by her; her soul accompanied me constantly.

On *the 11th* Clara returned. On the 13th we celebrated Clara's 24th birthday quite amiably. Two little children already? They came to the bed early with floral wreaths. Later Mendelssohn, David, Hauptmann, and by chance Heinrich Dorn. We played a little music.

On *the 14th Streicher* from Vienna with a young composer Pauer. We didn't see them.

On *the 15th Kirchner,* a talented young musician in whom I have always been very interested, went to Winterthur in Switzerland, where he obtained a good organist position.

On the 18th new misfortune in the Carls' house. He had to take to his heels. Carelessness, kindness, and *far too much* reliance on an invisible helping hand have brought him to that.

Marx from Berlin. The music director *Skraup* from Prague, *Fischhof* from Vienna. *Hiller's* arrival.

On *the 25th,* examination at the conservatory; my best pupils are Fräulein *Jacobi* from Altenburg, *Preuss* from Gotha, *Ergmann* from Breslau. Almost no composition talents can be found.

A ball at Schletter's. An evening at Dr. Härtel's

On *the 1st of October,* the 1st subscription concert under Hiller's direction.

Dorpat [CS]

The 18th of February/1st of March 1844[29]

Here in Dorpat [Tartu, Estonia] I can finally get to our somewhat neglected diary; it will be difficult for me on the one hand, because there is much I have to catch up with, and I will not be able to do it completely because there is much I've again forgotten. Today I will try to report up to the day of our departure.

November 1843

This month was a very restless one; I traveled back and forth to Dresden 3 times, Robert had many *Peri* rehearsals, and so both of us were always in motion.

On *the 20th* in Dresden I gave a very well attended concert at the *Hôtel de Pologne,* and played among other things Robert's Quintet with *Schubert, Kummer,* and two other gentlemen whose names I cannot remember. It was exceptionally well liked and was received with the loudest testimonials of applause; I was sorry that Robert did not hear it, because he surely would have been happy with our collaboration. In the same concert Marie (my sister) also made her first public *debut* and specifically with the *E-Flat Sonata by Moscheles* together with myself. She played very well, but was very anxious, which made me worry about the future, because it cannot be foreseen that the anxiety will diminish rather than increase. Incidentally, we had much fun with her, because she did not want to come out until the last minute, and only Father's permission *not* to curtsy in front of the audience enabled her to come out with downcast eyes, and also to leave in the same way at the conclusion of the piece, which was received with the greatest applause. But Father was happy, which I granted him in my entire soul; surely he has long wished for this moment, and once again has earned some joy for his many efforts.

On *the 23rd* yearning drove me back to Leipzig, even though the second concert was supposed to be on the 30th. I found everyone quite well, my little children happy, little Marie with dark red little cheeks, as usual in the evening.

The 24th was a little farewell soirée at *Mendelssohn's,* who wanted to leave the next morning. He seemed very distressed and saddened to be parting from Leipzig, but still played several sonatas by *Beethoven* wonderfully, *Dr. Frege's wife* (with what seemed a heavy melancholic heart) also sang a few lieder by *Mendelssohn,* and I too played a few things.

The rehearsals of the *Peri* gave me endless pleasure; I always lap up that music with truly sensual delight.

On *the 29th* I drove to Dresden again, where various ordeals awaited me.

The 30th was the second concert, the applause just as great as, if not even more than, the first time, and the audience always a fine, well-selected one.

December 1843

On *the 1st* I again drove to Leipzig, actually in order to hear an orchestral rehearsal (which I thought the last) for the *Peri,* but unfortunately it was on the

2nd in the afternoon, when I had to leave again exactly at the same time, since in the evening I was supposed to play in Dresden at court. In addition to this inherently great ordeal, I almost had the bad luck of missing the steam train; with the greatest urgency and effort, half unconscious, breathless, on my feet that threat-

Marriage Diary III   *207*

ened to break down any moment, I got to the car just as it was ready to leave. Never will I forget that.

The court concert was brilliant, many titled guests attended! The king and queen spoke with me in a very friendly way, also the duchess of *Cambridge* at whose house in *Hanover* I had played before.[30] At 12 o'clock I returned home and on the 3rd in the morning back again to Leipzig, where my mother from Berlin and Frau Stegmayer expected me.

On *the 4th* Robert performed his *Peri* for the first time (for the benefit of the music conservatory), and at the same time made his first debut as a conductor. The magnificent orchestration had delighted me already in the morning at the rehearsal, and anyone can imagine how happy I was in the evening—words cannot describe it at all. The applause was great, but it was enthusiastic at the second performance, which took place on

the 11th. Robert was acclaimed already when he made his appearance and found a beautiful laurel wreath on the conductor's podium, which consternated him somewhat, but must have given pleasure. He was called back after every section. The most beautiful singing was *Frege's* of the *Peri;* after the virgin's one aria (*Sachs* was out of town, therefore *Frege* had taken over this aria) the public could not resist giving her the loudest applause. Also Herr *Schmidt, Kindermann,* as well as the entire chorus performed most beautifully; everyone sang with body and soul—I did it [inwardly] for all of them! if ever I've wanted to have a beautiful voice, it was now! What I wouldn't have given to be able to sing the *Peri*.

On the day following the first performance the *Härtels* requested the work for publication; Robert sold it to them immediately on the condition that a score of it be printed. The piano arrangement will appear first.

Mother unfortunately could not attend the second performance, she had to leave already on the 5th. After the first performance we all ate together at the *Hôtel de Bavière, Frege* as well; after the second we were there alone with *David,* who behaved in the most friendly way toward Robert, and at the second performance (on that very day) made his big contribution by eliminating the obstacles that the theater had put in the way.

On *the 15th* we had a most merry party at our home, where in our little room we danced into the night. We were happier than if it had been the biggest ball. Our guests were *the Freges, the Seeburgs, the Preussers, Gade, David,* etc. etc. With *Gade* I played his sonata for piano and violin dedicated to me, and with *Hiller Bennett's* overture to the Wood Nymph, in which *Hiller,* however, thought to find more tree trunks than nymphs.

On *the 16th* Robert received a letter of conciliatory content from my father, and thus my most yearned-for wish was fulfilled. Robert was reconciled with my father in Dresden, where we went on

the 19th. From Herr *von Lüttichau,* stage manager of the theater, Robert had received a request to perform his *Peri* on the *23rd* for a benefit concert at the theater, which then also took place, although the performance was not as good as in Leipzig. The participants consisted only of theater members who are happy when they do not have to sing, and thus make no effort whatsoever to penetrate a work. Madame *Kriete* sang the *Peri* well, but not with the same noble feeling as *Frege; Mitterwurzer* was good, *Bielcizsky* bad, however, irresponsibly negligent in preparing himself—I believe at the rehearsal he did not yet know the poem. *Tichatscheck* behaved shabbily, like a *nonartist!* his part wasn't big enough for him, not enough shouting effects, and that's what someone like him wants. The audience was very animated, but I would have wished for a second performance, since only then would the audience have really understood the whole thing, although my dear Robert obtained rich applause already the first time. He con-

Marriage Diary III

209

ducted beautifully, as in Leipzig, with such a quiet attitude that it was a pleasure to see it. *Raimund Härtel* had come from Leipzig for this performance, since he hadn't heard it there.

On *the 24th,* for the presenting of gifts, we stayed at Father's, where we were generously provided for, too. I thought of my dear children quite a bit, whose gift giving I had to postpone.

On *the 26th* we went back to Leipzig, and found little Marie and little Elise to be well.

On *the 31st of December* we gave presents with special pleasure to little Marie, who was overjoyed. On days like that one really feels God's blessing in such children as we have—there cannot be any greater happiness. Later in the evening *Reuter, Wenzel, Herrmann, Teschner* from *Berlin,* and *Lorenz* joined us.

January 1844

We entered the new year with pleasure and cheer—may Heaven protect us and our children in the future as well!—

With the new year our preparations also began for the Petersburg trip, with which Frege stood loyally at my side, tirelessly ran around town with me, generally took great interest, and seemed sincerely pleased that this long-cherished wish of mine should be fulfilled. The most difficult thing about the journey stands before us, the separation from our children.

On *the 18th Pauline* [Schumann] came from Schneeberg to pick up the children; a female relative of [aunt] *Carl,* Pastor *Groebe's* wife, who had been engaged to stay with the children, we did not like at all, she did not handle little Marie at all affectionately and gently; simultaneously Carl [Schumann] wrote that we may send the children to him in Schneeberg, and thus we naturally preferred that decision.

Robert still had much work to do on the *Peri,* which he wanted to deliver before our departure. He still found much to correct in the piano arrangement and did so with untiring zeal. He delivered it to Härtel's the day before our departure—how I look forward to the printed version!

On *the 21st* Pauline took our darlings with her—that was an awful day, as were all that followed in Leipzig. Any paternal and maternal heart can imagine how both of us felt at the time of separation, the pain was indescribable! as they were thus driving away, what a pain that was! may Heaven return these dear children to our arms healthy and well maintained. *Pauline* will certainly nurse and cherish them with total love, what great joy the reunion will be!—

Our departure was ever and ever postponed day after day. God, were those dreadful days without our children!

Father arrived a week before our departure and stayed until the end, when he accompanied us with many friends to the train.

1. Robert and Clara Schumann's Inselstrasse residence in Leipzig.

2. A page from Marriage Diary I (13 September 1840).

3. The singer Sophie Schloss.

4. The sisters Elise and Lina List.

5. *Hammerclavier by Conrad Graf, belonging to Clara and Robert Schumann. Courtesy of the Kunsthistorisches Museum, Vienna.*

6. The Bastei Bridge in the Saxon Alps. Courtesy of the Saxon Landesbibliothek.

7. *The Royal Theater in Copenhagen. Lithograph by C. F. Christensen, ca. 1830, courtesy of the Teatermuseet, Copenhagen.*

8. *A view of Carlsbad from the south.*

9. *Königswart Castle.*

10. Courtyard in Königsberg, showing the entrance to the "Blutgericht."

11. *Adolph Henselt, portrait medallion.*

12. *Nevsky Prospect and the Anichkov Bridge, Petersburg.*

13. View of the city of Tver (Kalinin).

14. Concert program of the Petersburg Philharmonic Society.

15. Honorary diploma given to Clara Schumann.

16. *Ivan's Square in the Kremlin, Moscow. Etching by A. Finlen.*

17. *Ivan's Square from the south. Ink sketch by Robert Schumann. To the left is the Cathedral of the Assumption. To the right is the Bell Tower of Ivan the Great and the bell walls.*

18. Robert Schumann, after a portrait of 1844.

19. *Clara and Marie Schumann, circa 1844.*

Four

THE TRIP TO RUSSIA

25 January – 31 May 1844

[CS]

The 25th. Beginning today I will copy from Robert's travel diary; if we were to write everything down in detail, we would have no time left over, therefore just the notes, as they follow:

June 1844

I will start recording everything experienced during the past 4 months, a huge amount of work; you must be tolerant, dear Robert, if I often merely copy from your notebook.

January 1844

On *Thursday the 25th of January* we departed at 11 o'clock in the morning for Berlin, and arrived there quite bored by the trip at 6:30 at the *Hôtel* de Brandenburg. Mother and *Mendelssohn* with *Gade* soon arrived.

On *Friday the 26th* in the morning we visited the *Mendelssohns* and were received very amicably—it seemed that the air of Leipzig was good for them. *Mendelssohn* surprised me with the dedication for his 6 newest Songs without Words,[1] including also the lovely, gracious Spring Song.[2] We talked together for a long time, also a great deal about *Richard Wagner,* about whose music *Mendelssohn* was quite indignant. Toward the evening he visited Robert and also took him out for a glass of Bavarian beer, which made Robert happy. I stayed with Mother, where Frau *Stegmayer* also visited—she now seems to seek her life's joy in finery—sad consolation for lost peace!—

Saturday the 27th we visited Madame *Schröder-Devrient,* our apartment neighbor. She was amusing as usual and told us many funny stories about Liszt, whom she thoroughly hates with a vengeance.

Further visitors were Marie Lichtenstein (old and cold, as Robert says) and Friedrich Rückert—magnificent head, like that of a legislator. He received us very amiably, inquired with much interest about the *"Peri,"* and invited us to his place in the country in *Neusess* near [Coburg]. I'm happy that Robert has gotten to know this man, whom he has always loved so much as a poet.

With Mother we were for dinner at *Mendelssohn's; Taubert* was there also, but compared to *Mendelssohn* he strikes one as terribly prosaic and insignificant, perhaps he just seemed so to us because he was embarrassed and therefore made a few very senseless remarks.

Toward the evening Devrient came to us to say good-bye, and around 7 o'clock we left very comfortably by mail coach for Königsberg [now Kaliningrad, Lithuania] (after we had had much trouble with our luggage, however). *Mendelssohn* bid adieu to us at the carriage and seemed to take much interest in our trip, for which he heartily wished us the greatest success.

Mother and the children were also at the carriage.

Madame *Mendelssohn* gave me a pair of very pretty wrist warmers, which were very useful.

Throughout the first day the trip to Königsberg was most boring, ugly region, sand everywhere, but on

the 29th in the morning it became somewhat more interesting because of the drive, luggage and all, over the frozen Weichsel [Vistula River], later because of the view from the Nogat [River] to Marienburg [Malbork, Poland], which is very nicely and romanti-

The Trip to Russia   231

cally located on a hill. We crossed the river on foot, then went to the castle and looked at the magnificent *Remter*, completely restored, which made a great impression on us. A privy councillor from Danzig [Gdańsk, Poland], *Heyne*, who was a friendly, cultivated man, joined our company from Marienburg on. Robert conveyed greetings through him to a former colleague *"Tilly"* with whom he had studied in Heidelberg. *Elbing* [Elblag, Poland], *Frauenburg* [Frombork, Poland] were other nice towns that we passed. Interesting was the *Copernicus* Tower in Frauenburg, where the famous astronomer lived, also the place of execution of Kühnapfel, who murdered the bishop of [Ermland]. At 7 o'clock in the evening we arrived in Königsberg and took rooms in the "Deutsches Haus." The first impression unpleasant and dreadful, the inn an old, gray building. At the carriage, reception by Engelhardt, an unpleasant, intrusive man, who in addition strikes me as quite nasty.

On *Tuesday the 30th* in the morning Robert visited *Sobolewski,* who seems to be a spirited, energetic man, but not happy in his position. Later we went to *Schindelmeisser,* where negotiations were pursued with the theater director, and actually in the presence of a number of witnesses, regarding a concert at the theater; a formal contract, to which a trustee (a wealthy landowner) even added his signature. The whole scene that Sobolewski had arranged was ridiculous, although with the intention that the theater director could not cheat us, as he had recently done a number of times with other artists.

On that same morning we visited the *Lobecks,* to whom I am distantly related, and Robert [visited] Herr *Dibowski,* whom I got to know only in passing, but who is supposed to be a great music enthusiast. In the evening Robert went to the *Café National,* whose owner had previously been at *Felsche's* [café] here [in Leipzig].

On *Wednesday the 31st* we made visits to Consul *Adelsohn, Op-*

penheimer, Lork, and the *music director Sämann,* the last of whom has something mean about him, but may well be a capable director. Robert received a visit that made him happy from Civil Councillor *Sabbarth,* with whom he had studied in Heidelberg.—I found fairly good pianofortes at *Gebauer* and *Marthy,* the latter I preferred for the concert. The instrument makers here have [their own] carriages, which was very convenient for me, since I used *Marthy's* carriage a lot. Everyone here moved around on sleighs, but we did not have to suffer much from the cold as yet, although we still had to buy ourselves a big fur blanket and foot warmer for the winter journey.

The midday meal we ate at the inn together with *Sabbarth* and finished with champagne. Robert writes at this point—"peculiar internal discords in the evening on account of the *Lobecks*—Clara much too ignorant for the world and always soupçonnois"[3]—I no longer know what gave rise to this reproach. In the evening we were at the *Lobecks'* and found a nice circle there, all of them open to each other, which probably was partly due to the hostess, who is a happy, cheerful woman. The music teacher Kahle, a sophisticated man with a pretty, red-cheeked wife, who sang dreadfully, however, were there also.

February 1844

On *Thursday the 1st* before noon old *Lobeck* visited us—*Haller* from Vienna (her real name is *Meiner*) had a lieder rehearsal at our place; she is very pretty and has a beautiful voice. To Sobolewsky's—"household for musicians"[4] (it would be awful if all musicians had households like that, because this one was unprecedented)—wandering around the town—to *Sabbarth's*— *Laidlaw's* story about *Liszt's* cigar ashes, which the women of

The Trip to Russia

Königsberg guard as relics for themselves—*I*[mmanual] *Kant's* house—visit from the Russian consul *Adelsohn*—extraordinarily friendly people everywhere. In the evening at *Sobolewsky's* Academy[5]—the G Minor Symphony by Mozart, compositions by *Sobolewsky* (very mediocre); after dinner in the company of many, headed by *Dr. Zander* as director of the society. Engelhardt's pretty wife was there too.

On Friday the 2nd in the morning, rehearsal of the concert with a very weak orchestra—abominable theater, terribly cold— Robert in the "Blutgericht"[6] (I don't understand this) with Englehard—in the evening, concert for a full house—*Demoiselle Wurst* (a beginner), *Demoiselle Haller,* and a violinist, *Schuster,* assisted me—here Robert writes: "observations about Clara's playing and art and the audience"—an old Heidelberg acquaintance, *Jacoby*—the actor and horn player *Schuncke,*—after the concert at *Adelsohn's,* where the entire political elite, headed by *Jacoby,* was assembled. The latter a man with beautiful forehead and eyes—Robert conversed with him a lot—conversations about politics occupied the evening. The *director Ellendt* (whose wife and daughter we had met at the *Lobecks'*), we also met the piano teacher *Cavalieri* there—all kind and educated people, particularly *Adelsohn* himself. We didn't get home until 12:30.

On *Saturday the 3rd* in the morning Robert went shopping with *Adelsohn,* needed protection against cold on the trip,—later breakfast in the "Blutgericht" (now I know of course that the restaurant was called that—tasteless advertisement) with *Sobolewsky, Dibowsky,* and old friendly *Marty,* a postal secretary and a court counselor—much champagne—in the evening 2nd concert— the D Minor Sonata [by Beethoven] and my distress at the time— (i.e., Robert's distress—why, I don't know)—farewell from *Haller,* who was swimming in tears (for reasons unknown to us)—with Englehardt and Sabbarth yet in the *café.*—Farewell from the

234   *The Marriage Diaries of Robert & Clara Schumann*

friendly people here was difficult for us—considering the first impression, we would never have believed that.

The night from Saturday to *Sunday the 4th* went by rather restlessly; after the concert I had to pack everything, and at 6 o'clock in the morning we drove by post chaise and *Marty's* sleigh to Tilsit [Sovetsk, Lithuania], where after spending a snowy, drab day we arrived at 7 o'clock in the evening. The high privy councillor *Nernst,* to whom we had been referred by his sister (here in Leipzig), was already waiting for us, and thus we had to spend the evening with him at his house. We found kind hosts and in addition a very cultivated circle, charming daughters (one a wife and one a bride), a singer from Königsberg (a very musical woman, who also knew about Robert's compositions, which surprised us, so close to the Russian border), and I played (as Robert says) very well.

On *Monday the 5th* at 4 o'clock in the morning we went by post chaise to *Tauroggen* [Taurage, Lithuania] —a gruesome trip across the Niemen [Neman River] and audible palpitations before getting to the so very much dreaded border. Well before the border we were met by a border cossack with pistol in his belt, who accompanied us as far as the custom house. What a pretty, friendly place! was this the same place we imagined would be so awful?—we were treated with greatest consideration, the trunks merely opened and then quickly closed again, so that it took us barely ½ an hour. The customs director *Wilken* (to whom *Adelsohn* in Königsberg had most warmly referred us) greeted us politely, and an official named *Kresslowski* in a plain overcoat rendered us every service regarding the endorsement of passports and our subsequent travel, since here already no one spoke German. From his appearance one would never have guessed this man's importance! he knew almost every artist, because he has helped all of them as he did us. The inn was excellent and gave us some courage for the journey to

The Trip to Russia

come, which was completely taken away from us [at] the first stop, however, because there we found a lunch, dreadful, not a bite to be enjoyed, and paid more than a thaler for it. It's good that things did not continue that way! we never again found it as bad as that on the whole trip. Our carriage (the mail coach) was most comfortable, but the trip boring due to the deep snow, since we could only move slowly from one spot to the next. Here we were on Lithuanian [territory]—we found most of the villages half buried in snow, but on the streets much activity, much more than at home; here at night as well as during the day one encounters entire caravans of one-horse peasant sleighs, on which they take their grain and other crops to the market in *Mitau* [Jelgava, Latvia] (capital of *Kurland,* where we arrived at 5 o'clock in the morning). After *Mitau* it seemed more intensely cold to us, and already we became quite afraid about our noses, which really wouldn't have been necessary as yet. Around 10 o'clock we came to *Riga* and while entering across the *Düna* [Daugava River] had the great experience of seeing an entire timber market on the river—I let go of the carriage door, which I had opened in order to jump out in case of an emergency break in the ice, because I was sensible enough to realize that the ice would think we're just a bit of straw. There was pushing and shoving, there were Jews, and there was the shouting of drivers—what a repulsive impression the inner city made on us with its narrow dirty alleys, on which one could barely walk because of peasant sleighs, and in addition such deep holes in the snow that one could have one's neck and legs broken. Everything here was bad and disagreeable! not even the slightest convenience for travelers was to be found at the depot—no porters, no carriage, nobody whom one could ask for anything—it was terrible. Together with another gentleman we took a large peasant sleigh that happened to be standing in the courtyard, loaded our luggage on it all by ourselves, and mounted it ourselves; *that* was how we arrived in front of the Stadt *London,* a dirty, mean-looking house, where they assigned us to a room on the 4th floor, which we of course did not accept and immediately got back onto our trunk in order to go to what we thought might be a better inn. We got to the Stadt Petersburg—God, what was it like there! a hole way toward the back, not a single chair that wasn't broken, torn blankets; in one word, we found a robber's cave there. Robert immediately went to Herr von *Lutzau* (to whom we had been referred by *David*) to call him for help; during that time I kept standing in the middle of the room, dressed as I was in a fur coat, locked myself in, and when I couldn't stand any more I sat down on a trunk. What a terrible hour that was! *Lutzau* arrived and took us back to the Stadt London, which was supposed to be the best(!) inn in Riga, and where he had already reserved lodgings for us, which had not been given to us, though, since we hadn't told them our name. We got a gloomy room on the ground floor, for which, after the experience we had just had, we thanked God nevertheless.

In the afternoon we visited the merchant *Julius Behrens,* incidentally also a pianist and composer, who offered Robert good cigars but otherwise did not appeal to us very much personally, as in general nobody did, except *Lotz* (violinist) and maybe also Cantor Löbmann, [who] really pleased us.

On *Wednesday the 7th (26th January* according to Russian accounting) Robert went out for a ride with Herr von *Lutzau,* in 10 degrees below freezing; he returned home annoyed because he had fallen into a hole, which is quite easy in *Riga* during the winter; the bustle is too repugnant, in order to get from one place to another one must often climb over the sleighs. He had gone with Lutzau to the chief of police and the mayor for the permit for the concert, and on top of that they demanded an advance payment of 25 rubles silver for the poor—Robert did not pay it, as can well be imagined, since that of course would mean treating artists like

The Trip to Russia 237

vagabonds!—Later we went to see Doctor *Kaull,* Governor General von *Pahlen,* but only found his wife, Consul General *Wöhrmann,* etc. In the evening there was supposed to be music at the *Behrens',* it nearly didn't happen at all; during the first piece I played the hostess was clumsy enough to let tea be passed around, which naturally made me get up as soon as the piece was over (I should have done it on the spot) and not play anymore. *Lotz, Löbmann, Säuberlich, Dr. Sodoffsky,* [and] *Lutzau* were there, several of them to accompany a trio, since after many pleas and apologies from the host I finally did play, namely the Mendelssohn [Trio]. To this entire incident must be added that the Schwarzhäupter (an organization of bachelors who have jurisdiction over the large concert hall) did not want to make the hall available on the announced concert day because the next day there would be a session for which the hall would have to be scrubbed; this put us into a most severely unhappy mood, and we would have preferred to leave immediately, and Herr *von Lutzau* (who is on bad terms with many people and later would have liked to run them down) strongly advised us to do so, but not the others, and thus the majority won out. A tedious tea brought the soirée to an end—that was enough to consolidate Robert's disgust. We spent the days in *Riga* most greatly bored, we did not like any parties, the people were so stiff, so dull, didn't have anything to talk about, and if they ever spoke about the emperor, they did that with gestures, as if spies with a whip were standing over them—we ourselves became quite anxious and in our room hardly dared to say an honest word. I thought, how much worse are things going to be once we get to Petersburg! how very mistaken I was! never again on the entire trip did I feel such discomfort, never again did I think of not saying what I was thinking. The most pleasant hours we spent at the theater director *Hoffmann's,* who was just the one all our acquaintances berated in the worst way; generally in *Riga* there is mischief making, which is intolerable, and the worst one is *Lutzau,* whom Robert once quite strongly tried to put straight. The people of *Riga* are completely lacking in finer education and even the governor's wife, a kind and pleasant woman, knew how to behave only stiffly and awkwardly with guests—nevertheless, she had to prove she was the wife of the governor.

On *Thursday the 8th (January 27)* we received various visits, also Robert made one to the theater director *par excellenc*e with a mustache. Acquaintance with a *Frau Richter,* who in one hour teaches anyone how to make freehand drawings, and showed great interest in taking a sleigh all the way to Petersburg with us, but nothing came of it later, which was just as well, because to my taste the mother and daughter really smelled too much of perfume, which I don't like at all.

In the afternoon at *5 o'clock* we made an excursion on the *Düna* in *Kaull's* sleigh, which I thought would be really nice, but soon the wind cut our faces so terribly that we now became seriously afraid about our noses, and got them to turn back as fast as possible. At home one has no idea what a cold wind in Russia is like, it feels as if lots of knives are cutting one's face in two; we again experienced that quite strongly in *Dorpat* during a pleasure trip that unfortunately had enough bad results that we would prefer to forget it. A cup of tea at *Kaull's* was supposed to warm us up again. After that Robert went with *Kaull* to the Musse [a club], where, although a lot of newspapers were lying around, the most interesting political reports, probably, were blacked out with printer's ink. That seemed rather tyrannical and narrow-minded to us—we almost would have started hating Russia already, had things not soon gotten so much better.

On *Friday the 9th (January 28)* for dinner at *Kaull's;* except for Rector *Uhlmann,* who had been expelled from Dorpat, and the Baron Schulz's dull company, to which must be added that men and women sit separately at the table (Russian style), which just is

The Trip to Russia   239

not conducive to conversation. The superintendent, among many others, arrived after dinner, but when we left we were in just as bad a mood as when we had arrived, and as we were all the time in *Riga*—this disagreeable emotional state really made me completely ill.

In the evening we drank champagne at our place with *Behrens* and Cantor *Alt*—the people of *Riga* don't get very far in the pleasures of life.

Saturday the 10th (January 29). At 8 o'clock in the morning we drove by stagecoach to *Mitau*. The day was magnificent and thus we had the most friendly view of *Mitau*. The castle outside the town (where *Ludwig* the 18th lived during his exile) looks very nice, and now serves, I believe, for assemblies and conferences. One could well think of *Mitau* as rather a large village, so small are the houses and so open is its location, but the people here made us feel good after those in *Riga*. We took lodgings here at *Zehr's* [inn], very bad, and immediately after our arrival at 12 o'clock visited, with Herr *Dunio* (an official and a great friend of music as well), Herr *Maczevsky*, a handsome man but, as Robert says, a bit like an army provost. His wife and children are very musical; the wife astonished me with her exact knowledge of every classical composition and her good sense of music—too bad that she is no longer young!—toward the evening we went to *Maczevsky's* brother, who gave me his Graf piano for the concert. Pleasant family.

I spent the evening at *Maczevsky's* and Robert in the aristocratic *club* with *caviar* and *hazel hens*. The company consisted of noblemen and officers—all educated people, as one hardly expects in this small town.

On *Sunday the 11th (January 30)* Robert made a pretty parody "how the people of *Mitau* storm *Zehr's* hotel for concert tickets"—since they were really not quite so eager to attend!—

Rehearsal at the *club* and in the evening the concert, which was as well attended as it could possibly have been at just this time, since only a few of the nobility were in town. The audience was a very grateful and musically sophisticated one. Bad night afterward, since Robert suffered from a severe headache. I was revived again here—I dreaded returning to *Riga*. —Count *Kayserlingk* invited us to *Mitau* for a 2nd concert.

On *Monday the 12th (January 31)* we drove back to *Riga* in the morning (Robert still very unwell). In the evening I gave my first concert in the Schwarzhäupter Hall, a melancholy place with amusing decorations. Large and attentive audience, but incidentally not artistically sensitive at all—Henselt always said that only *Dreyschock* is acceptable for the people of *Riga*. —The following night the Spanish dancer *Lola Montez* held a *bacchanalia* with *Riga's* principal officers and aristocrats, and just on the floor above, so that we couldn't shut an eye. She was accompanied by military people who on command of the Kaiser took her out of the country.

On *Tuesday the 13th (February 1)* in the morning, visit by *Hollander* and stories about the Schwarzhäupter. *Matinée* at *Löbmann's* where I played Robert's quintet, which didn't go especially well, however. In the evening I gave a private concert at the *Musse*—Robert says "Clara played some things wonderfully."

By the way, a formal businessman's atmosphere reigned over the entire gathering.

Wednesday the 14th/2. At 9 o'clock in the morning we went to *Mitau* again; despite thawing weather we drove on the ice across the *Düna*, which was really very unpleasant for me.

Herr von der *Ropp* received us in the hall and had a *Lichtenthal* piano put there for me, which that evening, since the heat had made it completely unusable, put me in great despair; it was barely possible to play a single piece on it, and yet I had to—to that was added yet another misfortune—I fell on the stairs, which had gotten very slippery because of the snow, and completely tore my

The Trip to Russia 241

velvet dress, so that we spent half an hour repairing it so that I could at least play; I hadn't brought a second dress—once again a new lesson for the future.

The audience was small (they had not publicized the concert sufficiently) but very animated. After the concert we ate a small *supper* with Herr *von Kienitz, Baron Rönne,* and Count *Kayserlingk.*

At the *Maczevskys* we got to know a Madam *Berndt* with a talented daughter (in very unfortunate circumstances, but a very kind woman). The daughter is supposed to go to the music conservatory in Leipzig.[7]

On *Thursday the 15th/3,* after *Dunio* accompanied us awhile, we left for *Riga* again. The Countess *Pomarovska* with daughter (Polish women) were already waiting for us at the inn—we had them come to the theater rehearsal, where we too went right after our return. Madame *Hoffmann* (the director's wife) accompanied me in this last concert. Small theater and mediocre orchestra. In the evening we almost missed the concert by oversleeping—we were so exhausted by the stresses of many consecutive days, otherwise this wouldn't have happened to us. So I just flew into my clothes, and the concert still began at the right time after all. The Concertstück by *Weber* I played partly wonderfully (in Robert's opinion), but the piece by *Scarlatti* and Henselt's "Vöglein"[8] that much worse. It just simply was not possible for me to have any fresh energy left.

After the concert we drank a glass of punch with *Behrens* at our place.

On *Friday the 16th/4,* big confusion about our departure, since we wanted to spend some time in Dorpat. Finally *Behrens* obtained a private stagecoach with German driver, which we could keep until Petersburg, and let us stay for a week in Dorpat.

For dinner we were at the *Hoffmanns'*—fine meal and pleasant stay. In the evening, visit from *Löbmann*—a good but boring person.

On *Saturday the 17th/5*, in the morning we drank champagne at our place with *Löbmann* and *Behrens*—in the evening farewell from them as well as *Kaull, Lutzau,* and others. At 7:30 in the evening we left—God, how good we felt when we drove out the gate!—At first we sat quite comfortably, but that was quickly to end, since soon we were stuck in the snow with stormy and cold weather, and after that had happened several times in a row, we turned around and stayed at the station [we had] left a few hours earlier. After we had rested for a few hours and the morning had arrived,

Sunday the 18th/6, in the morning we drove on in at least 10 degrees [below] freezing. Amid snowdrifts constantly driven by the wind we had the most beautiful sunrise, several times more got stuck in the snow, but found very good stations everywhere (they are all alike—all built according to the same plan), where one could well regain one's strength and also stay for the night. On this journey the region was less inhabited than in Kurland, and we were always surrounded by many birch forests—wolves did not want to make an appearance, even though we promised the coach-man a tip if he would show us one. In the evening we saw a starry sky, shimmering more magnificently than we have ever seen it at home—we were already more in the north, probably that was the reason.

Monday the 19th/7. At 5:30 in the morning we started up again in quite cold weather. In *Uddern* we found a letter from Pro-fessor *Broeker* that was supposed to tell us where to stay in *Dorpat*. We arrived there before noon and put up at the *Stadt London.* The city immediately made a very pleasant impression on us; it has a broad and friendly location, all the streets bright, small pretty houses, and above all affectionate people. *Broeker* came to see us

The Trip to Russia   *243*

immediately and had *a lot* to say, but was entertaining. He also brought us the Petersburg newspaper right away, where we were mentioned and our arrival was announced. This immediately made us cheerful. *Broeker* also had already written much about us in newspapers, can in any case be very useful for artists in *Dorpat.*—he is the town trumpet. We rather liked him, because he is really quite kindhearted and took care of us with complete friendship.

Robert immediately obtained a piano for the room, but it was pretty bad.

Broeker visited us in the evening for a long time and entertained us quite well.

Tuesday the 20th/8. In the morning the music director *Brenner* from Eisleben visited us—a somewhat arrogant-appearing man. Later we looked at the Aula with *Broeker,* visited Madame *Broeker,* Frau *von Wahl,* who had a good *Hasse* pianoforte, the curator of the university, *Baron von Krafftström,* and Herr *von Liphardt, David's* brother-in-law. We went for lunch at the latter's; before that I had played for a few people at his place, whereupon while leaving he pressed into Robert's hand an envelope containing 150 rubles *in bills.*[9] Robert wanted to return it, but at my suggestion kept it. We spent several very pleasant hours there, found the interior arrangements very beautiful, only the Russian meal just did not taste good to us. After the meal the gentlemen played *billiards* in a solarium and smoked—thus Robert felt good.

In the evening, after I had attended a ladies' tea party where I was the foreign animal to be looked at, we had to go with *Broeker* to a carnival ball at the Academic Club, where for half an hour we were very bored and then fled.

Wednesday the 21st/9. Visit from Frau *von Vietinghoff* and Fräulein *von Lilienfeld*—two very dear ladies. Robert was sick the whole day and also in the evening during my concert. That took

244   *The Marriage Diaries of Robert & Clara Schumann*

place in the large auditorium and was very well attended. I received much more applause than I deserved, since I played very miserably, especially the *F Minor* Sonata by *Beethoven*, for which the very heavy but otherwise good *Hasse* pianoforte (belonging to Frau *von Wahl*) was much to blame. I was very disconsolate after the concert and a few tears flowed.

Thursday the 22nd/10. Visits by *Broeker*, Frau *von Menzenkampf*, Fräulein *von Wahl*, Fräulein *von Lilienfeld*, and Baroness *von Wolff*, daughter of Frau *von Knorring*.

Toward noon Herr *von Liphardt* drove us in an open sleigh at 20–22 degrees [below] freezing to the princely estate of his father, who at the time was not in *Dorpat* but in *Berlin*. The cold weather cut our faces as if with many knives, at home no one can conceive of anything like that. In Rathshof [the Liphardt family estate] we saw a *malachite vase* worth 30,000 rubles silver, and in addition beautiful floral arcades in the rooms, magnificent furniture, *etc.*, not to mention a small but very interesting gallery of paintings. On the return trip my husband developed such a severe attack of rheumatism that he had to lie down in bed immediately and even ran a fever, which subsided in the evening, however. We were invited for lunch by Frau *von Wahl*, but of course couldn't go.

Friday the 23rd/11 Robert spent in bed, and of course couldn't attend my second concert in the evening. It took place in the *Ressource* [restaurant with a concert hall] and was very well attended—the applause was stormy. All the people shouted "another concert," and only with the promise of a third concert was I allowed to leave the hall. In the meantime Robert had gotten up, but was too weak to stay out of bed.

Saturday the 24th/12 quiet day—Robert was lying down—hopeless condition, since he felt very weak. The concern of the Dorpat women was extraordinary; they knew that our hotel was bad, and the food as well, *etc.* The Countess *Sievers*, Frau *von*

Wahl, the *Baroness von Üxküll,* and Frau *von Vietinghoff* took turns sending food, good soups, meat, jellies, wine, stewed fruit, in short everything that strengthens and refreshes someone who is sick. Even two sets of bedding and a beautiful large quilt arrived anonymously, so that a better sickbed could be made. To be sick here was much less horrible for Robert than it would have been in any other place. Actually it was anxiety that made him sicker and weaker than he was; he thought he would never get up again, might contract typhus, or something else. That put me in a terrible position, and at the same time I also had to give three concerts, during which I had to turn Robert's care over to our coachman, who incidentally was a good old fellow. Professor *Walther* treated him, but didn't take his condition seriously enough, so that later we took yet another physician, who then also brought the whole matter to an end with the first visit.

On *Sunday the 25th/13* Robert wasn't yet any better, was discouraged and sad. *Chevalier Buroschi* came to see him, in addition he read many compositions by *Latrobe,* Faust by *Goethe,* etc.—

On *Monday the 26/14* I gave my third concert, with exactly the same enthusiastic applause as the second. Robert was waiting for me out of bed—1 hour after the concert the students serenaded us beautifully and also sang several of his choruses for men's voices. I had to thank them—a beautiful moment!—

On *Tuesday the 27th/15* Robert was somewhat better, but always very weak. Visit from Frau *von Wahl,* an intelligent woman. She told us how in the winter they once drove right over a farmhouse without noticing it, until they tipped over, after which they saw it, of course.

Wednesday the 28th/16 always Robert's poor health—continuous concern of the people of *Dorpat.*

On *Thursday the 29th/17* we made a brief excursion—Robert with the greatest effort.

246   *The Marriage Diaries of Robert & Clara Schumann*

Young *Pavlowski* played for us; we had to draw up a certificate for him, so that he will receive a stipend from the emperor.

We sent for another doctor, who explained Robert's condition to him.[10] Later *Walther* and *Broeker* came as well, and Robert's spirits improved.

On *Friday the 1st of March (February 18)* we made farewell visits in the morning, and at 4:30 in the afternoon during mild weather left *Dorpat,* where despite all the big inconveniences it had gone well for us. We spent the night in *Torma.*

On *Saturday the 2nd of March (February 19)* Robert already felt much better, the joy of life had returned. Interesting on this tour were the enormous caravans of as many as 100 distillery wagons, which one sometimes could barely pass, occasionally they ruin the road in a terrible way, along the way there are large potholes, so that one could faint because of all the horrible bumping.

Today we drove along Lake Peipus and a long distance along the Baltic Sea to *Narva* [Jõesuu], where we passed through on

Sunday the 3rd of March (Feb. 20) at 2 o'clock in the morning. A very ancient castle, *Ivangorod,* looked interesting, also a beautiful bridge. At 6 o'clock we came to the first real Russian place, *Jamburg* [Yamagrod], where we saw the first Greek church with 5 cupolas, painted green and yellow, which are the Russians' favorite colors. We stayed overnight in *Kipen* [village near Ropsha, south of Peterhof]. The weather was mild, together with a beautiful moonlit night! good stations everywhere, as well as good midday meals almost everywhere.

On *Monday the 4th of March (February 21),* departure at 6 o'clock in the morning with dew in the air—in *Ropsha* [a country estate near Petersburg built by Peter the Great] we got stuck in the snow (Robert said he believes this was the place where Paul III met his demise,—you must be mistaken? he was actually murdered in Petersburg?).[11] We saw many German colonial villages, and the

The Trip to Russia

region was not without charm, birch forests made the region attractively varied.

In *Strelna* there is an imperial castle, also a large monastery of St. [Sergei]—the country houses of Petersburg now started coming into view—tasteless construction and all yellow or green—charming woodlands up to the triumphal gate outside *Petersburg.* That is a magnificent entrance!! we got out and after the easygoing *inspection* of the carriage (wine and liquor are most severely forbidden and not a drop may enter) drove to the stagecoach *office* and from there immediately to the *Henselts',* whom we found only after a lengthy search. From one street to the next the city grew more magnificent, and we found it wonderful when arriving at the *Hôtel Coulon,* where the Henselts had taken quarters for us. The square was called *Michailovsky's*—the Grand Prince *Michael* has his beautiful palace here. The *Hôtel Coulon* is 250 feet in length—the building forms a whole street. Our lodgings cost 30 rubles silver a week. Robert immediately went out and took a look at the imposing *Nevsky Prospect,* which was quite close to us.

For dinner at the *Henselts'*—Doctor *Adam,* an intelligent man, and *Gross* the *cellist* were there. The son of Henselt, intelligent but rude. At 11 o'clock we came home.

On *Tuesday the 5th (February 22)* we had a complete thaw; in the morning we drove along the *Nevsky Prospect,* past the Winter Palace, then along the *Neva* [River] and were amazed by this most wonderful city in the world (as Robert says).

Later we visited the *Viardots,* who received us in the most friendly way. How happy I was to find Pauline [Viardot-Garcia] here, and how affectionately and cordially she behaved toward me!—From there we went to the rehearsal of an evening concert that was supposed to take place in the *Assemblée de la Noblesse* for hospital patients. We found a magnificent hall that accommodates 4,000 people. The *music director Maurer* greeted us immediately, as did the brothers *Vielhorsky,* also the conductor *Heinrich Romberg,* whom at the beginning we found intolerable, and later quite pleasant and very useful!—

For dinner we were at the *Viardots* and found a lot of Italians there—at the top of the list their little Prince *Rubini,* to whom they show great reverence. After dinner Pauline showed me her beautiful presents—sable, Turkish shawl, and lots of cut diamonds, everything from the court, chiefly from the emperor couple.

In the evening we were to have the most impressive view that we have ever had of this kind; we entered the completely filled Hall of the *Nobility,* which was illuminated with thousands of lights and everyone most elegantly dressed, all the ladies in ball costumes and holding floral bouquets (one of which, by the way, often costs 100 rubles in bills—that's 30 thalers), furthermore the imperial loge completely decorated with the most beautiful fresh flowers, the same on the orchestra level, the diplomats' loge across from the imperial loge, above the orchestra a platform completely occupied by preciously attired Asians, the imperial loge occupied by the [Grand Princess von] *Leuchtenberg, Prince von Hessen,* the Grand Princess *Olga* among others. One cannot sufficiently describe this splendor—Paris has nothing like it to offer, for one thing there are no assembly rooms like that.

The concert was most average. Overture to Oberon [by Weber] went badly, the Italians sang one to death with *ini,* the Invitation to the Dance [by Weber] orchestrated by *Berlioz,* in which he eliminated the ending, however, because it probably does not work (!).

The audience consisted only of the highest *nobility.* After the concert we had a quarrel with our servant, whom we had missed and had to go home on foot in satin shoes (i.e., *I* [did]). We ate in the dining room while the manager, Herr *Bruno,* told us that he pays 80,000 ruble bills yearly for renting his place.—In the

The Trip to Russia   249

morning we were visited by Herr *Wirth* (a native of Augsburg, from whom I obtained a beautiful grand piano for my room) and *Martinov,* a good pianist.

During the night we had dance music overhead, which from now on repeated itself almost every night—it was a wealthy Polish woman and her daughters who were so rowdy.

On *Wednesday the 6th of March (February 23)* we began making visits and delivering our letters to *Vielhorsky, Lvov, Colloredo, Seebach, James Thal* with amiable wife and children, etc. etc. Always and every day we looked with astonishment at the great Winter Palace, General Staff, Senate Building, *Alexander* Column, and yet many other things.

For dinner we were at Henselt's, where Robert never felt really well, however. Henselt's concerto—which will *never* be finished! he's been working on it already for years.[12]

In the evening we drove to Engelhardt's *Hôtel*—much effort to find it, since our arch-Russian coachman didn't know it and always drove straight ahead, which is what all coachmen do with the greatest rigidity when they don't know where to go. Concert by *Böhm*—little to be seen of the *nobility! Carl Mayer* played in a mediocre way the 2nd and 3rd movements from *Mendelssohn's G Minor Concerto.* How eager I was to see this man, whom Father had often praised as *Field's* best pupil!—

On *Thursday the 7th of March (February 24)* in the morning, visits at *Count Colloredo's* (to whom we had a letter from *Metternich,* which contrary to expectation did us no good at all, however), at *Baron Stieglitz's* (wonderfully furnished, with a view of the *Neva*), at *Wirth's* (who had a large number of beautiful instruments, more beautiful than any I know in Germany, standing there), at *General Gedeonov's* (director of all the theaters in Petersburg and Moscow), at *Bulgarin's* (editor of the ["Nördliche Biene"]), at *Maurer's,* and in the afternoon to Countess *Voron-*

tzov-Dashkov's (who was sick with measles), to the *Stöckhardts'*, Frau *von Sauerweid's* (not very pleasant), and *Senkovski's* (wealthy journalist with princely accommodations).

Before noon we attended the rehearsal of Pauline's concert—in the evening we were at a small quartet soirée at the Counts *Vielhorskys'*, where we found *Molique, Gross, Maurer, Heinrich, and Ciprian Romberg.* They played quartet[s] by *Spohr* [and] *Beethoven,* and *Mathieu Vielhorsky* [played] a solo on the violoncello, as a dilettant quite competent, especially with good comprehension. We were received there in a very friendly way and didn't get back home until 1:30.

In the afternoon we were also visited by *Seebach* and a secretary of *Count Colloredo. Martinov* belonged to our daily visitors.

On *Friday the 8th of March (February 25)* in the morning, visit from the *Stöckhardts,* then to the rehearsal of the singers of the Imperial Court, which takes place every Friday, and for which tickets are given out. This is the finest chorus we have ever heard, the basses resemble organ basses at times, and the [male] sopranos often sound quite supernatural, more beautiful than the most beautiful women's voices. The nuancing and shading are most exactly prepared, sometimes almost too refined and elaborate—an excess of shading must finally be tiring. Unfortunately they sang really mediocre compositions, surely including some by *Lvov,* who is director of the institution. We returned on foot—we hadn't walked for a long time.

At the Henselts' for dinner—in the evening, concert by Viardot. For us very boring! nothing but Italian music, and that which was better couldn't be heard, because the audience talked loudly throughout, even—can one believe this is possible—during the Egmont Overture by *Beethoven.* Pauline sang a Russian folk song very prettily and stimulated not enthusiasm but fanticism. It went too far not to make a reasonable person and connoisseur indignant who surely acknowledges Pauline's art but also knows it is

The Trip to Russia
251

lacking. *That's* what happened to us, we became annoyed, and grew even more so while having to wait on the steps for at least one hour with Madame Henselt, who had gone there with us, because the coach couldn't drive up owing to the large number of carriages. The ladies and gentlemen generally have endless patience for that, to wait hours after a full concert for their carriages—with such prospects no one could bring me to a concert. To get back to the enthusiasm of people in Petersburg for the Italians, that really becomes unbelievable. The opera season cost the public half a million this winter, and a new subscription for next winter (when those [Italian singers] and also [the bass] *Lablache* want to come again) was offered immediately after its closing, for which just as much was paid in advance. The leading families are supposed to have gotten money at a pawnbroker's just to obtain a loge, since it was the fashion, after all, and *that* makes the people of Petersburg into *what* and *how* they are. One can well imagine that under such conditions it was a poor time for concert performers, and thus I could nonetheless be satisfied with what I had earned. Molique contributed to his first concert, and from the second and last 2 thalers were left over for him, despite his having driven around for 2 weeks to deliver the tickets personally to the people's homes, which I never would have done.

On *Saturday the 9th of March (February 26)* in the morning, visit from Count *Mathieu Vielhorsky,* then visits to General *Doubelt,* State Councillor *Meyer,* Baroness von *Krüdener,* and the English embassy secretary *Bloomfield.* Visit from *Lvov,* who talked much with Robert about his opera, which he wants to have performed in Germany in the summer.[13]

At noon we ate at the *table d'hôte* in the *Hôtel Coulon,* where a fixed meal costs 1½ rubles silver. One cannot eat à la carte here at all, one has to pay just as much, and at the end one isn't even full—it has been prudently arranged that way.

In the evening Madame *Henselt* talked to us quite pleasantly about the emperor and his deeds during the revolution following his ascension to the throne.[14]

On *Sunday the 10th of March (February 27)* in the morning Robert took a walk to the Catholic church, the Lutheran church with good church choir, and the Kazan Cathedral with barbaric church music. The latter is built in the shape of a cross; flags and keys that were captured in the war hang on the walls.

Visits from Herr *von Sauerweid* (just as unpleasant as his wife), State Secretary Meyer with sister, Count Michel *Vielhorsky, Wirth, James Thal,* and General *Bolkhovskoi,* the former governor of *Tver* [Kalinin], who brought Robert the first and very gratifying news of his uncle [Carl von Schnabel], who is still alive, but quite aged.

At noon we drove with Madame *Henselt* and Herr *Gehling* on the *Neva,* then through the *Fortress* and back. The wind cut forcefully into one's face and today Robert actually thought that his mental power had been frozen, but soon, after we got warm, it thawed out again.

For dinner at *Henselt's*—Robert spoke with him a lot about his concert. He is a terrible pedant, and must be a terribly embarrassing and tormenting husband, although basically he's really good at heart. His heart hides completely behind his moods and capriciousness and it peeps out only now and then.

On *Monday the 11th of March (February 28)* in the morning Robert wrote to his uncle—with a happy heart, one would think.

We made calls on Count *Volkonsky* (the emperor's treasurer) and *Seebach* and received visits from Count *Mathieu Vielhorsky,* the instrument maker *Lichtenthal, Koberwein* (who was very useful and obliging to Robert in regard to our passports, residence permit, and all police matters), and General *Doubelt.* Later we again went to see *Gerke* (pianist), the wife of General *Rönne,* and General *Schubert.*

For dinner at General *Bolkhovskoi's,* who has a very pretty daughter who also plays the piano quite superbly. We thought, how

The Trip to Russia

253

is this going to turn out, if the first one we hear already plays like that! but it was just that we had heard the best one first.

In the evening Madame *Henselt* had her day for entertaining guests; we went there only to be most greatly bored by the women's tea and card games, in which Madame Henselt was tactless enough to participate—namely, with the game.

On *Tuesday the 12th of March (February 29)*, visit from young *Schuberth*, worthy brother of the *Schuberth* from Hamburg. Later we looked at several *Broadwood* and *Lichtenthal* pianos, which, compared to those by *Wirth,* we didn't like very much, however. In addition to that we also made many futile visits, which really was partially to our liking; all the while we had the the most beautiful weather.

For lunch we were at Stöckhardt's, where we found a lot of Germans. Stöckhardt is a thoroughly kind man but nevertheless, or perhaps just because of that, extremely bothersome with his sugary friendliness! therefore one often feels inclined to be unfriendly to him, which one later regrets, because it was only his abundant goodwill that drove one to do that.

His wife resembles him, but she is easier to take because she is reserved; he, however, is highly intrusive and at every moment says something stupid, especially about music. Along with that he is a gushing music enthusiast.

In the evening we were at *Vielhorsky's* together with Pauline *Viardot.* We were only a few people and therefore I decided to play several little things on *Vielhorsky's* thoroughly deteriorated *Erard.* *Michel Vielhorsky* sang for us various songs and choruses from his opera,[15] which proved to be of significant originality. *Pauline* surprised us with her extraordinary memory: she still remembered the theme of Robert's Variations for 2 Pianofortes, as well as several of the variations, from last summer, when I had played them with *Mendelssohn* at her concert.

On *Wednesday the 13th (March 1)* Robert was very weak, he

felt it in every part of his body. Visits to *Böhm* (violinist), *Romberg*, and *Carl Mayer*. We received visits from *Bolkhovskoi, Martinov, Bloomfield*, and *Gasser*, the latter a banker, a Saxon by birth but a Russian citizen for a long time now. For dinner at State Councillor *Meyer's*—friendly, simple people—the daughter played much for us by her late mother, born *Schiatti*, who had a significant talent for the older sonata style—she played that really with the greatest veneration, and generally strikes me as a girl of exceptional character.

On *Thursday the 14th (March 2)* in the morning, visits from Knecht (cellist), Carl Mayer, Madame Beer (sister of Grund in Hamburg), Madame Gerke, *etc.* Later we drove to Madame *Reichwald* in the [St. Mary's] Institute [for the education of girls]. For dinner at the Henselts'—melancholic, quiet day—writes Robert. The weather constantly warm.

Friday the 15th (March 3) a day of expectation for things that are about to happen! today was my first concert, I had great anxiety, I was also afraid to find an empty hall, which wasn't the case at all, however. I played well despite all the anxiety and received great applause. But the Englehardt Hall is very ugly, dark, dirty, so one must wonder why the elegant world goes there. The Grand Princess von *Leuchtenberg* (I had been recommended to her by our queen) and Prince von *Oldenburg* were there.

On *Saturday the 16th/4 Lvov* visited us, later we went to [Baron von] *Stieglitz's* and on the way back took a really close look at the statue of Peter the Great, the St. Isaak Cathedral, and went with *Stöckhardt* into the *Kazan* Cathedral, where we were most favorably impressed by an image of the Virgin made of numerous precious stones, then the balustrade in front of the altar, made entirely of pure silver, and the keys to various captured cities, among them also Dresden and Leipzig.

At home we found *Michel Vielhorsky*. He played sections from his opera for us that reveal much talent.

The Trip to Russia

255

In the evening I had promised to play in the concert of the Philharmonic Society,[16] but half an hour before the concert *Fuchs* came and asked me instead to play twice, since Herr *Versing* and Madame *Schoberlechner* had suddenly left him in the lurch. I did it, and for that I was given thanks in really a very honorable way. After the last piece, to accompany the enthusiastic applause the orchestra three times sounded a fanfare that made me feel quite shocked and embarrassed. The grand princesses *Leuchtenberg* and *Olga* were there.

On *Sunday the 17th/5* in the morning I rehearsed Robert's Variations for 2 Pianofortes with Henselt. He is so pedantic, though, that it makes one feel desperate; all of his effort goes into technique, for hours he practices one spot, and that's just what he did in the variations. Robert was not very satisfied; Henselt lacks the gentle and poetic playing especially necessary for these variations—thus the perfume that drifts over the whole thing eludes him completely, and he doesn't feel it. What he plays best are pieces that demand much power, overtures, polonaises, *etc.*, but one can't stand that for long—it tears my nerves to have to listen to the piano played for hours with maximal power, and with that he himself loses fine sensitivity ever more.

At home we found the wife of State Councillor *Mandt* and *Mlle. Reichwald* and Fräulein *Thun*. Later we rehearsed Robert's quintet with *Maurer* and son, *Hager* and *Gross*. We had invited the brothers *Vielhorsky,* Bolkhovskoi with his daughter, the *Henselts;* Frau *Thun,* State Councillor *Meyer* with his sister, *Frau Müller,* daughter of *Johann Heinrich Müller* (composer), came also by chance and stayed. The interest and enthusiasm for the quintet was widespread, and the *Vielhorskys* were so delighted that they immediately planned to invite an orchestra to their place in order to hear Robert's symphony as well, to which Robert naturally agreed gladly. Another thing I'd forgotten, that *Rubinstein,* coming from Moscow, also showed up by chance for the quintet.

From the Philharmonic Society I received an honorary diploma in recognition of my service on their behalf[17]—I found that really too much for the little that I had done, but naturally was very pleased. For dinner we were at Henselt's.

Monday the 18th/March 6. In the morning visits from *Böhm, Court Councillor Grimm* (teacher of the young grand princesses), *Rubinstein,* a pianist *Schiller,* Count *Michel Vielhorsky,* General *Schubert, Maurer,* and *Romberg.* At noon I played the [cello] sonatas of *Mendelssohn* with *Mathieu Vielhorsky.* Playing with him is like playing with an artist.

We had dinner at *Bolkhovskoi's* with *Henselt.* In the evening Robert went for half an hour to the St. Michael Theater, where Madame *Fink-Lohr* gave a concert, but sang in a very mediocre way.

On *Tuesday the 19th/March 7* in the morning we visited the *Kazan* Church, then the [Sts.] *Peter-Paul* Church in the *Fortress,* where the graves of the Russian imperial families since *Peter* are located. At the grave of *Peter* we were overcome by holy terror— what a great man rested here!—in the same church Robert went to see the Most Holy Sanctuary (women may not go there), where a cross made of a *single* diamond can be seen. A chandelier carved of ivory by *Peter* also hangs at the altar. From there we visited *Peter's* little Dutch house on the *Neva* with a small garden, and also saw a fairly large boat there, which he had constructed himself; this was an interesting morning!—In addition I must point out that the enormous spires of the Fortress Church, as well as the Admiralty, were presents from the Dutch to the Emperor *Alexander,* and were covered with real solid gold.

For dinner we were at General *Schubert's,* who seems musically quite well educated but one-sided. He has two very inquisitive and uneducated sisters staying with him, but pleasant daughters who disguise their curiosity somewhat (since this seems common to the entire family) with their kindness and comfortable external

The Trip to Russia

257

demeanor. A few others were there as well, also *Knecht,* who, ever since I refused to play in his concert, looks at me only sideways.

Martinov has not come for several days anymore. He had behaved discourteously toward me, had engaged in silly, insulting conversation, and therefore we snubbed him soundly during the quintet morning at our place, which he happened to attend.

In the evening we went to *Lvov's,* and truly enjoyed ourselves with his magnificent quartet playing—if he were only as human as he is artistic! I played Robert's quintet there, but to our great dismay it went miserably. A violoncellist *Beer,* who comes from the Paris Conservatory, played with much French emotion and pomp, but remarkable facility.

Lvov's residence is one of the most aristocratic houses that we have seen in Petersburg—but [he] is not rich, on the contrary is supposed to be heavily in debt. Who would have believed that of this adjutant to the emperor, who in Germany traveled like a prince.

At his place we met *Mr. Wartel* from Paris, whom we never saw again, however.

Wednesday the 20th/8. In the morning old Stein came to see us, the father of *Carl Stein*, who toured as a pianist 10–12 [years] ago. He is a nasty person, whom everyone steps on like a worm, however. His son ran away from him, and now the old man gives a few lessons.

At noon we drove along the *Nevsky* [Prospect]; we had no real goal and gave free rein to our coachman, who naturally drove straight ahead and thus brought us to the *Nevsky* Monastery and actually up to the furthest wall, where he then had to stop. We got out, pleased with our coachman's intuitive understanding, and looked around the very friendly cloister courtyard. We also went into the church and saw the monument of the saintly *Nevsky* there, which is of solid silver.

In the afternoon we were in a bad mood—it seemed that the

concert wouldn't be fully attended. In the evening, 2nd concert in the Engelhardt Hall. Like the first the attendance was average, which distressed us. The Italian opera, for which people had spent everything, was again to be blamed for that. We in Germany would call a mediocre concert here a good one, because there were always at least 4–500 people. *Leuchtenberg* and *Olga* were there again, which made up for it somewhat, as this honored me.

Thursday the 21st/9. In the morning *Romberg* arrived, with whom we then went to *Vielhorsky's,* where Robert rehearsed his symphony. After the rehearsal we drove, as usual, for a ride in a small sleigh, which was one of my greatest pleasures in Petersburg.

In the evening, *soiree* at *Vielhorsky's.* I played *Mendelssohn's G Minor* concerto there, and Robert conducted his symphony with the most general appreciation, and considering the one rehearsal it went very well. The gathering was not big, but well chosen. Prince von *Oldenburg*—a thoroughly kind man, whose goodness is inscribed on his face—*Nesselrode,* a short man with sharp nose, were those who interested us the most.

Molique also played a concerto written by himself—beautifully, but with a disagreeable face and freezing coldness.

After the concert, *supper*—*Michel Vielhorsky* amused all of us with his original, humoristic way of singing banquet songs. That is a man whom I truly love and honor. One may only rarely find a man in so high a position, who at the same time is so sociable, so completely the artist among artists, with whom one could completely forget what rank he is, who is full of kindness, in short has everything to make him dear and valuable to others. Robert won't be angry at me for these confessions, he shares these feelings with me, loves and honors him as I do. We came home at 1 o'clock, after both of the brothers [Vielhorsky] gave us their autographed portraits.[18]

Friday the 22nd/10. In the morning, visit by *Homilius* and

General *Pesavorius,* then with *Michel Vielhorsky* to the *Sheremet-yev Chapel,* where we attended part of a Russian mass, which made a disgusting impression on me, however, because the prostration of one's whole body 3–4 times a minute is really too much, as generally the Russian service is tied up far more with ceremonies than the Catholic, which already seems exaggerated enough at times. But we heard a magnificent choir here (the best after the court singers), the one that Count *Sheremetyev* maintains primarily *for himself alone.* In this choir the sopranos seemed especially magnificent to me, often they really sounded like voices from another world.

In the afternoon we visited *Herr von Grimm,* whose wife is a singer. I found this man always disagreeable, just looking at him—I know of nothing more repulsive than a *young* decrepit man. Later we still had to call on Herr *von Gasser,* who complained about, among other things, the improvement of the mail coaches; on *Sinovyev* and *Mandt.* For dinner we were at the Henselts'—in the evening we went with *Stöckhardt* to the concert of the law school, to which Prince von *Oldenburg* (*chief* of this institution) had personally invited us.

The concert was performed almost entirely by law students, whom the prince allows to have musical instruction, so that they have something useful to do in their spare time.

Molique played, with the greatest annoyance, one could see that.

The prince treated us with the greatest honor all evening, greeted us immediately on arriving, and at the end himself accompanied me to the instrument, so that I should play something for the law students. He was delicate enough not to urge me, but from a third person I found out that it was his wish. Among those present we were very interested in a *Georgian princess* who is a Russian prisoner, but treated as a princess by the emperor, also receives a princely stipend. Robert found her very beautiful—she had much resemblance to *Napoleon,* which immediately astonished one.

Lvov revealed himself as a hypocritical courtier among the guests. I snubbed him quite coldly—he really behaved just too shabbily toward us.

On *Saturday the 23rd/11* we obtained a ticket for a certain Countess *Tolstoy,* who had asked for tickets to the concert—prior to the first concert we had received a similar [request] from the Princess *Gortchakov* and sent the tickets, for which we haven't yet been paid, however. We sent the servant out and discovered later, when we compared both handwritings, that it was one and the same, and therefore—a fraud. How repulsive!—

Henselt took me this morning to the empress's maid of honor, *Frau Bortenyev,* with whom he had spoken about my playing for her [Highness]. I visited her because she was so good and friendly and had suggested that I be offered letters for Moscow. Now I had been here so long, but had not yet played at court—*Vielhorsky* always said I should just wait quietly, we can make it to court in due time, it's just that the empress is always indisposed; but in that case I could have waited for a long time yet, Henselt made an effort and went right to the source, and that was good.

Had I played for the empress right at the beginning, then my concerts would have been much more successful—in Petersburg everything must emanate from the court if the nobility is to participate.

Visit from Herr *von Seebach, Bloomfield,* and Prince *Vyasemsky,* who was a great enthusiast for me, which I would never have expected of him—later he even wrote poems about me.

Today we visited the *bazaar,* where there are innumerable shops, but one doesn't find the elegance there that one would have expected.

Before dinner, rehearsal of the quintet in the hall, afterward

The Trip to Russia 261

at *Henselt's* for dinner. In the evening I went with *Stöckhardt* to *Chambeau,* secretary of the empress. That was another fine trick that *Stöckhardt* played on me, asked me for God's sake to go with him to these people because they are most anxiously wanting to make my acquaintance, while he probably put on airs and said "I will bring Madame Schumann here to you." How I later regretted this visit! I had played on a rattletrap that evening, and on top of that invited the daughter, who is very weak and not allowed to go to any concert, to come to see me because I wanted to play some more for her. That again was one of those stupid acts of kindness on my part!—She arrived with her mother, and after I played for her the mother told me her husband would be able to give me good letters to Moscow, *only I should go there and ask him for them.* Such insolence really hasn't happened to me for a long time! while the most highly placed people sent and offered letters to me, this secretary's wife demanded that I should ask her husband for them. And can one really imagine that I had so little presence of mind, that I didn't even give this woman an answer that she would have had to remember! I wasn't used to such impudence, as I'm generally too stupid in such cases, so that I feel like hitting myself afterward.—Of course I did *not* go to Herr von *Chambeau.*

Today we decided in any case after the 3rd to give yet a fourth, final concert in the *Michael Theater,* which later proved to be a fortunate decision. Mainly I had prevailed upon Robert for that.

Sunday the 24th/12 at 2 o'clock I gave my third concert; it was well attended and the audience a very fine one. The quintet went very well and had an extraordinary reception; incidentally, however, the audience was in a colder mood, despite my having played very well that day. But surely that was due to the daylight— in the day the mood is much colder than at night, which is quite natural.

Vielhorsky brought me an invitation for the evening at the empress's, I had also promised *Gross* to play in his private concert the same night, so it turned out to be a hectic day.

For dinner we went to the Henselts', from there immediately home again, where I just had time to get dressed so as to drive right away to Herr *von Grimm*, where *Gross* gave his soirée; I played Adagio and *Finale* from the *F Minor* Sonata [by Beethoven], and from there drove immediately with *Vielhorsky* to the empress's.

That was some splendor in the palace! there were chamberlains, servants, Moors, lots of *Circassians*—it could have been most intimidating!—

The imperial family received me most graciously; it was a small circle, and assembled in the empress's living room (called the Golden Room), where I then also played. I played much, among other things the *Mendelssohn* Spring Song 3 times in a row, in addition to a lot of other pieces. *Leuchtenberg* herself plays much, and also seemed most interested in what I played. The three princesses, *Olga, Marie,* and *Alexandrine* enchanted me more than any beauties have for a long time. They surely are the most beautiful creatures I've ever seen. *Olga* is really imperially proud—a great beauty; *Alexandrine* is the highest loveliness, delicacy, and grace. *Marie (Leuchtenberg)* is the least beautiful, but interesting and the most lively of the three. The emperor was there as well, and spoke with me in a very friendly way—he too is a very handsome man. The empress is very sickly and thin, but still has a lovely face, and is so cordial and kind that I completely lost my earlier aversion for her (in Weimar[19] she had seemed terribly proud to me)—she took notice of me with the greatest friendliness, sat next to me at the piano the whole evening, and spoke with me a lot. The prince of *Hessen* was also there—I was glad to see him again.[20] I returned home completely satisfied and delighted by the good reception, and over a bottle of champagne told Robert at length about my experiences.

The Trip to Russia   263

Monday the 25th/13. Visits from *H. Romberg, Henselt,* the *Grimms,* and the *Chambeaus* —later we went to *Stieglitz's, Olde- cop's* (editor of the Petersburg paper), *Vielhorsky's,* and *Baron von Zoller's.* For dinner we were at General *Schubert's.* In the evening *Molique* gave his truly miserable farewell concert. I felt sorry for him, even as unbearable as he is. An overture by Lvov, bad, as wasn't at all to be expected, opened the concert. *Molique* played some things very beautifully today, but he is cold.

Tuesday the 26th/14. Visit from *Versing,* with whom we went through lieder of Robert's. Later Herr von *Ribeaupierre* (the diplo- mat) came for us to take us to the Winter Palace. How magnifi- cent, how glorious that is! one cannot describe it! The room of the empress (where I had played) delighted us especially, with the malachite tables and columns on the walls, then her garden, in which one believes oneself to have been transported to a fairy gar- den. It is decorated with the most beautiful exotic plants, as well as fish and birds that live and sing there. I was carried away by this view, and would have wanted to see nothing else, just spend a short fifteen minutes there. In brief I just want to mention yet the great [St.] George Hall, also called the Golden Hall,[21] where there are *Buvets* [i.e., buvettes = serving cabinets] completely filled with golden and silver table settings and goblets, including [one] by *Cel- lini,* furthermore the Field Marshalls' and Generals' Hall, where portraits of all the generals since *Peter's* time are displayed. In one of these halls we encountered Prince *Volkonsky,* secretary to the emperor, who was on his way to the emperor. Immediately adja- cent to the Winter Palace is the Hermitage, formerly Empress *Catherine's* favorite residence, now devoted to the exhibition of famous paintings and incredibly magnificent vases. We found among other things a room full of *Rembrandts,* as well as one by *Wouvermann,* furthermore a room full of various antiques discov- ered in the *Crimea,* golden laurel wreaths, bracelets, *etc.* At the end we came yet into a room filled with diamonds and other precious stones. Never have I seen such a treasure, such large *diamonds*, and pearls one inch big! Only one diamond like that and our trip would have been completely paid for.

It was most interesting for us to have Herr *von Ribeaupierre* as a guide; he showed us the castle chapel where under the rule of *Catherine* he was baptized; he still clearly remembered certain festivities in the throne room where he saw *Catherine,* as well as Emperor *Paul* I.

This man was kind enough to show us around for fully 3 hours (we needed that long just to see everything superficially), to show us everything with the greatest friendliness and patience, to explain, and at the same time to tell us many things of interest about his own life experience. That once again was a man of genuine nobility, of a sort unknown in our country! where in Germany would a high-ranking count like Ribeaupierre guide us around a palace for 3 hours? When I got back to our place, I received a beautiful jeweled bracelet from the empress.

In the evening I went with *Henselt* to Minister of War *Tchernyshov's,* in order to thank him for the letters to Moscow he wanted to give me. Robert did not feel like coming along, which he later regretted when he heard that that was the famous war minister. As he himself puts it, in the meantime he had escaped to a coffeeshop in a melancholic state, and given me quite a shock when I did not find him at home.

Wednesday the 27th/15. Robert received a letter from his uncle in *Tver,* which gave him great pleasure.[22]

Around 1 o'clock at the invitation of Prince von *Oldenburg* we drove to the *Smolny* Convent, where aristocratic young women are educated and for whom, since they are not allowed to go out, I was supposed to play.

Because of his fear of so many young ladies, Robert had not gone inside with me, and was already on the point of returning

The Trip to Russia   265

home, when the prince had him sent for, [and Robert] had to sit right next to him. Incidentally, many listeners were still there. I played a lot, and afterward had to make a tour among all the ladies, all of whom wanted to thank me—I could well have been like a queen if my face hadn't revealed my embarrassment and the unfamiliarity of this role. Later we made the tour through the inner rooms of the institute, always accompanied by a troupe of young girls, one of whom wanted to carry my gloves, another my wrist warmer, the third my shawl, etc., and wouldn't give these back until we had arrived at the staircase, where a unanimous chorus of repeated thank-yous rang out.

Despite the many embarrassments that followed one another here, the thing did give me much pleasure, as in general agreeable things easily make one forget what is disagreeable.

For dinner we were at Herr von *Gasser's*—a wealthy *banker.* He has an unpleasant wife, who is essentially rude and mean in her nature, but at the same time crammed full of jewels. I found her so disgusting that I was happy when I no longer heard her voice.

In the evening we were at Prince von *Oldenburg's*—one of my most pleasant evenings!—with Henselt I played the prince's symphony, then Robert's Variations for Two Pianofortes, in addition yet many solo pieces, and Henselt, after much pleading from the princess, played some things as well, among others a polonaise by *Chopin* beautifully. Herr *Versing* sang some of the prince's lieder— the prince took great delight in that, these are his happiest hours, when one plays or sings his music for him, and for this reason as well Henselt composes with him most patiently twice a week. The princess is the kindest person one can imagine! one rarely finds this simplicity and kindheartedness in a woman of such high rank. She was most friendly to me, and I also admire her as much as him.

266 *The Marriage Diaries of Robert & Clara Schumann*

After this *soirée* we went to our place together with Henselt and conversed with him until late at night.

Thursday the 28th/16. Very early in the morning Robert received an anonymous, indescribably nasty letter, which undoubtedly came from old *Stein,* who from that time on also did not put in another appearance. He had brought me one of his young students who was completely incompetent and played pieces that were much too difficult—this I told him openly, hence his rage probably. The letter disconcerted me at first, but then it made me laugh.

Visits to *Nesselrode, Ribeaupierre,* who had also visited us the day before, *Vyasemsky,* etc.

At the *bazaar* there was a *Palm Sunday market,* which couldn't be of any interest to us at all, however, only very poor things were there.

For dinner at State Councillor *Meyer's,* —unfortunately it always turned out that after the meal we could not stay there longer, almost every time we had to leave immediately instead, and every time the daughter would really very much have liked to play something for us by her mother, whom she really adores in a touching way.

On *Friday the 29th/17* in the morning, rehearsal at the theater. At Romberg's request the orchestra played for nothing, but we had to pay the singer 100 rubles *in bills.*

The concert in the evening was completely filled, and also attended by the court again. We made a clear profit of over 1,000 rubles silver—that was pretty! without that we would have had trouble leaving Petersburg.

After the concert the Henselts and the two *Rombergs* were with us for the evening meal.

On *Saturday the 30th/18* as a result of the night's carousing we felt very poorly. At 10 o'clock we went to the rehearsal at *Viel-*

horsky's, who had again arranged for orchestral music in the evening.

For dinner at *Stieglitz's*—a fine *dinée* [*sic*]—not very fine hosts. This man has 40,000, and after I had brought him 4–5 letters took 10 tickets for my first concert—that was all!—

In the evening at *Vielhorsky's.* Symphony by *Mendelssohn*—3 Leonora overtures by *Beethoven.* Among the guests were Prince *von Oldenburg, Lvov, Nesselrode,* General *Laskovsky, Glinka* (composer), Herr *von Lenz, Robert Thal,* the music director *Behling,* etc. Several songs by the latter were performed during the meal, which were quite pretty but not exceptional. We were terribly tired, but stayed until 3 o'clock in the morning.

On *Sunday the 31st/19* in the morning we went with *Stöckhardt* to take a closer look at the house of Prince von *Oldenburg.* A magnificent, at the same time most comfortable, palace. The prince himself, with his spouse, greeted us, and the two charming children were fetched as well, so we should see them. The prince led us to his organ, which is located next to a small house chapel and is used during the service (he is Lutheran). Then he showed us a statue by [Bien-Aimé] that represents a Spanish woman dancer. From a corner window one has a charming view across the *Neva,* from which it was difficult for us to leave.

When we came home, we found *Michel Vielhorsky, Ribeaupierre, H. Romberg,* the latter with whom Robert later went to have breakfast, and thus encountered the emperor *by himself* in a one-horse sleigh.

Henselt gave a musical *matinée*—we arrived there just as he had finished, had been delayed by visits. We stayed there for dinner.

Monday the 1st of April/March 20. Terrible dirt in the streets because of the thaw, during which we partly walked, partly drove, in order to book a carriage to Moscow, and that with a German coachman. We were so stupid as to let ourselves be talked into a square box with two little holes for looking out, which we later regretted bitterly. We had been told that it is good to ride in— what a deception was waiting for us!—

Today Robert's journal celebrated its 10-year jubilee—Robert celebrated it with *Romberg*.

We stayed home the entire day, in the evening Henselt came to see us, and we then chatted with him pleasantly for a long time.

On *Tuesday the 2nd of April/March 21* we still had terribly much to do, visits to make to *Stieglitz*, the *Vielhorskys*, and others, to pack, go to the Henselts' once more for dinner, in brief, not until 10 o'clock in the evening, when we left, did we get our thoughts together. Both Prince von *Oldenburg* and the [Grand Princess] *Leuchtenberg* sent me wonderfully valuable bracelets.

So we finally left in the evening, but *never* will I forget this first horrible night! That was a road the likes of which is unknown in Germany, nothing but holes, but yard-deep holes, so that when one fell into them, one didn't think it would be possible to get out. In this way we were almost completely battered to pieces as far as Moscow, not for one minute could we sit quietly in one spot,—at the beginning Robert believed he would faint, and would gladly have turned back again, but this carriage had already been paid for, his uncle was also expecting us in Tver, thus we had to accept our fate. We weren't very cheerful on this trip, as anyone could imagine. Fortunately because of their wide runners the Russian sleighs can never turn over, otherwise we could well have broken our arms and legs. Unfortunately we were also very dissatisfied with our coachman—every moment something in the wagon broke, which he wouldn't get fixed because he thought it would still work like that, until we finally got stuck in villages several times in order to have repairs made. Oh God, if we could only have beaten this careless person up, how often we would have liked to do that!—

The Trip to Russia

Wednesday the 3rd of April/March 22 was spent in the awful agony of traveling. In the evening we passed through *Novgorod,* interesting city, already constructed somewhat in the Moscow style.

On *Thursday the 4th of April/March 23,* continuous bad countryside up to the Volkonsky Mountains,—a chain of small hills that the Russians call a mountain range. Volkonsky itself a small village with pretty girls. The weather was always beautiful, but that couldn't diminish our suffering. We traveled nonstop this night as well.

On *Friday the 5th of April/March 24* by noon we were in *Torzhok*—well known for its shoes. We found a good inn there that had a reputation for good cutlets—which we ate, of course, and found them good but not outstanding. Approaching *Tver* the countryside became more agreeable; for a long time we drove along the river, the *Tvertsa,* we also passed a forest with a pretty monastery. Toward the evening we saw *Tver* lying on a hill beautifully illuminated. A peculiar city, very expansively built, situated quite romantically. We drove (by now it was already evening) to Robert's cousin *Carl's,* son of the old man *Schnabel,* but found, as Robert says, the nest empty. Husband and wife had already gone to the country, in order to be able to greet his uncle first thing in the morning on his 71st birthday.[23] Everything had been arranged most comfortably for our arrival, the servants rushed around for us, and a friend of the family who spoke German also came by so that we could communicate with them. The domestic servants were all very Russian. We enjoyed being here by ourselves at first, so that we could quietly orient ourselves somewhat within the family; we discovered that *Carl* has married his third wife, that the old aunt (a native of Meissen) is also still alive, and many other things as well that interested us. One can well imagine how happy we felt that evening, in such a strange land to arrive in the home of such close relatives, to find everything prepared in order to provide us the greatest comfort! We completely gave in to our enjoyment and went to sleep most satisfied in comfortably soft German beds— even the moon shining into the little room greeted us in a friendly way.

On *Saturday the 6th of April/March 25* at 7 o'clock in the morning we drove in the uncle's sleigh, harnessed with 3 horses, one behind the other, to *Seskovitz* in the most beautiful sunny weather; halfway there we had breakfast in the carriage—the servant had taken along wine, rolls, meat, eggs, *etc.*—where it tasted quite superb to us. At one o'clock we arrived for the uncle's 71st birthday—there was great joy on all sides! The old man had not seen any members of his family for years and didn't know Robert at all yet. The young Schnabels are nice people, he a great hypochondriac, but she a most affectionate woman, *a native of Tallinn.* The day was spent gossiping; the uncle is very weak physically, but mentally still very lively.

On *Sunday* the serf women arrived early as on Easter and brought Easter eggs, a ceremony that always ends with a kiss. A young pretty serf woman interested me especially; the old aunt had gotten her as a present from a friend; the aunt had formally adopted her, had taught her German, writing, reading, and regarded her as her child, had been with her to Petersburg, where she took her along to all social events; this girl, only 12 years old, suddenly started behaving so abominably, became so disorderly, that the aunt, after all kinds of punishment failed to help, sent her back to the serfs, where she finally also married a very poor serf. With this girl one could say that birth factors cannot be ignored. Now this girl arrived to give us her Easter eggs as well. The aunt told me it gives her pain each time to see this woman for whom she had done so much with the highest expectations.

The relationship of the serfs to their masters is in no way as terrible as one thinks of it at home. If the master is good, then he is a father to the serfs, who worship and love him; if the master is bad, then our peasants might live just as poorly as the Russian ones.

Robert had a lot to tell the uncle, and a lot to listen to; he showed him letters from his parents and came to life, it seemed, in the pleasure of having yet seen, before the end of his life, the darling of his sister, whom he loved very much.

On *Monday the 8th of April/March 27,* farewell from the uncle, whom we will probably never see again.[24] The aunt drove to the town with us, the young *Schnabels* had already left the day before. The old aunt drove behind us in a *kibitka,*[25] we on ahead. It's amazing—after we had made such a big trip without any accidents, this little tour might have had an unfortunate outcome. First the driver ran into a pole so violently that, had we not by chance bent backward, both of us might have been crippled. Right after that he again drove (probably consternated by the first accident) into a puddle that, only lightly frozen over, broke immediately, so that one of the horses stumbled and was scraped. Then for two hours we drove on the water across ice in the warmest weather, and while ascending from the river we could still have had an accident because one horse became skittish. Those were a lot of misfortunes all at once—God be praised, whose protection we for once had felt very clearly here. Even during our departure from Seskovitz we were happy that everything had turned out so well— which proved to be unjustified.

In the middle of the day we had breakfast in a very shabby serf house, that was quite an establishment! The aunt conversed much in Russian with the serf woman, who stared at us like strange animals. The aunt is excellent company, and always in good spirits. I've really grown to like her. We arrived in *Tver* in a very bad mood because of the horrors, but were soon cheered up by our kind cousins. Later we went for a brief excursion; in the evening I played before a few music lovers. Specifically I very much liked a major with his wife. We were quite cheerful and comfortable together.

On *Tuesday the 9th of April/March 28* in the morning Carl gave us presents, Robert a beautiful Bulgarian robe, a cap with large tassel, and Russian shoes, and me a Russian tea machine, which gave me much joy.

At noon we took a ride through the town, visited a state councillor, and looked at the old aunt's former house and garden. Formerly the uncle had lived in *Tver*, and retired only at an older age to Seskovitz, which he purchased along with 200 serfs, and which Carl, who is currently a police chief, will take over after his death. In the afternoon I played in traveling clothes for some more of *Carl's* friends—then at 7 o'clock we left, again in our little wooden box. We had to endure new travel problems, which lasted nearly a day as yet. There was nothing of interest until the view of Moscow from *Petrovsky* [castle], which gave us the greatest surprise. It was here where *Napoleon* stayed during the burning of Moscow, which he thought he had already captured. It [i.e., Petrovsky with its castle and amusement park] is constructed in a most unusual way, and one really feels transported into "The Arabian Nights" when one sees it. From there until Moscow one drives between peculiar Russian country houses, until one then finally enters Moscow. It looks completely different from Petersburg, the houses are less magnificent and the streets irregular— the first impression isn't what one expects. We put up at Shevaltishev's, but I was so ill that I couldn't accompany Robert on his tour of the Kremlin.

He returned completely enchanted; I shared his delight as soon as I too had appreciated the magnificent view of the Kremlin. One arrives there through a main gate through which no man may go with his head covered,[26] then when one emerges one can see over the entire Kremlin with its many golden cupolas, the great cathe-

The Trip to Russia   273

dral, the great bell tower, the new palace that the emperor is currently having built for himself, the old *czar's palace,* the great armory, and much else still, but above all at the base of the Kremlin one can see a large part of the city, separated from the base of the Kremlin by the *Moskva* [River]. This view is indescribable, the city is so peculiarly oriental with its countless towers that one thinks one must be in Constantinople. Before one gets to the Kremlin, one sees an odd church, something I've never seen before, with 9 towers and each one different, one looks like a tulip, the other like a pineapple, yet another like all sorts of beautifully bordered ribbons, etc. This church is called [St. Basil's Cathedral]. At the Kremlin Robert was very interested in the great bell of *Ivan Veliky,* which he later also celebrated in verse.[27] This Kremlin stimulated us anew each time we saw it—we visited it nearly every day.

On *Thursday the 11th of April/March 30* we felt better—Robert too had become ill the night before. We immediately went to the Kremlin in the morning, by way of the shops, where one sees authentic Russians and where all the traffic takes on a wholly Asian character, then across the *Moskva,* in order to look at the Kremlin from below as well. The Moscow merchants and women wear a very pretty costume. The men long coats held shut by a band at the waist, and the women silk cloths wound around their heads, never in a hat; it often looks rather strange when one sees a woman walking like that in a silk dress and a kerchief. Very conspicuous to us were the women serfs (it happened to be Easter week, when everyone came in from the country to have fun) in silk cossack jackets covered with the most beautiful fur, and underneath for instance an ordinary cotton dress. Everything here in Moscow interested us, because everything is so unusual—Moscow is truly unique in its own way, and nothing in Europe equals it.

As we were returning from our walk, Herr Reinhardt came to

see us, to whom we had been urgently referred by *Vielhorsky*. He used to be the most prominent piano teacher in Moscow, but for some time gives lessons only in the orphanage, to which he dedicates body and soul. He immediately took us to the *Hôtel de Dresde*, where we then also felt much better than before—at *Shevaltishev's* we had suffered so much from the heat. Our new landlord was named *Shor* and spoke German. We paid 15 ruble *bills* daily for the room, for the servant 25 rubles a week, 1 meal 4 rubles, *etc*. As in Petersburg everything was enormously expensive, but driving especially so—if one wants to make a visit one has to take the carriage for half a day and pay 3 rubles silver.

After dinner we drove for an hour's excursion around the Kremlin and back. At 6 o'clock we returned home and delighted ourselves with the setting sun from a corner window in our room (where one could also see part of the city, which gave us much pleasure, for the little there was nevertheless had lots of cupolas).

We went to bed very early, at a time when here life really picks up.

On *Friday the 12th of April/March 31* in the morning *Reinhardt* came with *Marcou* (violoncellist) to confer with us about the first concert. There were a few little debates, Robert was supposed to visit some bachelors without me, which he didn't want to do, thus I went along, to *Verstovsky*, the theater director, and *Grösser*, the music dealer. The distances here are enormous, one cannot go on foot at all, much less so than in Petersburg.

Our servant *Friedrich* was a German from Bremen; he had gone to Moscow (under Napoleon) with a French general, became sick there and had to stay, and hasn't gotten away since, and specializes in serving foreigners who do not understand Russian.

After the meal we went to a pastry shop and read German newspapers; in the evening we were at home.

On *Saturday the 13th/April 1* Robert was very ill. We received

The Trip to Russia   *275*

visits from Madame Reinhardt, *Villoing,* the teacher of Rubinstein, Reinhardt, and Grösser, and made visits to *Nebolsyn,* Count
Sherbatov the vice governor, and others.

For dinner we were at the Reinhardts. A *Dr. Nov* entertained
us very pleasantly by telling us much about *Field,* also Reinhardt,
who was one of his better pupils. He must have been a genial
person!—

After dinner we drove to the *Promenade,* where we found an
incredible crowd of carriages. It was the end of Easter week, where
the people amuse themselves with swings and jugglers. We got
home at 8 o'clock.

On *Sunday the 14th/April 2* in the morning we went with *Marcou* to the Kremlin; it is surrounded by a notched wall on which
there are iron hooks in order, as the saying goes, to display the
Strelitzs' heads, as ordered by Peter the 1st.[28] Right at the entrance to the Kremlin is a small watchtower that was used during
wartime, with the approach of the Tartars. Unfortunately, almost
all the churches were closed, so that we were only able to walk
around the Kremlin in the most awful mud, since for two weeks
we had already had the most beautiful sunshine, which then
melted the snow, however.

Visit from *Nebolsyn*—nice old man, who has married a young
capricious wife, however.

In the evening we looked for a café, where we read newspapers,
it was at the Smith's bridge and we found the Berlin Vossische
Zeitung there.

At the Kremlin we also saw the oldest church in Moscow, which
is already half sunken into the ground, and which the emperor
won't have demolished.[29]

On *Monday the 15th/April 3* we made many visits, but found
few people at home. We found Madame *Siniavine* to be a pleasantly elegant woman, and magnificently established. The post-

master *Bulgakov* seems to be a man of the world, but probably doesn't have much interest in music.

For dinner we were at *Nebolsyn's,* whose wife I found most unpleasant. He too is very beautifully established and has a beautiful room for music, which he put at our disposal, but we never used it, because for other reasons it never suited us.

While driving home, Robert had such an attack of dizziness that he suddenly was unable to see, and we became most anxiously concerned. It went away, but during our whole stay in Moscow he was always inclined to be dizzy. We couldn't explain this to ourselves at all, until later someone said this is a result of the Moscow beer that we drank every day, and had exactly this effect on Robert's strong body.

On *Tuesday the 16th/April 4* we were visited in the morning by Noble Marshall *Tcherkov,* who behaved very amiably toward us and whom we had much to thank for, because the *season* was completely over here, a large part of the nobility already in the country, and the few who were still around had no money and no longer any interest in the concerts. In Russia everything is a matter of fashion! it is fashionable to go to concerts until Easter, at that time the people assign a certain sum for this sort of entertainment, but after Easter God Himself can descend from heaven, he could achieve nothing; I couldn't have gotten anywhere without *Tcherkov,* because this man took a large number of tickets and distributed them, actually dragged people there by their hair. How much more I would have earned before Easter, it would have been altogether different.

We wanted to call on people, but couldn't because of Robert's dizziness. We walked around in the streets and amused ourselves with that quite well. We also visited the Kremlin again and Robert made a beautiful poem "The Bell Maker [*sic*] of Ivan Veliky," followed later by two others that were about Napoleon, about whom

The Trip to Russia 277

one is always automatically reminded in the Kremlin.[30] In the evening we chatted a lot with Reinhardt.

Wednesday the 17th/5. In the morning Robert always wrote poetry, while I played and received visitors. Today came: Fischer von Waldheim, a good old man, but disagreeably intrusive, who seems to me downright mad for females, even though he already has married children; Baron *Meyendorff*, an intelligent, interesting but at the same time very confused man.

At midday we drove to *Serge Golitsyn,* to whom we had been referred by Prince von Oldenburg, but who was of no use to us whatsoever, on the contrary he cost me a pair of gloves and Robert 3 rubles silver (for the carriage), since he had invited us to his home just to bid us "good day." Are these Moscow's elite? and Governor General Sherbatov, who has a loge at the theater but didn't buy a single ticket for any concert? are these Moscow's protectors of artists?

Later we drove to the road from *Smolensk* whence the French had come. We couldn't cross the *Moskva* because water showed beneath the ice.

Robert got it in his mind to settle in Moscow longer, but one must first examine each city more closely, since later on we did find quite a few drawbacks that would spoil one's stay as well.

We looked at the water tower from which all of Moscow obtains its water.

In the evening we went to the large theater. It is a beautiful, large, magnificently illuminated building, but was quite empty. They presented *Cosimo* by *Prévost* (?)—partly clever music and beautifully orchestrated; pretty playing and singing by the Russians. After the concert we went to the *Passage Gagarin* and had a glass of punch there.

On *Thursday the 18th/April 6* we went walking a lot. In the morning Robert always wrote poetry, and then our way always led to the Kremlin, which aroused ever-new fantasies in Robert and always presented new delights to our eyes.

We paid a visit to Lehnhold and discovered a beautiful warehouse for pianos there, mostly those by Wirth and Stutznagel.

Later we looked at the Hall *de la noblesse*, which is quite magnificent and like the one in Petersburg holds 3–4,000 people. In terms of its decorations Robert found it to be even more elegant that the one in Petersburg. On the way back we passed an enormously large house that was almost as long as an entire street is at home, but which had only 4 walls. It had been burned out during the [great Moscow] fire, and the present owner had let it stay like that on a whim (there may well have been another special reason), though painted from the outside, because it is located on the biggest street of Moscow, the *Tverskoy*, but from the inside, as mentioned before, completely hollow and desolate. How rich must a man be who leaves such a large piece of land unused.

The evenings we always spent quietly at home—the season for *soirees* was already at an end here.

On *Friday the 19th/April 7* thirst directed us to a beer dive, where we listened to two men singing horribly. They seemed to be coachmen.

For dinner we were at *Fischer von Waldheim's*. Here Robert writes "insults that could barely be endured, and Clara's conduct at the time." I know of nothing, but it seems to me now, while reading through the pages of notes, that I often aroused Robert's ill will—surely never with bad intentions, but always through awkwardness and absence of quick wit. Often it's only after thinking about it calmly that I find what others who are smarter know immediately.

On *Saturday the 20th/April 8* we received visits from *Amatov* (violinist), *Marcou,* and *Tcherkov,* who usually came on the day of the concert in order to pay for the purchased tickets himself. Rob-

The Trip to Russia

ert called on *Genischta,* the leading piano teacher in Moscow as well as a man talented in composing, but he strikes me as very conceited, which made me feel uncomfortable every time I saw him.

In the evening I gave my first concert in the little theater; it was empty, but the great attentiveness of the audience made up for that somewhat. The audience was most enthusiastic and a beautiful lady, Madame de *Kiriev,* even sent me a bouquet of flowers. During the intermission Prince *Sherbatov, Tcherkov,* and many others came onstage.

On *Sunday the 21st/April 9* we went, after we had many visits, through the imperial garden at the foot of the Kremlin and then up to the Kremlin itself, where we climbed the big bell tower, but soon left again, since neither of us are heroes in climbing heights. Then we saw the arsenal, where some small Saxon cannons can also be found that Robert thinks look so peaceful, so bright and new, as if they had never been used.

In the evening we again wandered around the streets until 9 o'clock, when Baron *Meyendorff* came to see us. (We had been referred to him by Liszt, with whom he seems to be very good friends.)

Monday the 22nd/April 10 uneventful day. In the evening, brief walk to the Kremlin.

It was very noticeable to me here never to receive visits from ladies of the *nobility;* Madame *Siniavine* always wrote me how much she would wish to be able to express to me her delight about my playing, *would I please come to see her.* That astonished and hurt me quite a lot, since I wasn't used to that; in the largest cities the leading ladies did not think they were too good to visit me, and here not a single one did it. Reinhardt later explained to me that in Moscow it is not the custom to visit women artists, and one *never* does it. That soothed me somewhat, although it always hurt me anew when Madame *Siniavine* wrote I should come to see her. And later, when we gave a matinee at our place, and had invited all these prominent ladies, all of them came—how was that? wasn't that contrary to the custom?—

Tuesday the 23rd/April 11. Constant illness of Robert. For dinner at *Tcherkov's* (noble marshall),—an excellent meal, a most affectionate hostess, who incidentally seemed quite odd but good-natured to me. She wore glasses and smoked cigars after dinner, as did her sister the princess [Dolgoruky]. The gentlemen also had to do this *sans gêne,* and found themselves *con amore* while doing so. I also got to know the amiable Countess *Bobrinsky* here.

After the meal we paid a visit to Herr *von Stryk,* director of the Home for Foundlings. That was a friendly couple, which made the stay in Moscow pleasant for us, and also much that was unpleasant, of which there could be no lack during this unfavorable time for concerts, after everyone had gotten sick and tired of music, although the public, once they did come to my concerts, honored me in every way.

In the evening Robert usually read the newspapers at *Pedolli's.* At home we found *Genischta,* who in Robert's notes is described as a boring Philistine, which I sincerely agree with.

On *Wednesday the 24th/April 12* Robert completed another poem—this collection of poems shall follow as an appendix to this book.

For dinner we were at Baron *Meyendorff's,* where Frau *von Kiriev* and the young Herr *von Tzinoviev* were the only guests. This woman is very beautiful and at the same time has a very pleasant personality. Her son was with her—a child as pretty as a picture. After dinner we went with *Meyendorff* and the lady to the instrument maker *Talarnov,* whose instruments are nice but enormously expensive; one of them costs 1,000 rubles silver.

We walked home along the *boulevards* with *Meyendorff,* who al-

The Trip to Russia   *281*

ways amused us with his absentmindedness. The evening was wonderfully beautiful—our furs started to be a burden to us.

At home we found a letter from *Schneeberg*—always our favorite surprise.

Thursday the 25th/April 13 was the first birthday of our little Elise, which we now had to celebrate far away. I felt quite sad at heart. For dinner we were at Reinhardt's, but we could never feel really at home there.

In the evening grand ballet in the theater—boring.

Friday the 26th/April 14. Nothing of any importance happened today, and because of that we were amused by a little scene with our Friedrich. This man had gotten to be so old and pedantic, and had these old attitudes of his, so that for instance we couldn't get him to buy anything except in the so-called shopping booths, but these were half an hour away from us. He thought that what he wanted couldn't be bought anywhere else. Now when we got back home late in the evening, i.e., 9:30, Robert had an appetite for *caviar;* Friedrich insisted one could get that only in the shopping booths. We argued why in Russia one shouldn't be able to get *caviar* at any store, and that it's a disgrace, etc., until it got to be too much for our Friedrich and he left, and then did actually get some right away. He had rescued his honor.

May this little unimportant adventure receive leniency in these pages—it was our most important experience today.

In the evening we bought postcards of *Moscow.*

On *Saturday the 27th/April 15* at 1 o'clock I gave my second concert in the Hall of the *Nobility,* which again was poorly attended, although better than the first. The audience most enthusiastic, however, even though the piano wasn't at all clearly audible, since the hall is generally unfavorable for music, and we had placed the piano in the center of the hall, as everyone had advised us, but which we bitterly regretted. I was very unhappy about it, as well as about the small audience, which of course seemed even smaller in this enormous place than it actually was.

Toward the evening we drove—everyone knows where—to the Kremlin. Today we saw Moscow in the last light of the evening—what a magnificent view! (I made a mistake, Robert drove by himself, I was too tired due to the concert.) Then he went into one of the churches of the Kremlin and heard disgusting church music there, consisting of nothing but fifths and octaves. Then he inspected the cannons, of which the many marked with an *N*, which had also been badly shot up, interested him the most. Furthermore he found those from the revolution *"liberté et egalité"* (in the Kremlin?) as well as Saxon ones by [Prince] *Xaverius*.

In the evening Reinhardt and Marcou came to our place, with whom we had many debates about the orchestra that we had wanted for the last concert, especially also in order to play Robert's symphony. Can one really believe that in Moscow it was impossible to get the people together? The music director *Johannes* was insulted that Robert did not visit him, also the cellist *Schmidt, Marcou* had damaged his finger, in one word, it didn't work out. Robert also became impatient and therefore dropped any further efforts.

Today a travel book that Robert had left at the station was returned to him. He was very pleased.

Sunday the 28th/April 16. We had constant rain for several days. Today Robert took care of the above-mentioned orchestra operations, but without any success. It's a disgrace to call such people as *Johannes* and *Schmidt* artists—they are simply mechanics, and just as uneducated as people like that. *Kudelski* (violinist) was really the only one with whom one could do anything, and he then finally brought it to the point where we could at least put Robert's quintet together, for which to be sure we had to be satisfied with a *hired* cellist, poor devil, who only plays for his daily bread, and barely knows what music is. At Schmidt's Robert sud-

The Trip to Russia   *283*

denly stood up and left as a consequence of this reckless behavior. It was probably the best signal he deserved after that. I was furious at the whole Moscow music world, *Marcou, Reinhardt,* everyone included.

At noon I played at the Home for Foundlings for a large number of orphans, of whom one class is given lessons by Reinhard. After that we inspected the entire institute, one of the most impressive I've ever seen. Herr *von Stryk* and Frau *von Hoymar* took us around, both people of magnificent character. First we attended the children's classes, where everything is most properly organized; pretty are the little tents in which the young girls do their exercises. Then we entered a room for making drawings, where we were surprised by the skillfulness of the girls. Several young girls there presented Robert with an embroidered folder, as they had done for me earlier, right after my playing, when Robert wasn't present. This courtesy made us very happy. Then we went up a flight of steps, always an iron floor, to the wet nurses, where we found the highest degree of cleanliness, and among the 540 nursing children didn't hear a single one scream. The nurses were all most properly dressed in white linen, and wore red or blue velvet caps. All the children have their little beds and their little linen presses with their own number, which is also marked on the children's laundry. Then we also saw several actual orphans, whose parents were unknown, which made a sad impression on me. From there we went into the classrooms for boys and into their large hall, where they also sang a few things. After that I also played a little bit, since the boys never get to go where the girls are. From there the boys led us to their gymnasium, where they demonstrated some of their skills. Now we returned to the lower floor, where we inspected the beautifully organized kitchen, where everything really seemed as if it had been licked clean, so bright and shiny.

[As RS indicates in his notebook, after that the chapel of the house was inspected.] Most of the Russian churches are rich with gold and diamonds—the people contribute to their churches, even if it's the last thing they have.

Finally we went to the lowest floor, where we found the reception room for the little (only newborn) children; year after year one man and one woman are there; one of them registers the children in the book and gives their number to the mother of the child or to whoever brings the child in, the same number that is then also hung around the child's neck; the other immediately takes charge of the child and carries it into the adjacent room, where it is immediately bathed, dressed, and turned over to the wet nurse, about 20 of whom come every morning and wait for children. And a minister is also available to baptize it right away, if that hasn't already been done. The mother doesn't have to tell either her name or anything else, she is asked about nothing except what the child is called or supposed to be called, what religion it should have, and that's all. While we were there two children were brought *numbers* 2359 and 2360 for this year. At least 20 arrive every day, and 7–8,000 are accepted every year. They stay there for 6 weeks and are then sent with their wet nurses to the country where they remain until their 10th year, i.e., that is how long the wet nurse receives 2 silver rubles a week. If she wants to keep the child longer, she may do so, but has to pay for that herself. Rarely do the wet nurses return the children, who are then brought up to be serfs, as all foundlings generally are. Each month a physician goes around to the villages to look after the children, whether they are well cared for and healthy. If that is not the case, then they are taken back and cared for in the hospital, which is also located in the foundling home. This building is like a self-sufficient city; it has its hospital rooms, its doctors, its laundresses, seamstresses, in short 7,000 people live there. One can't have any idea of the grandeur of this institute, if one hasn't seen it himself. And in

The Trip to Russia   285

this large house and for these many children Herr *von Stryk* is
the father and Frau *von Hoymar* the mother, both of the noblest
character, and loved and honored by everyone. The ones who are
educated and raised there up to their confirmation or perhaps even
longer are the orphans of officers; the girls are raised to be govern-
esses and when they leave must serve for 6 years in the governor's
province, before they may return to Moscow or Petersburg.

I will never forget the impression that this day has made on me!
First the grandeur of the institute, of the building, but then the
succession of good deeds that are practiced here every day and then
also the accompanying sadness, that all these children are without
parents and for the most part have been voluntarily abandoned by
them. That is terrible but really is softened when one observes the
kindheartedness of both directors.

This institute is a deathless sign of the kindheartedness of the
Empress Catherine, who donated it.

After this powerful excursion, which lasted close to three hours,
we sat down for dinner at Herr *von Stryk's*. He had led us around
these three hours despite his wooden leg; one of his legs was shot
off in the war. Our meal was excellent, as always at *Stryk's*, but
we left around 8 o'clock to go home, where we arrived immensely
tired.

On *Monday the 29th/April 17* in the morning we had visits
from *Dr. Lehnhold* and the piano teacher *Lemoc*, a Bohemian, who
also once accompanied [the soprano Angelica] *Catalani* on her
travels. Later Baron *Meyendorff* picked us up to go to the Kremlin,
where we looked at the Treasury. But we saw so much there in
a very short time that very little remained in my memory. What
interested me the most was the Polish constitution in a little box
at the feet of the emperor,[31] furthermore crowns of immense
splendor, especially that of *Ivan III,* then a scepter and crown also
of great value, a gift of the Byzantine emperor. We also saw the

sedan chair of *Charles* XII for the battle of *Poltava,* [and] many remarkable things of *Peter* the Great. A bowl by *B. Cellini* attracted our attention with its most tasteful work in mother of pearl, which revealed the master.

Many swords of noteworthy people, thrones, blindingly bright precious stones, finally we also saw a hall filled with all kinds of imperial and royal carriages, but one just can't remember it all.

For dinner I was at the Countess *Bobrinsky's,* whom I liked very well; Robert did not accompany me, since he was not well. She gave me a few really nice little things for my children.

In the evening Reinhardt and *Marcou* were at our place—Robert writes correctly at this point "two negative friends, who do nothing, but talk a lot."

Tuesday the 30th/April 18. For dinner to *Dr. Lehnhold's,* then at home played some sonatas by *Beethoven* with *Kudelski,* and the one by *Gade. Genischta* joined us—always a disagreeable visit for us.

On *Wednesday the 1st of May/April 19* in the morning I rehearsed Robert's double variations with Reinhardt, which he played quite well, some things at least more in the character of the piece than Henselt. At 1 o'clock, rehearsal of the quintet with *Kudelski, Kretschmann, Amatov,* and *N. N.,* the last of whom scratched a lot.

Robert went to the English *Club* for the midday meal with Herr *von Stryk.* It was a Russian meal; hazard was played for high stakes after the meal, as at all parties like that in Russia.

In the evening soirée at Madame *Siniavine's;* distinguished and large party. I played much and beautifully, as Robert says; at the same time, however, always talking and whist playing of the gentlemen in the next room. At the end of the *soirée* Madame *Siniavine* had quite tastefully arranged a little lottery, where some nice winnings came my way too. Robert was deeply preoccupied the

The Trip to Russia   287

whole evening with looking at the princess [Bariatinsky], who is called "angel" both in his notebook and in his heart. But she really was beautiful. This evening Robert found a good description of his favorite bell *by Ivan Veliky.* The next day Frau *von Siniavine* had it sent to my husband as a present. That made him very happy, me along with him.

On *Thursday the 2nd of May/April 20* at 1 o'clock we gave a *matinée* at our place. We had invited 30–40 people, and it was actually here that the most aristocratic ladies also showed up, and gladly, as it seemed. The quintet constituted the beginning and was exceptionally well liked; I would have liked to play it at my last concert, but the hall is too big for quartet music. The quintet was followed by several solo pieces played by myself and Robert's variations with Reinhardt at the end. We were in a really cheerful mood today, also received letters from home.

Reinhardt stayed with us for dinner, which did not suit Robert, however, since he just as I was very exhausted.

In the evening for a walk on the Tver *Boulevard.*

Friday the 3rd of May/April 21. Name day of the empress— magnificent beautiful weather. At 10 o'clock in the morning we went to the Home for Foundlings, where today the archbishop himself held services. We were in a gallery with Frau von Stryk, Reinhardt, and a Fräulein *von Osorov,* whom I liked very much; from there we could witness everything without being disturbed. It was a grand ceremony—partly barbaric chanting, but partly modern as well. The archbishop was dressed up as Jesus Christ, which was very disgusting, even more the hand kissing at the end, which the governor had started. The most prominent people of the city (men only, of course) were present and had a big breakfast right after the service, in a beautiful hall where the portrait of the empress, decorated with the most magnificent flowers, was displayed. While they were having breakfast with Herr *von Stryk* at the head of the table, we went to the front house to look at the obstetrics school, whose director is Reinhardt's stepmother. Any woman in advanced pregnancy can go there and receive the best care, a wet nurse immediately for the child, and can stay there for 6 or more weeks after the delivery, until they know where to go next. If they don't want to reveal their name, no one will ask them for it, and if they want to remain completely incognito and invisible, then they wear a mask and are immediately given a single room for themselves, can also bring their own female servants along. Everything is arranged so properly and beautifully that it gives one pleasure to see it. How many women, maybe even affluent ones, there are who cannot permit themselves to have the rest and care at home that everyone receives here. This institute is a worthy companion to the Home for Foundlings.

When we returned, the dignitaries were nearly finished with their breakfast, and after they finally left we sat down at a small table, Herr *von Stryk* kept the band there, and thus we spent that noon festively. After the meal another little dance was performed.—Yet I shouldn't forget to mention the beautiful strawberries we received *in jelly* for dessert.

In the evening we went to the big theater to see Glinka's opera "All for the Czar."[32] The first act with much graceful music, especially the pretty trio, sounding somewhat like nationalistic music—the orchestration weak and the brass too prominent—apart from that [Glinka] is a happy, well-organized musical person. The second half of the opera was lame in every respect and barren of any dramatic progression, in addition a storm set that was most shabby while at the same time funny. This would never have been allowed to be shown on a German stage.

After the theater we went to a Berlin sausage and ham store that our Friedrich had found for us, to our great delight.

Saturday the 4th of May/April 22. Magnificent weather again.

The Trip to Russia 289

Visit to Frau *von Siniavine,* to whom Robert gave his poems; then rehearsal *entre nous* in the aristocratic hall. After dinner drove with the *Stryks* to the *Simonov* monastery. A Russian monastery, bright colors everywhere—trees and graves inside the courtyard. We climbed up to the platform of the single church, where we had a wonderful view over Moscow with its countless cupolas and towers. Visit to the abbot, a jovial man, who served us tea and then also gave us postcards of *Simonov.* At 6 o'clock we went to the vespers. The singing of the monks is quite unusual, *piano,* with hollow voice and very monotonous—for 5–6 hours they sing always the same thing. The composition is partly barbaric, partly childish, full of octaves and fifths. Robert escaped after 2 hours of martyrdom because of this singing (which is famous nonetheless, just because of the peculiar sound), I soon followed him and the others with me as well. The Russian church service is the most strenuous I know. It lasts at least 2 ½ hours, during which all those present must stand, and prostrate themselves any moment. I can't imagine how weak natures can stand that! and then the service itself is so monotonous, so uniform, the same thing is repeated over and over, and they may cross themselves 1,000 times, as do people on the street in front of each holy icon, of which there are many more here than in the Catholic countries.

Robert was able to escape early enough to see Moscow at sunset, which surely was more uplifting than this horrible church singing.

Then we went to have tea at the Stryks, where Herr *von Ozorov* sang Russian folk songs dreadfully, but otherwise he was a kind man.

The yearning to leave Moscow for home tortured us terribly the last week of our stay here, we counted the hours.

On *Sunday the 5th of May/April 23* at 1 o'clock, my last concert at the *Assemblée.* Small audience but very enthusiastic. In the notebook it says—Clara played consistently beautifully—I also played a new Fantasy by Thalberg, which I had just learned in Moscow. Also a *Notturno* by *Field* gave much pleasure.

NB. I almost forgot to remember Madame *Field,* who had looked me up. But she was separated from *Field* during the last years of his life, and is not supposed to be worth anything. I saw her only once.

Toward the evening we went for a nice walk across the Tver Boulevards up to the Moskva Bridge, where we looked at the Kremlin once more for a really long time, and truly feasted our eyes on this singular view. From there we went to restore ourselves at the confectioner *Pedolli's,* Robert with newspapers, I with ice cream.

On *Monday the 6th of May/April 24* we had daguerrotypes of ourselves made for the cousin in *Tver;* one of them was a good likeness, and so that was the one we sent.[33]

Today we took our breakfast in the Berlin sausage booth—it tasted superb to us, and what's more, we also had goat cheese— surely a rarity in Russia.

Farewell from *Tcherkov,* a kind nobleman.

For dinner at Reinhardt's with the *Vehs.*

Tuesday the 7th of May/April 25. Always magnificent weather. Today our preparations for departure began. To the banker Brandenburg, a little shopping at the Armenians and in the Russian shop, then I went with *Lemoc* to the Cholera Institute and played there. Great anger over the bad piano there and *Lemoc's* foolishness that he hadn't put another one there, so that I should have to loudly express my judgment about this instrument, on which one could barely move—he had told me earlier that it is quite good, but just to achieve his purpose. I was furious!—

Farewell from *Villoing,* then with Herr *von Stryk* and Reinhardt to the Kremlin to see the Coronation Cathedral and the old *Palace*

The Trip to Russia

of the Czars, called *Terem.* In the cathedral the portrait of The Mother of God was especially precious. The *Palace of the Czars* is quite peculiar, in Tartar and Chinese taste. We also saw the window that the false *Dmitry* had jumped out of, and a beautiful, very precious house chapel. All of the rooms are decorated in a very colorful way, and everything has been left the way it was ages ago. From there we went along for dinner at Herr *von Stryk's,* where he had a suckling pig, most delicate, set before us—he definitely wanted us to get to know this authentic Russian food.

After dinner, shopping in the [Gostini Dvor] and farewell from the Kremlin. At home we found Madame Reinhardt, who wanted to bid us adieu for the last time.

On *Wednesday the 8th of May/April 26,* farewell from *Marcou* and *Lemoc.* Before the departure we went to a Russian restaurant where we found the people truly in their national character. Coachmen, craftsmen, *etc.,* came there and drank tea—we ate a cutlet there, but with much disgust, since the dirt here was terrible.

Reinhardt made it to the coach, and finally at 10:30 we left, after we had bidden adieu to our good-hearted Friedrich.

While driving out we saw green for the first time—how happy we were to be going back home!—

The weather was magnificent! every day of traveling we had the most beautiful spring warmth, and magnificent bright nights.

On *Thursday the 9th of May/April 27* at 6 o'clock in the morning we arrived in *Tver* and had the good fortune to stay there long enough to look up *Carl* [von Schnabel]. We had breakfast with them and they then accompanied us across the Volga by boat to the stagecoach. Soon we got to *Torzhok*—in the evening to *Vyshni Volochek,* the latter a nice town with many canals.

Friday the 10th/April 28. The weather always glorious, the nights charming, but life in the stagecoach intolerable, terribly long stops at the stations, and after a brief stretch of road something would always tear in the saddle and harness, which in Russia consists only of ropes. Sometimes we were beside ourselves.

At 11 o'clock in the evening to Great *Novgorod*.

Saturday the 11th of May/April 29. Good midday meal in Pomerania. We often met German hosts at the stations.

This time the road was much better than when we had come here, consequently despite its great length the trip not as exhausting. Toward evening we passed through the charming *Sophia* and at 10 o'clock we arrived at Petersburg. We stayed at the station inn.

Sunday the 12th of May/April 30. In the morning we went to the Henselts'. How entirely different we found Petersburg again in the summer. On the *Nevsky Prospect* we were surprised by the beautiful wooden pavement, on which the carriages just flew by.

At Henselt's we met with *Gross*—a hypochondriacal, disagreeable person. Henselt played from his concerto, later we went with the Henselts for dinner at Wirth's, where *Gehling* with his wife were as well. After dinner we climbed the Admiralty Tower, which has a magnificent view—one can look out as far as the sea. But it was very dangerous to climb the stairs, and we were glad when we got down safely. In the evening we promenaded along the *Neva* and then to a pastry shop, where we read newspapers.

Monday the 13th/May 1. In the morning, visit by Gross—boring in his remarks. Later we went to the *Vielhorskys'*, who received us with the customary friendliness.

At *Bernard's* Robert met *Haumann,* who had given concerts in Petersburg while we were in Moscow. *Bernard* told Robert about an amusing adventure that *Haumann* had with Stieglitz.

Later we went to the steamship counter, but couldn't find it. The *Neva* delighted us. For dinner at the Henselts'. *Madame Henselt* is sometimes quite ill-mannered, nasty, and often *very*

The Trip to Russia   293

stingy. I teased her a bit because of her horses, which she pampers so much that she prefers not to let them run at all.

After dinner we inspected the instruments at *Wirth's*—it's difficult for one to make a choice, since all of them are so beautiful.

Tuesday the 14th/May 2. A rainy day. In the morning we went to the Zoological Museum with Madame Henselt and Doctor Schultz. We sat down in a hansom cab, but Madame Henselt with Doctor Schultz preferred crossing the Neva by boat, where they were surprised by terribly rainy weather. We met again at the museum. We also had a small fight with our driver, whom in the initial shock I began to assault.

The Zoological Museum is surely one of the biggest and most beautiful in the world. An enormous mammoth interested me the most. We had a little argument whether the teeth lying next to it aren't horns rather than teeth?

The Chinese cabinet also was of great interest to us—what magnificent fabrics it contained!—

From there we went to Stöckhardt to take our farewell, since we now wanted to leave Russia in earnest. But how we fought each other! Robert couldn't make up his mind to travel by sea, and it was just too difficult to get away by land, and so much more strenuous!—

In the evening Robert went with Gross to a quartet evening at *Albrecht's* (a native of Breslau). They played among other things one of his quartets. He came back in the evening at 11 o'clock.

Wednesday the 15th/May 3. Today was the aforementioned sea war with Robert.

Dinner at the Henselts'. In the morning I went shopping with Madame Henselt and Madame Gehling—presents for our acquaintances. The horn player Eisner came to see Robert and asked him to listen to the daughter of State Councillor *Simonsen* play the piano, in order to give advice whether it's worth the effort to send her to the conservatory in Leipzig. *Eisner* is an honest, excellent person! unfortunately Robert could not, on account of obstacles, fulfill his wish.

In the evening we went to *Vielhorsky's,* where Robert's quartets were played, unfortunately badly. We got to know the daughter of *Michel Vielhorsky* today—an amiable lady. It was the last evening today with our distinguished protectors. *Michel* amused us with his absentmindedness, which at times is probably an affectation, often in order to avoid certain unpleasant invitations.

At 1:30 we got home. The night was magnificently bright. Here the sun doesn't set before 10 o'clock and rises again at 2 o'clock.

Thursday the 16th/May 4. Visit by State Councillor *Michelson* with daughter—I was not at home. At 10 o'clock we drove with Romberg and *Mathieux Vielhorsky* to Tsarskoye Selo [Pushkin]. The station was not at all elegant, but the road from Tsarskoye to Pavlovsk charming. This is the property of the Grand Prince *Michael,* but is open to the public as a place of amusement. We were not able to look around any further, since we wanted immediately to drive back to Tsarskoye Selo again. Having arrived there again, we took in a nicely prepared breakfast in the home of Count *Vielhorsky* (as the [Grand Princess] Leuchtenberg's adjutant he has to go out there every day), and then drove around in the park in a long line (a carriage like a sofa, with seats on both sides), a favor that does not come to everyone, because only those who belong to the court are allowed to drive in the park. Unfortunately, we were so pressed that we could see everything only superficially, since I was supposed to play that very evening at the Grand Princess *Helene's.*

Today we luxuriated in spring, only I was unfortunately very ill. First we looked at the new castle, but only from the outside, since it was inhabited. It is fairly simple, especially by contrast to the

The Trip to Russia

old, colossal, and overly ornate one. It is immensely wide and built in impure taste, but on the inside offers much of interest. The most interesting was the room of the Emperor Alexander, his bedroom, where everything still was the way he had left it. Then a room, or better yet a salon, completely faced with amber, walls, everything. What large sums must have been put into that!—

From there we drove to the arsenal, which is small but most exquisite, and beautifully maintained.

The luxury was enormous, mostly it was gifts to the emperor. Most astonishing to me were 2 riding saddles whose edges were completely oversewn with diamonds. One of them was a present that the sultan had given the emperor after the peace [treaty of 1829] at Adrianople [Edirne, Turkey]. We also found many things of *Napoleon's*.

From there we drove to the artifical ruin in which Dannecker's Jesus Christ is erected. The posture was not wholly desirable, and the lower half of the figure almost too big in relation to the head. The ruin was ridiculous.

At 3 o'clock we drove back, and at 7 o'clock to the Grand Princess *Helene* with Henselt. Robert writes—"beautiful woman with regal bearing, very intelligent, educated and lovable in conversation." (in fact she conversed almost exclusively with Robert— she's supposed to like conversation with men better than with women.) I played well, despite my not having touched a pianoforte for nearly 2 weeks.

We met a Count *Pahlen* (son of the conspirator against Emperor *Paul*)[34] and Count *Oseyev,* a friendly man. In the evening at the Henselts' until 11 o'clock. There one constantly has to witness fights between husband and wife.

On *Friday the 17th/May 5* in the morning, farewell visits from *Böhme* and *Stöckhardt.* Then to *Wirth,* where I selected a piano for myself—it cost 1,200 rubles *in bills.* From there I went to the

foundlings' home, where I played as a favor for *Michel Vielhorsky.*
We had much awkwardness over the passport, but Herr Koberwein
cleared it all up.

For dinner at the Henselts'—farewell there from the Geh-
lings—Madame Gehling proved to be very obliging toward me
during the last week, and ran around with me to do shopping for
3 hours every day. We had a big thunderstorm after dinner, which
unfortunately kept us from going to the islands, which are supposed to be so magnificent.[35]

In the evening, farewell from *Michel Vielhorsky. Mathieu* [Viel-
horsky] was in Tsarskoye Selo, therefore we did not see him again.
This farewell was difficult for us—we had really come to like
these people!—

Late in the evening Gross and Henselt came to bid us adieu.
Henselt had actually made us more sad than happy, because by
earning [so much] money he ruins himself as an artist.

Saturday the 18th/May 6. I still had a lot of packing to do in
the morning, then Robert went to Stieglitz, where he had a run-
in with a rude clerk. At 1 o'clock we left on the steamboat, after
we had finally said good-bye to the two Rombergs and Madame
Henselt (who had arrived only one minute before departure with
all sorts of commissions, *etc.*) How gladly she would just have
sailed away with us to Germany! What a commotion that was at
the quay! these people!

Petersburg now disappeared bit by bit with its beautiful golden
towers, which did make us feel somewhat tenderhearted. The
shores of the Estonian coast were beautiful, we passed by Peterhof
[Petrodvorets] and Oranienbaum [Lomonosov], but at too great a
distance to be able to see it.

At 4 o'clock we arrived in Kronstadt [Kronshlot], where we
landed right next to the big steamship *"Alexandra."* There a large
midday banquet awaited us, which could barely accommodate all

The Trip to Russia 297

the guests, since very many had sailed along just to accompany their relatives. After the meal both of the smaller steamboats went back to Petersburg (one of them had also brought passengers to the "*Nicolaus,*" which was supposed to leave for Lübeck at the same time as we did); there were still many farewell scenes, until the bell sounded, and now it was over! those of us who were now on the big ship had to stay there. We were (I believe) 59 passengers.

The port of Kronstadt is imposing with its Russian fleet, but despite its many ships it seemed desolate to me.

The evening was magnificent! Because of passport matters we had to remain in Kronstadt until

Sunday the 19th/May 7 at 3:45, when we finally departed. We had interesting travel company, among which we got to know especially Prince *Metchersky* from Moscow, a young piano teacher Hermes from Moscow (a native of Mecklenburg), Frau and Fräulein von *Chambeau* (who were mentioned previously, in Petersburg), a young Portuguese named [Borges di Castro] (Robert's cabin mate), various Russian generals, and Frau *von Schloezer* with 3 children. Prince *Metchersky* was the leader of the conversation—full of humor and spirit.

Soon the coast completely disappeared, and only now and again did we encounter ships and in the Gulf of Finland still much ice. Our captain was named *Schütt* and was making the first voyage to *Swinemünde* [Świnoujście, Poland]. The *Nicolai* always went ahead of us, until we lost her on the side.

In the afternoon the clouds towered into a thunderstorm, which to my great horror we had to sail directly into—I would have preferred to turn around!—The thunderstorm became very severe and inundated us so quickly that it wasn't possible to pull the sails down, and the storm broke one of the masts, which crashed onto the deck with a terrible noise; fortunately, the sailors were occupied at the other side of the vessel, otherwise it might have killed some of them. The shock affected everyone, although Prince *Metchersky* tried to make light of the whole thing. Almost all of us were crowded together in the small pavilion on the deck, only a few, including Robert with admirable repose, had fled into the lower room of the ship. After ¾ of an hour it let up, but returned all-powerfully during the following night and lasted 3 hours, through which all of us slept, however. In the evening we had Hochland Island to our left and sailed along it all night.

Monday the 20th/8. Several people seasick—cold, unpleasant weather in the morning and the company in a thoroughly bad mood. Very thick fog until 12 o'clock, when the sun finally broke through. Today we were in the open sea—one always has an excellent appetite on the ship, and fortunately we were not seasick, although Robert was not well on the first and second morning. Beautiful sunset—in the evening we passed Gotland Island. Passable sleep during the night.

Tuesday the 21st/May 9 always very cold—the ship's movement became more notable today—pretty groups on the deck— Frau von *Schloetzer's* 3 children happy as larks, played with oranges—the equality of social positions on the ship is pleasant, no one is embarrassed in front of others.

Toward evening the rocking of the boat became so prominent that I developed great anxiety. At 11 o'clock at night we passed by Bornholm [Island]. During the night probably nobody enjoyed the most restful sleep, since first of all the ship rocked so badly that one could not stand on one's feet, and then the impatience for [the] next morning!

On *Wednesday the 22nd of May* at 6 o'clock in the morning we got up and found the most magnificently mild air outside and the ship magnificently approaching our beloved Germany. The entire company was in the most cheerful mood. At 6:30, first appearance of the Prussian coast. The beautiful spring morning, not a

The Trip to Russia 299

single cloud in the sky. The pilot boat soon arrived, the pilot jumped onto our ship, and now we proceeded directly to Swinemünde, where we finally arrived at half past ten. A lovable place—happy landing—funny confusion of the customs officials and my anxiety, which had been quite unnecessary. On a small steamboat we now went to Stettin [Szczecinek, Poland], through the lagoon and then along the most delightful villages—the left bank of the Oder charming!—Never will I forget this pleasure trip! this blessed security and along with that this magnificent weather, a completely new, clean steamship, in which one doesn't feel any motion from the engine, since it was taken into tow by another engine. Arrival at 4 o'clock in Stettin—accommodations at the Hôtel *de Prusse,* unpleasant lodgings.

In the evening we took a bath at the Moritz Baths. Unpleasant rocking motion that remains with one even after one has left the ship. A strong thunderstorm during the night, and anxious state in our small room.

Thursday the 23rd. At 2 o'clock in the afternoon, arrival in Berlin. We spent much time with Mother until

Friday the 24th noon, when we left for Leipzig. Arrival there at 7 o'clock.

Saturday the 25th we spent unpacking and

Sunday the 26th of May, the first Pentacost holiday, at 3 o'clock in the afternoon we left for Schneeberg, where we arrived around 10 o'clock.

We found our children asleep—a lovely, gratifying sight! Little Marie had remained exactly the way she was earlier, just as lovely and cute; Elise, however, has turned into a husky girl, but unfortunately she was always ill during our stay in Schneeberg.

Carl and *Pauline* [Schumann] had cared for the children with tender love, one surely could see that!—

Monday, Tuesday, and Wednesday we had such terribly rainy

weather that we could not get out of the house. Only on Wednesday we were at the Uhlmanns' for dinner, and in the evening at Dr. Otto's, where I had to play on a chopping board.

On *Thursday the 30th of May,* the children's farewell from Schneeberg. *Carl* [Schumann] very unwell and both very sad now to have to give up the children.

In Zwickau with little Marie we looked at the newly restored church,[36] visited old Superintendent Lorenz's widow, Robert also a few acquaintances, and then we headed for Leipzig, where Aunt *Carl* expected us. We had also taken along a young housekeeper from Schneeberg, *Elwine Breuel,* so that in the future I can live more for art.

So now we were with our dear children again within our 4 walls! what luck that we are reunited in such good health—God's protection went with us on our journey and guarded our children.

Friday the 31st of May was the last day of our vacation and heavenly weather.

Five

RUSSIAN CUSTOMS

[RS][1]

At banquets men and women always sit separately.

Only a few of the high-ranking Russian women made a return visit to Clara; this is in accordance with an old custom; one prefers to be a protector, not a friend, to artists.

Smoking, also in the company of women, is something we found in the most elegant homes.—

It is a degree of intimacy among the Russians to address each other by first name, after which the name of the father also is customarily used, thus: "Paul Ivanovich."—

Probably no people bow lower than the Russians—men as well as women.—

The disgraceful tyranny of the theater and the orphanage over the concert performer.—

Between the different wines, beer is also passed around at banquets.—

One can wager that 5 minutes after departure, something breaks down in the carriage of every Russian coachman.—

Mendelssohn on the 26th of January in Berlin told me and Gade:

When shall we three meet again . . .

(Macbeth)

Except for *Taubert* there is no musical person in Berlin—the [soprano Henriette] Sontag-Rossi a musical anti-Christ—everything seems to be *shaky* in Berlin—*Rückert* was certainly in a bad mood when speaking about his stay in Berlin, invited us to Neusess, his country estate.

Sobolewsky, an unusual person, who had a strange education, did not learn until an advanced age to spell correctly. His views on music are not always the most educated—somewhat tired of music—has finished an opera.[2]

Dr. Jakoby. That we would run into him at the Russian Consul's is characteristic of Königsberg; he even used "Du" in speaking to him [the consul]. He spoke very clearly and sharply. Story about Lola Montez and Prince Paskevich. Liszt and Schröder[-Devrient], like fashion and genius to one another—*Löbmann* in Riga tells a cute anecdote about Leopold Schefer and his current wife.

von Lutzau's description of the local [in Riga] conditions of servitude—

Kaull: Story about the serf who saved a man's life and is supposed to pay 5 rubles silver for the medal: "he doesn't want to save anyone else."

Uhlmann: "the government doesn't like temperance associations because they don't like associations in general and are also afraid of damage to their monopoly on brandy."

✻✻ in Mitau: "The vacation of an official in a foreign country must be personally authorized by the emperor"—that one cannot get away, even if one's own mother were dying—

A passport to a foreign country costs 25 rubles silver.

Postal arrangements still very infantile, the way they were about 25 years ago in our country—

According to orders by the governor of Livonia, a virtuoso may not set an admission fee of more than 1 ruble silver. By contrast,

Russian Customs

they demanded an advance of 25 silver rubles from me for 2 concerts.

In Mitau there is much talk about the woman violinist *Berner,* who is now in Naples; similarly in Riga about *Frau von Brüloff,* née Timm.

von Broeker in Dorpat talks of a nice gesture from *Liszt,* who arranged a good concert here for a poor student. The enthusiasm for him is supposed to surpass anything one has ever heard about enthusiasm. A bride demanded one of Liszt's gloves from her bridegroom, etc. etc. Before the start of the 1st concert the women rushed into the hall like crazy.

For staying in a foreign country, every Russian must pay a head tax of 50 rubles silver a year.

The students of Dorpat serenaded Liszt with the Marseillaise.—

Broeker finds the constitution of the Russian Baltic Sea provinces more German than the German one; the old [pre-Russian] one was more primitive.

The Liphardt Quartet in Dorpat had a very good influence on the local musical culture.[3]

Fühllos selbst für ihrer Künstler Ehre,	Itself insensitive to its artists' honor,
Gleich dem todten Schlag der	Just like the pendulum clock's
Pendeluhr,	lifeless beating,
Dient sie knechtisch dem Gesetz der	The law of gravity is slavishly
Schwere,	served
die entgötterte Natur.	By nature deprived of Gods.

The one thing whom she serves emerged from behind the curtain that hid its brilliance, and look what had been shimmering in the dark was now dark, incapable of radiating any warmth. Beautiful are the fruits that the warm world produces; happily do we exchange them for the colorful baubles that had been in their place before.

This comment about a part of a masterpiece ["Die Glocke" by Schiller] may perhaps remind you, beautiful lady, about hours much too brief, that your presence at the observatory of the stars has made more beautiful to

Your admirer,
F. W. Bessel

Königsberg,
the 27th of September 1840.
(From the album of the wife, née Witte, of Professor Mädler in Dorpat)

> Le Beau—c'est la splendeur *du vrai,*—
> L'art—c'est le résonnement [*sic*] de la pensée.[4]

Dorpat,	F. Liszt
the 31st of March 1842	(from that very place)

So a sort of "end-rhyme verse" can also be found in paintings. In the album of Frau von Mädler I discovered three little drawings by A. Ramberg that were very cleverly done "following each of 5 given endpoints."

On the origin of the Russian folk hymn by Lvov.

The little Russian word "nichevo"—

A woman tells of Rubini's stinginess and greed for money and that he said he didn't want to stop singing until he had earned a sum of I don't know how many millions. Henselt said, "And then I would hope he would burst like an animal."—

Count Vielhorsky's idea of a Petersburg Music Festival.

They talk about the emperor supposedly having kissed Rubini.

Russian legal conditions explained by Stöckhardt.

The emperor cannot stand long hair; Liszt, on hearing this, is supposed to have had his cut shorter and shorter.—

Glinka is celebrated by everyone as an extremely talented musician. Incidentally, he is a nobleman. The word "musician" still has a bad smell here.—

Vielhorsky's story about a pupil of Field's who is supposed to have practiced so hard she died: in this respect Field is supposed to have created quite a bit of damage and unhappiness.

Count Nesselrode is a great friend of music.

Pigeons are a sacred bird for the Russians and may not be slaughtered.—

The emperor is supposed to have said about Molique that he is a vacteur (scratcher)—

Count Vielhorsky has a complete string quintet (2 violins, viola, cello, and bass) by Stradivari.

Prince Yussupov has assembled an orchestra completely made of his serfs.

About Listz's playing the emperor is supposed to have said:—
"*Beaucoup de difficultés, mais pas d'agrément*"—[5]

My uncle told me that ordinary Russians would not shoot any wolves.

Uncle's story about Grand Prince Constantine (the emperor's son), how he would want to take his farewell as admiral—also the story about General Gomalov, when the emperor showed him the Winter Palace and Gomalov missed the Russian sacred icon.

The story of the serf (my aunt's foster daughter) in Seskovitz and her speaking German.

Henselt's playing in the Hall of the Nobility in Moscow—very droll story—

Reinhardt in Moscow owns a superb portrait of Field when he was still young; the head is genial and shows quite the Englishman.

Prince Tchernyshov is also a great friend of music.

Why especially among musicians does one encounter so many unhappy and ill-humored artists?

No one knows why one bares one's head under the great Kremlin gate.[6] It is a *more holy custom* than the hidden holy custom [i.e., tabernacle or *hostia*] in the churches, based on nothing more than a fear of the priests.

At the "great bell" there arose within me the thought of a poem that I would like to carry out. The bell is supposed to have failed while being cast.[7]

A striking phenomenon, to encounter so many familiar faces (like Verhulst, Poppe yesterday). Are the same faces found over and over?[8]

Six

POEMS
FROM
MOSCOW

by Robert Schumann

Die Glocke von Iwan Welikii

I (1735)
Moskau, Wunderstadt im Osten
Hundert Kirchen ragen aufwärts,
Hundert Glocken nah' und ferne
Schweben tönend in den Höhen.

"Christ ist auferstanden" klingt es
Fromm von abertausend Lippen,
"Ist wahrhaftig auferstanden"
Tönt es fort im Bruderkusse,
Und es geht die Sonn' des ersten
Ostertags auf über Moskau.

Ich auch,—spricht ein Künstler sinnend,—
Zu des Höchsten Ehre möcht' auch
Ich ein Denkmal gründen, das mit
Ries'ger Zunge seinen ew'gen
Namen allerorten künde:
Eine Glocke sei's, wie nimmer
Sie die Welt geseh'n; sie rage
Von des Kreml's höchster Spitze
Segenläutend den Geschlechtern,
Meinen Namen auch von Jahr zu
Jahr bescheiden fortvererbend.

Töne, Glocke, wenn durch deine
Pforte, Moskau, ein dein Kaiser zieht,

The Bell of Ivan Veliky

I (1735)
Moscow, wondrous city in the East
Churches by the hundreds rising upward,
Bells by the hundreds near and far
Swaying, tolling way up high.

"Christ has risen" intone
Many thousands of pious lips,
"Truly has risen"
Rings out in fraternal kisses,
And the sun rises over Moscow
On the first day of Easter.

I too,—says an artist contemplating,—
To honor the Almighty I too want
To raise a monument, which with
Gigantic tongue will proclaim
Everywhere His eternal name:
Let it be a bell, the likes of which
The world has never seen; may it rise
From the Kremlin's highest point,
Blessing each new generation,
And also year after year
Modestly passing on my name.

Toll, bell, when through your gate,
Moscow, your emperor enters,

Töne warnend, wenn des Aufruhrs
Flamme dir im Innern glüht,
Töne, wenn der Feind sich naht,—
Töne, töne früh und spat.

Wie das Werk im Innern lebt,
Der Vollendung entgegenstrebt!
Es schafft der Meister Tag und Nacht,
Mit Liebeswarmer Künstlertreu
Die starre Masse oft umarmend.

Schon wachsen um den Saum der Form
Blumen hervor im lieblichen Gewinde,
Schon rundet sich der Meisterhand
Des *Czaren Bild* mit Kron' und Scepter,
Der *Czarin* auch, und dass das Werk
Gesegnet sei, in erster Reih'
Steht auch das Bild von Jesus Christ.

So ruht die Glocke in ihrer Gruft,
Bald einzuathmen Himmelsluft,
Es harrt der Meister der sel'gen Stunde,
Die die Form hervor aus der Erde ruft,
Und in der Stadt von Munde zu Munde
Vom grossen Werk geht schon die Kunde.

Und tausend Glöcklein grüssen festlich,
Den Tag, zu feiern ihrer Schwester
Erstehungstag; in dichten Schaaren
Zum Iwansplatz zieht das Gedränge,
Metropolit und Priesterschaft
Umsteh'n die Stelle, wo der Meister

Poems from Moscow

Sound the alarm when the flame
Of revolution glows within you,
Toll when the enemy draws near,—
Toll, toll early and late.

How the work lives internally,
Striving toward completion!
The master creates day and night,
With the loving heat of artistic faith
Repeatedly embracing the rigid mass.

Already round the edge of the form
Flowers grow in lovely garlands,
Already the master's touch rounds off
The *czar's image* with crown and scepter,
Also the *czarina's,* and so that the work
May be blessed, first of all
There appears also the image of Jesus Christ.

Thus the bell rests in its vault,
Soon to inhale the air of heaven,
The master awaits the blessed hour,
Which summons the shape from the earth,
And in the town, from mouth to mouth,
The great work already is announced.

And a thousand tiny bells greet festively
The day, to celebrate their sister's
Resurrection Day; tightly pressed together
The crowd moves toward Ivan's Square,
Archbishop and all priests
Surround the place where the master

Den Guss vollbringen soll, wo Hebel
Und Winden schon sich zeigen, aus
Der Tiefe in die luft'ge Höh'
Die ungeheure Last zu ziehen.

Es knistern die Flammen; zäh und weich
Schmilzt das Metall im glüh'nden Ofen;
Das widerspänstige Erz zu zähmen;
Es braucht der Zeit; es rinnt der Schweiss
In Tropfen von des Meisters Stirn;
Die singend an die Arbeit gingen,
Die lustigen Gesellen auch,
Verstummen all, stumm steht das Volk,
Und stumm vor Allen schafft der Meister.

Nun ist's vollbracht, die Form gefüllt,
Nun kühle sich die gähr'nde Masse,
Die Bilder, die der Künstler schuf
In reiner Treue aufzunehmen.
Und bald in allvereinter Kraft
Rühr'n sich die Hände, Flaschenzug
Und Hebel greifen ineinander,
Von seiner Stelle, dass er schwebe,
Den riesigen Koloss zu rücken.

Nun hebt er sich, der Knopf zuerst
Mit schön gewund'nen Tragebändern—
Doch um des Meisters Sinne dunkelt's,
Das Erz, es deckt ein fahles Grau
Und halb unkenntlich springen die
Gebilde auf der Fläche vor,
Und nun zur Hälfte in die Höh'

Poems from Moscow

Shall do the casting, where levers
And winches can already be seen, to raise
From the depth to the breezy height
This enormous load.

The flames are roaring; viscous and soft
The metal melts in the glowing oven,
Taming the refractory ore;
It takes time; the sweat is running
In drops from the master's brow;
And those who went to work singing,
The joyful apprentices as well,
Everyone speechless, the people stand in silence,
And mute before them all the master toils.

And now it's done, the mold completely filled,
Now the boiling mass may cool,
In order to faithfully receive
The images created by the artist
And soon in strength united
The hands will move, pulleys
And levers grasping one another,
To move the gigantic colossus
From its place, so it may swing.

Now it lifts up, first the hook
In beautifully coiled carrying straps—
But in the master's mind a darkness grows,
Because the ore is covered by pale gray
And barely recognizable emerge
The images from the surface,
And now the bell has been raised

Die Glocke weiter aufgezogen—
Ganz nahe des Erlösers Bild
Es klafft ein Sprung, es fehlt ein Stück,
Und unbeweglich in der Tiefe
Ein Rest bleibt stehn—Entsetzen
Fasst rings das Volk und fasst den Meister.

Und wie er trauernd seine Augen
Abwendet, das Gesicht verhüllt,
Das Schreckliche nicht mehr zu schau'n—
Die Mutter, die im stummen Schmerz
Das todtgeborne Kind betrachtet,
Ihr Antlitz mag nicht schmerzensvoller sein—
Da drängt ein Mann sich im Talar
Zu ihm und spricht:

Du hast versucht, was du nicht solltest,
Mit Heil'gem nied'ren Sinn beschönt:
Nicht Gott ist's dem du dienen wolltest'
Der *Eitelkeit* hast du gefröhnt:
So sei dein Nam' fortan verhöhnt,
Du, tausend Andren gleich vergessen.
Soll dir ein Werk mit Gott gelingen,
Lern' erst zur Demuth dich bezwingen.

Und schweigend hört's der Künstler an,
Und wie die Menge sich verlor,
Verlor er mit sich im Gedränge.

II (1836)
In Moskau, Russlands Wunderstadt,
Von einer Glocke ging die Sage,

Poems from Moscow 319

Halfway further to the top—
Very close to the Savior's image
There forms a gap, a piece is missing,
And immovable at the bottom
A remnant stays behind—horror
Seizes the people and seizes the master.

And how he mournfully casts his eyes
Away, covering his face,
To see that terrible thing no more—
The mother, who in silent pain
Views the stillborn child,
Her face cannot look more tormented—
Then a man in a long robe rushes
Toward him and says:

You've attempted what you should not have tried,
Covering vulgar spirit by sacred things:
It was not God whom you wished to serve
It was vanity to which you submitted:
So henceforth your name shall be mocked,
You, forgotten like thousands of others.
Should a work of yours succeed with God,
Then first learn to force yourself to be humble.

And in silence the artist listened to that,
And as the mass of people dispersed,
He too disappeared into the crowd.

II (1836)
In Moscow, Russia's wondrous town,
There was the saga of a bell,

So riesengross, dass sie im Sturze
Die Kuppel, die sie trug, hernieder
Gezogen in die Erde, wo
Sie selber nun vergraben, jährlich
Sich tiefer in die Erde bohrend.

Noch andre Sagen gab's von ihr,
So: dass ein Künstler sie erdacht,
Der wohl den Besten beizuzählen,
Und das beim Gusse sie missglückt—
Und andre noch.

Es hört der Kaiser von dem Riesen,
Der ihm in seinem Kremlin schläft—
Er spricht "ich will die Glocke sehn"
Und milden Sinnes fügt er bei:—
"Der Künstler der das Grösste dachte,
Sein Streben soll geheiligt sein,
Ob auch die That es krön', ob nicht—
Man zieh' sie an des Tages Licht,
Die lang genug im engen Schrein
Geschlummert, von des Künstlers Streben
Der Welt ein sprechend Bild zu geben."

Und wie der Kaiser dem Entschluss
Die rasche That wohl angewöhnt,
Dass, was geschehn soll, muss geschehen,
Wie sich der Kleinmuth auch entgegenstemme—
So sieht man rüst'ge Arme bald
Am Werke der Befreiung schaffen,
Dass sie, die Sclavin niedern Bodens,

Poems from Moscow 321

So gigantic that when it fell,
The cupola holding it
Was dragged into the earth
And buried there as well,
Boring deeper into the earth each year.

There were yet other stories about it,
Thus: it was conceived by an artist
Who may have been among the best,
And that an accident occurred while casting it—
And others yet.

The emperor hears about the giant
Who sleeps in his Kremlin for him—
He says: "I want to see the bell"
And adds the gentle thought:—
"The artist who conceived the greatest,
His endeavor shall be blessed,
Whether or not the deed succeeds—
One should take into the daylight,
What too long in a narrow shrine
Has slumbered, so the world may be given
A fitting idea of the artist's striving."[1]

And since the emperor is in the habit
Of deciding as well as quickly acting,
So that what shall happen, must happen,
No matter how much opposed by timidity—
So one soon sees vigorous arms
Working to achieve liberation,
So that this slave beneath the earth

In ihre Würde eingesetzt,
Aufleb' im Licht lebend'gen Odems.

Wo Moskau wie aus hundert Bächen
Vom Kreml herab sich in das Thal
Endlos ergiesst nach Osten zu,
Auf seiner höchsten schönsten Stelle—
Inmitten mancher Cathedrale
Dem Schatz nah' mit den Reichs-Kleinodien—
Dort steht sie nun, zwar schwebend nicht,
Zwar klingend nicht—
Doch wenn am Ostermorgen früh
Die jungen Schwesterglocken all
Dem heil'gen Tag entgegensingen,—
Ein rührend leises Klingen
Hat mancher Gläub'ge da gehört,
Als träumte sie ein still Gebet
Zu Ehren Christi des Erstand'nen.

III
Wie ähnelt, Glockengiesser, dir
Und deinem Loos ein andrer Meister,
Dess' Bild mir durch den Sinn fährt, hier
Grad hier, wo mich auf Schritt und Tritt
Verfolgt der Ruf erschlagner Geister.

Zwar war sein Handwerk Glockengiesser nicht,
Doch dem Metall verwandt; am liebsten mit
Kanonenschrift dictiert' er Reichen
Und Völkern sein "Ich wills" und dass
Er wisse was er wollt' auch zu erreichen,
Zu seinen Füssen kündeten's die Leichen.

Poems from Moscow 323

In its dignity is installed,
Revived in the light of living breath.

Where Moscow, as if from a hundred creeks
Flows from the Kremlin down into the valley
Endlessly heading east,
At its most tall and beautiful place—
Amid many a cathedral
Near the treasure with its imperial jewels—
That's where it now stands, although not moving,
Although not ringing—
But when on early Easter morning
All the young sister bells
Greet the holy day with song,—
A touching soft sound
Has been heard there by many a believer,
As though it were dreaming
A quiet prayer honoring Christ.

III
How much, bell caster, you resemble
With your lot another master,
Whose image is on my mind, here
Just here, where my every step is pursued
By the summons of slain spirits.

Although his trade was not bell casting,
It was related to metal; he preferred using
The language of cannons to dictate to empires
And to nations his "I want it" and that
He also knew how to achieve what he wanted,
This was indicated by the corpses at his feet.

Ich seh' ihn mit verschränkten Armen,
Kremlin auf deinen Zinnen stehn—
Ein Gluthmeer rings der Himmel, auf
Mit neuer Kraft die Flamme lodernd,
Wo kaum gelöscht—die Stadt ein Grab,
Und hie und da ein heul'nder Hund,
Den Herren suchend und betrunkner Pöbel
Und (selten nur) ein Siegsgeschrei,
Als press' der Tod es aus der Kehle . . .

Dir aber auf dem Kremlin, raunte nicht
Ein finstrer Geist dir in das Ohr:
Hast du auch Wort gehalten auf dem Thron,
Hast deinen Völkern Freiheit du gegeben,
Du, der du's konntest, du von dem ein Hauch
Hinreicht, Millionen zu erheben,
Mit deinem Geist du, deinem Adleraug'—
Hast du gehalten auf dem Thron,
Was du versprachst, Napoleon?

War's auch das *Volk,* das du bedacht,
Wenn siegsgewiss du sie zur Schlacht
Anführtest, war's zu *seinem* Heil,
Als Enghien dem Blei der Henker
Du übergabest, wars zu *seiner*
Erhebung, dass du Legionen
Aushubest, sie nach fernen Zonen
Entsendetest—*und nicht zu deiner?*

Nicht länger kann er's tragen, was
Ihn aus den Flammen anspricht, blass
Und blässer wird die Wange, wie

Poems from Moscow   325

I see him standing with folded arms,
Kremlin, on top of your battlements—
The sky a fiery ocean, the flames
Ignited with new energy where
They have just been extinguished—the city a grave,
And here and there a howling dog,
Searching for its master and drunken mobs
And (only rarely) a cry of victory,
As if death were squeezing it out of the throat . . .

But when you were at the Kremlin, did not
A dark spirit whisper into your ear:
Did you keep your word while on the throne,
Did you give freedom to your people,
You, who could do that, you from whom one breath
Suffices to call up millions,
With your spirit, you, with your eagle's eye—
Did you keep your word on the throne,
To what you had promised, Napoleon?

Was it really the *people* that you considered,
When certain of victory you led them
Into battle, was it for *their* welfare
That you turned Enghien over to
The executioner's bullets, was it for *their*
Benefit that you conscripted legions
To send to far distant regions?
And not for yours?

No longer can he tolerate what
The flames tell him, pale
And paler grows his cheek, as

Die Flamme roth und röther lodert.
Aus allen Häusern flammt's hervor;
Er aber mit verhängtem Zügel
Sprengt durch Petrowski's brennend Thor,
Als säss' das Feu'r ihm schon am Bügel.

IV
Er hat gebüsst auf hartem Stein,
Wie du mein Glockengiesser; nein,
Vielleicht nicht ganz rein war sein Streben—
Was kümmert's dich—er hat gebüsst,
Als mit gebrochnem Aug' auf Sanct
Helena er das Bild geküsst
Von seinem Kinde, das man ihm
Vom Vaterherz genommen; Cherubim
Im Himmel sahn das Leid und sprachen:
Was noch kein Sterblicher, er hat's getragen.

So ruht' er lang im fernen Meer;
Der Ruf der Schildwach nur eintönig
Erschallt am Grabe; dass ein König,
Ein Kaiser hier begraben wär'—
Der stille Ort verrieth es wenig.
Und ruhte Jahrelang. Wie gleicht,
O Glockengiesser, dir und deinem
Geschick das Loos des Schlachtengott's!

Des Lobs der Freunde satt, des Spotts
Der Feinde überdrüssig, *ganz*
Den Menschen nehmend, reicht
Klio, des Spruchs Vollzieherin
Der Weltgeschichte, ihren Kranz

Poems from Moscow 327

The flame glows red and redder.
From every house the fire blazes;
He, however, galloping at full speed,
Bursts through Petrovsky's burning gate,
As though the fire had already reached his stirrups.

IV
On a hard rock he has atoned,
As you did, my bell caster; no,
Perhaps his aims were not entirely pure—
Why should you care—he has atoned,
As with broken eyes
He kissed, on Saint Helena, the picture
Of his child, that was taken
From his paternal heart; angels
In heaven saw the sorrow and said:
He has tolerated more than any mortal man.

Thus he continues to rest in the distant sea;
With only the monotonous shout of sentries
Sounding at his grave: that a king,
An emperor was buried here—
The quiet place barely reveals it—
And rested for years. How similar to you,
O bell caster, and to your fate
Is the lot of the god of battles!

Fed up with praise from friends,
Sick and tired of the enemies' mockery, *completely*
Taking charge of the man, Clio,
The executrix of historical verdicts,
Presents her wreath to the hero,

Dem Helden, mit gerechtem Sinn
Die Schatten sondernd und den Glanz.

Und einem König mässig, weise,
Sprach sie in's Herz: es ist die Zeit,
Ihn, der sein Blut zu Frankreichs Preise,
In Schlachten hundertfach geweiht,
Zurückzufordern, die Gebeine,
Eh' sie im fremden Land verstiebt,
Zurückzuholen zu den Borden
Der Seine, ins Land (wie er mit rühr'nden Worten
Verfügt' in seinem Testamente)
Ins Land, das er so sehr geliebt.
Vollbring's und Recht hast du geübt!

Als ob die süsse Last es könnte,
Der Ozean ebnet sich, es ein'gen
Sich freundlich Well und Wind', den Lauf
Des edlen Fahrzeugs zu beschleun'gen;
Mit seinen Masten prächtig still
Schwebt es daher die Wassergleise—
Brav, brav, mein Prinz von Joinville,
Dies war fürwahr die schönste Reise
Die du gethan zu Frankreichs Preise!

Im Dom der Invaliden
Da steht ein Grab noch neu,
Da regnet's frische Blüthen
An jedem fünften Mai.

Poems from Moscow

Separating, with righteous intent,
The shadows and the brilliance.

And to a king's heart
She, moderate and wise, said: it's time to reclaim
Him who has dedicated his blood
A hundredfold in battles to the glory of France,
To return his mortal remains,
Lest they be scattered to the winds
On foreign soil, instead of being returned to the banks
Of the Seine, into the country (as with touching words
He decreed in his testament)[2]
To the land that he loved so much.
Bring it about, and you have done justice!

As though the sweet burden were able to cause it,
The ocean grows calm, waves and wind
Are amiably united to speed the progress
Of the noble vehicle;
With its masts splendidly calm
It floats along the water's tracks—
Well done, well done, my prince of Joinville,
For sure this was the most beautiful voyage
That you have made for France's glory!

In the Church of the Invalides
There is a tomb, yet new,
There is a rainfall of fresh flowers
On every fifth of May.

Vor allem Immortellen
Es bringen sie in Schaaren
Die einstens Kriegsgesellen
Des tapfren Kaisers waren.

Und aus dem stillen Grabe
Ertönt's mit Geisterlauten:
"Habt Dank ihr meine trauten
Kam'raden für die Gabe."

Und leiser sprichts und leiser:
"Kommt bald zu mir, wie lange
Liesst ihr mich schon allein,
Ihr die ihr wie der Kaiser
Allzeit müsst fertig sein—
Kommt bald!"—Es kniet der letzte
Gardist an Kaisers Grab,
Die letzte Thräne netzte
Das vielgeliebte Grab.

Dass er nicht wank' und weiche,
Man braucht's ihm nicht zu sagen:
Er ward als stille Leiche
Alsbald hinweggetragen.

Die Franzosen vor Moskau

Über der Moskwa dort von der Höh',
Dort kam sie her die grosse Armee.
Als sie nun ausgebreitet ganz
Sahen die Stadt im Sonnenglanz,

Above all everlasting flowers
Are brought by hosts
Of those who once were war companions
Of the courageous emperor.

And from the silent tomb
With ghostly voice sounds out:
"Be thanked, you my loyal comrades,
For your gift."

And more and more softly it speaks:
"Come to me soon, how long have all of you
Left me alone already,
All of you who like the emperor
Must be ready at all times—
Come soon!"—The last guardsman
Kneels at the emperor's tomb,
The last tear splashed
The much-beloved tomb.

That he should not waver or yield,
One need not tell him that:
He was soon carried away
As a quiet corpse.

The French before Moscow[3]

Across the Moskva, from yonder hill,
From there came the great army.
Now as they saw the whole city
Spread out in the brilliant sunshine,

Endlos die Kuppeln am Horizont,
Schallt' es freudig von Front zu Front:
Moskau, Moskau, die Wunderstadt
Die sich nun auch ergeben hat.

Sie rückten näher, sie riefen laut:
Das ist auf Ehr' die schönste Braut,
Die uns geschenkt der General
Nach der verdammten Reisequal.
Hier mag ein lustig Leben sein,
Wir möchten je eher je lieber hinein.

Doch standen sie lange wie angebannt,
Sie dachten: es müsst' ein Rathsherr kommen
Die Schlüssel der Stadt in der Hand—
Es that kein Rathsherr kommen.

Sie harrten zwei Stunden lang,
Der Kaiser ward zornig; er sprang
Zuletzt in das Thor hinein,
Als wär' die Stadt schon sein.

Da war kein Mensch zu schaun,
Es überlief den Herr'n ein Grau'n,
Und wie er auf dem Kreml
Sich setzte in den Schem'l
Vom Kaiser Alexander,
Es war ihm da, als brannt' er.

Und als in weiter Fern'
Er sah ein lichtes Pünktchen—
Er sagt', das ist kein Stern.

Poems from Moscow

The cupolas endlessly on the horizon,
Shouts of joy were heard from front to front:
Moscow, Moscow, the city of wonders
That now has finally surrendered.

They approached closer, they called loudly:
That, on my honor, is the most beautiful bride
The general has given us after
The damned torture of travel.
Life may be joyous here,
We want to enter as soon as possible.

Yet they just stood as if enchained,
They thought: a councilman must come
With the keys to the city in his hand—
No councilman came.

They waited for two hours,
The emperor grew angry; finally
He galloped through the gate,
As though the city were already his.

There was nobody to be seen,
The emperor was horrified,
And when at the Kremlin
He sat down in the chair
Belonging to Czar Alexander,
It seemed to him the chair was burning.

And when in the far distance
He saw a small bright dot—
He said, that is no star.

Und wie er wieder hinsah,
Das Pünktchen was ein Fünkchen,
Er sprach "ich seh's nicht gern".

Und wie zum drittenmal
Er hinsah, da erscholl es
Von allen Seiten "Feuer"
Und immer grimmer schwoll' es
Das Flammenungeheuer.
Da war ihm klar der Rest:
Er sass in Feindes Nest,
Der Schwefel ihm und Feuer
Vermacht statt Sang und Feier.

Da rief der Kaiser laut:
Und in die Dielen hackt' er
"Rostopschin, du Vertrackter
Das hast du mir gebraut
Hätt' ich dir nie getraut
Und deinen falschen Thoren
Nun ist mein Krieg verloren."

Und auf der flachen Höh,
Wo sie zuerst geschaut
Die trügerische Fee,
Sah bald man die Armee
Zurückmarschieren.—Traut keiner Braut,
Die sich so schnell ergiebt, traut keiner,
Wie schön sie sei; die prächt'ge
Es wollte sie umarmen
Napoleon; das nächt'ge
Gespenst mit Flammenkuss

Poems from Moscow   335

And when he looked once more,
The small dot was a small spark,
He said, "I don't like to see that."

And when for the third time
He looked there, from every side
Sounded the cry "Fire"
And the monstrous flames
Grew ever more furious.
Then the rest became clear to him:
He was trapped in the nest of the enemy,
Who bequeathed him sulfur and fire,
Instead of song and celebration.

Then the emperor shouted loudly:
And into the planks he barked,
"Rostopschin, you cursed man,
You led me into this
If only I hadn't trusted you
And your treacherous fools
Now my war has been lost."

And on the flat hill,
From where it first saw
The treacherous sorceress,
One soon saw the army
Retreating.—Do not trust any bride
Who surrenders so quickly, trust none,
No matter how beautiful she may be,
Napoleon wanted to embrace the splendid one;
The nocturnal specter
Reciprocates the greeting

Erwidert es den Gruss
Und jagt ihn ohn Erbarmen
Den schwergeprüften Reiter
Durch Städt' und Länder weiter.

Moskau, den 13./25. April 1844.

With a kiss of fire
And pursues without mercy
The sorely tested rider
Throughout cities and countries.

Moscow, 13/25 April 1844.

❧ NOTES

Marriage Diary I

1. CS's twenty-first birthday.

2. Since Rudelsburg on the Saale is close to Naumburg, this probably refers to the excursion restaurant Gattersburg, near Grimma.

3. The first edition of the *Liederkreis,* op. 39, published in August 1842 by Haslinger in Vienna, did not have a dedication. Schumann dedicated none of his compositions to Elise List.

4. RS had already reviewed the first performance of this work in April 1840; his detailed discussion appeared in the *Neue Zeitschrift für Musik* on 1 January 1841 (*Gesammelte Schriften* 4.3ff.).

5. RS also expressed himself this way in the *Neue Zeitschrift für Musik* (*Gesammelte Schriften* 3.27).

6. *Translator's note:* The Trio No. 1 in D Minor, op. 49, composed in 1839. Mendelssohn would not compose the Trio No. 2 in C Minor, op. 66, until 1845; hence all subsequent references in the diaries are to the First Trio.

7. Sophie David came from a wealthy, aristocratic Baltic family, von Liphardt.

8. The first and second of three handwritten volumes of lieder, today preserved in the Deutsche Staatsbibliothek, Berlin.

9. This refers to *3 Gesänge,* op. 31; the manuscript by CS is now in the Pierpont Morgan Library, New York.

10. For Christmas 1840 CS composed the Burns lied "Am Strande" in addition to two Heine settings, "Ihr Bildnis" and "Volkslied." The dedication copy of the lieder can be found in the Robert Schumann Haus, Zwickau.

11. Chopin's Ballade in F Major, op. 38. RS had dedicated his *Kreisleriana,* published in 1838, to Chopin.

340   *Notes to Pages 13–23*

12. Elise List made her debut in the second concert, on 11 October.

13. RS's "Die Kartenlegerin" and "Die Rote Hanne," contained in his Lieder, op. 31, were based on Adelbert von Chamisso's translation of Béranger's poems.

14. The pianist Louis Rakemann, who went to America for several years in 1839, had been a persistent admirer of CS.

15. *Zigeunerleben,* op. 29, no. 3, for small chorus, piano, triangle, and tambourine ad lib.

16. Continuous conflict since 1831 between the Egyptian pasha Mohammed Ali and the Turkish sultan had become more acute in the autumn of 1840. It came to an end following military intervention by England and Austria and the capitulation of the pasha in February 1841.

17. In her debut at the second Gewandhaus concert Elise List sang arias by Donizetti and Bellini.

18. RS sketched a symphony movement (Andante in C Minor); the manuscript is now in the University Library of Bonn.

19. For Henry Fothergill Chorley's later remarks about RS and CS in the magazine *Athaneum,* see p. 47.

20. The booklet "Über Musik aus Shakespeare's Schriften" can be found in the Robert Schumann Haus, Zwickau; it was intended for the anthology "Dichtergarten für Musik" that RS prepared later.

21. The bookseller Friedrich Fleischer took over the publishing company Gebrüder Schumann (most recently owned by Eduard Schumann, who died in 1839) and married Eduard's widow.

22. A private musical performance for invited guests.

23. Following her marriage in 1836 Livia Frege had widely withdrawn from public concertizing. In December 1843 she sang the main role for the first performance of RS's *Das Paradies und die Peri;* see p. 207.

24. The second movement, Andante con moto, of Mozart's Symphony in E-Flat Major, K. 543.

Notes to Pages 25–46   *341*

25. The poem belongs to the "Kleine Verse an Klara" that RS had sent to her from Vienna in November 1838. The manuscript is in the Robert Schumann Haus, Zwickau.

26. "Blondels Lied," op. 53, no. 1; "Frühlingsfahrt," op. 45, no. 2; and "Der Deutsche Rhein," WoO 1. A second version from the annual *Orpheus* can no longer be traced.

27. On 23 March 1839, when Schubert's Great C Major Symphony was first performed at the Leipzig Gewandhaus (see *Gesammelte Schriften* 3.195 ff.), CS was in Paris.

28. Ferdinand Kufferath played, among other things, his Capriccio for Piano and Orchestra, op. 1 (see *Gesammelte Schriften* 4.77 f.).

29. This instrument, which CS had received as a "souvenir" from Conrad Graf after her stay in Vienna in 1838, was later used primarily by RS. After his death it was obtained by Johannes Brahms, who in 1873 gave it to the Gesellschaft der Musikfreunde in Vienna.

30. RS's composition, arranged by Hauschild as *Schottische Walzer,* was performed in Leipzig at Tannert's Dance Salon.

31. Henriette Voigt, born Kuntze (died in 1839); RS dedicated his Piano Sonata in G Minor, op. 22, to her.

32. The versions of the "Rheinlied" for male chorus as well as chorus and orchestra are lost.

33. Of the eight compositions that were performed, the one by Gustav Kunze received a prize by public acclamation.

34. The C Major Fantasy, op. 17, dedicated to Liszt and published in 1839.

35. See note 10.

36. This plan was realized not with the lieder mentioned here but with the ones CS composed for RS's birthday, 8 June 1841, to verses from Rückert's *Liebesfrühling.*

37. Presumably the *Geibel-Gesänge,* op. 29, published in three individual folios.

342   *Notes to Pages 47–70*

38. See note 19. CS gives this quotation in the original English.

39. "Fünf Andere" (Five others), from *Westöstlicher Divan,* Tefkir Nameh (Book of contemplations).

40. I.e., seven solo lieder (op. 37, nos. 1, 3, 5, 6, 8, 9, and 10) and two duets (op. 37, nos. 7 and 12), which were combined with the three composed by CS (see note 60).

41. This intention was not realized.

42. The last line of the poem, "Im Thale blüht der Frühling auf!" (In the valley spring blossoms forth), can be considered the basis for the motto at the beginning of the symphony.

43. Probably the *Gedichte aus dem Liederbuch eines Malers* (Poems from the songbook of a painter), op. 36, set to texts by Reinick. Schumann dedicated the first edition, published in 1842, to Livia Frege.

44. The Quartet, op. 74.

45. CS herself set the Goethe poem to music in July 1853.

46. CS's stepfather. Her mother was divorced from Friedrich Wieck in 1824 and married the music teacher Adolph Bargiel the same year.

47. In June 1840 RS had instigated a claim against Friedrich Wieck in the Dresden Civil Court for personal defamation, on the basis of which Wieck was condemned to prison for eighteen days. The additional accusation for restitution of Clara's property was dropped (see p. 68).

48. The program of the Gewandhaus concert on 25 February featured compositions by, among others, Bellini, Donizetti, and Meyerbeer.

49. Nevertheless, Wieck later returned fifty thalers of the freight expenses; see p. 201.

50. The diary of their wedding trip in 1837, kept by Cécile and Felix Mendelssohn, including text and drawings, has been partially published (1937 in French, 1947 in English). The original is in the Bodleian Library, Oxford.

51. Allegro brilliant in A Major, op. 92.

Notes to Pages 72–86   343

52. In addition to solo pieces by Scarlatti, RS, Chopin, and Mendelssohn, CS played the Adagio and Rondo from Chopin's Piano Concerto in F Minor as well as Mendelssohn's Duo, op. 92, with the composer. She probably also accompanied the singer Heinrich Schmidt.

53. The performance of the *St. Matthew Passion* on Palm Sunday, 4 April, was the first in Leipzig since Bach's death.

54. Of the performance in March 1837 in the Berlin Singakademie Clara had heard only the first part: she wrote, "all 77 choruses in lento and adagio at once, I haven't yet learned to tolerate that."

55. The texted version (1795/96) of Haydn's originally purely instrumental composition.

56. This plan was never actualized.

57. Julius Rietz's Overture to *Hero and Leander* and *Altdeutscher Schlachtgesang* for male chorus and orchestra were performed.

58. I.e., the Overture, Scherzo, and Finale in E Major, reworked in 1845 and published in 1846 as opus 52.

59. The Fantasy in A Minor, reworked in 1845 as the first movement of the Concerto for Piano and Orchestra, op. 54, published in 1846.

60. The lieder "Er ist gekommen in Sturm und Regen," "Liebst du um Schönheit," "Warum willst du andre fragen," and "Die gute Nacht, die ich dir sage." The first three were published in the fall of 1841, together with RS's seven lieder and two duets (see note 40) as their common opus 37/12; the last remained unpublished until 1992 (Clara Schumann, *Complete Songs,* vol. 2, ed. Joachim Draheim and Brigitte Höft [Leipzig: Breitkopf & Härtel, 1992]).

61. Mendelssohn's "Gondellied" in A Major (first publication in 1837, contained in none of the collections of *Lieder ohne Worte*), which appeared in vol. 14 of the *Musikbeilagen zur Neue Zeitschrift für Musik,* December 1841.

62. The Third North German Music Festival took place in Hamburg on 5, 7, and 8 July 1841, with the collaboration of Liszt and Wilhelmine Schröder-Devrient.

344   *Notes to Pages 89–117*

63. *Translator's note:* RS was chronically afflicted with a fear of high places stemming from his nervous breakdown at age twenty-three, when he nearly threw himself from a fifth-floor window.

Marriage Diary II

1. Presumably *Die Geschwister* (The siblings) by Ernst Raupach, on 7 July.

2. The first theater built by Gottfried Semper had been opened in April 1841 and was destroyed by fire in 1869.

3. RS completed the draft for a scenario, which today is in the Robert Schumann Haus, Zwickau.

4. *El magico prodigioso.* Goethe said in 1812 that in this drama "the subject of Doctor Faust is handled with unbelievable grandeur."

5. The symphony appeared on 10 November 1841, but for her birthday RS was able to give CS the proofs of the "first published part"; see p. 108.

6. See Diary I, notes 40 and 60.

7. Viktor, the four-and-a-half-year-old son of Livia and Woldemar Frege, had died in July.

8. An incomplete sketch of four movements of the symphony as well as an outline of the score for the main movement are now in the University Library of Bonn. In 1852 RS published a piano version of the scherzo in his *Bunte Blätter,* op. 99.

9. Probably CS's Scherzo, op. 14, published in 1845.

10. The rest of this entry has been made illegible by erasures.

11. The following two lines, which the next sentence refers to, have been made illegible by deletions.

12. The composition was missing until 1991 and then obtained by the

Notes to Pages 117–125 345

Heinrich Heine Institute in Düsseldorf. Only a setting for voice and piano (opus 64, no. 2, i–iii) was published by RS; the full score will be available in the Neue Schumann-Gesamtausgabe edited by the Schumann Society, Düsseldorf, and the Robert Schumann Haus, Zwickau.

13. The *Scottish* Symphony in A Minor, op. 56, conceived already in 1829, finished in January 1842.

14. A composition stemming from the collaboration in 1835 of Thalberg, Herz, Pixis, Czerny, Chopin, and Liszt—variations on a duet from Bellini's *I Puritani*. Liszt had transcribed it for two pianos.

15. The Symphony in D Minor (revised in 1851, published in 1853 as the Fourth Symphony, op. 120) and the Overture, Scherzo, and Finale, op. 52.

16. *Symphonie pathétique* by Gottfried Herrmann.

17. Adolf and Julius Stahlknecht presented their own composition for violin and violoncello, a "Fantastic Tone Portrait, *Die Walpurgisnacht*."

18. Allegro and Scherzo, the first two movements for the Sonata in G Minor, completed by CS in January 1842. See note 23.

19. Published in 1854 as "Schlummerlied" in the *Albumblätter*, op. 124. The manuscript can be found in the Schumann Family Album, Saxon Landesbibliothek, Dresden.

20. In addition to the Mendelssohn concerto, Clara played the *Moses Fantasy* of Thalberg.

21. In thanks for his dedication of the Symphony in B-Flat Major, Schumann received a golden tobacco box.

22. The Double Symphony for Two Orchestras *Irdisches und Göttliches im Menschenleben* (The worldly and the divine in the life of man) (see Gesammelte Schriften 4.228ff.).

23. See note 18. CS had composed an Adagio and Rondo in addition to the existing movements; only the Scherzo was published (in *Pièces fugitives,* op. 15, no. 4). The entire work was performed in 1989 by

346   Notes to Pages 125–140

Annerose Schmidt, and published in 1990 by Gerd Nauhaus according to the manuscript (Robert Schumann Haus, Zwickau).

24. This arrangement for piano four hands, made with CS's collaboration, appeared in June 1842.

25. Accordingly, the organization's series was called Private Concerts.

26. In addition to solo pieces, CS played the Konzertstück in F Minor by Weber.

27. In addition to CS's solo recital (pieces by Henselt, Chopin, Scarlatti, and Thalberg), the program featured only one song and one declamation.

28. By Bach, Mendelssohn, and Liszt (*Lucia* Reminiscences).

29. After the work received a preliminary rehearsal at the Leipzig Gewandhaus in November 1842 on RS's recommendation, he advised the composer "to write a friendlier symphony."

30. The Stock Exchange was erected 1839–41 in place of the former Maria-Magdelen Cloister.

31. Later addition by RS: "the 16th: in the evening saw Antigone [by Sophocles, with music by Mendelssohn] in Leipzig for the first time."

32. Later addition by RS: "morning of the 18th Pixis very eager to pick a fight with the critic of my newspaper—farewell from L. Anger, who has obtained a position as organist in Lüneburg."

33. Later addition by RS: "the 20th. miserable life. Much practicing of counterpoint and fugues during this time."

34. Later addition by RS: "Read a lot: Hauff's 'Fantasies in a Bremen Rathskeller,' Andersen's 'Improvisator.' "

35. Later addition by RS: "23rd: visit from H. Truhn, who wants to be a singer, with H. Schmidt."

36. Later addition by RS: "the 25th. in the Pauliner Church: heard Davide [penitente] by Mozart and Mendelssohn's 42nd Psalm."

Notes to Pages 141–145 347

37. Later addition by RS: "the 26th. received Clara's 1st letter from Copenhagen."

38. Later addition by RS: "Wenzel, Reuter, Becker for dinner at my place."

39. *Roberto Devereux* by Donizetti.

40. First performed on that day was the ballet *Napoli oder der Fischer und seine Braut* (Naples; or, The fisherman and his bride) (music by Gade, Helsted, Paulli, and Lumbye), which even now is still in the repertory of the Copenhagen Royal Theater.

41. Later addition by RS: "'melancholy times' it says in my notes for this day. Composing was out of the question."

42. Later addition by RS: "the 30th: The music director Berwald from Stockholm—not uninteresting, is supposed to be a good composer."

43. Later addition by RS: "Diligently studied scores of quartets by Haydn and Mozart during this time. Read 'Familie H.' by Friederike Bremer and 'Faustine' by the Countess Ida Hahn."

44. Later addition by RS: "On the 2nd at Voigt's for dinner. A woman pianist, Fräulein Wolfahrt from Weimar."

45. Later addition by RS: "the 4th in the theater: saw Fidelio [by Beethoven] with Schröder[-Devrient]."

46. Later addition by RS: "On the 8th: In the evening saw Gretry's 'Bluebeard' with Schröder-Devrient."

47. Later addition by RS: "the 9th afternoon G. Barth, husband of Hasselt, from Vienna. Terrible anger on account of Verhulst's malicious gossip."

48. The frigate *Thetis,* which under the command of Captain Zahrtmann transferred the works of Bertel Thorwaldsen from Leghorn to Copenhagen.

49. Later addition by RS: "On the 12th read 'Only a Fiddler' by Andersen with great pleasure, and thought about Clara a lot."

348 *Notes to Pages 146–152*

50. CS played compositions by Moscheles, Mendelssohn, Chopin, Liszt ("Erlkönig" transcription), Beethoven, Bach, and Thalberg as well as her own Scherzo, op. 10.

51. The concert took place in the Hôtel d'Angleterre.

52. CS dedicated her Lieder, op. 13, published in 1843, to Queen Caroline Amalie.

53. The lyrical drama *Preciosa* by P. A. Wolff, with music by Carl Maria von Weber, had been in the repertory of Copenhagen's Royal Theater since 1822.

54. Later addition by RS: "the 18th: Richard Wagner, who had come from Paris."

55. In letters to Leipzig Cranz had asserted that Schumann had "abandoned Clara in Hamburg when she was ill," that she had run up debts there, and that "no one had liked her." See also note 47.

56. Later addition by RS: "the 24th: surprising letter, that Clara will arrive already on Monday."

57. Later addition by RS: "the 25th: traveled to Magdeburg in the afternoon happy as a bridegroom and fearful at the same time."

58. The louis d'or, in Germany, referred to a gold five-thaler coin; thus less than a third of CS's gross earnings was left over.

59. The fire, which had broken out during the night of 4–5 May and did not cease until 8 May, destroyed 1,450 houses, including 24 hotels along the Jungfernstieg.

60. The house in which Schiller spent the summer of 1785 had been identified in 1841 through investigations by Robert Blum.

61. In May and June 1842 several extensive articles by RS appeared in the *Neue Zeitschrift für Musik* (see *Gesammelte Schriften* 4.125ff.).

62. "Liebeszauber" (Geibel) and "Sie liebten sich beide" (Heine), published in 1843 as part of CS's opus 13.

Notes to Pages 153–170 349

63. The house, Inselstrasse 5 (now 18), still exists, and now has a memorial plaque.

64. Thus CS remembered the custom practiced in many places of decorating graves on this day: Ludwig Schuncke was buried in the cemetery of St. John's Church in Leipzig.

65. The diary contains a printed page with the poem (dated Neusess bei Coburg, in June 1842), while Rückert's manuscript of it has disappeared.

66. CS visited her mother and her mother's second husband, Adolph Bargiel, for the first time in April 1835 in Berlin.

67. The exhibit was arranged for the benefit of the Tiedge Foundation, inaugurated in 1841, which was dedicated to the support of artists and their relatives.

68. The actress, a celebrated beauty, had met Liszt in Berlin and allegedly followed him secretly on his travels.

69. RS expressed himself about Reissiger's opera in the *Neue Zeitschrift für Musik* (see *Gesammelte Schriften* 4.167–73).

70. One of the two male choral festivals organized by the Dresden Choral Society, Liedertafel and Orpheus.

71. Although the letter—apparently by accident—was dated 15 August, RS and CS celebrated the fourteenth as their engagement day.

72. In connection with an encounter in Carlsbad in 1819, Goethe noted that he had found Metternich "as always to be a gracious gentleman."

73. *Linda di Chamonix,* written on commission for the Viennese court.

74. This favorite weapon of Ziska's had formerly been hanging over his tomb in Čáslav, which in 1623 was demolished on imperial orders.

75. The relics of a holy boy named Boniface, given to Prince Metternich by Pope Gregory XVI, were in an antique sarcophagus from Hadrian's tomb in Rome.

76. In the shafts of this former mine Prince Ernst of Saxony, who had

350 *Notes to Pages 171–185*

been kidnapped from Altenburg Castle, was temporarily hidden in 1455.

77. This birthday book, in which only a few pages have been filled out, can be seen in the Robert Schumann Haus, Zwickau.

Marriage Diary III

1. The premiere of RS's Quintet in E-Flat for Piano and Strings, op. 44, took place in the Gewandhaus on 8 January 1843, at a "musical morning conversation" by the Schumann couple.

2. In a letter Mendelssohn later remarked that RS's First String Quartet had "pleased him extraordinarily well."

3. The last guest performance by Theodor Döring, who appeared in comedies by Bauernfeld and Kotzebue.

4. These arias were conducted by Wagner himself, who had come with Wilhelmine Schröder-Devrient from Dresden.

5. Probably the officer von Döring, a gambler and spendthrift, whom Schröder-Devrient had met in 1840 and to whom she was unhappily married from 1846 to 1848.

6. With a letter on 21 January Wieck had invited CS to visit him; she left for Dresden on 11 February.

7. See note 1. In addition to RS's Piano Quintet, op. 44, the program included, among other things, the String Quartet in A Minor as well as lieder and duets by RS and CS.

8. The last two works appeared respectively as the *Fantasiestücke*, op. 88, in 1850, and as the Andante and Variations, op. 46 (a reduced version for two pianos), in 1844.

9. This probably refers to the *Pièces fugitives*, op. 15, nos. 1–3 (see also Diary II, note 23), and the Impromptu in E Major, first published in 1885.

Notes to Pages 186–199 351

10. In his concert on 4 February Berlioz had conducted, among other things, his *King Lear* Overture.

11. After the death of his first wife in 1854, Berlioz would marry the singer Maria Recio, with whom he had been living since 1842.

12. In December 1843 Agnes Semmel, née Fleischer, would die in childbirth.

13. By contrast, the *Fliegende Holländer*, first presented on 2 January 1843, was withdrawn after four performances.

14. Symphony No. 1 in C Major, op. 5.

15. On Mendelssohn's recommendation RS reworked the variations (see p. 200).

16. The name is missing.

17. Only six scholarships were available.

18. Among others the Orchestral Suite in D Major, the Cantata *Preise, Jerusalem, den Herrn,* and the "Sanctus" from the B Minor Mass.

19. Princess Alice Maude Mary, later grand duchess of Hesse.

20. RS and CS met the Wartel couple again in Russia; see p. 257.

21. See *Gesammelte Schriften* 4.237ff.; Schumann called Bazzini "a violinist of genius."

22. Alwin Wieck was also active as a piano teacher later on; he left behind a voluminous manual for piano study (manuscript in the Robert Schumann Haus, Zwickau).

23. CS gave RS the manuscript of her lieder "Loreley" (Heine), "O weh des Scheidens" (Rückert)—published in 1992 (*Clara Schumann, Sämtliche Lieder* [*Complete Songs*], vol. 2, ed. Joachim Draheim and Brigitte Höft, vol. 2, Breitkopf & Härtel EB 8559)—and "Ich hab in deinem Auge" (Rückert), op. 13, no. 5.

24. A collection of CS's songs, started in 1842, to which she added until 1853, can be found in the Deutsche Staatsbibliothek, Berlin.

352   *Notes to Pages 199–241*

25. The so-called Salziger Lake disappeared in 1893 as a result of flowing into excavations of the Mansfeld Mining District.

26. The *Allgemeine musikalische Zeitung*, which up to then had been edited by Moritz Hauptmann. RS declined the offer, as he would once more in 1846.

27. These scenario outlines can be seen in the Robert Schumann Haus, Zwickau. Both projects, for which RS had tried to obtain A. W. von Zuccalmaglio as librettist, remained unrealized.

28. This refers to Robert Franz's love for his eighteen-year-old student Luise Gutike, which probably remained unfulfilled owing to the question of rank.

29. While the "old style" Russian date is first mentioned here, it appears later, in Clara's subsequent notes (see p. 236).

30. In January 1835; until 1837 the duke of Cambridge had been viceroy of Hanover.

The Trip to Russia

1. Book 5, op. 62, published in April 1844.

2. In her concerts during the Russia trip, CS often played from manuscript the "Frühlingslied" and the "Venetianische Gondellied" in A Minor.

3. From the French *soupçon:* mistrustful, suspicious.

4. Citation from RS's travel notebook.

5. The Musical Academy was a choral society, founded by Sobolewsky in 1843, that continued into the twentieth century.

6. A well-known wine tavern in the cellar vaults of Königsberg Castle.

7. Beginning in June 1844 Minna Berndt studied piano and singing at the Leipzig Conservatory.

Notes to Pages 241–262 353

8. Adolph von Henselt's étude "Si j'étais oiseau" (If I were a bird), which CS frequently performed.

9. Paper money had less than one-third the value of coins; one silver ruble was worth three and a half in paper.

10. As RS's own notes reveal, his diagnosis was hemorrhoids.

11. There was no Czar Paul III; perhaps RS is thinking of Peter III, who in 1762 was murdered in Ropsha by partisans of his wife, Catherine II.

12. Henselt had worked on the concerto since 1837. In October 1845 CS performed it in Leipzig from manuscript; it was not published until 1847.

13. The first performance of Lvov's opera *Bianca e Gualterio,* in October 1844 at the Dresdner Court Theater, would be a failure.

14. The Decembrist revolution on 26 December 1825 had been put down by the personal participation of Czar Nicholas I.

15. Vielhorsky's opera *The Gypsies,* begun in 1838, remained unfinished.

16. See the program announcement (illustration 14). Instead of the opera arias shown there, CS played pieces by Scarlatti, Chopin, and Mendelssohn, in addition to the Fantasy by Thalberg.

17. That is, the board of directors of the society elected CS to be an honorary member. The diploma can be seen in the Robert Schumann Haus, Zwickau (see illustration 15).

18. These portraits can be found in the Schumann Family Album (Saxon Landesbibliothek, Dresden).

19. A reference to CS's concert on 11 August 1840 in the Weimar Belvedere Castle, which the Czarina Alexandra attended.

20. Prince Friedrich von Hessen-Kassel, whom CS had got to know in Copenhagen, had been married to the Grand Princess Alexandrine since January 1844.

354   Notes to Pages 263–296

21. An error on CS's part: the St. George Gallery and the Golden Hall of the Winter Palace are not the same.

22. The letter has been published in G. Eismann, *Robert Schumann: Eine Biographie in Wort und Bild* (Leipzig, 1964), 115.

23. In Carl von Schnabel's letter (see ibid.) is stated—probably erroneously—that he will have his *seventieth* birthday on 25 March.

24. He died the following year, 1845.

25. A vehicle used in Russia with a roof made of mats.

26. The custom of passing bareheaded through the Savior's (Spassky) Gate goes back to the year 1647, when an icon of the Savior of Smolensk was erected on this archway.

27. See pp. 312–23.

28. A reference to the Strelitz rebellion put down by Peter I in 1698.

29. The Church of the Savior in the Forest (thirteenth/fourteenth century) stood in the inner court of the New Kremlin, still under construction in 1844.

30. See pp. 322–37.

31. After the defeat of the Polish revolt of 1830–31, Nicholas I had "rescinded" the Constitution of 1815, an event that was supposed to be symbolized this way.

32. Actually, *A Life for the Czar* (premiere in 1836, performed 1941–89 in a mutilated version as *Ivan Susanin*).

33. The portraits are missing.

34. In 1801 Czar Paul I was murdered as the result of a conspiracy of officers led by General and Minister President Count P. L. von Pahlen. See also note 11.

35. Apparently the so-called Garden Islands and the Pharmacist Island; on the latter was located the botanical garden constructed by Peter I.

Notes to Pages 300–331

36. The Marienkirche (St. Mary's Church), which had been thoroughly restored in 1839–42.

Russian Customs

1. The following notes are from RS's travel notebook of the trip to Russia.

2. Probably the opera *Salvator Rosa*, which was performed in 1848 in Königsberg [Kaliningrad].

3. From 1829 to 1835 the first violinist of this private string quartet was Ferdinand David, who later married one of the daughters of the von Liphardt family.

4. "Beauty is the splendor of truth, art is the reasoning of thought."

5. "A lot of difficulties, but little pleasure."

6. See The Trip to Russia, note 26.

7. It was not while being cast, but during a fire in 1737, that a piece weighing about eleven tons broke from the Czar Kolokol bell.

8. *Translator's note:* It was probably symptomatic of RS's nostalgic yearning for home that he would occasionally see "familiar" faces of his Leipzig friends while visiting public places such as the opera in Moscow (see Peter Ostwald, *Schumann: The Inner Voices of a Musical Genius* [Boston: Northeastern University Press, 1985], 188). In addition, Schumann raises an interesting question here: is there only a finite number of facial designs to be found in different communities?

Poems from Moscow

1. On orders of Czar Nicholas I, in 1836 the bell was mounted on a granite base designed by Auguste Montferrand; see illustration 17.

2. The passage from Napoleon's will alluded to reads as follows: "I want

my ashes to rest on the bank of the Seine, amid the French people, whom I have loved so much."

3. The extremely hasty writing of this poem, with numerous corrections, indicates that it is a draft and not a fully completed work.

BIOGRAPHICAL DIRECTORY

(*Italics indicate the preferred Christian name*)

ALBRECHT, Karl, Born 27 August 1807 in Poznan, died 24 February 1863 in Gatschina. Violinist, conductor, and composer. Trained in Breslau; member of the orchestra of the local theater; conductor's aid in Düsseldorf, 1835; director of music for the dramatic theater in Petersburg (1838), then for the German and Russian Opera (conductor of the premiere of Glinka's *Russlan and Ludmilla*, 1842); director of the Philharmonic Concerts, 1845; voice teacher at the orphanage in Gatschina from 1850.

ALT, Karl. Choirmaster in Riga; local correspondent for the *NZfM.*

ALVENSLEBEN, Johann Ludwig *Gebhard* von. Born 7 September 1816 in Kalbe (Altmark), died 26 April 1895 in Kassel. Landowner, amateur composer and writer.

ANACKER, August Ferdinand. Born 17 October 1790 in Freiberg, where he died 21 August 1854. Studied in Leipzig and worked there as singer, pianist, and music teacher; choirmaster of the city and cathedral of Freiberg, 1821; founder of the city's Academy of Song; reorganizer of the Mountain Music Corps.

ANGER, Louis. Born 5 September 1813 in Andreasberg, died 18 February 1870 in Lüneburg. Pianist and composer; student of J. N. Hummel; music teacher in Leipzig, 1836–42; then organist and music director in Lüneburg.

AVÉ-LALLEMANT, Johann *Theodor* Friedrich. Born 2 February 1806 in Magdeburg, died 9 November 1890 in Hamburg. Music teacher in Hamburg from 1828; organizer of local musical events; committee member of the Philharmonic Society, 1837–44; friend of RS and CS.

BANCK, *Carl* Ludwig Albert. Born 27 May 1809 in Magdeburg, died 28 December 1889 in Dresden. Composer and writer on music; music critic in Magdeburg, Berlin, and Leipzig; voice teacher in Dresden from 1840. Collaborator on the *NZfM,* 1834–37. Called "Knapp" or "de Knapp" by RS.

BARGIEL, August *Adolph* Anastasius (*actual name* Anastasius Antonius Aloysius Bargel; change of name after conversion from Catholic to Lutheran faith, Easter 1807). Born 1 November 1783 in Bauerwitz, near Ratibor; died 4 February 1841 in Berlin. Violinist; member of the Leipzig Gewandhaus Orchestra, 1810–19; opened a singing school; to Berlin as music teacher, 1826. From 1824, second husband of Marianne BARGIEL.

BARGIEL, Ernst Amadeus Theodor *Eugen*. Born 28 February 1830 in Berlin, died 22 December 1907 in Bucharest. Son of Adolph and Marianne BARGIEL, half brother of CS. Emigrated to Romania.

BARGIEL, née Tromlitz, Marianne. Born 17 May 1797 in Greiz, died 10 March 1872 in Berlin. Pianist; student of Friedrich WIECK; his wife, 1816–24 (mother of Clara, Alwin, and Gustav WIECK); married Adolph BARGIEL after divorce.

BARGIEL, Woldemar. Born 3 October 1828 in Berlin, where he died 23 February 1897. Composer; half brother of CS. Studied with Dehn in Berlin and with HAUPTMANN, Moscheles, Rietz, and GADE at the Leipzig Conservatory, 1846–50. Music teacher in Berlin; at the conservatory in Cologne from 1859; conductor and director of the music school in Rotterdam from 1865; professor at the academy of music in Berlin from 1874.

BARTH, Gustav. Born 1818 in Vienna, died 12 May 1897 in Frankfurt/ Main. Pianist, conductor, and music critic. Conductor of the Vienna Musikgesangverein, 1843–49. Married to singer Wilhelmina van Hasselt.

BARTH, Johann Ambrosius. Born 1790 in Leipzig, where he died 1 December 1851 (suicide). Publisher in Leipzig; published in *NZfM* between 1 January 1835 and 30 June 1837.

BAUDISSIN, née Kaskel, Countess Sophie von. Born 27 July 1817 in Dresden, where she died 9 December 1894. Second wife of Count Wolf BAUDISSIN from 1840, friend of CS and godmother of Ludwig Schumann. Pianist and author of children's books (*pen name* Aunt Aurelie) and novels.

BAUDISSIN, Count *Wolf* Heinrich Friedrich Karl von. Born 30 January 1789 in Rantzau, died 4 April 1878 in Dresden. Initially diplomat (in the service of Denmark, 1810–14), then writer and translator. Translations from Middle High German (Hartmann von Aue), Eng-

Biographical Directory 359

lish (thirteen of Shakespeare's dramas, partly in cooperation with Dorothea Tieck), French (all dramas by Molière), and Italian (Gozzi, Goldoni).

BEAULIEU-MARCONNAY, Karl Olivier von. Born 5 September 1811 in Minden, died 8 April 1889 in Dresden. Diplomat and writer on history. Studied law in Heidelberg and Jena, 1831–33; in the service of the justice department of Oldenburg from 1834; member of the chamber of finance from 1841; in the service of the government of Weimar from 1843 (as director of the department of justice, 1848; majordomo in 1849; director of the court theater, 1851–57; chief educator of the grand duchess, 1853). Member of parliament, 1864–66; later in Dresden.

BECKER, Constantin *Julius*. Born 3 February 1811 in Leipzig, died 26 February 1859 in Oberlössnitz. Composer, writer on music, and music pedagogue. Studied philosophy in Leipzig, then student of C. F. Becker; music teacher in Dresden, 1843–56; in Oberlössnitz from 1846. Contributed to the *NZfM*.

BECKER, Ernst Adolph. Born 6 August 1798 in Dresden, where he died 31 July 1874. Studied in Leipzig, 1818–21; law degree. Examining judge (*Bergschreiber*) of the mining authority in Schneeberg, 1830–34; secretary at the Saxon department of finance in Dresden, 1834–36. Friend of RS; amateur pianist.

BECKER, Nikolaus. Born 8 October 1809 in Bonn, died 28 August 1845 in Hunshoven. Son of a merchant; studied law in Bonn from 1833; justice official in Cologne and Geilenkirchen; died of tuberculosis.

BEHLING (*also* Beling). Conductor and composer in Petersburg.

BEHRENS, Julius. Merchant, pianist, and composer in Riga.

BENDEMANN, *Eduard* Julius Friedrich. Born 3 December 1811 in Berlin, died 27 December 1889 in Düsseldorf. Painter of portraits and historical scenes; student of Wilhelm von Schadow; professor at the academy of art in Dresden from 1838; director of the academy in Düsseldorf, 1858–67. Friend of RS and CS.

BENNETT, William Sterndale. Born 13 April 1816 in Sheffield, died 1 February 1875 in London. British pianist, conductor, and composer. Several stays in Leipzig from 1836; student of Mendelssohn. Founder of the Bach Society of London in 1849; music director of the Philharmonic Society, 1856; director of the Royal Academy of Music, 1866.

BERGER, Ludwig, Born 18 April 1777 in Berlin, where he died 16 February 1839. Pianist and composer; student of Clementi and others; after concert tours and a trip to London he moved there from Berlin, 1815; cofounder of the more recent Berliner Liedertafel in 1819. Teacher of Mendelssohn, Fanny HENSEL, TAUBERT, HENSELT, C. BANCK, Henriette VOIGT, DORN, NOTTEBOHM, and others.

BERNARD, Moritz. Born 1794 in Kurland, died 9 May 1871 in Petersburg. Composer and pianist; student of Field and Hässler in Moscow, where he became Count Potocki's music director; in Petersburg from 1822, where he founded a publishing house for music (1829; taken over by Jürgenson, 1885) and the journal *Der Nouvellist*, 1840.

BLASSMANN, *Adolf* Joseph Maria. Born 27 October 1823 in Dresden, died 30 June 1891 in Bautzen. Pianist (student of Charles MAYER and Liszt) and composer of music for piano. Toured in Germany, 1843; taught at the conservatory in Dresden; conductor of the Euterpe in Leipzig, 1862–64; music director of the court in Sondershausen (1866–67); then conductor of the Dreyssig Academy of Song in Dresden.

BLOOMFIELD, Lord John Arthur Douglas. Born 12 November 1802, died 17 August 1879 in Ciamhallta, near Newport (Ireland). British diplomat; initially attaché in Stockholm; then secretary of the legate; later chargé d'affaires; special emissary and authorized minister in Petersburg, 1845; legate in Berlin, 1851–60; ambassador in Vienna, 1861–71.

BÖHM, Franz, Born 1789, died 1846. Violinist and teacher at the School of Dramatic Arts in Petersburg.

BOHRER, Max. Born 1785 in Mannheim, died 28 February 1867 in Stuttgart. Cellist and composer; toured in Europe, 1810–20; concertmaster of the court orchestra in Stuttgart from 1832.

BÖTTGER, Adolf. Born 21 May 1815 in Leipzig, where he died 16 November 1870. Poet and translator; arranged text for RS's oratorio *Das Paradies und die Peri*.

BOURNONVILLE, Auguste. Born 21 August 1805 in Copenhagen, where he died 30 November 1879. Son of ballet master Antoine

Biographical Directory

Bournonville (1760 Lyon–1843 Fredensborg); made his debut as dancer at the Royal Theater in Copenhagen in 1813; continued training as dancer and violinist in Paris; solo dancer and ballet master in Copenhagen in 1830; in Vienna, 1855–56; in Stockholm, 1861–64; in Copenhagen until 1877; finally director (first Wagner production, *Lohengrin,* in Denmark, 1870).

BRENNER, Freidrich. Born 1815 in Eisleben, died 1898 in Munich. Organist and composer; university music director and organist in Dorpat, 1839–93; credited for advancing local musical activities.

BROCKHAUS, Heinrich. Born 4 February 1804 in Amsterdam, died 15 November 1874 in Leipzig. Publisher; partner in the firm Brockhaus & Avenarius in Leipzig, 1823–49; later its sole owner.

BULGARIN, Faddej Venediktovic. Born 1789 in Minsk province, died 13 September 1859 at the Karlowa estate, near Dorpat. Russian writer and journalist; initially in the service of the Russian, Polish, and French armies; later writer in Warsaw (wrote in Polish); in Petersburg from 1832. From 1823, editor of the *Nordic Archive;* cofounder (1825) and editor of the *Nordic Bee* (*Severnaja pcela*).

BULL, *Ole* Bornemann. Born 5 February 1810 in Bergen (Norway), died 17 August 1880 in Lysø, near Bergen. Norwegian violinist; toured extensively in Europe and the United States.

BÜRCK, August. Born 1 February 1805 in Leipzig, died at the mental hospital in Colditz, 1862. Writer on music; wrote for the *NZfM.*

BUSCH, Friedrich Wilhelm. LL.D.; secretary of taxation in Hamburg. Amateur musician.

CANTHAL, August Martin. First flutist at the Hamburg City Theater; lived at the Dammtorwall.

CARL, née Tromlitz, Emilie. Born 4 March 1802 in Plauen, died 18 February 1885 in Dresden. Sister of CS's mother; married Julius CARL, 26 December 1828; lived in Dresden from January 1862.

CARL, *Julius* Eduard. Born 24 February 1800 in Falkenstein, died 13 May 1850 in Leipzig (found dead in water). Merchant and traveling salesman; married Emilie Tromlitz in 1828.

CATALANI, Angelica. Born 10 May 1780 in Sinigaglia, died 12 June 1849 in Paris. Italian coloratura soprano; made her debut in Venice, 1795; performed in Florence, 1799, and at La Scala (Milan), 1801; went to Lisbon in the same year, where she married French embassy attaché Valabrègue; then to Paris; to London, 1806; director of the Théâtre Italien in Paris, 1814–17; toured in Europe until 1828; no more performances thereafter.

CHORLEY, Henry Fothergill. Born 15 December 1808 in Blackley Hurst (Lancashire), died 16 February 1872 in London. British music critic, writer on music; in London from 1830; acquaintance of Mendelssohn and Moscheles.

CHRISTERN, Karl. Born 1812 in Hamburg, date of death unknown. Composer of songs and writer on music; editor of the *Hamburger Blätter für Musik;* wrote for *NZfM.*

COLLOREDO-WALLSEE, Imperial Count Franz de Paula von. Born 29 October 1799, died 26 October 1859 in Zürich. Austrian diplomat; legate in Petersburg, 1843–47; federal president in Frankfurt/Main, 1848; legate in London, 1852–56; ambassador to Rome until 1859; then representative at the peace conference in Zürich, where he died unexpectedly.

CONSTANTIN, *Bertha* Carolina. Born 17 September 1818 in Leipzig, date of death unknown. Daughter of shopkeeper Friedrich Wilhelm Constantin and Johanna Carolina, née Seidenschnur; godchild of Friedrich Hofmeister; married Carol VOIGT in 1841.

COURLÄNDER, Bernhard. Born 2 January 1815 in Copenhagen, died 1898 in Baltimore. Danish pianist; made his debut at the Royal Theater in Copenhagen in 1832; royal chamber musician in 1842; toured the United States in 1846; piano teacher at the Peabody Institute in Baltimore.

CRANZ, August Heinrich. Born 1789, died 1870. Founder (1813) and owner of the Cranz store for musical instruments, with publishing house and instrument rental, in Hamburg.

DAHL, Johann Christian Clausen. Born 24 February 1788 in Bergen (Norway), died 14 October 1857 in Dresden. Norwegian painter of landscapes; in Dresden from 1818; professor at the academy of fine art in Dresden from 1820.

DANNECKER, Johann Heinrich von. Born 15 October 1758 in Stuttgart, where he died 8 December 1841. Sculptor; sculptor at the court in Stuttgart from 1780; studied in Rome, 1785–90; professor at the Karlsakademie. Friend of Schiller, whom he portrayed several times.

Biographical Directory 363

DAVID, Ferdinand. Born 19 January 1810 in Hamburg, died 14 July 1873 in Klosters (Switzerland). Violinist and composer; student of Spohr and HAUPTMANN; member of the orchestra of the Königsstadt Theater in Berlin, 1826–29; then first violinist of the Liphardt string quartet in Dorpat; concertmaster of the Leipzig Gewandhaus Orchestra from 1835; teacher at the conservatory from 1843.

DECKER, Konstantin. Born 29 October 1810 in Fürstenau, died 28 January 1878 in Stolp (Pomerania). Pianist, composer, and music critic; studied archeology, natural science, and mathematics in Berlin; piano teacher in Petersburg from 1838; then in Königsberg; in Stolp from 1859.

DESSOIR, née Reimann, Therese. Born 12 June 1810 in Hanover, died 7 April 1866 in Mannheim. Actress; initially at the Royal Theater in Hanover; from 1832 in Leipzig, where she married actor Ludwig Dessoir (*actual name* Leopold Dessauer, 1810–74), with whom she went to Breslau, 1835. She then separated from him and returned to Leipzig; in Mannheim from 1845.

DEVRIENT, Gustav *Emil*. Born 4 September 1803 in Berlin, died 7 August 1872 in Dresden. Actor (at first, apprentice at his uncle's chemical factor in Zwickau); debut in Braunschweig, 1821; in Leipzig, 1823; in Magdeburg, 1828; in Hamburg, 1829; at the Hofbühne in Dresden, 1831–68; numerous tours, 1839–57.

DEVRIENT, née Loth, Johanne Christiane. Born 21 August 1785 in Leipzig, where she died 10 October 1857. Widow of manufacturer Johann Christian Devrient (1776–1823) in Zwickau; RS's landlady at the "Rotes Kolleg" in Leipzig, 1836–40. Godmother of Marie Schumann.

DÖHLER, Theodor. Born 20 April 1814 in Naples, died 21 February 1856 in Florence. Austrian pianist and composer; student of Czerny and Sechter in Vienna; concert tours in Europe, 1837–45; then in Petersburg, Moscow, and Paris; from 1848 in Florence.

DÖRFFEL, Alfred. Born 24 January 1821 in Waldenburg, died 22 January 1905 in Leipzig. Pianist and writer on music; studied at the conservatory in Leipzig. Custodian of the music department of the public library in Leipzig from 1860. Honorary doctorate, 1885.

DÖRING (actual name: Häring), Theodor. Born 9 January 1803 in Warsaw. Died 17 August 1878 in Berlin. Actor; debut in Bromberg,

1825; appeared at theaters in Breslau, Mainz, Mannheim, Hamburg, Stuttgart, Hanover; from 1845 at the Hoftheater in Berlin. Played comic roles, folk characters.

DORN, *Heinrich* Ludwig Edmund (or Egmont). Born 14 November 1804 in Königsberg, died 10 January 1892 in Berlin. Conductor and composer; student of L. BERGER, Zelter, and B. Klein; music director at the opera in Königsberg, Leipzig (where he was RS's teacher of music theory, 1831–32), Hamburg, Riga, Cologne, Berlin (music director of the opera at court, 1849–69); later teacher and critic.

DREYSCHOCK, Alexander. Born 15 October 1818 in Zak (Bohemia), died 1 April 1869 in Venice. Austrian pianist and composer; student of Tomásek; toured extensively in Europe from 1838. From 1862 professor and director of the conservatory in Petersburg.

DÜTSCH, Otto. Born c. 1825 in Copenhagen, died 1863 in Frankfurt/Main. Danish composer; studied at the conservatory in Leipzig, 1842–47; to Russia as military bandmaster, 1848; later choir teacher and conductor in Petersburg.

EBERWEIN, Karl. Born 10 November 1786 in Weimar, wher he died 2 March 1868. Violinist and composer; student of Zelter, to whom he had been recommended by Goethe. Led musical performances in Goethe's house; later music director in Weimar.

ECKERT, *Carl* Anton Florian. Born 7 December 1820 in Potsdam, died 14 October 1879 in Berlin. Violinist, conductor, and composer; quartet player in Leipzig, 1838–41; accompanied Henriette SONTAG on her tour of the United States, 1852; music director of the opera in Vienna, 1853–60; music director at court in Stuttgart, 1860–67; in Berlin from 1869.

EISNER, Karl. Born 19 June 1802 in Pulsnitz, died 23 January 1874 in Dresden. Horn player and composer; member of the royal orchestra in Petersburg until 1836; then with the royal orchestra in Dresden; toured extensively.

ERNST, Heinrich Wilhelm. Born 6 May 1814 in Brünn, died 8 October 1865 in Nice. Violinist and composer; student of Mayseder and BÖHM; lived in Paris and from 1845 primarily in England; gave concerts throughout Europe. Acquaintance with RS from 1830.

FAABORG, Rasmus Christian. Born 5 October 1811 in Naesbyhoved Mølle, near Odense, died 20 October 1857 in Copenhagen. Danish

Biographical Directory 365

opera singer; debut, 1835; employed at the Royal Theater in Copenhagen from 1841.

FÉTIS, François-Joseph. Born 25 March 1784 in Mons (Hennegau), died 26 March 1871 in Brussels. Belgian composer and musicologist; music director in Brussels, 1831; director of the conservatory from 1833.

FIELD, John. Born 26 July 1782 in Dublin, died 11 January 1837 in Moscow. English-Irish pianist and composer; student of Clementi, with whom he went to Paris and afterward to Petersburg in 1802, where he gave piano lessons; in Moscow from 1820; returned to London, 1832; numerous tours; returned to Moscow after falling ill in Naples.

FINK-LOHR. Singer in Petersburg; soloist at La Scala in Milan.

FISCHHOF, Joseph. Born 4 April 1804 in Butschowitz (Moravia), died 28 June 1857 in Baden, near Vienna. Austrian writer on music and music pedagogue. Studied medicine and music; professor of piano at the conservatory in Vienna from 1833.

FLECHSIG, Emil. Born 24 November 1808 in Wiesenburg near Zwickau, died 17 December 1878 in Zwickau. School and college friend of RS; studied theology in Leipzig; teacer at the lyceum in Zwickau, 1831–44; from 1838, also at the Bürgerschule. Deacon at St. Mary from 1844; from 1851, also last protodeacon at St. Catherine; retired in 1871. RS in part relied on his translation of Thomas Moore's *Lalla Rookh* for RS's *Das Paradies und die Peri*.

FLEISCHER, Eleonore Josephine *Agnes*. Born 12 January 1824 in Leipzig, died 8 December 1843 in Gera (in childbirth). Oldest daughter from the first marriage of Friedrich FLEISCHER; married (January 1843) Moritz SEMMEL, brother of her stepmother and a collage friend of RS.

FLEISCHER, Georg *Friedrich*. Baptized 8 April 1794 in Leipzig, died 22 September 1863 in Reudnitz, near Leipzig. Bookseller; city councillor in Leipzig, 1831–60. First marriage with Johanne Marie Friederike, née Schaumburg; divorced. Children: Agnes, Cäcilie Catherine (born 1825), Carl Friedrich (1826–74), Isidora Emilie (born 1828), Adele Henriette (born 1829), and Gustav Wilhelm (1832–59). From November 1840, second marriage with Therese Schumann, née Semmel.

FLEISCHER, née Semmel, *Therese* Marie. Born 2 September 1803 (or 1805) in Gera, died 22 February 1889 in Dresden. Married Eduard Schumann, brother of RS, 17 February 1825; second marriage (from November 1840) with Friedrich FLEISCHER.

FRANCK, Eduard. Born 5 December 1817 in Breslau, died 1 December 1893 in Berlin. Composer and music teacher; trained in Leipzig; student of Mendelssohn, 1834. Music teacher in Berlin from 1846; in Cologne, 1851–58 (music director from 1856); in Bern from 1859; teacher at the Stern Conservatory in Berlin from 1867.

FREGE, née Ferhardt, Virginie *Livia*. Born 13 June 1818 in Gera, died 22 August 1891 in Abtnaundorf, near Leipzig. Singer; debut, 1833; training with Wilhelmine SCHRÖDER-DEVRIENT in Dresden, 1834; engagement at the Königsstadt Theater in Berlin, 1835. Only occasional performances after she married (1836). First singer of the role of the Peri in RS's *Paradies und die Peri* in 1843.

FRIEDRICH, Eduard Ferdinand. Born 1816 or 1823 in Wiederau, near Leipzig; died February 1892 in Dresden. Pianist and salon composer; regarded as a student of Chopin in Paris. Undertook concert tours; in Magdeburg, Hamburg, and Dresden.

FRIESE, August *Robert*. Born 28 April 1805 in Dresden, died 7 November 1848 in Leipzig. Publisher in Dresden (took over his father's company in 1825) and Leipzig (firm of Robert Friese from 1833 and, in 1847, Robert Blum & Co.). Publisher of the *NZfM* from 1 July 1837.

FUCHS, J. Leopold. Composer and music teacher in Petersburg; originally from Saxony. Correspondent for the *NZfM*.

FÜCHS, Ferdinand. Born 11 February 1811 in Vienna, where he died 7 January 1848. Composer; student at the conservatory in Vienna; member of the orchestra of the royal opera.

GADE, Niels Wilhelm. Born 22 February 1817 in Copenhagen, where he died 21 December 1890. Danish violinist, conductor, and composer. With a stipend from the king, went to Leipzig (1843), where he became second conductor of the Gewandhaus Orchestra. Successor of Mendelssohn as director of the Gewandhaus concerts, 1847; returned to Denmark, 1848; director of the conservatory in Copenhagen. Friend of RS.

GARCÍA, Pauline. *See* Pauline VIARDOT-GARCÍA.

Biographical Directory 367

GENISCHTA, Josef (Josif Josifovich). Born c. 1810, died c. 1850. Russian pianist, cellist, conductor, composer, piano teacher, and (from 1837) conductor of the Moscow choir.

GERKE, Anton Augustovich. Born 21 August 1812 in Pulin, died 17 August 1870 in Petersburg (?). Pianist and music teacher; student of FIELD, Kalkbrenner, Ries, and Moscheles; lived in Petersburg from 1832; cofounder of the symphonic society, 1840; professor at the conservatory in Petersburg, 1862–70.

GLÄSER, Franz. Born 19 April 1798 in Obergeorgenthal (Bohemia), died 29 August 1861 in Copenhagen. Violinist, conductor, and composer; student of Pixis. Music director at various Viennese theaters; at the Königsstadt Theater in Berlin from 1830; royal music director in Copenhagen from 1842.

GOLDSCHMIDT, Otto. Born 12 August 1829 in Hamburg, died 24 February 1907 in London. Pianist and composer; student of Mendelssohn, Chopin, and others; married Jenny Lind in the United States, 1852; in Dresden until 1858; then in London; deputy director of the Royal Academy of Music, 1863.

GOLDSCHMIDT, Sigismund. Born 28 September 1815 in Prague, died 26 September 1877 in Vienna. Austrian pianist and composer; student of Tomásek; in Berlin and Paris; took charge of his father's banking business, c. 1850.

GÖTZE, Franz. Born 10 May 1814 in Neustadt/Orla, died 2 April 1888 in Leipzig. Violinist and singer; student of Spohr; member of the Weimar royal orchestra from 1831; then trained to become an opera singer; first tenor at the royal theater in Weimar, 1836–52; voice teacher at the Leipzig Conservatory, 1852–67, then private teacher.

GRIEPENKERL, Friedrich Konrad. Born 10 December 1782 in Peine, died 6 April 1849 in Braunschweig. Aesthetician; student of J. N. Forkel in Göttingen; from 1808, teacher of language and literature in Hofwyl (Switzerland); at the Catharineum in Braunschweig in 1816; from 1821 associate, from 1825 full professor of philosophy and humanities. Founder of an academy of song; editor of J. S. Bach's keyboard and organ works.

GRIEPENKERL, Wolfgang Robert. Born 4 May 1810 in Hofwyl (Switzerland), died 16 October 1868 in Braunschweig. Writer; son of Friedrich Konrad GRIEPENKERL; studied in Berlin; doctorate, Jena,

1839; assistant professor of history of art and literature, Collegium Carolineum; high school teacher in Braunschweig from 1844.

GRIMM, August Theodor von. Born 25 December 1805 in Stadtilm (Thuringia), died 28 October 1878 in Wiesbaden. Writer; studied philosophy, history, and (from 1827) languages in Petersburg. Journey to Germany, France, and Italy, 1832–35; after his return, director of studies and tutor to the Grand Prince Constantine and the Grand Princess Alexandrine; traveled through Russia, Syria, Greece, and Algeria with Constantine, 1845–47; from 1847 state councillor and tutor to the grand princes Mikhail and Nikolai; in Dresden from 1852; again royal tutor in Petersburg, 1858–60; then in Berlin.

GROSS, Johann Benjamin. Born 12 September 1809 in Elbing, died 1 September 1848 in Petersburg. Cellist and composer; member of the Liphardt string quartet in Dorpat (1833–35), then of the imperial orchestra in Petersburg.

GRUND, Friedrich Wilhelm. Born 7 October 1791 in Hamburg, where he died 24 November 1874. Cellist, conductor, and composer; founder of the Hamburg Academy of Song, 1819; conductor of the Philharmonic concerts in Hamburg, 1828–63.

GULOMY (*also* Goulomy), Jérôme Louis. Born 22 June 1821 in Pernau (Livonia), died 10 October 1887 in Bückeburg. Violinist of Russian origin; gave concerts in Germany (1842), in Holland, Great Britain, Norway, Sweden, and elsewhere, 1843–46. Concertmaster for the prince of Bückeburg from 1853; royal director of music and professor of music from 1866.

HAFNER, *Carl* Magnus. Born 23 November 1815 in Kornneuburg, died 15 January 1861 in Hamburg. Austrian violinist; student of Mayseder and Jansa in Vienna; in Hamburg from 1839, where he founded the first string quartet that regularly performed in public (with Löwenberg, Pollack, and SACK).

HALM, Friedrich (*actual name* Baron Eligius Franz Joseph von Münch-Bellinghausen). Born 2 April 1806 in Kraków, died 22 May 1871 in Vienna. Austrian playwright, poet, and novelist.

HARKORT, née Anders, Auguste. Born 1794 in Elberfeld, died 7 May 1857 in Dresden. Wife of Karl Friedrich HARKORT; presided over a cultivated household; sponsored writers and musicians.

HARKORT, Karl Friedrich. Born 1788 in Elberfeld, died 29 February

Biographical Directory

1856 in Leipzig. Merchant and manufacturer of cast-iron ware in Leipzig.

HÄRTEL, Hermann. Born 27 April 1803 in Leipzig, where he died 4 August 1875. LL.D.; lawyer and bookseller; from 1835, co-owner (with his brother Raimund) of the firm Breitkopf & Härtel, music publishers and piano makers; founder of the Association for Fine Art in Leipzig.

HÄRTEL, Raimund. Born 9 June 1810 in Leipzig, where he died 9 November 1888. Brother of Hermann HÄRTEL; music publisher; with the firm Breitkopf & Härtel from 1832; co-owner from 1835; retired in 1880. First marriage with Marianne Louise, née Göring; second marriage with Wilhelmine Friederike Louise, née Haufe (1835–82).

HARTMANN, née Zinn, Emma Sophie Amalia. Born 22 August 1807 in Copenhagen, where she died 6 March 1851. Song composer (pseudonym: Mrs. Palmer); became first wife of Jens Peter Emilius HARTMANN, 2 December 1829.

HARTMANN, Jens Peter Emilius. Born 14 May 1805 in Copenhagen, where he died 10 March 1900. Danish composer and conductor of German origin; trained as lawyer and musician; educational trip through Germany, 1836. Codirector of the conservatory in Copenhagen; father-in-law of Niels Wilhelm GADE.

HAUMANN, Theodor. Born 3 July 1808 in Ghent, died 21 August 1878 in Brussels. Belgian violinist and composer; studied law; received doctorate, 1830; to Paris; frequent concert tours from there. No public performances after 1836.

HAUPTMANN, Moritz. Born 13 October 1792 in Dresden, died 3 January 1868 in Leipzig. Violinist, composer, music theorist, and writer. Student of Spohr; violinist at the court orchestra in Dresden, 1812–15; music teacher of Prince Repnin in Petersburg, 1815–20; in Dresden, 1820–22; member of the court orchestra and teacher of music theory and composition in Kassel, 1822–42; choirmaster of St. Thomas (*Thomaskantor*) in Leipzig from 1842; teacher of music theory at the Leipzig conservatory from 1843; publisher of the *AmZ,* 1843.

HEINEFETTER, Sabine. Born 19 August 1809 in Mainz, died 18 November 1872 at the mental institution in Illenau. Singer; debut in

Frankfurt/Main, 1825, then engagement in Kassel; continued studies in Paris and Italy; engagement at the court theater in Dresden, 1835; tours, 1836; retired from stage, 1842.

HEJBERG (Heiberg), Johan Ludvig. Born 14 December 1791 in Copenhagen, died 25 August 1860 in Bonderup near Ringsted on Sealand. Danish writer; studied natural sciences in Copenhagen from 1809; Ph.D. (1817) with a dissertation on Calderón; studied music and theater in Paris, 1819–22; lecturer of Danish language and literature at Kiel University; playwright in Copenhagen from 1828; teacher of aesthetics and literature at the military academy in Copenhagen, 1830–36; director of the Royal Theater, 1849–56.

HEJBERG, née Pätges, Johanne Luise. Born 22 November 1812 in Copenhagen, where she died 21 December 1890. Debut as dancer at the theater in Copenhagen, 1823; debut as actress, 1826; worked there until 1864, as director until 1874. Married Johan Ludvig HEJBERG, 1831.

HELENE PAVLOVNA, née Princess Charlotte von Württemberg, Grand Princess of Russia. Born 9 January 1807 in Petersburg, where she died 2 February 1873. Married Grand Prince Mikhail Pavlovic, brother of Alexander I and Nikolai I, December 1823. Musically trained; studied with HENSELT, 1839; did great service to the musical community in Petersburg. Cofounder of the Russian Imperial Society of Music, 1859.

HELSTED, Eduard. Born 8 December 1816 in Copenhagen, where he died 1900. Danish violinist and composer; member of the Royal Orchestra in Copenhagen from 1838; concertmaster from 1863; teacher at the conservatory from 1869.

HENSEL, née Mendelssohn-Bartholdy, Fanny. Born 15 November 1805 in Hamburg, died 14 May 1847 in Berlin. Sister of Felix Mendelssohn-Bartholdy; married painter Wilhelm Hensel, 1829; pianist and composer.

HENSELT, Adolph. Born 9 May 1814 in Schabach (Bavaria), died 10 October 1889 in Warmbrunn (Silesia). Pianist and composer; student of Hummel and Sechter; went on concert tours; gave piano lessons in Petersburg from 1838.

HERING, Karl *Eduard*. Born 13 May 1807 in Oschatz, died 26 November 1879 in Bautzen. Music teacher, organist, and composer; studied

Biographical Directory 371

theology in Leipzig and couterpoint with Weinlig, then pursued his own studies in Dresden; organist at the main Lutheran church and music teacher at the seminary in Bautzen from 1839; composed oratorios and various other choral works.

HERRMANN, Friedrich August. Born 3 August 1814 in Dresden, where he died 31 October 1871. LL.D.; lawyer in Leipzig; later in Dresden; friend of RS. First marriage, from July 1839, with Antonie, née Schmidt, widowed Häussler (born 1811 in Leipzig, buried there 9 March 1842); second marriage, from April 1848, with Malwine Albertine, née Leonhardt (born 1827 in Grimma).

HERRMANN, Gottfried. Born 15 May 1808 in Sondershausen, died 6 June 1878 in Lübeck. Violinist, pianist, conductor, and composer; organist at St. Mary in Lübeck from 1831; director of the court orchestra in Sondershausen, 1844–52; then music director and intermittently director of the city theater in Lübeck; conductor of the Bach Society in Hamburg.

HESSE, *Adolph* Friedrich. Born 30 August 1809 in Breslau, where he died 5 August 1863. Organist, conductor, and composer. Organist at St. Elisabeth in Breslau from 1827; at St. Bernhardin, also in Breslau, from 1831. Conductor of the symphonic concerts of the theater orchestra there. Toured in England, France, and Italy as organ virtuoso from 1844.

HILF, *Christoph* Wolfgang. Born 6 September 1818 in Bad Elster, where he died 1 January 1912. Violinist and conductor. Trained as linen weaver; later student of DAVID in Leipzig; violinist in the Gewandhaus Orchestra, 1838–41; concertmaster in Bad Elster; successor of his father as director of the local spa orchestra, 1850–92.

HILLER, Ferdinand. Born 24 October 1811 in Frankfurt/Main, died 11 May 1885 in Cologne. Composer, pianist, conductor, and writer on music; friend of RS and CS. Active in Dresden from 1844; encouraged RS to conduct there. To Düsseldorf as kapellmeister, 1847; to Cologne, 1850. Recommended RS as his successor in Düsseldorf.

HIRSCHBACH, Hermann. Born 29 February 1812 in Berlin, died 19 May 1888 in Gohlis, near Leipzig. Composer, music critic, and writer; contributed to the *NZfM;* editor of the *Musikalisch-kritisches Repertorium* in Leipzig, 1843–45.

HOFFMANN, Johann. Born 1805, died 1865. Singer and intermittently

372 *The Marriage Diaries of Robert & Clara Schumann*

theater director in Riga; director of the theater in the Josephstadt, Vienna, from 1855.

HOFMEISTER, Johann *Friedrich* Karl. Born 24 January 1782 in Strehlen, died 30 September 1864 in Reudnitz, near Leipzig. Music publisher; founded the Hofmeister publishing house (1807), which was passed on to his sons (1852).

HOMEYER, L. Joseph Maria. Born 18 September 1814 in Kreuzeber (Eichsfeld), died 5 October 1894 in Duderstadt. Organist and composer; undertook many concert tours; at various times music director for the duke of Lucca.

HOMILIUS, Friedrich. Born 15 October 1813 in Saxony, date of death unknown. Horn player; member of a military band in Dresden, 1830–38; first horn player in the orchestra of the Imperial Theater in Petersburg; professor at the conservatory, 1873–99; also director of the Philharmonic Society.

HORSLEY, William. Born 15 November 1774 in London, where he died 12 June 1858. British organist and composer; cofounder of the club Concentores Sodales (1798–1847) and (in 1813) of the Philharmonic Society of London; organist at various churches in London; member of the professorial committee of the Royal Academy of Music from 1822; editor of the collection *Vocal Harmony,* the *Cantiones sacrae* by Byrd, and other works.

HORSLEY, Sophie. Born c. 1820. Youngest daughter of William HORSLEY; friend of Felix and Cécile Mendelssohn-Bartholdy.

JACOBY, Johann. Born 1 May 1805 in Königsberg, where he died 6 March 1877. Studied medicine in Königsberg and Heidelberg; general practitioner in Königsberg; wrote political commentary from 1830. Among other things, favored a constitution for Prussia. Member of the Prussian national assembly (1848), of the German national assembly (1849); accused of high treason, later acquitted. Member of the opposition in the second chamber of the Prussian parliament from 1863; imprisoned several times for falling out of favor politically; retired from public life, 1871.

JAHN, Otto. Born 16 June 1813 in Kiel, died 9 September 1869 in Göttingen. Classical philologist, archeologist, and father of musicology. Private lecturer in Kiel, 1839; associate professor in Greifswald, 1842; full professor, 1845; in Leipzig, 1847–51; in Bonn, 1855; in Berlin from 1867.

Biographical Directory 373

KAHLE, Carl Hermann Traugott. Born 1806 in Dessau, date of death unknown. Pianist and music teacher in Dessau; to Königsberg, 1831; organist there.

KAHLERT, Karl *August* Timotheus. Born 5 March 1807 in Breslau, where he died 29 March 1864. Writer and aesthetician of music, composer. Studied law, history, philosophy, and literary history; trained at the provincial high court, 1832; professor of philosophy at Breslau University, 1840–46; contributed to *Cäcilia, AmZ,* and *NZfM.*

KEFERSTEIN, Gustav Adolph. Born 13 December 1799 in Kröllwitz near Halle, died 19 January 1861 in Wickerstedt, near Apolda. Theologian and pedagogue; author and critic of music and musical aesthetics (pen names: Dr. K. Stein, Dr. Peregrinus Jocosus); initially deacon at the garrison church in Jena; then minister in Wickerstedt. Contributed to *NZfM.*

KELLNER, Gustav. Born 1809 in Weida, died 24 February 1849 in Weimar. Pianist and composer; music director in Potsdam; piano teacher in Weimar from 1838.

KINDERMANN, August. Born 6 February 1816 in Potsdam, died 6 March 1891 in Munich. Opera singer; first engagement at age sixteen as a member of the choir of the court opera in Berlin, where Spontini let him sing his first soli. At the city theater in Leipzig (as second bass, later first baritone), 1839–46; then at the royal opera in Munich.

KIRCHNER, *Theodor* Fürchtegott. Born 10 December 1823 in Neukirchen, near Chemnitz; died 18 September 1903 in Hamburg. Composer; student of RS at the Leipzig Conservatory; organist in Winterthur, 1843–62; then conductor and music teacher in Zürich, Würzburg, Leipzig, Dresden, and Hamburg.

KISTNER, Carl *Friedrich.* Born 3 March 1797 in Leipzig, where he died 21 December 1844. Publisher in Leipzig, owner of the music store H. A. Probst from 1831; from 1836 as the firm of Kistner. Cofounder of the Leipzig Conservatory.

KITTL, Johann Friedrich. Born 8 May 1806 at Worlik Castle (Bohemia), died 20 July 1868 in Polish Lissa. Studied law, later composition with Tomásek in Prague; pursued music exclusively from 1840; director (1842–46), then teacher at the conservatory in Prague.

KLENGEL, August Alexander. Born 27 January 1783 or 29 January 1784 in Dresden, where he died 22 November 1852. Organist and composer; student of Clementi, whom he accompanied to Petersburg. Stayed there until 1811; then in Paris, Dresden (1814), London (1815); organist at the court church in Dresden from 1816.

KLENGEL, Moritz Gotthold. Born 4 May 1794 in Stolpen, died 10 May or 14 September 1870 in Leipzig. Violinist; member of the Gewandhaus Orchestra, 1814–68; teacher at the Leipzig Conservatory.

KLOSS, *Carl* Johann Christian. Born 8 February 1792 in Mohrungen, near Eisleben; died 26 April 1853 in Riga. Organist and composer; student of Türk in Halle; also appeared as violinist and pianist. Worked in Leipzig, Königsberg, Elbing, Danzig, Dresden, and Kronstadt, mostly traveling from 1840.

KOSSMALY, Carl. Born 27 July 1812 in Breslau, died 1 December 1893 in Stettin. Composer and writer on music; student of Zelter, L. BERGER, and B. Klein; conducted theater orchestras in various cities; conductor and music teacher in Stettin from 1846. Wrote for the *NZfM.*

KRÄGEN, Philipp Heinrich *Carl.* Born 17 May 1797 in Dresden, where he died 14 February 1879. Pianist and composer; initially tutor in Warsaw; in Dresden from 1817; sponsored by Friederike SERRE; appointed court pianist in 1853. Godfather of Julie Schumann.

KREUTZER, Konradin. Born 22 November 1780 in Messkirch (Baden), died 14 December 1849 in Riga. Composer and conductor; student of Albrechtsberger in Vienna; music director in Stuttgart, Schaffhausen, Donaueschingen, at various Viennese theaters, 1822–40; music director in Cologne, 1840–46; returned to Vienna, 1846–49; then in Riga.

KRÜGER, Eduard. Born 9 December 1807 in Lüneburg, died 8 November 1885 in Göttingen. Organist, composer, and writer on music; studied philology in Berlin and Göttingen; high school teacher in Emden and Aurich from 1830; editor of the *Neue Hanoversche Zeitung,* 1848; music director and librarian of the university in Göttingen from 1849; professor, 1861.

KRÜGER, Wilhelm. Born 5 August 1820 in Stuttgart, where he died 17 June 1883. Pianist and composer; in Paris, 1845–70; then back to Stuttgart to become court pianist and teacher at the conservatory.

Biographical Directory

375

KUDELSKI, Karl Mathias. Born 17 November 1805 in Berlin, died 3 October 1877 in Baden-Baden. Violinist; student of E. Rietz and Lafont; initially member of the orchestra of the Königsstadt Theater in Berlin; member of the Liphardt string quartet in Dorpat from 1830; conductor at the Imperial Theater in Petersburg from 1839; concertmaster and conductor in Moscow, 1841–51; then in Baden-Baden.

KUFFERATH, Hubert Ferdinand. Born 11 June 1818 in Mülheim/Ruhr, died 23 June 1896 in Brussels. Composer; student of F. SCHNEIDER, Mendelssohn, and DAVID; conductor of the male choral society of Cologne, 1841–44; then in Brussels, where he was appointed professor of composition at the conservatory, 1871.

KÜHNE, Ferdinand *Gustav*. Born 27 December 1806 in Magdeburg, died 22 April 1888 in Dresden. Writer and critic; studied philosophy in Berlin, where he wrote for the *Preussische Staatszeitung;* editor of the *Zeitung für die elegante Welt* in Leipzig, 1835–42; in Dresden from 1856. Sympathetic to the "Young Germany" movement. Married Henriette Harkort, 16 May 1841.

KUMMER, *Friedrich* August. Born 5 August 1797 in Meiningen, died 22 August 1879 in Dresden. Cellist and composer; student of Dotzauer and B. Romberg; oboe player (1814), then cellist (1817–64) at the court orchestra in Dresden.

LABITZKY, Joseph. Born 4 July 1802 in Schönfeld, near Eger; died 18 August 1881 in Karlsbad. Composer of dances; violinist in the spa orchestra in Marienbad, then in Karlsbad, where he founded his own orchestra, 1834; went on concert tours with his orchestra.

LAMPADIUS, Wilhelm Adolph. Born 29 November 1812 in Freiberg, died 7 April 1892 in Leipzig. Ph.D.; cleric in Leipzig; catechism teacher at St. Peter's Church; teacher at the citizens' school. Author of a biography of Mendelssohn.

LANDSBERG (*actual name* Landsberger), Ludwig. Born 1807 in Breslau, died 6 May 1858 in Rome. Violinist by training; to Paris, 1832; to Rome (1835), where he sponsored all German musicians who came to the city.

LATROBE (de La Trobe), Johann Friedrich Bonneval. Born 1769 in Chelsea, near London; died 1845 in Dorpat. Studied medicine in Jena; to Livonia as private tutor, 1795; involved in music and supported musical activities primarily in Dorpat; composed church music (Mendelssohn published his Stabat Mater and Agnus Dei), songs, piano and chamber music. Owner of an autograph collection.

LEHNHOLD, Dr. Owner of a store for musical instruments in Moscow.

LEMOCH, Vinzenz. Born 7 February 1792 in Networzic (Bohemia), date of death unknown. Pianist and composer; trained in Prague; organist of the Benedictine monastary in Breunau, near Prague; private teacher in Lemberg; accompanist of Angelica CATALANI from 1820; once more took up studies in Vienna with Salieri; to Moscow as music teacher, 1824; returned to Vienna in his later years.

LENZ, Wilhelm von. Born 1 June 1809 in Riga, died 19 January 1883 in Petersburg. Pianist and writer on music; initially trained in Riga; student of Liszt in Paris (1828); of Moscheles in London (1829); studied law in Dorpat and Moscow; became imperial state councillor of Russia. Author of several books on Beethoven.

LEUCHTENBERG, née Grand Princess of Russia, Duchess Maria Nikolaievna von. Born 18 August 1819, died 21 February 1876. Oldest daughter of Czar Nikolai I; married Duke Maximilian Eugen Joseph Napoleon von Leuchtenberg, 14 July 1839. After his death (November 1856), married Count Grigori Stroganov; in Florence from c. 1860.

LEWY, Carl. Born 1823 in Lausanne, died 20 April 1883 in Vienna. Austrian pianist; composer of salon pieces. Son of Eduard Constantin LEWY.

LEWY, Eduard Constantin. Born 3 March 1796 in St. Avold/Moselle, died 3 June 1846 in Vienna. Horn player; first horn player in the orchestra of the Vienna court opera from 1822; professor at the conservatory. Father of Carl, Melanie, and Richard LEWY.

LEWY, Richard. Born 1827 in Vienna, where he died 31 December 1893. Horn player; member of the orchestra of the court opera from 1840; later superintendent and director of the court opera and voice teacher.

LICHNOWSKI, Prince Felix Maria Vincenz Andreas von. Born 5 April 1814, died 19 September 1848 in Frankfurt/Main (assassinated by revolutionaries). Prussian officer, 1834–38; in Spain, France, and Portugal; member of the Curia of Lords in the first unified Prussian parliament, 1847; member of the Frankfurt national assembly, 1848. Close friend and travel companion of Liszt; writer.

Biographical Directory 377

LICHTENSTEIN, Martin Heinrich Karl. Born 10 January 1780 in Hamburg, died 3 September 1857 at sea near Kiel. Natural scientist; studied medicine in Jena and Helmstädt; expeditions in southern Africa, from which he returned to Germany, 1806. Professor of zoology in Berlin, 1811; director of the museum of zoology, 1813; founder of the Berlin Zoo (built 1841–44). Music lover and sponsor of musical events in Berlin.

LIPHARDT, Carl von. Born c. 1778. Owner of an estate and lord of the majorate at the Rathshof near Dorpat; trained at the Pfeffel "school of war" in Colmar; later land marshal of Livonia.

LIPHARDT, Carl Eduard von. Born 1808 in Dorpat, died 15 February 1891 in Florence. Son of Carl v. LIPHARDT; owner of estate; art collector and patron; brother-in-law of Ferdinand DAVID. Studied natural sciences and medicine in Dorpat, literature, linguistics, and art history in Berlin and Bonn (there with A. W. von Schlegel). On year-long trips through Italy, acquired a collection of old paintings and copper etchings, which was exhibited in his house in Dorpat. After a trip through Germany and Italy, finally settled in Florence.

LIPINSKY, *Karol* Józef. Born 4 November 1790 in Radzyn, near Lublin; died 16 December 1861 in Orlow, near Lemberg. Polish violinist and composer; music director in Lemberg; numerous concert tours. Concertmaster of the royal orchestra and the church orchestras in Dresden, 1839–59.

LIST, Caroline (*called* Lin[n]a). Born 1828. Daughter of Friedrich and Caroline LIST.

LIST, née Seybold, Caroline. Wife of Friedrich LIST; emigrated to Paris with her children, 24 May 1838.

LIST, Elise. Born 1 July 1822 in Stuttgart, died 4 January 1893 in Munich. Daughter of Friedrich and Caroline LIST; received her training as a singer in Paris and Milan; married Austrian industrialist Gustav Moriz Pacher von Theinburg (1808–52), 27 March 1845; in Vienna and Schönau; to Munich after Pacher's death.

LIST, Emilie. Born 10 December 1818 in Tübingen, died 14 December 1902 in Munich. Daughter of Friedrich and Caroline LIST; friend of CS; later, tutor in the family of Count Rodiczky, president of the federal military commission in Frankfurt/Main. Later lived in Munich with her mother and sister.

LIST, Friedrich. Born 6 August 1789 in Reutlingen, died 30 November 1846 in Kufstein (suicide). National economist; emigrated to the United States, 1825; American consul in Leipzig, 1833–37, where he concerned himself with the construction of the railroad from Leipzig to Dresden; in Paris from 1837; in Stuttgart, 1840; in Augsburg, 1842; committed suicide on a journey to the Alps after fruitless attempts to gain a permanent position.

LOBE, Johann Christian. Born 30 May 1797 in Weimar, died 27 July 1881 in Leipzig. Musician, writer on music, and composer; member of the Weimar court orchestra, 1811–42 (flute and viola); professor and director of his own music school in Weimar from 1842; editor of the *AmZ* in Leipzig, 1846–48; then teacher of composition and writer on music in Weimar.

LOEBMANN, Franz. Born 1804 or 1811 in Volschau (Niederlausitz), died 1878. Violinist and composer; initially violinist at the orchestra of a theater in Berlin; then choirmaster and music director in Riga.

LORENZ, Oswald. Born 30 September 1806 in Johanngeorgenstadt, died 22 April 1889 in Winterthur. Organist, music teacher, and writer on music; studied theology in Leipzig, 1825–28; then organist at the churches of George and John. Friend of RS and his deputy as editor of the *NZfM* in 1838–39 and 1844. Settled in Winterthur, 1844; voice teacher and organist there until 1878.

LOSE, née Gottschalk, Arnoldine. Born 1787 in Leipzig, died 1861 in Copenhagen. Widow of the music publisher Carl Christian Lose (senior, 1787–1835); took charge of his publishing house with P. W. Olson (Lose & Olson) until her son Carl Christian Lose (junior, 1821–92) took over.

LÖVENSKIOLD, Baron Hermann Severin von. Born 30 July 1815 in Holdenjernvärk (Norway), died 5 December 1870 in Copenhagen. Danish organist and composer; trained in Copenhagen, Vienna, and Leipzig; returned to Denmark, 1841; court organist in Christiansborg from 1851.

LÜTTICHAU, Baron Wolf Adolf *August* von. Born 16 March 1786 in Ulbersdorf near Schandau, died 16 February 1863 in Dresden. Head forester at the Saxon court; general director of the royal orchestra and director of the court theater in Dresden, 1824–62.

LVOV, Alexej Fjodorovic. Born 25 May [5 June] 1799 in Reval, died 16

Biographical Directory 379

[28] December 1870 in Romanovo, near Kovno. Russian violinist, conductor, and composer; personal adjutant to Nikolai I from 1834; general director of the imperial church orchestras from 1837; director of court music until 1861.

LYSER, Johann Peter (*actual name* Ludwig Peter August Burmeister). Born 2 October 1803 in Flensburg, died 29 January 1870 in Altona. Writer of novels and pieces of music; painter; trained as an actor. Went deaf, 1821; in Hamburg; in Leipzig, 1831–35; in Dresden, 1835–45; in Vienna, 1845–53; then in Altona. Friend of RS and contributor to the *NZfM* (*pen name* Fritz Friedrich).

MACZEVSKY, Alexander. Born in Mitau, died 8 June 1879. Conductor, writer on music, composer. Student of HAUPTMANN in Leipzig, later music director in Zweibrücken and Kaiserslautern.

MARCOU, Charles. Cellist; studied with Duport at the Paris Conservatoire; in Moscow from 1822.

MARSCHNER, *Heinrich* August. Born 16 August 1795 in Zittau, died 14 December 1861 in Hanover. Composer and conductor; in Dresden from 1820 (music director, 1824); at the city theater in Leipzig, 1827; court conductor in Hanover, 1831–59.

MARTINOV. Officer and amateur pianist in Petersburg.

MARX, Adolph Bernard. Born 15 May 1795 in Halle/Saale, died 17 May 1866 in Berlin. Music theorist, writer on music, journalist, also composer. Worked as lawyer, then took music lessons from Türk and Zelter; editor of the *Allgemeine musikalische Zeitung* (which he had founded) in Berlin, 1824–30; associate professor there, 1830; music director of the university, 1832; cofounder of the Stern Conservatory.

MARXSEN, Eduard. Born 23 July 1806 in Nienstedten near Altona, died 18 November 1887 in Altona. Pianist, piano teacher, composer, and writer on music; trained in Hamburg and Vienna; teacher of Brahms; sporadically wrote for the *NZfM;* appointed royal music director, 1875.

MAURER, Ludwig (*Louis*) Wilhelm. Born 8 February 1789 in Potsdam, died 25 October 1878 in Petersburg. Violinist, conductor, and composer; concert tour to Russia, 1806; there became conductor for Chancellor Vsovoloshski; traveled, 1817; concertmaster in Hanover, 1824–33; return to Russia; conductor at the French Theater and director of the concerts of the Symphonic Society in Petersburg, 1835; general intendant of the imperial orchestras, 1841–62, but lived in Dresden for long periods from 1845.

MAURER, Vsevolod Vassilievic. Born 1819, died 1892. Violinist, oldest son of Louis MAURER and student of his father; member of the orchestra of the French Theater in Petersburg from 1835; concertmaster at the Italian Theater there, 1843–85; teacher of the class for instrumentalists of the court orchestra.

MAYER, Carl (Charles). Born 21 March 1799 in Königsberg, died 2 July 1862 in Dresden. Pianist and composer; student of FIELD; piano teacher in Petersburg, 1819–50; numerous concert tours; to Dresden, 1850.

MECHETTI, Pietro. Born 1777 in Lucca, died 25 July 1850 in Vienna. Austrian music publisher; partner in the company of his uncle Carlo Mechetti (1748–1811) from 1807; sole owner from 1811. After his death, his widow, Therese Mechetti, took charge of the business.

MEERTI, Elisa. Born 1821 in Antwerp, date of death unknown. Belgian soprano; soloist of the Leipzig Gewandhaus concerts, 1839–42; later voice teacher in Brussels. Married clarinet player Arnold Joseph de Blaës (born 1814).

MÉHUL, Étienne Nicolas. Born 22 June 1763 in Givet (Forest of Ardennes), died 18 October 1817 in Paris. French organist and stage composer; first intendant of the Paris Conservatory, 1794; member of the academy, 1795.

METTERNICH-WINNEBURG, Prince Clemens Wenze Lothar von. Born 15 May 1773 in Koblenz, died 11 June 1859 in Vienna. Austrian state chancellor, 1821–48; main proponent of the policy of restoration in Europe; forced to step down on 14 March 1848.

MEYER, Emma. Born 8 October 1818 in Leipzig, where she died 24 September 1881. Daughter of merchant Adolph Meyer (junior); friend of the young CS; married shopkeeper's assistant Albert Leppoc.

MOLIQUE, Bernhard Wilhelm. Born 7 October 1802 in Nürnberg, died 10 May 1869 in Cannstatt. Violinist and composer; student of Spohr and others; in Vienna and Munich; concertmaster and music director in Stuttgart, 1826–49; then to London; professor of composition at the Royal Academy of Music, 1861–66; finally settled in Cannstatt.

Biographical Directory 381

MONTAG, Carl. Born 1817 in Blankenhain (Thuringia), died 1 October 1864 in Weimar. Pianist, composer, and writer on music; director of church music in Weimar. Correspondent of the *NZfM*.

MONTEZ, Lola (*actual name* Rosanna Gilbert). Born 1820 in Montrose (Scotland), died 30 June 1861 in New York. Dancer; illegitimate daughter of a Scottish officer and a Creole woman; raised in Bath; from 1840, traveled through Europe as a dancer under the assumed name Lola or Dolores Montez; protégée of King Ludwig I in Munich; then predominantly in the United States (with trips to Australia and England), where she lectured on among other things sociopolitical questions, published her memoirs, and appeared in theatrical productions of her own life story.

MOODY, Marie. Traveling Englishwoman, temporarily student of CS.

MORIANI, Napoleone. Born 10 March 1808 in Florence, where he died 4 March 1878. Italian tenor and voice teacher; taught at the conservatory in Petersburg, 1853–69.

MÜLLER, Carl Friedrich. Born 11 November 1797 in Braunschweig, where he died 4 April 1873. Violinist and composer; concertmaster in Braunschweig for many years; retired, 1872.

MÜLLER, Elise. Born 1782 in Bremen, where she died in 1849. Pianist, piano teacher, and director of a boarding school for young women in Bremen; daughter of local organist, composer, and writer on music Wilhelm Christian Müller (1752–1831).

MÜLLER, Friedrich. Born 10 December 1786 in Orlamünde, died 12 December 1871 in Rudolstadt. Conductor and composer; clarinet player in the court orchestra in Rudolstadt, 1803; court conductor, 1831–54.

MÜLLER, Johann Heinrich. Born 19 March 1782 in Königsberg, died 19 March 1826 in Petersburg. Violinist, conductor, and composer; student of Türk in Halle and Kreutzer in Paris; member of the court orchestra in Vienna; to Petersburg (1803) to become director of the orchestra of the German theater there; then trained as pianist and worked as piano teacher and composer.

NATHAN, Adolph. Born 3 December 1814 in Copenhagen, died 19 July 1885 in Ålborg. Danish pianist and composer; temporarily student of Friedrich WIECK.

NAUENBURG, Gustav. Born 20 May 1803 in Halle/Saale, died 6 August 1875 in Neugersdorf (Oberlausitz). Baritone, voice teacher, and writer on music; after studies in theology, took music lessons from B. Klein; concert singer and voice teacher in Halle from 1832; contributed to various musical journals, including the *NZfM.*

NAUMANN, Johann Gottlieb. Born 17 April 1741 in Blasewitz, near Dresden; died 23 October 1801 in Dresden. Composer and conductor; conductor of the court orchestra in Dresden from 1776; also worked in Stockholm and Copenhagen.

NESSELRODE, Count Karl Vassilievic (*actual name* Karl Robert) von. Born 14 December 1780 in Lisbon, died 23 March 1862 in Petersburg. Russian diplomat and politician; held positions at the embassies in Prussia, Württemberg, Holland, and France; secretary of foreign affairs, 1816–56; vice chancellor and chancellor of the Russian empire under Nikolai I.

NETZER, Joseph. Born 18 March 1808 in Imst (Tyrol), died 28 May 1864 in Graz. Austrian conductor and composer; studied in Innsbruck and Vienna; music director of the theater and conductor of the Euterpe concerts in Leipzig from c. 1840; at the Theater an der Wien from 1845; then back in Leipzig; conductor of the Styrian Music Society in Graz, 1853–64.

NOTTEBOHM, Martin *Gustav.* Born 12 November 1817 in Lüdenscheid, died 29 October 1882 in Graz. Writer on music and composer; studied with L. BERGER and Dehn in Berlin; from 1840 with HAUPTMANN, Mendelssohn, and RS in Leipzig, from 1845 with Sechter in Vienna; there he established himself as music teacher and musicologist; mainly studied Beethoven.

NOVAKOVSKY, Józef. Born 1800 in Mniszek, near Radomsk; died 27 August 1865 in Warsaw. Polish pianist and composer; student of J. Elsner and others; concerts in Italy, Germany, and France, 1833; then gave piano lessons in Warsaw.

OLDECOP, Evstafij Ivanovic. Born 1 September 1786 in Riga, died 10 February 1845 in Petersburg. Russian journalist, censor, and translator; editor of the *St. Petersburgische Zeitschrift* and the *St. Petersburgische Zeitung.*

OLDENBURG, Prince Peter Georgijevic von. Born 1 August 1812 in Jarosław, died 2 May 1881 in Petersburg. Nephew of Czar Nikolai I; music lover and amateur composer; patron of several educational institutions in Petersburg. Married Princess Therese von Nassau, 1837.

Biographical Directory 383

OLDENBURG, née Princess von Nassau, Therese von. Born 1815; married Prince Peter von OLDENBURG, 1837.

OLGA NIKOLAIEVNA, Grand Princess of Russia. Born 11 September [30 August] 1822, died 1892. Second oldest daughter of Czar Nikolai I, married the crown prince (later King Karl I), of Württemberg, 1846.

OLSEN, Peter Wilhelm. Born 8 July 1791 in Copenhagen, where he died 16 March 1859. Dealer of musical instruments and publisher; worked for the C. C. Lose company from 1806; became partner, 1835 (Lose & Olsen); started his own company (P. W. Olsen), 1846.

OTTEN, Georg Dietrich. Born 8 February 1806 in Hamburg, died 28 July 1890 near Vevey (Switzerland). Composer and conductor; student of F. SCHNEIDER in Dessau; music teacher, choirmaster, and orchestra director in Hamburg; also wrote on music. Founded the Musical Society of Hamburg (1856), whose president he was until 1863.

PARISH, Charles (Carl). Brother of Harriet PARISH; merchant in Hamburg.

PARISH, Harriet (called Henriette). Born 29 January 1816 in Hamburg, died 7 August 1864 in Plön. Pianist; friend of CS.

PARISH, Richard. Born 1776, died 1860. Merchant in Hamburg; father of Charles and Harriet PARISH; lived in Nienstedten.

PARISH-ALVARS, Elias. Born 28 February 1808 in West Teignmouth (England), died 25 January 1849 in Vienna. English pianist and harpist; numerous concert tours from 1823; harp soloist at La Scala (Milan) from 1834; at the Vienna court orchestra, 1836–38; more traveling; gave lessons in Vienna from 1847.

PASTA, née Negri, Giuditta. Born 28 October 1797 in Saranno, near Milan; died 1 April 1867 in Blevio, on Lake Como. Italian soprano; debut, 1815; performed in Italy, Paris, and London; only sporadically from 1833. Concert tour to Russia, 1840; retired from stage in Milan, 1841.

PFUNDT, Ernst Gotthold Benjamin. Born 17 June 1806 in Dommitzsch, near Torgau; died 7 December 1871 in Leipzig. Nephew of Friedrich WIECK; like Wieck, first studied theology; later became piano teacher and tenor, as well as choirmaster at the theater in Leipzig and timpanist in the Gewandhaus and theater orchestras.

POHLENZ, Christian August. Born 3 July 1790 in Salgast (Niederlausitz), died 10 March 1843 in Leipzig. Conductor, organist, and composer; director of the Leipzig Gewandhaus concerts and the academy of song, 1827–35; replacement choirmaster at the Thomas school, 1842.

POTT, August. Born 7 November 1806 in Northeim, near Göttingen; died 27 August 1883 in Graz. Violinist and composer; student of Spohr; member of the court orchestra in Hanover from 1822; concertmaster and director in Oldenburg, 1832–61; then lived in Graz.

POTT, née Winkler von Foracest, Aloyse. Born 25 April 1815 in Vienna, date of death unknown. Wife of August POTT; pianist and composer; student of Czerny and Gyrowetz.

PRÉVOST, Eugène Prosper. Born 23 August 1809 in Paris, died 30 August 1872 in New Orleans. Composer and conductor; studied at the conservatory in Paris; music director of the opera in Le Havre; in New Orleans, 1838–62; then in Paris; returned to New Orleans, 1867.

PROBST, Heinrich Albert. Born 1791 in Dresden, died 24 May 1846 in Leipzig (suicide). Music publisher; dealt in leather in Leipzig, 1817–23; then founded a music publishing house with C. F. Kistner, who took over when Probst joined Pleyel Company in Paris, 1831. Returned to Leipzig in May 1846 and there committed suicide. Married to Christiane Juliette, née Gross (1793–1845).

RAKEMANN, Ernst. Brother of Louis RAKEMANN; clarinet player in Bremen.

RAKEMANN, *Louis* Christian. Born 1816 in Bremen, date of death unknown. Pianist; moved to the United States, 1839; back in Germany from 1844; in London, 1851; in Paris, 1852.

RASCHER, Eduard Moritz. Born 1807 in Zwickau, where he died in 1849. School friend of RS; attended the lyceum in Zwickau, 1822–29; studied law in Jena; lawyer in Zwickau from c. 1834.

RECIO (*also* Martin-Recio), Maria. Died 13 June 1862. Singer; lived with Hector Berlioz from 1842, and married him after his first wife's (Harriet, née Smithson) death on 19 October 1854.

REICHMANN, Henriette. Friend and travel companion of CS; later lived in Hull (England).

REINHARDT, (called) Ivan Ivanovich. Pianist and piano teacher in Moscow; student of FIELD.

Biographical Directory 385

REISSIGER, Carl Gottlieb. Born 31 January 1798 in Belzig, near Wittenberg; died 7 November 1859 in Dresden. Composer and conductor; first studied theology, then became student of Salieri in Vienna and P. von Winter in Munich; music director at the Deutsche Oper in Dresden from 1826; court music director, 1827–59; also artistic director of the conservatory in Dresden from 1856.

RETTICH, née Gley, Julie. Born 17 April 1809 in Hamburg, died 11 April 1866 in Vienna. Actress; debut (1825) in Dresden, where she took lessons from Tieck; engaged at the Hofburg Theater in Vienna, 1830–33; married Karl RETTICH (9 April 1833) and went with him to Dresden until 1835; returned to the Hofburg Theater and performed there until her death.

RETTICH, Karl. Born 3 February 1805 in Vienna, where he died 17 June 1878. Austrian actor; at the Hofburg Theater in Vienna, 1832–33 and 1835–72; also in Graz, Kassel, and Dresden; married Julie Gley in 1833.

REUSS-KÖSTRITZ, Count (Prince from 1851) Heinrich II. Born 31 March 1803, died 29 June 1852 in Erfurt. Music lover; friend of RS.

REUTER, Moritz Emil. Born 2 March 1802 in Elsterberg near Plauen, died 30 July 1853 in Leipzig. M.D.; general practitioner in Leipzig; friend of RS and CS.

RIBEAUPIERRE, Marquis Alexandre de. Diplomat in Petersburg; earlier legate in Constantinople; then imperial councillor and senator at the czar's court.

RIEFFEL, Amalie. Born 1822 in Flensburg, died 10 August 1877 in Hamburg. Daughter of Wilhelm Heinrich RIEFFEL; pianist; temporarily student of RS; married to the merchant Wage from Hamburg, 1850.

RIEFFEL, Wilhelm Heinrich. Born 23 October 1792 in Hoya/Weser, died 6 February 1869 in Flensburg. Organist in Flensburg from 1817.

RIEFSTAHL, Carl. Born c. 1800 in Stralsund, died 31 July 1845 in Greifswald. Violinist in Munich, Frankfurt/Main, Petersburg, Stockholm, and elsewhere; numerous concert tours; professor in Greifswald from 1844.

RIEM, Friedrich Wilhelm. Born 17 February 1779 in Kölleda (Thuringia), died 20 April 1857 in Bremen. Organist, conductor, and com-

386   *The Marriage Diaries of Robert & Clara Schumann*

poser; student of J. A. Hiller in Leipzig; organist of the New Reformed Church from 1807; organist of the cathedral in Bremen from 1814; founder (1815) and conductor of the academy of song in Bremen; music director of the city of Bremen.

RIETZ, Julius. Born 28 December 1812 in Berlin, died 12 September 1877 in Dresden. Cellist, composer, and conductor; city music director in Düsseldorf, 1836–47; music director of the opera in Leipzig, 1847; conductor of the Gewandhaus concerts from 1848; court music director in Dresden from 1860; director of the conservatory there, 1870.

RÖCKEL, August. Born 1 December 1814 in Graz, died of the plague 18 June 1876. Conductor; student of his uncle J. N. Hummel in Weimar; music director of the theater there; then music director in Bamberg; in Dresden, 1843–49; imprisoned for thirteen years for his participation in the May revolt; later lived in Frankfurt/Main, Munich, and Vienna as litterateur.

RÖCKEL, Eduard. Born 20 November 1816 in Trier, died 2 November 1899 in Bath (England). Pianist and composer; brother of August RÖCKEL and, like him, student of J. N. Hummel in Weimar; lived in Weimar and Erfurt; from 1848 in England; several concert tours.

RODA, Ferdinand von. Born 26 March 1815 in Rudolstadt, died 26 April 1876 near Kriwitz (Mecklenburg). Composer, conductor, and organizer of musical events; to Hamburg, 1842; founded the Bach Society of Hamburg, 1855; music director of the university in Rostock, 1857.

RÖLLER, Eduard Hermann. Born 1808 in Treuen (Vogtland), date of death unknown. School friend of RS; attended the lyceum in Zwickau, 1822–27; studied theology, first in Leipzig (until 1830), then in Heidelberg; teacher in Kloschwitz from 1843; later settled in Dresden.

ROMBERG, *Cyprian* Friedrich. Born 28 October 1807 in Hamburg, where he died 14 October 1865. Cellist and composer; soloist in Petersburg from 1835; in Bad Pyrmont from 1845; drowned while bathing.

ROMBERG, *Heinrich* Maria. Born 4 April 1802 in Paris, died 2 May 1859 in Hamburg. Brother of Cyprian ROMBERG; violinist and conductor; studied at the Paris Conservatory; concertmaster of the imperial

Biographical Directory 387

opera in Petersburg from 1827; later conductor there; returned to Germany, 1859.

RUBINI, Giovanni Battista. Born 7 April 1795 in Romano, near Bergamo, died 2 March 1854 near Romano. Italian tenor; choral singer; discovered as soloist, 1814; engagement in Naples, 1832–43; at the Théâtre Italien in Paris, 1825–26; performed alternately in Paris and London, 1832–43; in Petersburg, 1843 and 1844; returned to Italy as a millionaire and bought a small principality there.

RUBINSTEIN, Anton. Born 28 November 1829 in Wechwotynez (Podolia), died 20 November 1894 in Peterhof. Pianist, composer, and conductor; numerous concert tours (to western Europe, 1841–43); to Berlin for studies with Dehn, 1844–48; director of the Russian Music Society in Petersburg from 1859; founded the conservatory there (1862), which he presided over, 1862–67 and again 1887–90.

RÜCKERT, Friedrich. Born 16 May 1788 in Schweinfurt, died 31 January 1866 in Neusess, near Coburg. Poet, playwright, and translator; studied law and philology; private lecturer in Jena, 1811; professor of Asian philology in Erlangen, 1826; in Berlin, 1841–48.

RUSSO, Michel Angelo. born c. 1830 in Naples, date of death unknown. Pianist and piano composer; first performed as a nine-year-old after early training in piano and song; temporarily student of Moscheles; concerts in France, Germany, and other European countries; missing from 1846.

SABBARTH, Franz Ludwig. Born 1809 in Breslau, date of death unknown. Studied law in Breslau and, from 1828, in Heidelberg (with RS); later appointed state councillor in Königsberg.

SACK, Johann Christian *Theodor.* Born 25 April 1818 in Hamburg, died 20 December 1897 in Vienna. Cellist; to Stockholm, 1844; joined the court orchestra there, 1853; gave up his career after an injury, then became wine merchant; to Vienna after the death of his wife (Hedwig, née Berwald, died 1880).

SÄMANN, Carl Heinrich. Born 1790 in Königsberg, where he died 29 January 1860. Organist at the parochial church; music director and teacher at the university in Königsberg.

SCHÄFFER, Heinrich. Born 20 February 1808 in Kassel, died 28 November 1874 in Hamburg. Singer (tenor) and composer; in Magdeburg, Braunschweig, and the City Theater in Hamburg; retired from stage, 1838; then became conductor and composer (works for male choir, instrumental music).

SCHLADEBACH, Julius. Born 1810 in Dresden, died 21 September 1872 in Kiel. Medical doctor; composer and writer on music in Dresden; editor of the *Neues Universallexikon der Tonkunst* (1854); editor of various political journals; contributed to the *NZfM*.

SCHLEGEL (*also* Köster-Schlegel), Louise. Born 22 February 1823 in Lübeck, died 2 November 1905 in Schwerin. Soprano; engagements in Leipzig, Berlin, Breslau and elsewhere; in Berlin, 1847–62. Married writer Hans Köster.

SCHLEINITZ, Heinrich Conrad. Born 1 October 1802 in Zschaitz, near Döbeln; died 13 May 1881 in Leipzig. Lawyer and notary in Leipzig; friend of Mendelssohn; member of the board of directors of the Gewandhaus concerts from 1834; cofounder of the Leipzig Conservatory, 1843; president of its board of directors from 1849.

SCHLESINGER, Heinrich. Born 1810 in Berlin, where he died 14 December 1879. Music publisher in Berlin; after the death of his father, Martin Adolph Schlesinger (11 October 1838), ran the family's publishing business (founded 1795) with his mother, Philippine; sole owner, 1844–64.

SCHLETTER, Heinrich. Born 8 January 1793 in Leipzig, died 19 December 1853 in Paris. Merchant and silk trader in Leipzig.

SCHLOSS, Sophie (Sophia). Born 12 December 1812 or 1822 in Frechen, near Cologne; died 15 May 1903 in Düsseldorf. Alto singer; soloist in the Leipzig Gewandhaus concerts for some time; in Düsseldorf from 1850.

SCHLOSSBAUER (*also* Schlosbauer), née Kerstens, Adele. Born 9 December 1815 in Kiel, date of death unknown. Married Andreas Schlossbauer, 3 June 1835.

SCHMIDT, Maria (Christian) Heinrich. Born 18 February 1809 in Lübeck, died 3 May 1870 in Berlin. Tenor; theater director and writer on music, also composer; at the city theater in Leipzig, 1838–45; then opera director in Dresden; in Hamburg, 1847; then voice teacher in Berlin. Contributed to the *NZfM*.

SCHMIDT, née Möllinger. Singer; wife of Maria Heinrich SCHMIDT.

SCHNABEL, Carl (senior) von. Born 6 April or 25 March 1773 in Zeitz (?), died near Tver in 1845. Brother of RS's mother; to Russia as physician of a regiment; later owner of an estate in Tver.

Biographical Directory 389

SCHNEIDER, Johann Christian *Friedrich*. Born 3 January 1786 in Waltersdorf (Oberlausitz), died 23 November 1853 in Dessau. Organist, conductor, and composer; music director and court organist in Dessau from 1821, where he founded the academy of song, a forum for vocal music, and a music school, which he directed, 1831–46. Teacher of composition; music theorist.

SCHOBER, Franz Ritter von. Born 17 May 1796 at Torup Castle, near Malmö; died 13 September 1882 in Dresden. Lawyer and litterateur in Vienna; friend of Franz Schubert.

SCHRÖDER, née Bürger, Anna *Sophie*. Born 23 February 1781 in Paderborn, died 25 February 1868 in Munich. Mother of Wilhelmine SCHRÖDER-DEVRIENT; actress; also gave public readings of poetry; debut in Petersburg, 1793; later engagements in Vienna, Breslau, Hamburg, and Prague; at the Hofburgtheater in Vienna from 1815; in Munich from 1831; back in Vienna, 1836; retired, 1840.

SCHRÖDER-DEVRIENT (*actual name* Devrient, née Schröder), Wilhelmine. Born 6 December 1804 in Hamburg, died 26 January 1860 in Coburg. Actress and singer; debut in Vienna, 1821; soprano at the court theater in Dresden, 1823–47; evicted (1849) for her support of the May revolt; returned to stage, 1856.

SCHUBERT, Franz. Born 22 July 1808 in Dresden, where he died 12 April 1878. Violinist and composer for violin; trained in Dresden and Paris; candidate at the court orchestra in Dresden, 1823; vice concertmaster, 1837; second concertmaster, 1847; first concertmaster succeeding LIPINSKI, 1861–73.

SCHULTZ (*also* Schoultz de Torma), Georg Julius von. Born 22 September 1808 in Reval, died 16 May 1875 in Vienna. Physician and writer from the Baltics (*pen name* Dr. Bertram); from a family of preachers in the Mecklenburg area; educated by his grandfather, provost Asverus of Torma; attended the Domschule in Reval and (1826–33) the university in Dorpat. Practiced as a general physician in Russia; several trips through Europe; published stories, plays, Estonian sagas, and translations. Prosector at the academy of medicine and surgery; physician at the military hospital and at the mineral baths in Petersburg. Member of the committee of censorship for the minister of the interior (as state councillor), 1867.

SCHULZ (Schulze), Johann Philipp Christian. Born 1 February 1773 in Langensalza, died 30 January 1827 in Leipzig. Conductor and composer; student of Engler and Schicht in Leipzig; conductor of the Sekonda Theater Group, 1800; conductor of the Gewandhaus concerts in Leipzig from 1810.

SCHULZE, Heinrich Benjamin. Born 6 June 1798 in Werdau, died 29 March 1866 in Dresden. Choirmaster and music director at parochial churches St. Mary and St. Catherine in Zwickau, 1833–65 (had already had the position of choirmaster in Weida from 1821); voice teacher and supervisor of the choir at the local high school, 1833–59.

SCHUMANN, Carl (senior). Born 12 June 1801 in Ronneburg, died 9 April 1849 in Karlsbad. Second oldest brother of RS; publisher in Schneeberg.

SCHUMANN, Carl (junior). Born 16 December 1827 in Schneeberg, died 1 May 1846 in Zwickau. Only son of RS's brother Carl from his first marriage (1809–33) with Rosalie, née Illing; attended the high school in Zwickau, 1840–46.

SCHUMANN, Elise. Born 25 April 1843 in Leipzig, died 1 July 1928 in Haarlem. Second oldest daughter of RS and CS; married (1877) merchant Louis Sommerhoff (1844–1911).

SCHUMANN, Marie. Born 1 September 1841 in Leipzig, died 14 November 1929 in Interlaken. First child of RS and CS.

SCHUMANN, Therese. *See* Therese FLEISCHER.

SCHUNCKE, Christian Ludwig (*Louis*). Born 21 December 1810 in Kassel, died 7 December 1834 in Leipzig. Pianist and composer; friend of RS; cofounder of the *NZfM*.

SCHUNCKE, Julius. Born 1808 in Berlin, date of death unknown. Brother of Carl SCHUNCKE. Horn player; actor at the courts in Munich and Hanover; indpendent actor in Königsberg (1844–47), Hamburg (1847–48), and elsewhere.

SEEBURG, August Mortiz. Born 19 March 1794 in Torgau, died 31 October 1851 in Leipzig. LL.D.; lawyer and city councillor in Leipzig; member of the board of directors of the Gewandhaus concerts from 1840.

SEEBURG, née Baroness (Freifräulein) von Flögel, *Vera*. Born 21 December 1803 in Berensberg near Aachen, died 1856 in Leipzig. Married August Moritz SEEBURG, 25 November 1819. Children: Alexander (born 1821), Christoph, Wolfgang (1826–93).

Biographical Directory 391

SEMMEL, Carl *Moritz*. Born 27 March 1807 in Gera, where he died 20 March 1874. Friend of RS at the university; brother of Therese Schumann, née Semmel (later FLEISCHER), whose stepdaugher Agnes FLEISCHER he married, 1843. Local magistrate and secret councillor of the judiciary in Gera.

SENKOVSKI, Ossip Ivanovich. Born 31 March 1800 near Vilnius, died 16 March 1858 in Petersburg. Orientalist and writer; expeditions to the Orient, 1819–21; professor of Oriental languages in Petersburg, 1822–47; founded the journal *Library for Reading (Biblioteka za ctenie)*, 1834; worked for the journal *Son of the Fatherland (Syn otecestva)*.

SERRE, Friedrich *Anton*. Born 28 July 1789 in Bromberg, died 3 March 1863 in Maxen. Studied law in Frankfurt/Oder; volunteer in the military near Grossgörschen as major adjutant to the military governor of Saxony; retired from military career, 1817; married Friederike Hemmerdörfer; in Dresden, 14/15 Amalienstrasse. After traveling in England, Scotland, and Italy, acquired the castle and manor Maxen (1819), which, like the Dresden apartment, became a center of the artistic and musical world of Dresden, as well as of charitable activities (establishment of the Tied foundation [1841], of the Schiller-Lottery [1859]).

SERRE, née Hemmerdörfer, Friederike. Died 7 August 1872 in Maxen. Daughter of a merchant from Dresden; married Major Anton SERRE, 1817.

SHAW, née Postans, Mary (*called* Mrs. Alfred Shaw). Born 1814 in Lea (Kent), died 9 September 1876 in Hadleigh Hall (Suffolk). English contralto; traveled all over Europe; performed at the Gewandhaus concerts in Leipzig, 1838–42.

SIVORI, Ernesto *Camillo*. Born 25 October 1815 in Genoa, where he died 18 February 1894. Italian violinist and composer; student of Paganini; toured extensively from 1836; in the United States, 1846–48; in Germany, 1862–63.

SKRAUP, Franz. Born 3 June 1801 in Wositz (Bohemia), died 7 February 1862 in Rotterdam. Bohemian-Austrian composer and conductor; originally lawyer; second director (1827), first director (1837–57) at the Prague theater of guilds; in Rotterdam from 1860.

SOBOLEWSKI, Friedrich *Eduard*. Born 1 October 1808 in Königsberg, died 17 May 1872 in St. Louis. Composer and writer on music; student of C. M. von Weber, music director in Königsberg, 1830; organist at the Altstadt church, 1835; director of the Philharmonic Society, 1838; of the music academy, 1843; wrote for the *NZfM (pen name* J. Feski); orchestra director of the theater in Bremen, 1854–58; emigrated to the United States, 1859.

SONTAG (*also* Sontag-Rossi) (Countess) Henriette. Born 3 January 1806 in Koblenz, died 17 June 1854 in Mexico City. Soprano; debut in Prague, 1821; appeared in Vienna, Berlin, and Paris; married the Sardinian secretary of the legate, Count Rossi, in London, 1828; in Berlin from 1830; performed exclusively as concert singer until 1849; then returned to guest engagements at the operas in London, Paris, and Germany.

SOUBRE, Étienne Joseph. Born 30 December 1813 in Liège, died there 8 September 1871. Belgian conductor and composer; director of the Philharmonic Society of Brussels, 1844; director of the conservatory in Liège from 1862.

SPIEGEL UND ZU PICKELSHEIM, Karl Emil Baron von. Born 1783, died 1849. Majordomo in Weimar from 1815; temporarily in charge of the court theater; lived near the outwork (now Marstallstrasse).

STAGE, Johan Adolph *Gottlob.* Born 31 August 1791 in Copenhagen, where he died 3 October 1845. Danish actor and director; first studied law; debut 16 November 1815 at the Royal Theater in Copenhagen; married Ulriche Augusta Koefoed in 1836.

STAHLKNECHT, Adolph. Born 18 June 1813 in Warsaw, died 25 June 1887 in Berlin. Violinist and composer; chamber musician at the royal chamber orchestra in Berlin; concertmaster from 1840.

STAHLKNECHT, Julius. Born 17 March 1817 in Posna, died 14 January 1892 in Berlin. Cellist and composer; soloist with the royal chamber orchestra in Berlin from 1835; concerts and trio soirées with his brother Adolph STAHLKNECHT in Berlin from 1844.

STERN, Julius. Born 8 August 1820 in Breslau, died 27 February 1883 in Berlin. Violinist, voice teacher, and conductor; studied in Berlin, Dresden, and Paris; returned to Berlin, 1846; founded the Stern Choir there, 1847; with Kullak and A. B. MARX, founded the conservatory (1850) that was later named after him. Royal music director, 1849; conductor of the former Liebig chamber orchestra in Berlin, 1867–75.

Biographical Directory 393

STIEGLITZ, Baron Alexander von. Died 24 October 1884 in Petersburg. Owner of a trading and banking business in Petersburg that had been founded by his father, Ludwig von Stieglitz (1778–1843); business closed in 1863.

STÖCKHARDT, Heinrich Robert. Born 11 August 1802 in Glauchau, died 10 October 1848 in Petersburg. Lawyer; professor of Roman law at the pedagogical institute in Petersburg.

STREICHER, Johann Baptist. Born 3 January 1796 in Vienna, where he died 28 March 1871. Austrian piano maker; joined the firm of his mother, Nanette, née Stein (1769–1833), 1812; became partner, 1823; sole owner of J. A. Streicher Company, 1833.

TAUBERT, Karl Gottfried *Wilhelm*. Born 23 March 1811 in Berlin, where he died 7 January 1891. Pianist, conductor, composer, and music teacher; conductor of the concerts at the court in Berlin, 1831; music director of the court opera, 1842–69; founder of the symphonic soirées of the royal chamber orchestra in Berlin.

TESCHNER, Gustav Wilhelm. Born 26 November 1800 in Magdeburg, died 7 May 1883 in Dresden. Voice pedagogue and composer; student of Zelter and B. Klein; in Italy, 1829; voice teacher in Berlin; professor, 1873.

THALBERG, Sigismund. Born 7 January 1812 in Geneva, died 27 April 1871 in Naples. Pianist and composer, student of Sechter and Hummel; in Vienna from 1822; extensive concert tours, 1837–48; married the daughter of the singer Lablache, 1844; to the United States, 1855; founded a piano school in New York; in Naples from 1858.

THUN, Leontine. Pianist from Dorpat; student of CS.

TICHATSCHEK, *Joseph* Alois. Born 11 July 1807 in Oberweckelsdorf (Bohemia), died 18 January 1886 in Blasewitz, near Dresden. Austrian tenor; studied medicine in Vienna from 1827; tenor at the Kärtnertor-Theater, 1830; then in Graz; at the Dresden court opera, 1838–72.

TISCHENDORF, Lobegott Friedrich *Constantin* von. Born 18 January 1815 in Lengenfeld (Vogtland), died 7 December 1874 in Leipzig. Theologian and writer; studied theology and philology in Leipzig, 1834–38; expeditions to Palestine, Syria, Sinai (where he discovered the fourth-century Bible manuscript *Codex sinaiticus,* 1859), and elsewhere; associate (1845), then full professor (1859) of theology in Leipzig.

TÖPKEN, Albert *Theodor*. Born 8 March 1808 in Bremen, where he died 29 June 1880. Law student; friend of RS at the university in Heidelberg; lawyer in Bremen; member of the board of directors of the local subscription concerts, 1834–77.

TRUHN, Friedrich *Hieronymus*. Born 14 November 1811 in Elbing, died 30 April 1886 in Berlin. Composer, conductor, and writer on music; wrote for the *NZfM;* student of Ries, Zelter, Klein, Dehn, and Mendelssohn; music director in Danzig from 1835; in Berlin, 1837–45 (publishing and concert tours); music teacher and conductor in Elbing, 1848; in Berlin, 1852 and again from 1858; in Riga, 1854–58.

TUTEIN, née Siboni, Josepha Moisa Franciska Romalia Anna Maria (*called* Peppina). Born 6 February 1806 in Milan, died 25 December 1866 in Copenhagen. Pianist; daughter of singer and pedagogue Guiseppe Siboni (1780–1839), who was called to Copenhagen by King Christian VIII as director of the singing school at the Royal Theater, 1881. Married Ferdinand Tutein, 1824. Children: Frederik, Louise, William Axel (1829–1901), Fernanda Sophie Marie (1832–1913), Sophie Emma Marie (1833–48), and Josepha Anna Marie (1842–1906).

TUYN, J. A. Born 25 March 1816 in Amsterdam, where he died 29 December 1855. Dutch tenor; studied with I. G. Bertelman and Bandorali in Paris; soloist of the Leipzig Gewandhaus concerts, 1841–42.

UHLMANN, née Lorenz, widowed Schumann, Emilie. Born 1 June 1810 in Wittenberg, died 29 September 1860 in Schneeberg. Daughter of the superintendent Gottlieb Lorenz (1768–1836) in Zwickau; married RS's brother Julius, 1828; second marriage with Johann Freidrich Uhlmann, 1835.

UHLRICH, Karl Wilhelm. Born 10 April 1815 in Leipzig, died 26 November 1874 in Stendal. Violinist; student of Matthäi; joined the Leipzig Gewandhaus Orchestra, summer of 1841; later concertmaster in Magdeburg and Sondershausen.

ULEX, Wilhelm. Died 1858 in Hamburg. Music teacher in Leipzig, then in Hamburg.

UNGER, Caroline (*in Italy* Carlotta Ungher). Born 28 October 1803 in Vienna, died 23 March 1877 near Florence. Soprano; performed in

Biographical Directory 395

concerts and operas, mostly in Vienna (at the premiere of Beethoven's Ninth Symphony and the Missa Solemnis) and Italy; married François Sabatier in Florence, 1841; retired from stage in Dresden, 1843.

VERHULST, Johann Joseph Hermann. Born 19 March 1816 in The Hague, where he died 17 January 1891. Dutch composer and conductor; student of Mendelssohn and friend of RS; conductor of the Euterpe concerts in Leipzig, 1838–43; then royal music director at court at The Hague; conductor of various choirs and musical associations.

VIARDOT, Louis. Born 1800 in Dijon, died 5 May 1883. Writer and translator; studied law in Paris; devoted himself to the study of literature after a trip to Spain, 1823; director of the Théâtre Italien in Paris, 1838–41; married (1840) Pauline GARCÍA-VIARDOT, whom he accompanied as her tour manager.

VIARDOT-(née) GARCÍA, Michelle Ferdinande *Pauline*. Born 18 July 1821 in Paris, where she died 18 May 1910. Mezzo-soprano and voice pedagogue. Studied piano with Liszt and composition with Anton Reicha; debut in Brussels, 1837; debut as stage singer in London, 1839; friend of CS; engagement at the Grand Opera in Paris from 1849; appeared in many guest performances; to Baden-Baden, 1862; retired from stage, 1864; gave voice lessons; in Paris and Bougival from 1871.

VIELHORSKY, Count Mathieu (Matvej Jurievic). Born 26 April 1794 in Petersburg, died 5 March 1866 in Nice. Russian cellist; organizer and sponsor of musical events; student of C. Romberg, founder of the Symphonic Society (1840), of the Concert Society (1850), and of the Imperial Russian Music Society (1854) in Petersburg, whose director he was.

VIELHORSKY, Count Michel (Mikhail Jurievic). Born 11 November 1788 in Petersburg, died 9 September 1856 in Moscow. Russian composer and sponsor; studied with Cherubini in Paris, 1808–10; then in Petersburg; in Moscow, 1823–26; then once more in Petersburg, where his palace was a center of art and music.

VIEUXTEMPS, Henri. Born 20 February 1820 in Verviers (Belgium), died 6 June 1881 in Mustapha (Algeria). Belgian violinist and composer; student of Sechter and Reicha; public performances from

1830; many concert tours through Europe and the United States; soloist of the imperial orchestra in Petersburg, 1846–51; then in Paris; professor at the conservatory in Brussels, 1871–73; had to retire as virtuoso owing to paralysis.

VILLOING, Alexander Ivanovich. Born 1808 in Petersburg, where he died September 1878. Piano teacher in Moscow; teacher of Nikolai and Anton RUBINSTEIN from 1837; the latter he accompanied on his concert tour through western Europe, 1840–43.

VOIGT, Carl Friedrich Eduard. Born 26 November 1805 in Naumburg, died 15 June 1881 in Leipzig. Merchant in Leipzig; partner in the yarn and silk trading business Berger & Voigt; art and music lover.

VOIGT, née Kuntze, Henriette. Born 24 November 1808 in Leipzig, where she died 15 October 1839. Pianist, student of L. BERGER in Berlin; first wife of Carl VOIGT; friend of Rochlitz, Mendelssohn, SCHUNCKE, and RS, who dedicated his Sonata in G Minor, op. 22, to her.

VOSS, Carl (Charles). Born 20 September 1815 in Schmarsow, near Demmin; died 29 August 1882 in Verona. Pianist and composer; trained in Berlin; gave piano lessons in Paris from 1846; worked to improve the construction of pianos.

WAAGEPETERSON, Christian. Born 1787, died 1840. Wholesaler of wine and art sponsor in Copenhagen; host of one of the most important musical salons there. Married to Albertine Emmerentse, née Schmidt (1793–1864); six children.

WARTEL, Pierre-François. Born 3 April 1806 in Versailles, died August 1882 in Paris. Tenor; at the Grand Opera in Paris, 1831; afterwards undertook concert tours through Europe and gave voice lessons.

WARTEL, née Adrien, Atala Thérèse Annette. Born 2 July 1814 in Paris, where she died 6 November 1865. Pianist and teacher at the conservatory in Paris; published an analysis of Beethoven's piano sonatas. Married Pierre-François WARTEL.

WENZEL, Ernst Ferdinand. Born 25 January 1808 in Walddorf, near Löbau, died 16 August 1880 in Bad Kösen. Pianist and piano teacher; studied philosophy and philology in Leipzig; then student of Friedrich WIECK. Teacher at the Leipzig Conservatory from 1843; friend of RS; contributed to the *NZfM*.

WEYSE, Christoph Ernst Friedrich. Born 5 March 1774 in Altona, died

Biographical Directory 397

8 October 1842 in Copenhagen. Composer; student of J. A. P. Schulz in Copenhagen; teacher of GADE and J. P. E. HARTMANN; professor, 1816.

WIECK, Cäcille. Baptized 25 July 1834, died 1893. Daughter of Friedrich WIECK from his second marriage; mentally ill from her sixteenth year.

WIECK, née Fechner, Clementine. Born 1805 in Grosssärchen, died 24 December 1893 in Dresden. Second wife of Friedrich WEICK from 3 July 1828.

WIECK, Friedrich *Alwin* Feodor. Born 27 August 1821 in Leipzig, where he died 21 October 1885. Son of Friedrich WEICK from his first marriage; violinist; student of DAVID; to Reval, 1843; member of the orchestra of the Italian opera in Petersburg, 1849–59; later became music teacher in Dresden.

WIECK, *Gustav* Robert Anton. Born 31 January 1823 in Leipzig, died 1884 in Vienna. Son of Friedrich WEICK from his first marriage; journeyman instrument maker; to Vienna, 22 April 1838; to Weimar, 1845; later in Vienna permanently.

WIECK, Johann Gottlob *Friedrich*. Born 18 August 1785 in Pretzsch, near Torgau; died 6 October 1873 in Loschwitz, near Dresden. Music pedagogue and writer on music; studied theology on Wittenberg; then tutor; founded (c. 1817) a company for piano making and an instrument rental shop, which became the property of F. Whistling in 1835. Gave piano and—in Dreden after 1840—voice lessons; then settled in Loschwitz.

WILLMERS, Heinrich *Rudolph*. Born 31 October 1821 in Berlin (or Copenhagen), died 24 August 1878 in Vienna. Composer and pianist; raised in Copenhagen, where he made his debut (1834) and gave concerts (1840); then student of Hummel and F. Schneider; in Vienna from 1853; professor at the Stern Conservatory in Berlin, 1864–66; return to Vienna.

WIRTH. Piano maker from Augsburg; in Petersburg until 1844.

WITTMANN, Franz Carl. Baptized 23 October 1814 in Vienna, died 17 October 1860 in Leipzig. Cellist; member of the Leipzig Gewandhaus Orchestra, 1836–60.

WÖHLER, Gotthold (or Gotthard). Born 1818 in Rügen, date of death unknown. Pianist, conductor, and composer; first studied theology, from 1840 music; student of Mendelssohn and others; toured as concert pianist from 1842; music director of the university in Greifswald from 1847.

ZEDTWITZ, née von Fricken, Christiane *Ernestine* Franziska von. Born 7 September 1816 in Neuberg near Asch, died 13 November 1844 in Asch.

ZUCCALMAGLIO, Anton Wilhelm Florentin von. Born 12 April 1803 in Waldbröl (Siegerland), died 23 March 1869 in Nachrodt, near Altena (Westphalia). Writer, composer, and collector of folk songs; in Russia, 1832–40; then in Berlin; in Frankfurt/Main and Freiburg, 1847–54; then in Elberfeld, Wehringhausen, and Nachrodt. Contributed to the *NZfM (pen names* Wilhelm von Waldbrühl, Gottschalk Wedel, Dorfküster Wedel).

INDEX

Abendroth, Amandus Augustus, 132
Abrahams, Fräulein, 143
Adam, Dr., 247
Adam, Johann, 198
Adelsohn, Consul, 231, 233, 234
Albrecht, Karl, 293
Alexander Nevsky, Prince, 257
Alexander Pavlovich, Czar, 256
Alexandra, Czarina, 262, 353n19
Alexandrine, Princess, 262, 353n20
Alt, Karl, 239
Alvensleben, Gebhard von, 185, 198
Amatov (violist), 278, 286
Anacker, August F., 100, 203
Andersen, Hans Christian, 97, 138,
  139, 140, 141, 143, 145; *Only a
  Fiddler,* 347n49
Anger, Louis, 100, 203, 346n32
Art exhibits, 160
Avé-Lallemant, Louise, 188
Avé-Lallemant, Theodor, 131, 132,
  133, 135, 136

Bach, Johann Sebastian, 139; works:
  Chaconne, 54; Chromatic Fantasy
  and Fugue, 54; Concerto in D Minor, 21, 193; Concerto in E-Flat
  Major for two pianos, 73; concertos, 70; fugues, 8, 11, 92, 103,
  112; Mass in B Minor, 54; *St. Matthew Passion,* 73, 133, 343n53; sonatas, 157; Triple Concerto, 22, 23;
  Well-Tempered Clavier, 6, 12, 16
Bach, Wilhelm Friedemann, 128
Banck, Carl, 162
Bargiel, Adolph, 58, 342n46, 349n66

Bargiel, Eugen, 156–157, 158, 159
Bargiel, Marianne (Tromlitz), ix, 84–
  85, 229, 342n46, 346n66; birth of
  granddaughter, 107, 109–110; vis-
  its by, 5, 172, 173, 196, 198, 207
Bargiel, Woldemar, 156, 158, 159
Bariatinsky, Princess, 287
Barth, Gustav, 347n47
Barth, Johann, 107
Bartholdy, Anna, 76
Baudissin, Count Wolf von, 34, 69,
  75
Baudissin, Countess Sophie von, 27,
  34, 69; as performer, 75
Baudissin, Philippine von, 69
Bazzini, Antonio, 195, 198, 351
Beaulieu-Marconnay, Karl Oliver
  von, 130
Becker, Carl F., 150, 184
Becker, Ernst, 5, 92, 103, 104, 105,
  160, 161, 162
Becker, Julius, 6, 13, 37, 112, 124,
  204, 347n38; visits by, 45, 117,
  157
Becker, Lorenz, 6
Becker, Marie, 92
Becker, Nicolaus, 26; "Rheinlied,"
  30
Beer (cellist), 257
Beer, Frau, 254
Beethoven, Ludwig von, 139, 182,
  250; works: "Adelaide," 60, 105;
  Concerto in D Major for violin,
  60; Concerto in E Flat for piano
  (no. 5), 122; Concerto in G Major
  for piano (no. 4), 52; *Egmont*

Beethoven, Ludwig von (*cont.*), Overture, 98, 181, 250; *Eroica* Symphony, 14, 182; "Fantasy" for piano with chorus, 39; *Fidelio,* 31, 193, 347*n*45; *Leonora* overtures, 22, 267; Quartet in E Flat, 56; Quintet in C Major, 67; Scottish lieder with violin and cello, 67; Sonata in A Major, 53, 115, 117, 150; Sonata in A Minor for piano and violin, 44, 130; Sonata in C Major for piano, 16, 19; Sonata in D Minor for piano, 200, 233; Sonata in F Minor for piano, 12, 244, 262; Sonata in G Major for piano and violin, 113; sonatas, 103, 156, 206, 286; Symphony in A Major (no. 7), 31, 55, 116; Symphony in B Flat Major (no. 4), 98; Symphony in C Minor (no. 5), 48, 65; Symphony in D Major (no. 2), 81, 98; Symphony in D Minor (no. 9), 60; Trio in E Flat, 43

Behling (conductor), 267

Behrens, Julius, 236, 237, 239, 241, 242

Bellinghausen, Count Münch von, 155

Bellini, Vincenzo, 141, 342*n*48

Bells (in Moscow), 273, 287, 309

Benckendorff, Countess, 188

Bendemann, Eduard, 193, 198

Bennett, William Sterndale, 125, 126; works: "Diversions," 113; *Wood-nymph* overture, 31, 208

Béranger, Pierre de, 13

Berge, Caroline von, 43, 76

Berger, Ludwig, 170

Bériot, Charles-Auguste de, "Tremolo," 49

Berlioz, Hector, 185–186, 198, 248; "Offertorium," 189

Bernard, Moritz, 292

Berndt, Minna, 241, 352*n*7

Berner (violinist), 305

Bernhard, Lilli, 132, 133

Berry, Caroline, duchess de, 163

Berwald, Franz, 347*n*42

Bessel, Friedrich Wilhelm, 306

Bielcizsky (singer), 208

Bien-Aimé, Luigi, 267

Blassmann, Adolf, 162

Bloomfield, John Arthur Douglas, Lord, 251, 254, 260

Blücher-Altona, Gustav von, 140

Blum, Robert, 348*n*60

Bobrinsky, Countess Sofia, 280, 286

Bogenhard, Gustav Franz, 151

Böhm, Franz, 254, 256, 295

Bohrer, Max, 151

Bolkhovskoi, General, 252, 254, 255, 256

Borges di Castro, 297

Börsensaal (theater), 65–66

Bortenyev, Frau, 260

Böttger, Adolf, 55, 62, 112, 124, 125

Bouillon (singer), 37

Bournonville, Auguste, 141–142

Brahms, Johannes, 341*n*29

Breitkopf & Härtel. *See* Härtel firm

Bremer, Friederike, *Familie H.,* 347*n*43

Brenner, Friedrich, 243

Breuel, Elwine, 300

Brockhaus, Friedrich, 126

Brockhaus, Heinrich, 69, 122, 149, 181

Broeker, Erdmann Gustav von, 242–243, 244, 246, 305

Brüloff, Frau von, 305

Index

Bruno (hotel owner), 248
Bulgakov, Alexander, 276
Bulgarin, Faddej, 249
Bull, Madame, 38
Bull, Ole, 38, 40, 43, 51, 52, 53, 131–132
Bülow, Frau von, 128
Bunsen (lawyer), 140, 141
Bürck, August, 19, 118, 198
Burkhardt (singer), 76
Burns, Robert, 13
Buroschi, Chevalier, 245
Busch, Friedrich Wilhelm, 100, 132
Byron, George Gordon, Lord, 17, 124

Calderón de la Barca, Pedro, *El Magico Prodigioso,* 98, 101, 344n4
Cambridge, duchess of, 207
Canthal, August, 131
Carl, Emilie, 5, 8, 15, 33, 56, 114, 155, 195, 209, 300
Carl, Emma, 54
Carl, Julius, 5, 8, 13, 19, 33, 56, 114
Caroline Amalie, Queen (of Denmark), 142, 143, 144, 145, 146, 348n52
Carstensen, Georg, 146
Carus, Agnes, ix
Carus, Ernst August, ix
Catalani, Angelica, 285
Catherine Alexejevna, Empress, 285
Cavalieri (pianist), 233
Chambeau, Ivan, 261, 263, 297
Chélard, Hippolyte, 117–118
Cherubini, Luigi, 11, 73; *Wasserträger,* 119
Chopin, Fryderyk F., 345n14, 353n16; works: Ballade in F Major, 13, 16; Ballade in G Minor,

35; Concerto in E Minor, 9; Concerto in F Minor for piano, 343n52; études, 12, 91–92; mazurkas, 141; polonaises, 265; Waltz in A Minor, 34, 140
Chorley, Henry Fothergill, 19, 47–48, 340n19
Christern, Karl, 132
Christner, Pastor, 88
Colloredo-Wallsee, Count Franz von, 249, 250
Constantin, Bertha, 10, 37. *See also* Bertha Voigt
Constantine Nikolajevich, Grand Prince, 308
Costa, Count da, 74
Courländer, Bernhard, 140, 141
Cranz, August Heinrich, 80, 131, 132, 135, 136, 148, 348n55
Czerny, Carl, 345n14

David, Ferdinand, 21, 51, 59, 181, 190, 195, 208; as composer, 24, 105; concertos of, 15, 23; as conductor, 13, 102; as performer, 7, 44, 54, 67, 113, 157–158, 172, 177, 355n3; as teacher, 184; visits by, 8, 19, 100, 120, 204
David, Sophie, 8, 58, 339n7
Decker, Konstantin, 100
Dessoir, Therese, 181
Devrient, Emil, 155
Devrient, Johanne Christiane, 5, 9, 107, 172
Devrient, Wilhelmine. *See* Wilhelmine Schröder-Devrient
Dibowsky, F. W., 231, 233
Döhler, Theodor, 182–183
Dolgoruky, Princess, 280

402 Index

Donizetti, Gaetano, 141, 342n48; works: *Linda di Chamonix,* 168, 349n73; *Roberto Devereux,* 347n39
Donner, Sophie. *See* Sophie Zahrtmann
Dörffel, Alfred, 37
Döring, Theodor von, 181, 183, 350n3
Dorn, Heinrich, 105, 204
Doubelt, Leontij, 251, 252
Dreyschock, Alexander, 240
Duflot-Maillard (singer), 65–66
Dunio (official), 239, 241
Dünz (of Berlin), 79
Dütsch, Otto, 100, 112
Duvigneau, David, 10

Eberwein, Karl, 118
Eckert, Carl, 7
Eggers (in Bremen), 128, 129, 130, 131
Eichendorff, Joseph von, 26, 29
Eike (secretary to Ole Bull), 38
Eisner, Karl, 293, 294
Ellendt, Johann, 233
Elsner (pianist), 79
Engelhardt (in Königsberg), 231, 233
Engelken, Friedrich, 130
Ernst, Heinrich Wilhelm, 149, 150; "Elegy," 187
Eusebius, xiv
Euterpe concerts, 55, 65, 117, 186
Ewerlöf, Franz Anton, 139, 142

Faaborg, Rasmus Christian, 141
Fétis, François-Joseph, 156
Field, John, 175, 249, 290, 308
Field, Madame, 290
Fink-Lohr (singer), 256
Fischer von Waldheim, Gotthelf, 277, 278

Fischhof, Joseph, 165, 201, 204
Flechsig, Emil, 100
Fleischer, Agnes, 155, 186, 351n12
Fleischer, Friedrich, 21, 46, 55, 73, 124, 340n21
Fleischer, Therese, 73, 124; as godparent, 195; Italian trip, 97; Schumann visits to, 21, 35, 38, 41, 46, 48, 55; visits by, 34, 46
Florestan, xiv
Franchetti-Walzel (singer), 65
Franck, Eduard, 108, 165
Franz, Robert, 185, 199, 203, 352n28
Frauenkirche (Copenhagen), 140
Frege, Livia, 38, 63–64, 208, 209, 342n43, 344n7; Schumann visits to, 155; as singer, 22, 31, 50–51, 87, 156, 206, 207, 340n23; visits by, 55, 110, 120, 158, 198
Frege, Victor, 110, 344n7
Frege, Woldemar, 63–64, 110, 344n7
Fricken, Ernestine von, x, xi. *See also* Ernestine von Zedtwitz
Friedrich, Eduard, 31
Friedrich August II, King, 43
Friedrich (servant), 275, 281, 288, 291
Friese, Auguste Sophie, 6, 23, 27, 32, 35, 79
Friese, Robert, 6, 32, 37, 42, 43, 195
Füchs, Ferdinand, 156
Fuchs, J. Leopold, 255

Gade, Niels, 140, 141, 189–190, 208, 229; works: sonatas, 286; Symphony No. 1 in C Major, 189
García, Pauline. *See* Pauline Viardot-García
Garlichs, Marie, 133, 134, 136, 148
Gasser (banker), 254, 259, 265

Index   403

Gedeonov, General A. M., 249
Gehling (of Petersburg), 252, 292, 293
Genast, Edward, 118
Genischta, Joseph, 279, 280, 286
Gerke, Anton, 59, 252, 254
Gewandhaus: balls, 124; CS performances, 7–8, 10, 11, 18, 27, 29, 31, 113, 124–125; concerts at, 43–44, 52, 57–58, 60, 63, 69, 116, 181, 189; hundredth anniversary of concerts at, 190; RS symphony rehearsals and performances, 102, 105, 180; soirées at, 22, 43
Gläser, Franz J., 198
Glinka, Mikhail, 267, 307; *A Life for the Czar,* 288, 354*n*32
Glücksburg, Prince von, 144
Goethe, Johann Wolfgang von, works: *Autobiography,* 100; *Egmont,* 181; *Faust,* 101, 245; "Five Others," 50, 342*n*39; *Herrmann und Dorothea,* 66; *Iphigenia,* 155; *Truth and Poetry,* 97
Goetze (singing teacher), 98–99
Goldschmidt, Madame, 185
Goldschmidt, Otto, 185
Goldschmidt, Sigmund, 195, 198
Golitsyn, Serge, 277
Gomalov, General, 308
Gorchakov, Princess, 260
Göthe, Frau von, 118
Götze, Franz, 118
Göthe, Walther von, 174
Goulomy. *See* Jérôme Louis Gulomy
Grabau, Henriette, 5
Graedener, Carl, 136, 147, 148
Graf, Conrad, 33, 60, 341*n*29
Grenser, Friedrich Wilhelm, 7
Gretry, *Bluebeard,* 347*n*46
Griebel, Julius, 31

Griepenkerl, Friedrich Konrad, 128
Griepenkerl, Wolfgang Robert, 128
Grimm, August Theodor von, 256, 259, 262, 263
Groebe, Frau, 209
Gross, Johann Benjamin, 118, 247, 250, 255, 262, 292, 293, 296
Grösser (music dealer), 274, 275
Grund, Friedrich Wilhelm, 100, 128, 131, 132, 133, 254
Gulomy, Jérôme Louis, 60
Gutike, Luise, 352*n*28
Gutzkow, Karl, *Blasedow,* 126

Haase, August, 105
Hafner, Carl, 131
Hagemeister, Frau von, 201
Hager (violist), 255
Hagn, Fräulein von, 160
Hahn, Ida, *Faustine,* 347*n*43
Haindl, Joseph, 49
Haller (singer), 232, 233
Halm, Friedrich, 155
Hamburg fire, 150, 151
Hammer, Julius, 163
Händel, George F., 11; Variations for Piano, 54
Harkort, Auguste, 34, 51, 58, 64
Harkort, Gustav, 82
Harkort, Henriette, 28
Harkort, Karl Friedrich, 34, 64
Harkort, Madame, 82, 179
Härtel, Hermann, 82, 126, 190, 204
Härtel, Raimund, 6, 79, 107, 120, 125, 172, 173, 209
Härtel firm (Breitkopf & Härtel), 129, 143, 179, 202, 207, 210
Hartenstien, Gustav, 73
Hartmann, Emma, 137, 138, 141, 143, 144, 145, 147

404 Index

Hartmann, Jens Peter, 138, 141, 143, 144, 145, 147
Haslinger, Tobias, 45
Hasselt-Barth, Wilhelmina, 347n47
Haugk, August, Baron von, 198
Haumann, Theodor, 292
Hauptmann, Moritz, 100, 174, 178, 184, 204
Hauschild, Johann Gottfried, 37; *Schottische Waltzer,* 341n30
Haydn, Joseph, 11, 56, 347n43; works: "Seven Last Words of the Savior," 73; symphonies, 113
Heine, Heinrich, *Tragödie,* 116–117
Heinefetter, Sabine, 118, 193, 198
Heinrich, duke of Bordeaux, 163, 250
Hejberg, Johan Ludvig, 138–139, 140, 141
Hejberg, Johanne Luise, 138–139, 140, 141, 147
Helene Pavlovna, 294, 295
Helsted, Eduard, 45, 62, 65, 185
Hensel, Fanny, 198
Henselt, Adolph von, 12, 130, 173–174, 198, 260, 264; as pianist, 255, 265, 286; visits by, 263, 268, 296; Schumann visits to, 247, 250, 252, 254, 259, 261, 267, 292, 293, 295, 296; works: Concerto, 249, 353n12; études, 103; "Poème d'amour," 66; "Si j'etais oiseau," 241, 353n8; "Variations," 163
Henselt, Rosalie, 251–252, 253, 254, 255, 259, 261, 292–293, 295, 296
Hering, Eduard, 37, 100
Hering (singer), 52
Hermes (piano teacher), 297
Herrmann, Friedrich August, 5, 78, 85, 126

Herrmann, Gottfried: *Symphonie Pathétique,* 121–122, 345n16
Herz, Henri, 345n14
Hesse, Adolph, 183, 185
Hessen, Juliane von. *See* Princess Juliane Sophie Philippsthal
Hessen-Kassel, Prince Friedrich von, 144, 248, 262, 353n20
Hexameron, 120, 123, 345n14
Heygendorff, Caroline von, 118
Heyne (privy councillor), 231
Hilf, Christoph, 31, 32, 49
Hiller, Ferdinand, 204, 208; *Destruction of Jerusalem,* 6
Hirsch, Rudolph, 67
Hirschbach, Herrmann, 108, 112, 115, 117, 186
Hoffmann, Johann, 237, 241–242
Hofmeister, Friedrich, 65, 66, 79, 99
Hollander (in Riga), 240
Homeyer, L. Joseph Maria, 156
Homilius, Friedrich, 258
Horak (chamber musician), 160
Horlbeck, Emilie, 150
Hornemann, Johan Ole Emil, 143–144
Horsley, Sophie, 66, 71
Horsley, William, 52
Hoymar, Frau von, 283, 285
Hugo, Victor: *Hunchback of Notre Dame,* 64
Hummel, Johann Nepomuk, 15; works: *Oberon,* 113; Septet, 122
Huth, Louis, 198

Immermann, Karl Leberecht, *Münchhausen,* 157

Jacobi, Constanze, 204
Jacoby, Johann, 233, 304

Index

Jahn, Otto, 149
Jean Paul, 26, 74; festival, 117
Johannes (music director), 282

Kahle, Carl Hermann Traugott, 232
Kahlert, August, 6, 7, 179
Kalliwoda, Johann Wenzel, 105
Kaskel, Sophie, 27, 34
Kasten, Judge, 170
Kaull, Dr., 237, 238, 242, 304
Kayserlingk, Count, 240, 241
Keferstein, Gustav Adolph, 118
Kellner, Gustav, 13, 15
Kerner, Justinus, 42; works: "Lust der Sturmnacht," 36; "Stirb, Lieb' und Freud'!," 36; "Trost im Gesang," 36; "Waldgegend," 46; "Wanderlied," 49
Kienitz, von der, 241
Kietz, August, 9
Kindermann, August, 207
Kirchner, Theodor, 162, 179, 204
Kiriev, Madame de, 279, 280
Kistner, Friedrich, 6, 10, 20, 27
Kittl, Johann Friedrich, 6, 185
Klengel, August Alexander, 11, 75
Klengel, Moritz Gotthold, 7, 169–170
Klopstock, Friedrich Gottlieb, 133
Kloss, Carl, 193, 198
Klugkist, Julius, 128, 129, 130
Knecht, F., 254, 257
Knorring, Frau von, 244
Koberwein, (in Petersburg), 252, 296
Körner, Julius, 170
Kossmaly, Carl, 159
Krafftström, Baron von, 243

Krägen, Karl, 76, 103, 104, 105, 173
Krägen, Madame, 79, 161
Krause, Wilhelm Ernst, 34, 68, 92
Krausse, Theodor, 125, 126
Krebs, Karl August, 131
Kresslowski (official), 234
Kretschmann (violinist), 286
Kreutzer, Cäcilie, 81, 82
Kreutzer, Konradin, 81; works: *Nachtlager von Granada,* 81–82; "Rheinlied," 36
Kreutzer, Maria, 82
Kriete, Henriette, 208
Krüdener, Baroness von, 251
Krüger, Eduard, 199
Krüger, Wilhelm, 126
Kudelski, Karl Mathias, 282, 286
Kufferrath, Hubert Ferdinand, 27, 31, 39, 341n28
Kühnapfel (in Frauenburg), 231
Kühne, Gustav, 28, 34, 125, 179
Kummer, Friedrich, 188, 205
Kuntze, Henriette. *See* Henriette Voigt
Kunze, Gustav, 42, 341n33

Labitzky, Joseph, 164
Lablache, Luigi, 251
Lampadius, Wilhelm Adolph, 54, 62, 157, 159, 171, 179
Lampe, Dr., 82
Landsberg, Ludwig, 19, 204
Lang, Pauline, 119
Laskovsky, General, 267
Latrobe, Johann Friedrich Bonneval, 245
Lehnhold, Dr., 278, 285
Lemoch, Vinzenz, 285, 290, 291
Lenz, Wilhelm von, 267
Leppoc, Albert, 191

Index

Leuchtenberg, Grand Princess Maria von, 248, 254, 255, 258, 262, 268, 294
Levetzau, Joachim Godsche von, 140
Levy, Carl, 189
Levy, Eduard Constantin, 189
Levy, Richard, 189(?)
Lichnowsky, Prince Felix, 119, 120, 151
Lichtenstein, Marie, 179, 230
Lichtenstein, Martin, 179
Lichtenthal (piano maker), 252
Lilienfeld, Fräulein von, 243, 244
Limberger, Jacob Bernhard, 7–8
Lindenau, Leopold, 131
Liphardt, Carl von, 100, 243, 244
Liphart, von, family, 339n7, 355n3
Lipinsky, Karol, 38, 130
List, Caroline (mother), 5, 6, 10, 13, 15, 16, 30, 34
List, Caroline (daughter), 7, 8, 15, 30
List, Elise, 7, 9, 15–16, 30, 34, 185; departure in humiliation of, 28; depression in, 16, 17, 19, 24; Gewandhaus concerts, 18, 23; as singer, 5, 6, 10, 15, 20, 24, 26, 27, 35; singing debut, 13, 18, 19, 340n12; song dedications to, 339n3; vocal qualities of, 14
List, Emilie, 5, 6, 7, 8, 9, 12, 15–16, 17, 19, 30, 34
List, Friedrich, 5, 10, 13, 15, 16, 30
Liszt, Franz, xi, 26, 160–161, 230, 343n62; at Weimar, 119; cigar ash story, 232–233; in Leipzig, 27, 120, 121–123; musical dedications to, 43, 341n34; as pianist, 38, 122–123; Russia trip, 29, 305, 307, 308; works: fantasies, 103; "Serenade," 32
Lobe, Johann Christian, 118

Lobeck, Christian August, 231, 232, 233
Loebmann, Franz, 236, 237, 240, 242, 304
Loose. *See* Arnoldine Lose
Lorenz, Johanne Caroline, 300
Lorenz, Oswald, 27, 124, 209
Lork (in Königsberg), 232
Lose, Arnoldine, 139, 145
Lotz (violinist), 236, 237
Löwe (composer), 197
Löwenskjold, Baron Hermann von, 44, 45, 51, 54
Löwenskjold, Baroness Margarethe von, 140
Lüders, Conrad, 141
Lüttichau, Baron August von, 208
Lüttichau, Ida von, 188
Lutzau, Frau von, 105, 236, 237, 238, 242, 304
Lvov, Alexej Fjodorovic, 26, 30, 249, 260, 267, 306; visits with the Schumanns, 254, 257; works: 29, 250; *Bianca e Gualterio,* 251, 353n13; overtures, 263
Lyser, Johann Peter, 31

Maczevsky, Alexander, 239
Mädler, Frau von, 306
Mahlmann, Siegfried August, 13
Mainberger (of Hamburg), 37
Mandt, Ludowike von, 255
Mandt, Martin Wilhelm von, 259
Marcou, Charles, 275, 278, 282, 283, 286, 291
Marggraf (in Leipzig), 126
Marriage diaries: language of, xvi, xvii; poetry in, xvii; style and content of, 3–4; translation of, xiii, xiv, xv
Marschner, Heinrich August, 98, 99,

Index

407

105, 155–156; works: *Hans Heiling,* 156; *Klänge aus Osten,* 24; *Der Templer und die Jüdin,* 156; *Der Vampyr,* 156

Martinov (officer), 249, 250, 254, 257

Marty (piano maker), 233, 234

Marx, Adolf Bernard, 150, 204

Marxsen, Eduard, 132

Maurer, Ludwig, 247, 249, 250, 255, 256

Maurer, Vsevolod, 255

Mayer, Carl, 108, 249, 254

Mayer, von (councillor), 251, 252, 255, 266

Mechetti, Pietro, 79, 80

Meerti, Elisa, 112, 113, 114, 116, 125

Méhul, Étienne Nicolas, *The Two Foxes,* 131

Mendelsshon-Bartholdy, Cécile, 6, 19, 20, 58; diary of, xxi, 70, 342*n*50

Mendelssohn-Bartholdy, Fanny. *See* Fanny Hensel

Mendelssohn-Bartholdy, Felix, 51–52, 59, 139, 149, 190, 195, 203, 353*n*16; in Berlin, 229–230; as conductor, 14, 70, 102, 116, 181; as critic of RS's music, 177–178, 350*n*2; departures of, 100, 206; diary of, xxi, 70, 342*n*50; England, visit to, 13, 18; Gewandhaus soirée, 22, 43; as godfather of Marie Schumann, 107, 116; Jewishness of, 31; Liszt visit, 27; as performer, 39, 43, 44, 54, 56–58, 87, 157–158, 182, 186, 193; return to Leipzig, 81, 84, 85–86; Schumann visits to, 40, 198–199; on *Spring Symphony,* 65, 66, 70, 72; success

of, 184; as teacher, 184; visits by, 19, 66, 76–77, 117, 181, 204; works: Allegro brilliant in A Major, 70–71, 342*n*51; Capriccio, 118; Concerto in D Minor, 182; Concerto in G Minor, 124, 249, 258; Duo, 343*n*52; "Forty-second Psalm," 346*n*36; Fugue in E Major, 130; fugues, 11, 86; "Gondellied," 86, 343*n*61, 352*n*2; "Lobgesang," 39, 44, 73; *Melusine* overture, 113; Octet, 21; psalms, 73; Sonata for cello and piano, 115, 117, 256; "Song of Praise," 143; songs, 31, 206; "Songs without Words," 57, 71, 229; "Spring Song," 229, 262, 352*n*2; symphonies, 267; Symphony in A Minor (*Scottish*), 117, 345*n*13; Trio No. 1 in D Minor, 7, 51, 56; "Variations sérieuses," 117; "Wer hat dich, du schöner Wald," 162; "Wie der Hirsch schreit," 22, 73

Mendelssohn-Bartholdy, Paul, 73

Menzenkampf, Frau, 244

Metchersky, Prince, 297, 298

Methfessel, Ernst, 151

Metternich-Winneburg, Prince Clemens, 166, 167, 168–169, 249

Meyendorff, Baron von, 277, 279, 280–281, 285

Meyer. *See* von Mayer

Meyer, Emma, 9, 11, 34, 46, 191

Meyerbeer, Giacomo, 55, 342*n*48

Michaelis Church, 133

Michail Pavlovich, Grand Prince, 247, 294

Michelson (councillor), 294

Mieksch, Johann Aloys, 160

Miller, Julius, 204

Mitterwurzer, Anton, 208
Molique, Bernhard, 130, 250, 251, 258, 259, 263, 307
Montag, Carl, 13, 26, 27, 37, 42, 118
Montez, Lola, 240, 304
Moody, Marie, 15, 29, 32, 34, 46
Moore, Thomas, *Lalla Rookh,* 203
Moriani, Napoleone, 97, 99
Moscheles, Ignaz, xi, 18, 19; as pianist, 21; works: Concerto in G Minor, 22; "Hommage à Händel," 22; Septet, 21; Sonata in E Flat Major, 8, 20, 181, 205
Mozart, Wolfgang A., 139, 347*n*43; works: Concerto in D Minor, 57–58; *Così fan tutte,* 182; "Davide Penitente," 346*n*36; *Don Juan,* 109, 122; *Idomeneo,* 113; overtures, 98; Requiem, 191; sonatas, 67, 70; symphonies, 126; Symphony in C Major, 58; Symphony in E Flat Major, 23–24; Symphony in G Minor, 233; *Titus,* 39, 57; "Das Veilchen," 58; *Zauberflöte* overture, 48
Mühlburg, Pielsticker von, 164
Müller, Carl Friedrich, 128
Müller, Elise, 131
Müller, Friedrich, 115–116
Müller, Gebrüder, 148
Müller, Johann Heinrich, 255
Music, early, 98

Nathan, Adolf, 9
Nauenburg, Gustav, 185
Naumann, Johann Gottlieb, 92
Nebolsyn, Nikolai Andreievic, 275, 276
Nernst (councillor), 234

Nesselrode, Count Karl Vassilievic, 258, 266, 267, 307
Netzer, Joseph, 198
Nicholas I, Czar, 252, 353*n*14
Nottebohm, Gustav, 100
Nov, Dr., 275
Novakovsky, Józef, 100

Oesterlei, Dr., 6
Oldecop, Evstafij Ivanovic, 263
Oldenberg, Prince Peter von, 254, 258, 259, 264, 265, 267, 268, 277
Olga Nikolaievna, Grand Princess, 158, 248, 255, 262
Olsen, Peter Wilhelm, 137, 138, 144, 146, 147, 150
Oppenheimer (in Königsberg), 231–232
Oseyev, Count, 295
Otten, Georg Dietrich, 133, 136, 148
Otto, Dr., 300
Ozorov (in Moscow), 287, 289

Pahlen, Magnus Freiherr von, 237
Pahlen, Count Peter von, 295
Pahlen, Peter Ludwig von, 295
Parish, Charles, 86, 132, 133, 165
Parish, Harriet, 86, 133, 165, 179, 185
Parish, Richard, 133
Parish, Susanne, 165, 179, 185
Parish-Alvars, Elias, 126, 189
Paskevich, Prince Ivan, 304
Pasta, Giuditta, 108
Pauer (composer), 204
Paul, Frau, 79–80, 160, 161
Paul, Wilhelm, 79–80, 160, 161, 162

Index

Paul Friedrich, duke of Mecklen-burg-Schwerin, 135
Paul I, Czar, 264, 295
Paulli, August Wilhelm, 139, 141
Paulli, Frederikke, 139
Pavlowski (pianist), 246
Pechlin, Countess Elise von, 140
Pesavorius, General, 259
Petersen, Jens Peter, 141
Petersilie, Wilhelm, 118
Petschke, Hermann, 155
Pfundt, Ernst, 7, 61
Philippsthal, Princess Juliane Sophie, 144
Pixis, Peter, 345n14, 346n32
Pogwisch, Henriette von, 118
Pogwisch, Ulrike von, 118
Pohlenz, Christian August, 73, 162, 181, 184, 190
Pohlenz, Emilie, 191
Pomarovska, Countess, 241
Poppe, Maximilian, 209
Pott, Aloyse, 129, 130
Pott, August, 117, 129–130, 179
Prechtler, Otto, 156
Preusser, Gustav Louis, 208
Prévost, Eugène Prosper, 277
Probst, Heinrich, 57

Queisser, Karl Traugott, 118
Quenstädt, Caroline, 129

Rakemann, Ernst, 130
Rakemann, Louis, 15, 340n14
Ramberg, Arthur von, 306
Rascher, Eduard Moritz, 170
Raupach, Ernst, *The Siblings,* 344n1
Recio, Maria, 186, 351n11
Reichmann, Henriette, 46
Reichwaldt, Frau, 254

Reichwaldt, Fräulein, 255
Reinhardt, Ivan, 273–274, 275, 281, 282, 283, 286, 287, 290, 291
Reinick, 342n43
Reissiger, Carl Gottlieb, 105, 160, 162; *Adèle de Foix,* 161, 349n69
Rettich, Julie, 155
Rettich, Karl, 155
Reuss-Köstritz, Count Heinrich II, 20, 125
Reuter, Moritz Emil, 5, 49, 54, 97, 111; visits by, 8, 24, 32, 45, 62, 67, 85, 112, 117, 124, 209, 347n38
Rheinlied competition, 39, 42
Ribeaupierre, Marquis Alexandre de, 263, 264, 266, 267
Richter, Frau (artist), 238
Richter, Jean Paul. *See* Jean Paul
Ridderstolp, Frau von, 179
Rieffel, Amalie, 11, 13, 32, 49, 82, 117; lessons from RS, 100, 102, 106; as pianist, 9, 27–28, 35, 36, 42, 66, 115; visits by, 6, 23, 27, 31, 35, 52, 55, 79, 114
Rieffel, Wilhelm Heinrich, 100, 102
Riefstahl, Carl, 132, 151
Riem, Friedrich Wilhelm, 128–129, 131
Rietz, Julius, 198; works: *Altdeutscher Schlachtgesang,* 75, 343n57; *Hero and Leander,* 75, 343n57; overtures, 114
Röckel, August, 118
Röckel, Eduard, 113, 118
Roda, Ferdinand von, 133, 346n29
Röller, Agnes, 5, 30, 43, 56
Röller, Eduard Hermann, 170
Röller, Professor, 100
Romberg, Cyprian, 250, 266, 296

Romberg, Heinrich, 248, 254, 256, 258, 263, 266, 267, 268, 294, 296

Rönne, Baron, 241

Rönne, General, 252

Ropp, Baron von der, 240

Rossini, Gioachino, 10, 168

Rubini, Giovanni Battista, 248, 306, 307

Rubinstein, Anton, 255, 275

Rückert, Friedrich, 230, 303; works: 52, 108, 109, 153, 154–155; "Edelstein und Perle," 51; "Er ist gekommen in Sturm und Regen," 84, 85, 343n60; "Die gute Nacht, die ich dir sage," 84, 85, 343n60; "Liebesfruhling," 50, 341n36; "Liebst du um Schönheit," 84, 85, 343n60; "Warum willst du andre fragen," 84, 85, 343n60

Russia trip, xv, xvi, 16; Bell of Ivan Veliky, 273; Berlin visits, 229–230, 299; Home for Foundlings, Moscow, 283–285, 287, 296; Königsberg visit, 230–234; Kremlin, 272–273, 274, 275, 276–278, 279, 282, 290–291; Latvia visit, 235–246; Moscow visit, 272–291; obstetrics school, 288; Russian customs, 273, 279–280, 303–309; St. Petersburg visits, 247–268, 292–296; serfs and serfdom, 270–271, 273, 284, 304, 308

Russo, Michel Angelo, 196, 198

Sabatier, François, 123

Sabbarth, Franz Ludwig, 232, 233

Sachs, Marie, 207

Sack, Theodor, 131, 133

Sämann, Carl Heinrich, 232

Säuberlich (in Riga), 237

Sauerweid, von (in Petersburg), 252

Scarlatti, Domenico, 241, 343n52, 353n16

Schadow, Friedrich Wilhelm von, 198

Schäffer, Heinrich, 131

Schefer, Leopold, 304

Schiller, Friedrich, 150; works: *Don Carlos*, 155; "Die Glocke," 182

Schiller (pianist), 256

Schindelmeisser (in Königsberg), 231

Schladebach, Julius, 185

Schlegel, Louise, 27

Schleinitz, Heinrich Conrad, 11, 190

Schlesinger, Heinrich, 106

Schlesinger (musician), 169

Schletter, Heinrich, 121, 191, 204

Schloezer, Frau von, 297, 298

Schloss, Sophie: departure of, 81; as singer, 13, 14, 18, 21, 23, 24, 27, 31, 39, 48, 52, 64; visits by CS, 34; visits of, 31, 46, 179

Schlossbauer, Adele, 136, 147, 148

Schmidt (in Bremen), 128, 129, 131

Schmidt (cellist), 282

Schmidt, Friedrich Christian, 118

Schmidt, Heinrich, 23, 46, 83, 207, 343n52, 346n35

Schmidt, Madame, 23, 46–47, 56, 60

S(c)hmidt, Madame, 72–73

Schmidt, Pastor, 56

Schmitt, Aloys, 69

Schnabel, Carl von (senior), 252, 264, 269–270, 271, 272

Schnabel, Carl von (junior), 269, 291

Schnabel, Frau von, 269, 270, 271

Schneider, Friedrich, 100

Schober, Franz Ritter von, 123

Schoberlechner, Sophie, 255

Schröder, Sophie, 182

Schröder-Devrient, Wilhelmine, 25,

Index

60–61, 69, 181, 182, 183, 188, 343*n*62, 347*n*45; on Liszt, 160–161, 230

Schubert, Franz, 123, 189, 205; works: "Gretchen," 10; songs, 31, 69, 123; symphonies, 114; Symphony in C Major, 26

Schubert, Franz (violinist), 188

Schubert, General, 252, 256, 263

Schubert, Madame, 123

Schuberth, Carl, 253

Schuberth, Julius, 80, 131, 132

Schulhoff, Julius, 185

Schultz, Dr., 293

Schulz, Baron, 238

Schulze, Johann Philipp Christian, 177

Schumann, Carl (Sr.), 80, 107, 149, 170, 209, 299, 300

Schumann, Carl (Jr.), 170

Schumann, Clara (Wieck): birth of children, 107–109, 193–194; Christmas, 46, 123, 124; as composer, 44, 52; Copenhagen, concerts in, 142, 143, 144–145, 146, 147–148; courtship of, ix, x, xi, xii; depression of, 26–27, 41; diaries, personal, xxiv; domestic life, xxii; Dorpat, concerts in, 243, 244, 245; emotional dependence on RS, 17, 179–180; on French culture, 64; fugal studies, 11; Gewandhaus concerts, 7–8, 10, 11, 18, 27, 29, 31; illnesses of, 25–26, 294; interpretation of RS's compositions, 9, 12; jealousy, 46–47; Jews, attitude toward, 9, 132, 192, 235; marriage of, xiii; on marriages of others, 23, 37, 191–192; maternal role as obstacle to composing,

199; Mitau, concerts in, 239–241; Moscow, concerts in, 279, 281–282, 283, 289–290; as organist, 93, 112; Paris visit, 341*n*27; performing, fear of, 18, 38–39; physical pain, 50; as pianist, 20, 40, 45, 47–48, 65, 66, 71–72, 99, 102, 114–115, 178, 240; piano incident with father, 33–34, 60, 63, 68, 201, 342*n*47; playing for the empress, 262; pregnancy of, 46; quarrels with RS, 35, 114; return of money and belongings from father, 76, 87, 99, 104; St. Petersburg, concerts in, 254, 255, 265, 266; sympathy for father, xii, 40–41, 63; as teacher, 201; two-career family conflicts, 126–127; visits to father, 183, 187, 188; visits to mother, 204, 230, 299; works: "Am Strande," 13, 44, 45, 339*n*10; "Er ist gekommen in Sturm und Regen," 84, 85, 343*n*60; "Die gute Nacht, die ich dir sage," 84, 85, 343*n*60; "Ich hab in deinem Auge," op. 13, no. 5, 351*n*23; "Ihr Bildnis," 44, 45, 339*n*10; Impromptu in E Major, 350*n*9; "Liebesfrühling," 50, 341*n*36; "Liebst du um Schönheit," 84, 85, 343*n*60; Lieder, op. 13, 152, 348*nn*52,62; "Loreley," 351*n*23; "O weh des Scheidens," 351*n*23; *Pièces fugitives,* op. 15, nos. 1–3, 350*n*9; Scherzo, op. 10, 348*n*50; Scherzo, op. 14, 111, 344*n*9; Scherzo, op. 15, no. 4, 125, 345–346*n*23; Sonata in G Minor, 124, 345*n*18; "Volkslied," 44, 45, 339*n*10; "Warum willst du

Schumann, Clara (Wieck) (*cont.*), andre fragen," 84, 85, 343*n*60

Schumann, Eduard, 340*n*21

Schumann, Elise: baptism of, 194–195; birth of, 193, 197; infancy of, 196, 201, 204; separation from parents, 209, 210, 281, 296

Schumann, Johanne C., ix, xi

Schumann, Marie: birth of, 107–109; Christmas, 124, 185; illnesses of, 171, 179, 188, 192, 203–204; infancy of, 110; 114, 115, 125, 134, 153; learning to talk, 196, 198; music and, 111; separation from parents, 127, 149, 170, 206, 209, 210, 299; teething of, 152; weaning of, 151

Schumann, Pauline, 170, 209, 299

Schumann, Robert: acrophobia of, 89, 91, 344*n*63; alter egos of, xiv–xv; Christmas, 45; as conductor, 203; courtship of, ix, x, xi, xii; creative difficulties, 19, 22; death of mother, xi; depression of, xxiii, 24; diaries, personal, xiii–xiv, xxiv; emotional breakdowns, ix, x; fugal studies, 11; illness of, 53, 243–246, 274, 276; Jews, attitude toward, 31, 69, 165; marriage of, xiii; and marriages of others, 43; mysticism in compositions of, 47, 48; as organist, 93, 112; as pianist, 61; as poet, 273, 276–277, 280; reconciliation with Friedrich Wieck, xxiii, 42, 208; separation from Clara, 126–127; suicidal tendencies in, x, xii; as teacher, 184, 192, 197; travel possibilities, 30, 62, 63; two-career family conflicts, 126–127;

works: Andante in C Minor, 340*n*18; Andante and Variations, op. 46, 184, 190, 200, 253, 255, 265, 286, 351*n*15;"Blondels Lied," 26; Concerto for Piano and Orchestra, op. 54, 343*n*59; "Der Deutsche Rhein," 26, 30, 32; "Fantasiestucke," op. 88, 184; Fantasy in A Minor, 80, 101, 102, 106, 122, 343*n*59; Fantasy in C Major, 12, 43, 341*n*34; "Frühlingsfahrt," 26, 341*n*26; *Gedichte aus dem Liederbuch eines Malers,* 342*n*43; *Geibel-Gesänge,* 46, 341*n*37; "Herbstlied," 13; *Kreisleriana,* 12, 16, 45, 339*n*11; "Liebesfrühling," 50, 341*n*36; Lieder, op. 31, 340*n*13; *Liederkreis,* op. 39, 6, 29, 339*n*3; "Löwenbraut," 13; "Lust der Sturmnacht," 36, 42; Overture, Scherzo and Finale in E Major, 73–74, 78, 106, 120, 343*n*58; *Das Paradies und die Peri,* 101, 190–191, 192, 194, 196, 197, 198, 199, 201, 202–203, 205, 206, 207–209, 208, 210, 340*n*23; Quartet in A Minor, 152, 350*n*7; Quartet in E Flat Major, 192; Quartet in F Major, 152; quartets, 159, 172, 183; Quintet in E Flat for Piano and Strings, op. 44, 177, 178–179, 183, 205, 240, 257, 287, 350*n*1; "Der Schatzgräber," 29; Sonata in F Sharp Minor, 113; Sonata in G Minor for Piano, 341*n*31; "Stirb, Lieb' und Freud,'" 36, 42; Symphony in B Flat Major (*Spring*), xxiii, 53, 54–55, 57, 60, 61, 62, 64, 68–69, 70, 72, 86, 101, 109, 111, 117, 125, 180; Symphony in C minor (unfinished), 111; Symphony in D Minor, no. 4, 101, 109, 120, 345*n*15; "Tragödie," 116–117; "Trost im Gesang," 36, 42; "Wanderlied," 49; "Wenn ich ein Vöglein wär," 13; *Zigeunerleben,* 16

Schuncke, Julius, 233

Schuncke, Ludwig, xi, 153, 349*n*64

Schuster (violinist), 233

Schütt, Captain, 297

Schützenhaus, 39

Scott, Walter, *Heart of Mid-Lothian,* 41

Seebach, Baron, 249, 250, 252, 260

Seeburg, August Moritz, 208

Seeburg, Vera, 208

Seidendörffer (police inspector), 54

Semmel, Agnes. *See* Agnes Fleischer

Semmel, Moritz, 155, 186

Sengstake, Frau, 128

Senkovski, Ossip Ivanovich, 250

Serre, Anton, 42, 60, 62, 63, 76, 87, 99, 173

Serre, Friederike, 76, 77, 87, 103, 166, 169

Seydelmann, Eugen, 83

Shakespeare, William, 26; musical references in, 19–20

Shaw, Mary (Mrs. Alfred), 125

Sherbatov, Prince, 275, 277, 279

Sheremetyev, Count, 259

Sievers, Countess von, 244

Simon, Christian Friedrich, 54

Simonsen, Frau, 198

Simonsen (city councillor), 293–294

Siniavine, Frau, 275, 279–280, 286, 287, 289

Sinovyev (in Petersburg), 259

Sivori, Camillo, 111–112, 114

Skraup, Franz, 204

Smith (in Leipzig), 43

Smoking, RS on, 303

Sobolewsky, Eduard, 231, 232, 233, 303–304

Sodoffsky, Dr. W., 237

Sontag-Rossi, Henriette, 303

Sophocles, *Antigone,* 346*n*31

Soubre, Étienne, 156

Spiegel und zu Pickelsheim, Baron Karl Emil von, 118

Spohr, Louis, 11, 157; works: *Berggeist* overture, 23, 24; Double Symphony for Two Orchestras, 125; *Historical* Symphony, 51; quartets, 250; *Zemire und Azor,* 114

Stage, Gottlob, 138, 140, 141

Stahl, Fanny, 132

Stahlknecht, Adolf, 122, 345*n*17

Stahlknecht, Julius, 122, 345*n*17

Stegmayer, Ferdinand, 79

Stegmayer, Frau, 79, 207, 230

Stein, Carl, 257

Stein, senior, 257, 266

Stengel, Wilhelm Ferdinand, 73

Stern, Julius, 100

Stieglitz, Baron Alexander von, 249, 254, 263, 267, 268, 292, 296

Stockfleth, Daniel, 132, 179

Stöckhardt, Heinrich Robert, 250, 253, 254, 259, 261, 267, 293, 295

Streicher, Johann Baptist, 112, 204

Strohmeyer, Karl, 118

Stryk, General von, 280, 283, 285, 286, 287, 288, 289, 290, 291

Talarnov (piano maker), 280

Taubert, Wilhelm, 230, 303

Tcherkov, Marshall, 276, 278, 279, 280, 290

Tchernyshov, Prince Alexander, 264, 308

Temperance, RS on, 304
Teschner, Gustav Wilhelm, 209
Thal, James, 249, 252
Thal, Robert, 267
Thalberg, Sigismund, 130, 345n14; as pianist, 59; travels of, 59–60; visits by, 62; works: fantasies, 66, 103, 118, 290, 353n16; *Moses* Fantasy, 32, 345n20
Thomaner (choir), 48
Thomas Church, 48, 73
Thorwaldsen, Bertel, 87, 140, 145, 347n48
Thun, Leontine, 78–79, 84, 87, 255(?)
Tichatschek, Joseph, 161, 162, 182, 188, 208
Tilly, Theodor von, 231
Tischendorf, Constantin von, 23, 26
Tobacco, RS on, 303
Tolstoy, Countess, 260
Tomaschek, Eduard Freiherr von, 171
Töpken, Theodor, 128, 129, 131
Travels, of RS and CS: America proposal, 127, 128; Bremen, Hamburg, 126–134; Connewitz, 80, 82, 104, 110, 113–114, 150, 153, 157; Copenhagen (CS), 133–149; Dresden, Bohemia, 159–170; Dresden, Pillnitz, Bastei, Schandau, 88–93, 97; Grimma, 5; Halle, 78; proposed trips, 30, 62, 63, 86; Salzburg, 153; Weimar, 115, 117–119; *see also* Russia trip
Tromlitz, Marianne. *See* Marianne (Tromlitz) Bargiel
Truhn, Hieronymus, 151, 346n35
Tutein, Johann Friedrich, 144

Tutein, Josepha (Peppina), 137–138, 140–141, 142, 147
Tuyn, J. A., 105, 108, 112, 113, 116, 126, 179
Tzinoviev, Herr von, 280

Uhlmann, Emilie, 300
Uhlmann, Johann Friedrich, 15, 300
Uhlmann, Rector, 238
Uhlrich, Karl Wilhelm, 15
Ulex, Wilhelm, xi, 132, 133
Unger, Caroline, 97, 99, 123

Veit, Wenzel Heinrich, 79
Veliky, Ivan, 273, 287
Verhulst, Johann Joseph Herrmann, 21, 22, 35, 43, 75, 115, 309, 347n47; as performer, 55, 125; visits by, 79, 85, 97, 105, 112, 117, 180
Versing, Wilhelm, 255, 263, 265
Verstovsky, Alexej Nicolaievich, 274
Viardot, Louis, 199, 200, 247
Viardot-García, Pauline, 10, 25, 52, 123, 199, 200, 247, 248, 250–251, 253
Vielhorsky, Mathieu, 248, 249, 250, 251, 252, 253, 255, 256, 258, 267, 268, 292, 294, 296, 307
Vielhorsky, Michel, 250, 254, 255, 256, 258, 259, 261, 266–267, 268, 292, 294, 296; works: *The Gypsies,* 253, 353n15
Vietinghoff, Frau von, 243, 245
Vieuxtemps, Henri, 38, 49
Villers, Alexander Heinrich von, 198
Villoing, Alexander Ivanovich, 275, 290
Voigt, Bertha, 37, 56, 81, 114, 115,

117, 121, 126, 157, 186. *See also* Bertha Constantin
Voigt, Carl, 7, 37, 45, 56, 66–67, 114, 115, 117, 121, 125, 126, 157, 186, 195, 347*n*44
Voigt, Henriette, 10, 37, 341*n*31
Volkonsky, Prince, 252, 263
Vorontzov-Dashkov, Countess, 249–250
Voss, Carl, 174, 185
Vyasemsky, Prince Peter Andreievich, 260, 266

Waagepetersen, Christian, 142
Waagepetersen, Mozart, 142
Wagner, Richard, 188, 229, 348*n*54; *Rienzi,* 182, 187–188
Wahl, Frau von, 243, 244–245
Waltersdorff, Wilhelmine von, 140
Walther, Professor, 245, 246
Wartel, Atala Thérèse, 194, 198
Wartel, Pierre François, 194, 198, 257
Weber, Carl Maria von, 55, 113; works: "Freischütz," 188 "Invitation to the Dance," 248; "Jubel-Overture," 39; Konzertstück in F Minor, 132, 241; *Oberon* overture, 44, 248; *Preciosa,* 147, 188, 348*n*53
Wedderkopp, Herr von, 130
Wedel, Gottschalk. *See* Anton Wilhelm von Zuccalmaglio
Wenzel, Ernst Ferdinand, 5, 78; visits by, 8, 24, 45, 54, 61, 62, 113, 117, 124, 209, 347*n*38
Weyse, Christoph Ernst Friedrich, 138, 139, 140, 146
Wieck, Alwin, 160, 162, 187, 195, 196–197, 201, 351*n*22

Wieck, Cäcilie, 187
Wieck, Clara. *See* Clara (Wieck) Schumann
Wieck, Clementine, 187
Wieck, Friedrich, 76, 160; court trial of, xii, xiii, 60, 75, 342*n*47; as godparent, 195; opinion of RS, xii; "*Opposition* Symphony," xxiii, 81; piano incident, 33–34, 60, 63, 68, 201, 342*n*49; as piano teacher, x, 205–206; reconciliation with Schumanns, xxiii, 42, 60, 99, 104, 208; visits to the Schumanns, 19, 67–68, 186, 195–196, 201, 210
Wieck, Gustav, 179
Wieck, Marie, 187, 188, 196, 201, 205
Wilken (customs director), 234
Willkomm, Ernst Adolph, 126
Willmers, Rudolph, 140
Winter, Amalie, 118
Wirth (piano maker), 249, 252, 292, 293, 295
Wittmann, Franz Carl, 115, 117, 172
Wöhler, Gotthold, 43, 112
Wöhrmann, Consul General, 237
Wolfahrt, Fräulein, 347*n*44
Wolff, Baroness von, 244
Wolff, P. A., *Preciosa,* 147, 348*n*53
Wurst, Bertha, 233

Xaverius, Prince, 282

Yussupov, Prince, 307

Zahrtmann, Christian Christopher, 141, 347*n*48

Zahrtmann, Sophie, 139, 140, 141, 144

Zander, Friedrich, 233

Zedtwitz, Ernestine von, 164. *See also* Ernestine von Fricken

Zoller, Baron von, 263

Zuccalmaglio, Anton Wilhelm von, 20, 352*n*27

Zwickau, ix, 88, 160